JUN 2 3 2020

D1736959

FROM HOPE TO HORROR

ADST-DACOR Diplomats and Diplomacy Series

Series Editor

Margery Boichel Thompson

Since 1776, extraordinary men and women have represented the United States abroad under widely varying circumstances. What they did and how and why they did it remain little known to their compatriots. In 1995, the Association for Diplomatic Studies and Training (ADST) and DACOR, an organization of foreign affairs professionals, created the Diplomats and Diplomacy book series to increase public knowledge and appreciation of the professionalism of American diplomats and their involvement in world history. In this sixty-ninth series volume career diplomat Joyce E. Leader analyzes the failed diplomatic efforts to achieve democracy and peace in Rwanda as the country careened along the path to genocide.

FROM HOPE TO HORROR

DIPLOMACY AND THE MAKING OF THE RWANDA GENOCIDE

JOYCE E. LEADER

Foreword by PAULINE H. BAKER

An ADST-DACOR Diplomats and Diplomacy Book

Potomac Books

AN IMPRINT OF THE UNIVERSITY OF NEBRASKA PRESS

© 2020 by Joyce E. Leader

The opinions and characterizations in this book are those of the author and do not necessarily reflect the opinions of the U.S. government, the Association for Diplomatic Studies and Training, or DACOR.

Portions of this book are based on "Rwanda's Struggle for Democracy and Peace: 1991–1994," a study written by the author under the auspices of the Fund for Peace.

All rights reserved. Potomac Books is an imprint of the University of Nebraska Press.
Manufactured in the United States of America.

Library of Congress Cataloging-in-Publication Data
Names: Leader, Joyce E., author.
Title: From hope to horror: diplomacy and the making of the Rwanda genocide / Joyce E. Leader; foreword by Pauline H. Baker.
Other titles: ADST-DACOR diplomats and diplomacy series.
Description: Lincoln: Potomac Books, an imprint of the University of Nebraska Press, 2020. | Series: ADST-DACOR diplomats and diplomacy series | Includes bibliographical references and index.
Identifiers: LCCN 2019027688
ISBN 9781640122451 (hardback)
ISBN 9781640123236 (epub)
ISBN 9781640123243 (mobi)
ISBN 9781640123250 (pdf)
Subjects: LCSH: Democracy—Rwanda—History—20th century.
| Genocide—Rwanda—History—20th century. | Rwanda—History—Civil War, 1994—Causes. | Rwanda—History—Civil War, 1994—Diplomatic history. | Rwanda—Politics and government—1962–1994. | Rwanda—Ethnic relations—History.
Classification: LCC DT450.435 .L43 2020 | DDC 967.571042—dc23
LC record available at https://lccn.loc.gov/2019027688

Set in Arno Pro by Laura Ebbeka.

CONTENTS

FOREWORD

PAULINE H. BAKER

Although much has been written about the Rwanda genocide of 1994, there has been no previous analysis available to the public by a high-level diplomat who was on the ground at the time. Joyce Leader served as deputy chief of mission at the U.S. Embassy in Rwanda from 1991 to 1994. She was deeply involved in the peace process and had access to many of the top leaders in Rwanda. This is her personal account of what happened in the years leading up to the genocide.

It is a first-person narrative by an insider who strove personally to make democratization and the peace process work. The narrative begins in August 1991, with Leader's arrival in Kigali, the Rwandan capital. It runs through 1992 and 1993, a period of intermittent violence and intensive negotiations, and ends in April 1994, as waves of genocidal killings broke out, forcing the evacuation of Americans and the closing of the U.S. Embassy. It also provides a glimpse into the aftermath of the calamity during her brief return after the killings in August 1994, exactly three years after her arrival.

Her principal thesis is that the precipitating events that triggered the genocide were rooted in the intense jockeying for power among the ruling and newly emergent opposition political parties. The Arusha Accords, which she worked on, were intended to accommodate these Rwandan parties in a pathbreaking power-sharing agreement that would have institutionalized greater equity between the two major ethnic groups: the ruling Hutu majority and the Tutsi minority, many of whom had been driven out of the country and festered in refugee camps in Uganda and elsewhere for three decades. Had they been implemented, the Arusha Accords would have ushered in a shift in power in Rwanda—by redressing inequities against a minority—as revolutionary as the peace accords in South Africa had been in redressing inequities against a majority. Though the population ratios were different, the goals of achieving equitable political representation were the same.

Rwandan opposition political parties were fragile entities, split by personal, regional, and ethnic differences. Hutu Power nationalists drew supporters from these parties, cultivating ethnic extremism as a way to unite right-wing factions in the competition for dominance. Even some moderate Hutu were captured by this tactic because there was no credible moderate Hutu leadership to follow. Extremists maintained that the peace accords were paving the road to Tutsi domination and would convert Hutu, a demographic majority, into what they regarded politically as a "permanent minority." Playing the "ethnic card" was a convenient way for extremist Hutu to generate political mobilization against the peace process. It proved a deadly tactic.

U.S. embassy officers had been aware of the danger but concluded that potential spoilers, including extremists, would be brought along once the Rwandan president adopted the Arusha Accords and the agreement was implemented. This was a devastating miscalculation that resulted in a perverse outcome: the peace agreement itself was a trigger for the genocide. The United States had vastly underestimated the organization, armed strength, and backing that extremists could command, not only to sabotage the Accords but also to eliminate perceived ethnic enemies and bring ruin to the entire country.

Many observers have noted that there were plenty of early-warning signs weeks and even months before. However, Leader shows that there were persuasive early-warning signs years before the genocide. Trends pointed toward a pattern of deterioration that was either not detected or not taken seriously.

Leader concludes that deeper societal trends could have been identified nearly two years in advance, alerting the international community to the high risk of mass violence. Her narrative notes menacing developments, such as the ruling party's formation of the Interahamwe, a violent youth group that Leader describes as a government-backed militia that took its violence to the ultimate level when it became the vehicle for killing Tutsi in several massacres and, finally, for carrying out the genocide.

Leader asks the big questions: Why didn't policymakers see these signs of deterioration? Were they so wedded to their policies that they lost objectivity? Did they focus on elites to the extent that they failed to see what was going on at the grass roots? Had they been so absorbed by day-to-day negotiations that they underestimated the significant trends of political decay? Did they not consider whether the peace process itself could inspire conflict?

This work is a significant contribution to the literature on Rwanda, U.S. diplomacy, and international responses to internal conflict. Leader's personal insights and reflections present a strong case study of why the international community should rethink the strategy and tactics of dealing with internal war.

The Fund for Peace is proud to have had the opportunity to work with Joyce Leader during her 2000–2001 tenure as a senior fellow.

PREFACE

Twenty-six years have passed since the genocide in Rwanda. For one hundred days in 1994 killers terrorized the country, brutally murdering up to one million men, women, and children. No Rwandan who lived through the 1994 genocide escaped the trauma of this catastrophic nightmare and its aftermath. Survivors still carry the scars of this tragedy. They still mourn the loss of loved ones. They remember the images, the fear, the shame, and the terror. For those who experienced this horror, the memories remain vivid despite the intervening years.

My memory of the first days of the genocide in Rwanda and, indeed, the years leading up to it, remain etched in my mind, too. A career diplomat in the U.S. Foreign Service, I served as deputy chief of mission—deputy to the ambassador—at the U.S. Embassy in Kigali, Rwanda's capital, from August 1991 until April 1994. Political liberalization announced in the summer of 1990 was just getting off the ground when I arrived. Armed conflict had been simmering at the northern Rwanda-Uganda border for about a year as well.

Rwanda's quest to transition to democracy and to peace would dominate the next three turbulent and challenging years. U.S. support for these two profoundly disruptive transitions would form the centerpiece of U.S. policy. The path, however, would not be smooth. Even though many Rwandans seemed genuinely committed to working for the success of the transitions, violence would escalate with every small step toward political liberalization and peace. Hope, frustration, and despair marked my time in Rwanda before the genocide forced the evacuation of American diplomats and other U.S. citizens in April 1994.

Once back in Washington and assigned to a different office at the State Department, I followed events in Rwanda as best I could in the U.S. press. I noted that most observers of the genocide and its aftermath generally began the story at the moment when the president's plane was shot down over Kigali on April 6, 1994. They had little if any knowledge of the preceding power struggles that had been under way inside the country. Nor did they realize that these struggles had their origins in the failed efforts to transition to democracy and peace that we at the embassy had been witnessing and championing for several years.

I felt compelled to put on the record this pre-genocide story of the political wrangling, peacemaking, and violence that was integral to Rwanda's efforts to transition to democracy and peace. I needed to understand what had gone so terribly wrong to enable such brutal killing to take root and spread so quickly throughout the country. I also wanted to describe the U.S. policies that had encouraged and supported these Rwandan initiatives toward peace, greater political openness, and collaboration across ethnic lines. Why had we diplomats and our diplomacy failed so abysmally to prevent the escalation of violence to mass atrocities and genocide? I wanted to explore what had gone wrong and whether the U.S. government and our international partners might have been more effective at avoiding mass violence and genocide had we done some things better or differently.

In 2000–2001 the Fund for Peace, a Washington DC nonprofit organization committed to ending violence and war, offered me the opportunity to spend a year as a senior fellow reflecting on and writing about my Rwanda experience. In 2001 the Fund published the result of my initial efforts under the title "Rwanda's Struggle for Democracy and Peace: 1991–1994." It told the story of Rwanda's attempts to transition to democracy and peace and how we at the U.S. Embassy in Kigali, in partnership with others in the international diplomatic community, were supporting those efforts. It also showcased the Fund for Peace's conflict-risk assessment tool by applying it to the Rwanda situation.[1]

Just before retiring from the Foreign Service in September 2003,

I discovered that Rwanda's 1994 genocide had become a watershed event for numerous policymakers, academics, humanitarian workers, and development specialists. Once a scarcely noticed event in a little-known African country, Rwanda's tragedy had become the focus of reflection among aid workers and international organizations seeking to understand why the genocide had happened and whether they might have contributed to it. Rwanda's genocide had become a major subject of study at Washington think tanks and some universities. Conflict prevention as a diplomatic and development strategy was gaining attention. In light of this new interest, I committed myself to revising and expanding my 2001 study detailing the pre-genocide years in Rwanda.

This book took shape over many years. Opportunities to speak about the origins and the lessons of the Rwanda genocide kept me engaged and thinking about where we as diplomats in Kigali had gone wrong. A return to State Department diplomacy from 2005 to 2009 as coordinator of a peacebuilding initiative involving Rwanda and its neighbors—the Democratic Republic of the Congo, Uganda, and Burundi—gave me a firsthand look at the ugly, regional legacy of the genocide. These experiences reinforced my determination to delve more deeply into why diplomacy had failed to avert the horror of genocide. I also wanted to do what I could to keep alive the memory of Rwanda's tragedy and its devastating aftermath to make such catastrophes less likely to ravage other societies in future.

Part 1 of the book recounts the three-way struggle for control of democratization and the peace process in Rwanda before the genocide. It discusses the impact of U.S. policies in support of democracy and peace on the course of these transitions. I tell this story as I experienced and understood it at the time from my field perspective as a U.S. diplomat at the embassy in Kigali. Analytical commentary puts events into a larger context.

Part 2 examines some of the larger questions about why diplomacy failed to prevent the escalation of conflict to mass atrocities and genocide. It examines challenges diplomats faced in Rwanda during profound social change and raises the troubling issue of unintended consequences of well-intentioned policies. It explores ways diplomats might use diplomacy and assistance activities more effectively to mitigate conflict and prevent escalation of violence in conflict or conflict-prone areas.

The conclusions and recommendations draw on my insight at the time of the events and have been stimulated by hindsight, reading, conversations, lectures, and analyses of conflicts in Rwanda and elsewhere. I conclude that our steadfast support for Rwanda's transitions to multiparty democracy and peace blinded us to evidence that our policies were leading to neither. Instead each advance toward democracy or peace provoked a backlash of violence against those supporting change from entrenched forces opposed to losing or sharing their power and privilege. Our policies supporting change contributed to the ever-escalating violence that became mass atrocities and genocide. With these lessons as a guide, diplomats should be alert to the unintended consequences of policies promoting change. Diplomacy must prioritize preventing conflict over promoting profoundly disruptive change in conflict-prone, transitioning societies.

To tell the story of the pre-genocide years, I rely heavily on my 2001 study, notes of meetings, my calendar of appointments, official documents, and my memory. In 2011 the Department of State declassified and posted on the internet embassy and department cables from the 1990–94 period in Rwanda. These archival documents were invaluable in helping me recapture details regarding what I and others who worked on these issues were thinking and reporting as events unfolded. For some specific dates and the content of exchanges where I was not present, I have turned to conversations with participants and to the meticulous research and writings of others referenced in the notes and included in the bibliography.

A few years after the 1994 genocide, a Rwandan Tutsi friend told me his story of survival. It was our first meeting after the genocide. When the Americans left Kigali a few days after the killing began, I had already lost phone contact with him. I knew nothing about his fate until several months later, when I saw his name on a list of persons successfully evacuated by United Nations troops from the besieged Hôtel des Milles Collines in central Kigali.

His mood was despondent as he recounted the terror he had experienced trying to stay alive in those first few days. For several days he hid in the ceiling of his home. Fearing the killers were closing in on him, he made his way to a large Catholic church near the center of Kigali. The church, l'Église de la Sainte-Famille, was sheltering many Tutsi families who would eventually perish there. For some unknown reason, staff at this church had separated him from the others that night, putting him alone in a small room. He said the room had terrified him; machetes, the farm tools that had become implements of slaughter, lined the walls just above his head.

Following a sleepless night, he escaped from the church to the nearby Milles Collines hotel, the setting for *Hotel Rwanda*, the 2004 film that captured the harrowing experiences of frightened Tutsi and some Hutu who had taken refuge there. After enduring nearly two months of living in perpetual fear and deteriorating circumstances, he and many others in mortal danger from the Hutu killers were successfully transported by a United Nations convoy across the front lines of the renewed war into the security of Tutsi-controlled territory. From there he joined his wife and children, who had been living outside Rwanda for several years for security reasons.

Out of the blue my friend asked, "Do you believe that some people are inherently evil?" His penetrating question hung in the air as I contemplated the possibility of "inherent evil." His story awakened in me memories and thoughts I was still trying to keep at bay. Could the people who had planned and executed the genocide have been inherently evil? My upbringing taught me to look for good in all people, but after what I had seen and experienced, could I still believe this? I didn't really know what I thought. I had seen the faces of the killers as we, the representatives of the international community, evacuated Kigali, and they looked decidedly evil as they waited patiently for us to leave town. But *inherently* evil? What could I answer a friend who faced that evil and survived? What could I answer honestly, I wondered, that would help him in his agony?

Finally I replied cautiously, "No, I do not think there are inherently evil people, but I do believe people can do evil things. The *genocidaires*," as the killers were called, "had done evil things." He didn't respond. His melancholy was still apparent. To this day I can only suspect what he believed at the time. About a decade after that conversation, when I returned to Rwanda under the auspices of the

State Department, I had several occasions to visit with him and his family. During one conversation he gave me a clue to his thinking then: "I can never forgive and I can never forget what happened. But I will not teach my children to hate all Hutu. I just want to move on."

My hope is that this book will help readers understand what drove some Rwandans to choose the path of genocide and why neither their compatriots nor the international community was able to prevent it from happening. Perhaps this story of the competition for power that marked the years prior to 1994, from the perspective of one foreign diplomat, can contribute to creating a fuller picture of the origins of the genocide and to stimulating thinking about how diplomacy might be more effective in future transitional and conflict situations. Perhaps it can help us as concerned citizens of the world come closer to realizing the elusive goal of "Never Again."

ACKNOWLEDGMENTS

Let me extend my sincere thanks to all my Rwandan friends and colleagues who patiently helped me understand *what* was going on in Rwanda during those turbulent years from 1991 to 1994, and *why*. I have also benefited enormously from conversations over the years with Rwandans who survived the genocide, some of whom now live in Rwanda and others who are living in exile. They helped me penetrate some lingering mysteries about the early 1990s in their country that had continued to confound me.

Diplomatic colleagues in Kigali, Arusha, and elsewhere took time to share their observations and insights with me to further our mutual understandings of events in Rwanda. I am grateful to each of the ambassadors who led the embassy in Kigali while I was in Rwanda—Robert Flaten (1990–93) for most of my tenure and David Rawson (1994–96) until our departure in 1994. Both were supportive during the turbulent, challenging times we faced. Because we each had a wide network of Rwandans and others we generally spoke with, there was a synergy in our discussions that helped each of us inform and sharpen our assessments of events occurring at any given time before the genocide.

Let me acknowledge a few of the many people who have encouraged me in this undertaking. I am grateful to the Association for Diplomatic Studies and Training (ADST) for its invaluable assistance in preparing the manuscript of this book for publication. I have greatly appreciated both the prodding and the patience of ADST's publications director, Margery Thompson. She has been instrumental in bringing this project to fruition as a volume in the ADST-DACOR Diplomats and Diplomacy series.

I am forever indebted to the Fund for Peace and its President Emeritus Pauline H. Baker, who first gave me the opportunity to pull together my thoughts on my experiences in Rwanda. I am grateful to the Fund for assigning to me all rights to the work I wrote that was published under its auspices in 2001.

My special thanks to the Institute for the Study of International Migration (ISIM) at Georgetown University. Dr. Susan Martin, ISIM director until June 2016, assigned several student interns to help research trends in conflict-resolution thinking and activities. She also supported my participation in an international political science conference, where I presented a paper about diplomacy in Rwanda before the genocide.

I cannot forget Alison Des Forges, an academic and expert on Rwandan history and human rights, who died prematurely in 2009. Our conversations always helped me achieve a deeper understanding of Rwanda and Rwandans. I greatly appreciate all the American and foreign academics who, through conversations over the years and through their writings, have stimulated my thinking on these issues.

Echoing in my head throughout has been the voice of Gen. Roméo Dallaire, the Canadian commander of the UN peacekeeping force in Rwanda at the time of the genocide. When our paths crossed at a conference on Rwanda in 2012, he insisted that I complete this writing task.

These individuals and organizations, among many others, urged me to keep going with this endeavor. For this they have my deepest gratitude.

ABBREVIATIONS

ADL
: Association Rwandaise pour la Défense des Droits de la Personne et des Libertés Publiques (Rwandan Association for Human Rights and Civil Liberties), the second most important human rights organization in Rwanda.

AMASASU
: Alliance des Militaires Agacés par les Séculaires Actes Sournois des Unaristes (Alliance of Soldiers Annoyed by the Underhanded Acts of the Unarists), a clandestine group within the Rwandan military that espoused Hutu supremacy views in anonymous tracts.

APB
: Atrocities Prevention Board, a U.S. government interagency panel established in 2012 to identify and coordinate government responses to atrocity threats.

ARDHO
: Association Rwandaise Pour la Défense des Droits de l'Homme (Rwandan Association for the Defense of Human Rights), the principal human rights organization in Rwanda.

AVP
: Association des Voluntaires du Progrès (Association of Volunteers for Progress), a primarily Tutsi human rights organization.

BBTG
: Broad-Based Transitional Government, the interim government that was supposed to be established in accordance with the Arusha Peace Accords of August 4, 1993.

CDR   Coalition pour la Défense de la République (Coalition for the Defense of the Republic), a Hutu supremacist party that broke with President Juvénal Habyarimana for being too moderate on the peace process.

CLADHO   Collectif des Ligues et Associations de Défense des Droits de l'Homme au Rwanda (Collective of Leagues and Associations for the Defense of Human Rights in Rwanda), an umbrella organization of five Rwandan human rights groups, namely, ADL, ARDHO, AVP, LICHREDOR, and Kanyarwanda.

CND   Conseil National de Développement (National Development Council), Rwanda's legislative body under the Habyarimana government.

CSO   U.S. State Department's Bureau of Conflict and Stabilization Operations, established in 2011 to strengthen strategy, policy, and programs for conflict prevention where U.S. security interests are threatened.

DMZ   Demilitarized zone, an area in northern Rwanda created by the March 1993 cease-fire agreement between the government forces and those of the Tutsi-led RPF.

DPKO   UN Department of Peacekeeping Operations, responsible for recruiting, equipping, and overseeing peacekeeping forces deployed throughout the world, including in Rwanda in 1993.

DRC   Democratic Republic of the Congo, Rwanda's western neighbor, previously known as Zaire. Its eastern region along the Rwandan border has known only conflict and violence since the Rwanda genocide.

FAR   Forces Armées Rwandaise (Rwandan Armed Forces), of the government of Rwanda that fought the RPF armed forces of the Tutsi exiles and participated in the genocide.

ICRC   International Committee of the Red Cross, a private organization based in Switzerland responsible for protecting victims of war under the terms of the Geneva Conventions.

IDP   internally displaced person, a person displaced within the borders of his or her own country, in contrast to a refugee who crosses a national boundary.

LICHREDOR   Ligue Chrétienne de Défense des Droits de l'Homme (Christian League for the Defense of Human Rights), a human rights organization close to the Catholic Church.

MDR   Mouvement Démocratique Républicain (Democratic Republican Movement), the principal opposition party strongest in south-central Rwanda that filled the positions of prime minister and foreign minister in the multiparty government formed in April 1992.

MRND   Mouvement Républicain National pour le Développement et la Démocratie (National Republican Movement for Development and Democracy), Rwanda's former single party of President Habyarimana, strongest in his home area, the northwest; heavily involved in planning and carrying out the genocide. Originally called Mouvement Révolutionnaire National pour le Développement (National Revolutionary Movement for Development).

NGO   nongovernmental organization, a national or international nonprofit group often having humanitarian or development goals.

NIF   Neutral International Force, called for in the Arusha Peace Accords to be organized by the United Nations and present prior to installation of the transitional institutions.

NMOG   Neutral Military Observer Group, a small force established by the Organization of African Unity to observe implementation of the July 1992 cease-fire.

OAU   Organization of African Unity, the all-Africa political and security organization with headquarters in

	Addis Ababa, Ethiopia, which supported the Arusha peace process.
PDC	Parti Démocrate Chrétien (Christian Democrat Party), the smallest of the four principal Rwandan opposition parties.
PL	Parti Libéral (Liberal Party), the third largest Rwandan opposition party composed primarily of businessmen, including many Tutsi.
PSD	Parti Social Démocrate (Social Democrat Party), the second largest of the four principal Rwandan opposition parties based primarily in the south.
RPF	Rwandan Patriotic Front, an armed guerrilla movement composed primarily of Tutsi refugees who had lived in Uganda for a generation. The RPF invaded Rwanda from Uganda on October 1, 1990, and concluded a peace agreement, the Arusha Accords, with the government on August 4, 1993.
RTLM	Radio Télévision Libre des Mille Collines (Free Radio and Television of the Thousand Hills), Rwanda's only privately financed radio station, established in mid-1993 by Hutu extremists. It broadcast virulent anti-Tutsi propaganda and encouraged the genocide.
TNA	Transitional National Assembly, the legislative body called for in the Arusha Peace Accords of August 3, 1993.
UNAMIR	United Nations Assistance Mission for Rwanda, the peacekeeping force established by the United Nations Security Council October 5, 1993, to help provide security during implementation of the Arusha Peace Accords.
UNHCR	Office of the United Nations High Commissioner for Refugees, that, with countries of origin and countries of asylum, develops and implements plans for the repatriation and reintegration of refugees.

UNOMUR	United Nations Observer Mission in Uganda-Rwanda, a military force deployed in September 1993 to monitor the Uganda-Rwanda border.
USAID	U.S. Agency for International Development, promoted good governance, provided economic support, and delivered humanitarian assistance in Rwanda before the genocide.
USIA	U.S. Information Agency, now part of the State Department Bureau of Global Public Affairs, promoted democracy in Rwanda through programs, workshops, and visiting speakers.
USUN	U.S. Mission to the United Nations, comparable to an embassy, based in New York City.

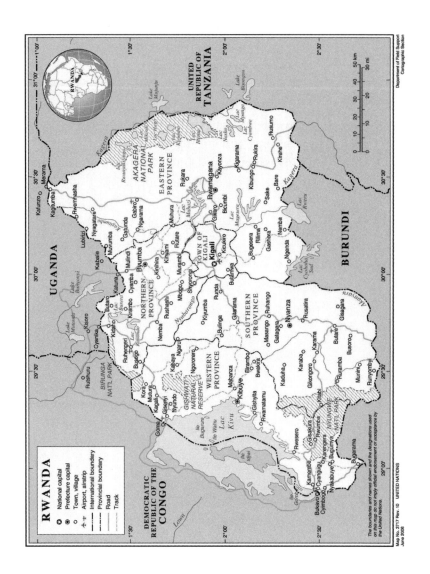

Fɪɢ. 1. Map of Rwanda. Map No. 3717 Rev.10, July 2008, United Nations.
Used with permission.

FROM HOPE TO HORROR

Introduction

Genocide in Rwanda was born of fear and hate. It grew out of the struggle for power among ethnic and geographic groups during a time when two transitions were under way—one to democracy and another to peace. Both transitions aroused expectations within and among ethnic and regional groups that would exacerbate existing social fissures. Both—if successful—would lead to profound changes in power relationships among ethnic and regional groups. At stake was the future governance of Rwanda. Some from the Hutu majority who were determined to hold onto power resorted to genocide against the Tutsi minority—"the enemy"—they feared intended to dominate or destroy them.

A lack of trust nurtured the possibility of genocide. Government authorities used their monopoly of power to exhort loyalists and intimidate opponents. Media propaganda intensified the fear and hate. Human rights abuses were grist for the power mill. Ethnicity became a tool to rally followers against "the other" and to instigate massacres. The absence of the rule of law gave free rein to those determined to control Rwanda's destiny. Human rights activists, democracy advocates, and opposition politicians had no way to hold abusers accountable.

Scarcity set the stage for competition among various ethnic and geographic groups: scarcity of land for cultivation, of natural resources to shore up the economy, and of opportunity for those without power. Forging a peaceful, united future was not a goal shared across ethnic and geographic groups. Polarization along political, ethnic, and geographic fault lines left no room for moderates. Hope turned to horror when nearly an entire ethnic minority—the Tutsi—was brutally slaughtered during one hundred days of a killing frenzy in the spring of 1994.

Historical Overview

Rwanda, a mountainous, landlocked country in the heart of the Great Lakes region of Central Africa, shares borders with the anglophone countries of Uganda and Tanzania to the north and east and the francophone countries of the Democratic Republic of the Congo and Burundi to the west and south. Its population includes two major ethnic groups: the Hutu account for about 84 percent and the Tutsi about 15 percent. A third group, the Twa, comprises about 1 percent. In the early 1990s the population numbered about 7 million; twenty-five years later it was estimated to be about 10.5 million.

A Tutsi monarchy ruled most of the area now known as Rwanda for hundreds of years before the Europeans colonized Africa. Germany colonized Rwanda in the late 1800s. After World War I, Belgium replaced Germany as Rwanda's colonial power. Both European powers favored the Tutsi with education and administrative positions, and both sidelined the monarchy, though it continued to be an important social institution for many Tutsi.

Rwanda gained its independence from Belgium in 1962. National and local elections brought the Hutu to power. For the next thirty years, first Hutu from the south and then, after a military coup in 1973, Hutu from the north dominated Rwanda's politics and economy. They imposed discriminatory laws that limited Tutsi participation in education and the civil service. The early years of independence saw multiple armed Hutu attacks against the Tutsi that left thousands of Tutsi dead. Thousands upon thousands fled to safety in neighboring countries. By 1990, when an armed Tutsi-led group invaded Rwanda, the Tutsi diaspora numbered around a million persons, living mainly in countries in Africa, Europe, and North America. About 600,000 of these were officially registered as refugees in countries neighboring Rwanda.

Kinyarwanda is the common language of both Hutu and Tutsi. French became the official national language under the Belgians. Following the genocide, however, English-speaking Tutsi refugees who headed the government made English an official language as well as the language of education. Swahili too, a lingua franca of commerce in central and east Africa, is another official language in Rwanda. Subsistence agriculture, the commercial production of tea and coffee, and tourism form the base of the country's small economy. Since fiber optic cables were laid in the country following the genocide, telecommunications has become a growing economic sector.

Since the genocide, Rwanda has had a minority Tutsi-led government. President Paul Kagame, who commanded the insurgent Tutsi-led forces that had invaded Rwanda in 1990 and later stopped the 1994 genocide, was twice elected to seven-year terms by overwhelming majorities, in 2003 and 2010. Constitutional changes to presidential term limits, approved by a 2015 referendum, made Kagame eligible to run for two additional five-year terms. He ran in 2017 and won handily. Rwanda is the only country that belongs to both the British-led Commonwealth of Nations and the French-led Francophonie, which groups together all French-speaking nations. The country is also a member of the East Africa Community, the African Union, and the United Nations.

Historical Seeds of Genocide

Three elements from Rwanda's history greatly impacted its efforts at democratization and peacemaking in the early 1990s. First, a legacy of ethnic and regional antagonisms had, over time, created distrust between the Hutu majority and the Tutsi minority and between northern and southern Hutu. Although tensions had existed in precolonial times, two decisions of the Belgian colonists significantly intensified interethnic, interregional distrust. One decision was the introduction of identity cards that categorized all Rwandans as either Hutu or Tutsi. This ended a precolonial custom of intergroup social mobility that allowed Hutu peasants who accumulated enough cattle to accede to the Tutsi ruling class. The other decision was to send Tutsi administrators to northern Rwanda; knowingly or unknowingly, in doing so the Belgians extended Tutsi authority for the first time to areas never conquered by Tutsi kings. Northern Hutu deeply resented their new Tutsi overlords.

Violence associated with pre-independence jockeying for power among ethnically based political parties further exacerbated historical distrust. Once in power, the victorious southern Hutu fueled interethnic anger through discriminatory laws and periodic anti-Tutsi violence. After their 1973 military coup, the Hutu from the north officially declared a single-party state, doubled down on anti-Tutsi discrimination, and favored northern over southern Hutu. Deep distrust among ethnic and regional groups was well established by 1991, when the president legalized multiple parties, and in 1992, when a coalition government committed to peacemaking to end an armed conflict.

A second element was Rwanda's lack of historical experience of power-sharing, collaboration, or cooperation across ethnic or geographic divides. The pendulum of power always swung from one extreme to the other. The precolonial Tutsi monarchy lost its dominance to the colonial powers, who ruled through Tutsi administrators. Colonialism gave way to elected Hutu supremacist governments, first from the south and then from the north. Both Hutu governments practiced anti-Tutsi discrimination and favored Hutu from their own region. What began as political pluralism before independence devolved into effective one-party rule afterward, regardless of the regional origin of the governing leaders. What democratic institutions existed—the national assembly, the single political party—functioned to support the government in power.

Third, by 1990 cycles of violence associated with Hutu and Tutsi efforts to gain and maintain power were also well established. Government pogroms against Tutsi inside Rwanda were intended to assert Hutu authority over their former Tutsi masters. Tutsi flight to neighboring countries to escape the carnage created an incipient Tutsi diaspora. Periodically, armed Tutsi refugees tried to fight their way back into Rwanda. The Rwandan army regularly defeated these forays, which generally provoked more Tutsi massacres at the hands of government soldiers, followed by more Tutsi flight. Tutsi in the refugee communities had mixed success at integrating into neighboring countries and elsewhere; many hoped to return one day to Rwanda.

In the early 1990s, armed Tutsi refugees again launched an attempt to fight their way back into Rwanda from Uganda. This invasion by the Rwandan Patriotic Front (RPF) provoked a strong anti-Tutsi response within the country. The Hutu government of President Juvénal Habyarimana arrested thousands of Tutsi professionals, launched an anti-Tutsi media campaign, and exploited interethnic distrust to carry out massacres of Tutsi in several parts of the country. The historical pattern was well established and well known to all.

Pressure for Change

By the early 1990s internal and external pressures threatened the power monopoly of the northern Hutu government, led since 1973 by President Habyarimana. Internal pressure came from the southern Hutu, who had been marginalized after the 1973 coup. They supported the president's announced political reforms and seized the opportunity to form multiple political parties to join in the anticipated, more open political process. The terms of democratization were initially negotiated in Kigali almost exclusively among Hutu politicians. Little thought was given to a role for the minority Tutsi population.

The external threat to the Habyarimana regime came from the RPF, the armed group composed primarily of Tutsi refugees who had grown up in Uganda. On October 1, 1990, a few months after the president first announced political liberalization, the RPF attacked Rwanda from Uganda, claiming it sought the right of refugees to repatriate. For the next year and a half, the RPF and the Rwandan army fought a low-intensity armed conflict near the Rwanda-Uganda border. A battlefield stalemate finally prompted both sides to accept peace talks.

The process of democratization and the search for peace—two profoundly destabilizing transitions—would dominate Rwandan political life during the three years prior to the catastrophic genocide. Throughout that time the international community supported Rwandan efforts to achieve both democracy and peace.

Three Groups Vie for Power

Three principal political groups were vying for power in Rwanda during the transitions toward democracy and peace. The first group, primarily Hutu from the north, included the president and his political party. They had monopolized power—dominating the government, the civil service, and the military through the apparatus of their one-party state—for nearly twenty years before democratization and the search for peace began. The president and his party loyalists apparently expected to maintain their grip on power despite the destabilizing transitions.

The second group vying for power consisted of the emerging internal opposition parties, composed primarily of Hutu from the south whom the 1973 coup had forced from power. Businessmen, civil servants, and former managers of quasi-governmental economic entities under President Habyarimana regarded their newly legalized political parties as vehicles for gaining power in the democratization process.

The third group vying for power in the early 1990s was the armed Tutsi-led Rwandan Patriotic Front that had invaded from Uganda and fought the Rwandan army to a stalemate. Initially it had no political presence or official representation in Rwanda. Nevertheless it purported to speak for both Tutsi refugees and Tutsi inside the country. For the RPF, the peace process and a negotiated settlement would become its avenue for securing a place in Rwanda's proposed new political order.

The democratization debate in Kigali pitted the two Hutu groups against each other without much thought of a role for the Tutsi. Once peace talks began in Arusha, Tanzania, the Tutsi-led RPF gained a voice in democratization and peacemaking decisions equal to that of the two Hutu groups inside the country.

The Peace Agreement Does Not Bring Peace

A peace agreement, known as the Arusha Accords, was hashed out over a year of discussions between Rwandan government negotiators and the RPF. It was signed on August 4, 1993, even though Hutu supremacists had rejected its power-sharing provisions on grounds that they gave too great a role and too much power to the minority Tutsi. Although implementation went forward, it stalled repeatedly over one controversial issue after another.

On April 6, 1994, eight months after the signing of the peace agreement, unidentified assailants shot down the president's plane as it was landing at the Kigali airport, killing all on board. Extremist Hutu soldiers and civilian militia immediately unleashed a well-orchestrated killing rampage that escalated into mass atrocities and genocide.

The Role of Diplomats and Diplomacy

Kigali's large, diverse diplomatic community also played a part in the Rwandan political scene prior to the genocide. On the diplomatic roster in the early 1990s were Belgium, France, the United States, and Germany, several neighboring African countries, and Russia, China, and Libya, among others. Whether as individuals from single diplomatic missions, subgroups, or a unified bloc, diplomats sought to influence Rwandan leaders through their support and encouragement for Rwanda's transitions to democracy and peace. Major Rwandan political actors were obliged to take the interests and actions of the diplomatic community into consideration when making their own calculations.

U.S. Policy toward Rwanda

U.S. interests in Rwanda were minimal. Neither the State Department nor other foreign affairs agencies in Washington gave much thought or attention to this small Central African country, even though reporting from the embassy in Kigali circulated throughout the bureaucracy. As a francophone country and former Belgian colony, it fell squarely within the Belgian and French spheres of influence. At the State Department, policy decisions on Rwanda rarely rose higher than the assistant secretary for Africa, three levels below the secretary of state in the department's policymaking hierarchy. Few interests translate into few resources for conducting policy. That meant minimal personnel and minimal funding for embassy and assistance activities in Rwanda.

Although its interests in Rwanda were few, the United States did care about national and regional stability. U.S. policy goals when I arrived in Rwanda in August 1991 were to support the democratization process and urge an end to the incipient war at the border. We reasoned that political liberalization would offer Tutsi—from both inside and outside the country—an incentive to lay down their arms and join the political process. Marginalized Hutu too would be able to participate in governance. Democracy would offer a framework for inclusion.

U.S. diplomats in Kigali knew there would be no additional funding or personnel coming from Washington for an embassy in a country where the United States had few interests. Therefore the few embassy officers had to concentrate on a limited number of priority policy issues. To enhance U.S. influence, we often worked closely with Western and African counterparts on select issues.

The Functioning of the Diplomatic Corps

During the three years prior to the genocide, the modus operandi of the diplomatic missions in Rwanda evolved from consultation to cooperation, and then to coordination.[1] Frequent consultations—to share understandings and interpretations of events in Rwanda and to compare notes on respective diplomatic interventions, development strategies, and policies aimed at supporting democracy and peace—were characteristic of the period between the October 1990 RPF invasion and July 1992, when the Arusha peace process began. Once peace negotiations were under way in Arusha, diplomatic strategies and policy goals for supporting Rwanda's two transitions coalesced around the success of the peace process. This prompted greater cooperation among the diplomatic missions on their policy positions. After the Arusha Accords were signed in August 1993, the Kigali diplomatic community united around the common policy goal of helping to facilitate implementation of the peace agreement. The entire diplomatic corps coordinated policies on joint diplomatic overtures to urge prompt implementation of the Arusha Accords.

Glass Half Full?

If asked whether Rwanda's glass was half full or half empty during those three years before the genocide, I would have replied that it was half full. At the U.S. Embassy we were optimistic that the processes of democratization and peace negotiations could eventually overcome the conflict and violence and bring stability to the country. We were convinced that an inclusive government based on multiparty elections would be able to contain the violence and abuses that were tearing the country apart. We believed that the moderates in the political spectrum could prevail over the extremists. Even when Rwandan society became polarized around the extremes, as happened during the nine months before the genocide began, we thought that implementation of the Arusha Accords would calm the situation and end the downward slide.

How wrong we were! We overestimated the willingness of the parties to share power, and we underestimated the determination and ruthlessness of those who did not want to relinquish it. We no doubt put too much faith in the peace agreement, hammered out in excruciating detail as a blueprint for Rwanda's future. When the breakdown came, few moderates were left: most were flirting with the fringes of one extreme or the other. Inclusiveness as a principle was seriously compromised. With the downing of the president's plane, the killing began, and hopes among Rwandans and diplomats for democracy and peace collapsed.

What Did We Miss?

Why did those of us living and working in Rwanda, with its ever-escalating violence, fail to anticipate that a horrible catastrophe might be coming? Perhaps we believed too strongly that the transitions could and would successfully transform the country. Perhaps it was because we were so fully engaged in supporting Rwanda's democratization and peacemaking that we closed our eyes to the unintended negative consequences of our policies promoting change.

We failed to realize or accept that neither democracy nor peace was a panacea for resolving deep-seated conflicts among groups within Rwandan society. The country's efforts to transform its authoritarian political system into a multiparty democracy unleashed animus and hatred from those who would lose power and privilege. Without addressing the root causes of these latent animosities, creating a vision of a common future, or accepting "the other" as an opponent rather than as a sworn enemy, successful change that profoundly alters power relationships is unlikely.

Is there something inherent in diplomacy that caused us to overlook the factors that were building toward genocide while we thought the country was building toward democracy and peace? Why did we diplomats fail to realize or accept that our policies of support were leading to neither? This book will attempt to answer some of these questions by revisiting the struggle for power under way in Rwanda before the genocide in an attempt to determine where diplomacy went wrong and how we could do better in future situations at risk of conflict escalation.

PART 1

RWANDA'S STRUGGLE FOR DEMOCRACY
AND PEACE, 1991–1994

[1]

Political Liberalization Takes Off

Political change was in the air when I arrived in the Rwandan capital, Kigali, in August 1991. The U.S. Department of State had assigned me to serve at the embassy in this small, mountainous African country as deputy chief of mission, the ambassador's deputy. I knew armed conflict was simmering at the northern border between government forces and the Rwandan Patriotic Front (RPF), a group of mostly minority Tutsi refugees who said they were fighting for the right to return to their homeland. I also knew that an exciting political transition was just getting off the ground. The country was beginning to move from nearly twenty years as a one-party state to a more inclusive participatory democracy. The formation and positioning of political parties was in full swing in Kigali.

Within a few days of my arrival, I met two of Rwanda's newly minted politicians and experienced firsthand their enthusiasm for Rwanda's transition to political pluralism. U.S. Ambassador Robert Flaten had invited me to lunch at his residence with two leaders of the Liberal Party (Parti Libéral; PL). Ambassador Flaten was eager for me to get acquainted with the leaders of the various political parties as soon as possible because in one month he and his wife would fly to the United States for a month's vacation. He wanted to prepare me to carry on the embassy dialogue with these important players in Rwanda's democratic transition during his absence.

The four of us sat on his screened-in porch overlooking a walled garden where tall red and yellow canna lilies turned their blooms toward the bright sun and the deep blue sky. I was more focused on our guests, Justin Mugenzi, PL president, and his colleague Stanislas Mbonampeka. The ambassador drew them out with questions about their plans and goals for the party and their assessment of the current situation in Rwanda. Mugenzi was the more talkative of the two, but Mbonampeka seemed the more erudite. Both talked enthusiastically about their fledgling party and were highly critical of the Habyarimana regime. I was impressed by their openness and apparent unity of purpose. Even though they sounded committed to a multiparty, democratic process, I was somewhat skeptical of their sincerity. None of the rivalry that was later to characterize their relationship was apparent that day.

I had a steep learning curve ahead of me. Foreign Service officers never get quite enough time between posts to prepare fully for the next assignment. I had left behind an absorbing, challenging, and fulfilling three years as a refugee officer at the U.S. mission in Geneva. After three weeks of home leave, two weeks of consultations at the Department of State in Washington, and two weeks of training for my new position, I was on a plane to Kigali. Now I needed to prepare myself as quickly and fully as possible before the ambassador went on vacation, leaving me in charge.

Although I did not yet have a good grasp of the contemporary Rwandan political scene, I was generally familiar with the country and the region. From Geneva, where my portfolio included African refugee issues, I'd twice visited Rwanda to confer with embassy personnel about the local refugee situation. Two decades earlier I had traveled to Rwanda occasionally in conjunction with my Peace Corps associate director position in neighboring Zaire (now the Democratic Republic of the Congo). My responsibilities then had encompassed supervising education volunteers not only in Zaire but also in Rwanda.

It felt good to be back. I was looking forward to the challenges of gaining a broader and deeper understanding of the country and its people, who the volunteers had always claimed were difficult to get to know.

The Ruling Party Promises Political Reform

In July 1991, a couple of months before I arrived in Kigali, President Juvénal Habyarimana, a northerner from the majority Hutu ethnic group, had issued a new constitution legalizing the formation of multiple political parties. This act had officially ended Rwanda's single-party state. For nearly twenty years the president and his political party, then called the National Revolutionary Movement for Development (Mouvement Révolutionnaire National pour le Développement; MRND), had monopolized all the levers of power in the country. MRND stalwarts, primarily Hutu from the president's home area in the north, had dominated all decision making in Rwanda through the MRND's total control of the government, legislature, civil service, local administrations, and security forces. At every level, power was concentrated in the hands of the president and his party.

Rwanda had not, however, escaped the wave of political pluralism sweeping through Africa's one-party states in the early 1990s. Under pressure to democratize from France and other Western countries, including the United States, President Habyarimana promised political reform and multiparty politics in a July 1990 speech to the nation. The MRND even changed the "R" in its name from "Revolutionary" to "Republican" and added the word "Democracy," becoming the National Republican Movement for Development and Democracy (Mouvement Républicain National pour le Développement et la Démocratie), though it still went by the acronym MRND.

Despite the president's promise of political reform, considerable pressure and cajoling from his political opponents and the diplomatic community had been necessary before Habyarimana had actually taken steps to legalize multiple parties. Now, a year later, the revised constitution had lifted the prohibition on parties other than the MRND. Any future elections would require the ruling, omnipresent MRND to compete for the power it had monopolized for so long.

The prospect of broader political participation had created excitement and offered new hope to those who had been shut out of the Rwandan political process. Since the 1973 coup and the ascension of northern Hutu, the southern Hutu had lost their access to key government and military positions.

Minority Tutsi had been excluded from the political arena since 1959, when the Hutu Social Revolution had overthrown the Tutsi king. Discrimination and violence had been the lot of the Tutsi ever since at the hands of Rwanda's elected Hutu governments, first from southern Hutu and then from northern Hutu. Periodic pogroms against them between 1959 and 1973 had forced hundreds of thousands of Tutsi—up to half the Tutsi population of the time—to seek refuge and safety in neighboring states. Substantial Tutsi refugee communities were still in place in 1990.

Political Parties Multiply

By June 1991 three opposition parties and one party of undefined allegiance were poised to register. In anticipation of political liberalization, they had been organizing in earnest for several months. These mostly Hutu southern-based parties modeled themselves on parties that had competed in elections in the late 1950s to lead the pre-independence government and then in the early 1960s to lead the first postindependence government. The winner in both cases had been the party of Rwanda's first president, Grégoire Kayibanda, a southern Hutu.

Generally party leadership of these new opposition parties comprised former MRND insiders from southern Rwanda who had had some falling out with President Habyarimana. Each of these leading politicians brought considerable historical baggage to their political leadership roles. These party leaders were intent on breaking the Habyarimana government's monopoly on power and decision making by gaining seats at the governing table.

Principal among the four opposition parties was the Democratic Republican Movement (Mouvement Démocratique Républicain; MDR), the successor to President Kayibanda's party, the Party of the Hutu Emancipation Movement (Parti du Mouvement de l'Émancipation Hutu; MDR-Parmehutu Party). The revived party dropped "Parmehutu" from its name in order to distance itself from the Hutu-supremacist notions of the earlier party. Like the old party, though, the new one had its geographic roots in the south-central town of

Gitarama. The new one also attracted adherents from Ruhengeri, a northern town not far from the Ugandan border, as well as from the southwest.

The MDR president was Faustin Twagiramungu, a dapper Hutu businessman turned politician from Cyangugu, the southwestern town bordering Zaire. Under the Habyarimana government, Twagiramungu had been the general manager (1977–89) of a quasi-governmental agency, the Association of International Rwandan Transport (Societé des Transports Internationaux Rwandais). In that position, however, he had been accused, but never convicted, of taking bribes from companies seeking cheaper licenses to bring freight into Rwanda.[1] The MDR party attracted primarily southern Hutu, many of whom had held important private-sector positions during Habyarimana's rule. Twagiramungu graduated from McGill University in Montreal in the 1960s. His wife was the daughter of Grégoire Kayibanda.

Another key opposition party was the Social Democrat Party (Parti Social Démocrate; PSD), based in the southern university town of Butare, hometown of its general secretary, Félicien Gatabazi. Tall and taciturn, Gatabazi too had a tarnished record. In 1982 he had been convicted and served eight months in jail for embezzling funds for food from a refugee emergency program when he served as minister of public works (1976–82) under President Habyarimana. The PSD tended to attract intellectuals, civil servants, and other professionals. Its members were more comfortable than MDR adherents with the easy mixing of Hutu and Tutsi characteristic of the university culture in Butare.

The third opposition party was the Liberal Party (Parti Libéral; PL). The PL had no particular geographic base but drew followers primarily from among urban businessmen. Unique to this party was the participation of Tutsi businessmen and persons of mixed Hutu-Tutsi heritage. Its leader, Justin Mugenzi, a jovial Hutu businessman from the southeastern town of Kibungo, also had a skeleton in his closet. Although he denied the charges, he had been convicted and sentenced in 1976 to life in prison for murdering his wife. President Habyarimana, however, pardoned him five years later, in 1981. Despite embracing the political opposition, Mugenzi still owed a great debt to the president. Stories circulated about his antics as a student in Bujumbura, Burundi, when he allegedly absconded with a military jeep. He was also said to be perpetually in debt.

Mugenzi had two key colleagues in the PL leadership. Stanislas Mbonampeka, sometimes described as his rival, was a Hutu lawyer. Landoald Ndasingwa, a Tutsi businessman and former professor at the University of Rwanda in Butare, was widely known for the popular nightclub and bar he owned near the airport in Kigali. Lando, as he was familiarly known, was instantly recognizable by his broad, ever-present smile and his distinctive limp, the result of polio. Lando, like Twagiramungu of the MDR, had graduated from McGill University; his wife, Hélène, was Canadian.

The fourth party to register soon after multiple parties were legal was the much smaller Christian Democrat Party (Parti Démocrate Chrétien; PDC). Although this party never developed a large following, it became important because it joined the political fray early. Initially the PDC was regarded as close to the ruling MRND. "Christian" in its name evoked the close relationship between the Catholic Church and President Habyarimana's regime. Gradually, however, the PDC adopted positions akin to those of the other three main opposition parties. This solidified its position in their ranks and helped boost the numbers of ministerial portfolios and assembly seats assigned to the opposition in the eventual coalition government and later in the peace accord. Its founder and leader, Jean-Népomuscène Nayinzira, a civil servant, reportedly claimed to have formed the party in response to a dream telling him to do so.

The U.S. Embassy supported the formation of these newly legalized political parties. Ambassador Flaten kept in close touch with their leaders, urging them to stay the course when negotiating with the ruling MRND became difficult and frustrating and seemed to get nowhere. He also had close ties to key MRND leaders and encouraged them to persist in discussions with the opposition parties.

To help strengthen these newly established political parties as well as their relationship with the ruling party, the embassy and the United States Information Service devised a study tour of the United States for key party leaders. The program would include one representative from each of the five registered political parties—four from the opposition and one from the ruling party. This two-week program took place in the fall of 1991. It had two principal benefits: it gave party leaders an opportunity to see how political parties and other democratic institutions functioned in the United States, and it gave the participants a chance to get to know each other better.

In a joint press conference at the Kigali stadium upon the group's return, the party representatives expressed enthusiasm for the trip to a large, raucous crowd of their respective supporters. They told of their support for the transition to multiparty democracy and committed to leading that process responsibly. At a dinner later that evening hosted by Ambassador Flaten at his residence, each participant acknowledged the importance of getting to know the others as a first step toward civil dialogue between the ruling and opposition parties and toward cooperation among them. Not long after this dinner, the opposition party leaders would formalize their cooperation in the face of intransigence by ruling party leaders.

Prime Minister Named

On October 13, 1991, President Habyarimana took the next step in Rwanda's political liberalization process: he appointed the MRND minister of justice Sylvestre Nsanzimana to the newly created position of prime minister, with the task of forming a multiparty government. Nsanzimana, a Hutu who had joined the cabinet just six months earlier, was known as a moderate. His achievement had been to discreetly engineer the release of thousands of prisoners—mostly Tutsi—arrested and detained without charge following the October 1990 armed invasion from Uganda by the mostly Tutsi RPF.

However, Nsanzimana ran into difficulties in putting together a multiparty government. Despite his prior diplomatic experience as Rwanda's ambassador to the Organization of African Unity in Addis Ababa, his negotiations with political party leaders soon bogged down over differences of approach between the ruling and opposition parties. The ruling MRND party was apparently willing to incorporate additional parties into the government only if its own decision-making majority remained intact. Opposition parties, to the contrary, held out for fundamental changes in the balance of power before they would agree to enter a new cabinet.

As this impasse dragged on, the opposition parties formed a Committee of Coordination to press their demands jointly. In their view, the prime minister should have been named not from the president's party but from one of the opposition parties. The prime minister should be accorded real power, they argued, which would necessitate changing the constitution that concentrated all power—executive, legislative, and judicial—in the president. And the national assembly, known as the National Development Council (Conseil National de Développement; CND), should resign because its composition reflected the single-party politics of the past rather than the multiple parties that would form the new government. The opposition parties wanted the president to meet with their Committee of Coordination to discuss these matters, but this did not happen.

In mid-November the opposition parties issued a joint statement complaining about the MRND's continued disregard for its political opponents and demanding a national conference as a path to true democracy. By that fall of 1991, five Francophone African countries had already held national conferences as stepping stones from authoritarian to elected government. These countries were Benin (February 1990), Republic of Congo/Brazzaville (February 1990), Gabon (March 1990), Zaire (February 1991), and Togo (July/August 1991). The Rwandan opposition leaders hoped a national conference would help level the political playing field by reducing MRND dominance.

To underscore their demand for a national conference, the opposition parties mounted a demonstration in Kigali that brought out ten thousand members and supporters who marched peacefully through the main streets of Kigali. The MRND replied a week later with a march of twenty thousand of its own against a national conference.[2]

When Prime Minister Nsanzimana finally announced the formation of his multiparty government on December 30, 1991, the only participating party other than the ruling MRND was the small, inconsequential PDC that had little credibility at that time as an opposition party. Its decision to join the Nsanzimana government reinforced the view of opposition parties that the PDC was nothing more than a tool of the ruling MRND.

Opposition politicians were outraged. In this climate the opposition mounted the largest demonstration Kigali had ever seen. On

January 8 an estimated fifty thousand persons turned out to show their opposition to the new cabinet. Though large and noisy, this march snaked peacefully through the center of Kigali. Thousands also marched in the southern cities of Gitarama and Butare, strongholds of the opposition political parties MDR and PSD, respectively.

Opposition leaders, elated by their success, called for another demonstration one week later. This time, however, MRND-controlled security authorities declared the demonstration illegal, even though the intent was only to peacefully bolster the opposition message of dissatisfaction with the new, nominally multiparty government. Those who dared to march anyway were stopped by police, and many were arrested.

A related report indicated that the Butare-based PSD had refused to participate in planning or implementing the second march. Its reasons for breaking opposition solidarity were unclear. Speculation within the diplomatic community hinted at possible infighting among opposition leadership as the cause. Much later, however, rumors circulated that the Butare-based PSD may have broken ranks with its opposition colleagues in order to negotiate separately with the MRND for a cabinet position in the new government. The rumors focused specifically on the PSD vice president, Félicien Ngango, as the individual who may have been holding private discussions with the prime minister about a cabinet position for himself. This apparent break in opposition ranks was short-lived; the opposition coalition soon got back on track and was working together again.

A New Party Forms

On March 6, 1992, while negotiations were under way over reconfiguring the so-called multiparty government to include opposition politicians, a new, radical Hutu supremacist party announced its formation. The Coalition for the Defense of the Republic (Coalition pour la Défense de la République; CDR) drew most of its support from discontented members of the ruling MRND. Martin Bucyana, CDR secretary general, headed this overtly Hutu supremacist group. It rejected power sharing with the Tutsi on grounds that the majority Hutu should continue to rule Rwanda. The CDR maintained that the Habyarimana government was too soft on the RPF and its presumed internal Tutsi supporters. Ironically, concurrent with the CDR's joining the Rwandan political fray, a Hutu massacre of Tutsi was taking place in the Bugesera area south of Kigali.

The CDR carved out a position to the right of the president's MRND party by taking a more hard-line, pro-Hutu, anti-Tutsi stance. Nevertheless the relationship between the two remained somewhat obscure. Many observers, including some in the Kigali diplomatic community, considered the CDR's creation a ploy to add ballast to the president's side of the political equation rather than to establish a totally separate political entity. A radical party on the president's side of the political spectrum, so the argument went, would allow him to espouse conciliatory positions that would be acceptable to the international community. The CDR could take the hard-line positions the president was believed to support but might find impolitic to articulate.

One of the CDR's foremost ideologues, Jean-Bosco Barayagwiza, was well-known to me. In his civil service position as director of political affairs at the Ministry of Foreign Affairs and Development, Barayagwiza had been my key interlocutor on a range of U.S. concerns ever since my arrival six months earlier. I had met with him on several occasions to solicit Rwanda's support for U.S. positions on issues before the annual meeting of the United Nations General Assembly. He had seemed affable and receptive to U.S. messages. Our discussions had not, however, given me any insight into his attitudes toward the political situation in Rwanda. Once his hard-line views became public, I realized that he had inevitably played a key role in formulating the Foreign Ministry's hard-line policies impeding government cease-fire agreements and peace talks with the RPF during the year and a half of failed international community efforts to bring the two sides together.

Civil Society Expands

While Ambassador Flaten worked with political party leaders to help strengthen the democratic institution of political parties, I was busy getting to know and support emerging civil society groups. In response to the promise of a more open political environment, a host of new citizen-led groups came to the fore, most of them newly formed: human rights organizations, journalism groups, women's groups, and an organization that supported cooperatives. My portfolio at the U.S. Embassy included offering these human rights organizations encouragement, moral support, and modest contributions for their activities. I identified potential recipient groups, discussed their proposed projects with them, and then helped them refine their plans into something their organizations could accomplish with available funds. Drawing on funds from the Department of State's Democracy and Human Rights Fund, the embassy was able, for example, to buy office equipment for one organization and fund a conference for another.

Human rights activists representing various political persuasions created five new human rights organizations to monitor and report on the actions of both the government and the armed insurgent group, the RPF. Each of the five human rights groups had ties to one or another of the opposition parties or to the Catholic Church. The goal of each was to promote respect for human rights and hold government officials and institutions, as well as RPF forces, accountable for abuses of human rights. They focused their attention primarily on the victims of those acts committed in the course of the expanding conflict between the government armed forces and RPF invading forces. They also investigated cases involving alleged abuse of power by the government or government-related groups.

Rwanda's first human rights organization, the Rwandan Association for the Defense of Human Rights (Association Rwandaise pour la Défense des Droits de l'Homme; ARDHO), formed just prior to the invasion of the RPF in October 1990. Its founder, Alphonse-Marie Nkubito, a Hutu, was the attorney general (*procurer général*) of Kigali at the time. ARDHO gained prominence and credibility as a result of its strong advocacy on behalf of the more than six thousand Rwandans—mostly Tutsi—arrested on suspicion of being accomplices of the RPF in the wake of the October 1990 invasion.

For speaking out strongly against these mass arrests and using his position to free many, Nkubito was transferred from his high-profile position in the capital to one of lesser importance in a distant rural area. His exile from Kigali lasted about a year. When he returned to the capital, he resumed his former position and was as outspoken as ever. ARDHO and Nkubito remained staunchly committed to holding the government accountable for any unjust treatment of civilians. Politically ARDHO allied itself closely with the Butare-based PSD.

A second human rights organization, the Rwandan Association for Human Rights and Civil Liberties (Association Rwandaise pour la Défense des Droits de la Personne et des Libertés Publiques; ADL), appeared in September 1991, about a year after ARDHO came on the scene. ADL had political ties to the most prominent opposition party, the Gitarama-based MDR. Among its founders was Abbé André Sibomana, a priest, journalist, and outspoken human rights activist. Although he had helped found ARDHO in 1990, he subsequently turned his attention to ADL and in 1993 became its second president. Sibomana trained a cadre of ADL investigators in the use of techniques he had learned as a journalist conducting human rights investigations. He also had the foresight to establish a network of regional human rights reporters who would alert ADL headquarters to cases of abuse in their areas.

A major driving force in the ADL was Monique Mujawamariya, a Hutu social activist. Energetic, articulate, and charismatic, Mujawamariya led many ADL field investigations at sites of reported human rights violations. Characteristically she collected moving testimony from victims, released blunt public statements, and issued well-documented reports that were often chilling in their graphic detail.[3] They were not well received by government officials or MRND party leaders.

Mujawamariya developed a close personal relationship with an American human rights advocate, Alison Des Forges, an international expert on Rwanda and frequent visitor to Kigali in connection with her work for the American advocacy group Human Rights Watch. Des Forges served as a strong role model for Mujawamariya, who became widely known for her solid human rights investigations and her willingness to challenge government claims that it had committed no abuses. In late 1993, a few months before the genocide began, she was among several human rights activists from around the world received by President Bill Clinton in the Oval Office in recognition for their remarkable work.

A third human rights group was the Christian League for the

Defense of Human Rights (Ligue Chrétienne de Défense des Droits de l'Homme; LICHREDOR). It was led by Innocent Mazimhaka and associated with the Catholic Church. The leadership and most members of ARDHO, ADL, and LICHREDOR were Hutu. This did not inhibit them, however, from documenting and denouncing human rights abuses against Hutu as well as Tutsi victims.

Two other groups composed primarily of Tutsi leaders and members tended to focus on Hutu injustices perpetrated against Tutsi. The Association of Volunteers for Progress (Association des Voluntaires du Progrés; AVP) was led by a Tutsi businessman named Charles Shamukiga. Its ties were to the PL party that had several prominent Tutsi among its mainly Hutu members. Fidel Kanyabugoyi, an outspoken Tutsi from the north, headed the fifth human rights group, Kanyarwanda, which took pro-RPF positions on many issues and defended the RPF against government allegations of human rights abuses. Kanyarwanda was scorned by the ruling Hutu for its overt sympathetic stance toward the RPF and its insurgency.[4]

The five human rights groups eventually joined together in an umbrella organization called the Collective of Leagues and Associations for the Defense of Human Rights in Rwanda (Collectif des Ligues et Associations de Défense des Droits de l'Homme au Rwanda; CLADHO). By bringing together both Hutu and Tutsi rights groups, CLADHO gave enhanced credibility to claims of abuse. With its own executive secretary, CLADHO investigated reports of human rights abuses, drawing on personnel from its member groups. The umbrella organization also, singly and with other groups, issued statements and reports urging government action to curb rights abuses.

Once these human rights groups were up and running, they functioned primarily by making public statements denouncing human rights abuses and issuing detailed reports of their investigations. While their primary concern was to expose abuses of the government and the military, some called the RPF to account when evidence suggested their involvement. This was the case when ADL found a mass grave in an area where RPF attacks had occurred.

Individual human rights activists, whether Hutu or Tutsi, took tremendous personal risks to do this critical work. Nkubito, for example, escaped at least two assassination attempts in the years prior to the genocide. Mujawamariya received several death threats. Not long before the genocide, the newly established, private Hutu-supremacist radio station RTLM named her along with several other human rights and democracy advocates "enemies" who should die. Nkubito and Mujawamariya, both Hutu, managed to escape Hutu militia killers in the early days of the genocide.

As ethnic tensions mounted and human rights abuses multiplied, new groups emerged in January 1993 to defend the government, the military, the MRND, and the CDR against allegations of abuses and wrongdoing leveled by the existing human rights groups. Calling themselves human rights organizations, these groups blamed the RPF for all human rights transgressions. They wanted the population in general—and diplomats in particular—to believe that the RPF, not the government, was behind the escalating violence and turmoil in the country. However, their political rhetoric and ideological claims did little to discredit the well-documented field research of the original human rights organizations.

Women's organizations also flourished. Some were more or less associated with the government, through the Ministry of Women's Affairs. Others were independent. One of these independent groups, Haguruka, the Association for the Defense of the Rights of Women and Children, received funding from the embassy for a series of workshops to educate women about their civil and human rights. The project used the multiplier concept—training women who would in turn train other women—to reach target audiences in remote rural areas. The group's aim was eventually to provide counseling and legal assistance for women victims of domestic violence. Haguruka's leaders told me they could not address this goal directly or openly, however, because the issue was such a culturally taboo subject in Rwanda at that time. Through its grassroots work, Haguruka built a network that would serve as a foundation for addressing this issue when the climate for such action was more favorable.

Five women parliamentarians, all members of the MRND, formed an ad hoc group to seek embassy support for a series of workshops on women's civil rights. The concept was a good one, and I worked with them to transform the idea into action. However, the planning never evolved into a project that could be implemented. As a result, we were unable to provide funding.

The Media

When I first arrived in Rwanda, the government monopolized information dissemination through the Rwandan Information Office (Office Rwandais d'Information), which managed the production and dissemination of all government-owned print and electronic media. This included a national radio station, Radio Rwanda; an official press agency, Rwandan Press Agency (Agence Rwandaise de Presse; ARP); and, later, a television station.

Radio Rwanda was the government's flagship media operation. Because a significant portion of the population was illiterate, radio was the most important medium for ensuring that messages and information about government activities reached not only the townspeople but also those whose homes were scattered across the country's many hillsides. As almost all of its programs were in the local language, Kinyarwanda, Radio Rwanda was the major source of information about what was happening in the country. Battery-operated radios owned by most households in rural areas made Radio Rwanda broadcasts accessible to people living in areas where electricity was limited. I listened to Radio Rwanda's French-language news broadcast each morning as I prepared for work.

The government press agency ARP distributed a weekly Kinyarwanda-language newspaper, *Imvaho*, and two French-language products, a weekly newspaper, *La Relève*, and the daily *Bulletin de ARP*. Each provided a synopsis of the news and the government's key messages. Because of its virtual monopoly on press outlets, the government used the media for its propaganda. The messages were decidedly pro-Habyarimana, pro-MRND, and pro–Hutu supremacy. Virulent anti-Tutsi messages denigrated this minority group and denounced the RPF.

The government's only real media competition had always come from *Kinyameteka*, a twice-monthly Kinyarwanda-language newspaper published since 1933 under the auspices of the Catholic Church, a major force in Rwandan life and politics. The paper was widely distributed through the dioceses. At the time of my arrival in Rwanda, the editor of the paper was Abbé André Sibomana, the Hutu from the south-central area of Gitarama who was also an outspoken human rights advocate and leader of the human rights group ADL. Earlier the church had sent Sibomana to Lyon, France, to complete a two-year journalism course. When he returned from his studies in 1988, the Catholic bishop appointed him editor of *Kinyameteka*. He held this position until the genocide began in 1994.[5]

When Abbé Sibomana took over as editor of *Kinyameteka*, the newspaper was losing readership for its anodyne reporting in troubling times. Under Sibomana's leadership, however, the readership expanded from seven thousand to over thirteen thousand by 1994. He transformed the newspaper by publishing well-documented articles exposing human rights violations and other government abuses of power. He took great risks in his efforts to hold the government accountable for its decisions and actions. For publishing articles unfavorable to the president and the MRND, Sibomana received several death threats. In September 1990, before my time in Rwanda, he and three other journalists were brought to trial for publishing reports of government corruption. They were acquitted, however, after presenting substantial evidence to support their published allegations.[6]

In the best tradition of the craft, Sibomana practiced both investigative and adversarial journalism. His approach demonstrated his commitment to both justice and respect for human rights. Within the international community, Sibomana became well known and respected for his integrity and courage in challenging the government's line on a broad range of issues. In 2000 the International Press Institute named him posthumously one of the fifty World Press Freedom Heroes of the past fifty years.[7]

Another publication with Catholic ties was *Dialogue*, a monthly French-language news magazine published under the auspices of the Dominican Friars. Its editor was a Belgian priest, Father Guy Theunis. Because of its magazine format, *Dialogue* was able to delve more deeply into the controversies of the day. Each issue tended to include several articles exploring a single theme from a variety of perspectives. Contributors could include Rwandan academics, politicians, civil society representatives, and many others. Because it was published in the French language and appealed to academics, *Dialogue*'s circulation was somewhat limited among Rwandans. Nevertheless Father Theunis, like Abbé Sibomana, had a deep understanding of Rwandan society.

Privately owned newspapers began to make inroads into the government's domination of the print media in the late 1980s, even before President Habyarimana's 1990 promise of multiparty politics and democracy. After the promise of pluralism, the trickle of private newspapers became a flood. Many papers consisted of little more than one or two staff members with access to a telephone and a printing press. Some would appear and then disappear in rapid succession. Their orientation spanned the spectrum from pro-Habyarimana and his MRND party to pro-opposition positions and pro-RPF.

Once the new political parties were established, they tended to adopt one of these new papers, depending on which party the editors belonged to. The parties may have provided some funding for these private papers linked to them, even though several parties published their own party bulletins. Most of the papers, though, were beholden for funding to wealthy businessmen or groups of like-minded individuals who wanted a voice in the new, more open political environment. These private papers therefore generally became mouthpieces for political or individual interests.

Most notorious among the newspapers supporting the president and his MRND party was *Kangura*. Run by Hassan Ngeze, a former bus driver, it had gained notoriety for publishing the "Hutu Ten Commandments" in December 1990, a few months after the RPF invasion. This unabashedly racist manifesto exalted Hutu supremacy and became a primary point of reference for Hutu propaganda demonizing the Tutsi as the enemy. This manifesto was one of the earliest indications of sentiment within the country that totally opposed the democratization and peace processes which the United States and much of the diplomatic community supported so strongly.

Among the new newspapers reflecting opposition political party views, several stood out. *Isibo*, a weekly paper edited by Sixbert Musamgamfura, echoed the point of view of the Gitarama-based MDR and its leader, Faustin Twagiramungu. *Umurangi*, also linked to the MDR, eventually took an anti-Twagiramungu position, reflecting internal MDR disagreements. Some new newspapers advocated for the Butare-based PSD, some for the business-based PL. A few risked openly supporting the RPF. One such paper was *Rwanda Rushya*, edited by André Kameya, a Tutsi and member of the Liberal Party. Another was *Kanguka*, edited by the RPF militant Vincent Rwabuk-wisi and funded by a Tutsi businessman and RPF member named Valens Kajeguhakwa.[8]

This lively private press scene, however, was characterized across the board by ideological content that often denigrated, demonized, or ridiculed other perspectives. Scathing political cartoons, easily understood by both literate and illiterate Rwandans, inflamed passions and stoked hatred of the other, whether political or ethnic. Responsible, objective journalism was rare; instead the prevailing operational mode for these new papers was "no holds barred."

The government monopoly of radio airwaves weakened with the introduction in 1991 of Radio Muhabura, the clandestine radio station of the RPF, the armed, Uganda-based, primarily Tutsi rebel group. Its broadcasts from the mountainous region at the Rwanda-Uganda border provided a potential counterpoint to the dominant government radio and TV messages. The station's impact was limited, though, because its programs were in English and its frequency could not reach southern Rwanda, where opposition to the Habyarimana government was strongest. Nevertheless the station became quite popular, particularly among Tutsi who regularly risked tuning in, albeit clandestinely. If caught, persons listening to Radio Muhabura could be liable to punishment as RPF sympathizers. As the border conflict intensified, more and more people, mainly Tutsi, wanted to hear the RPF message. Radio Muhabura routinely denied government accusations of RPF responsibility for human rights abuses in connection with violence inside Rwanda or warfare at the border.

Despite the multitude of start-up newspapers and the existence of Radio Muhabura, the government radio station continued to overshadow both the print media and other electronic media. The new newspapers were constrained from extending circulation much beyond Kigali by limited funding and transport difficulties. Even the introduction of government-controlled television near the end of 1991 was unable to displace radio as the preferred communication medium. Television broadcasts initially aired only on weekends for two hours a day and reached viewers only within a thirty-mile radius of Kigali. The lack of electricity in the rural areas also limited television access. The president's cohorts controlled the government radio and dictated the government messages reaching most Rwandans, especially those outside Kigali with little access to the array of new newspapers. Only after the 1992 coalition government created a Ministry of Information with responsibility for both the radio and government news briefs was this hard-line Hutu media monopoly broken. With the leadership of the new information ministry in the hands of the opposition MDR party, the tone at the radio began to change.

Most media reports in Rwanda, whether printed or electronic, were inaccessible to most in the diplomatic community. Only the government's daily radio ARP news bulletin, its weekly press summary, *La Relève*, and the monthly magazine *Dialogue* were available in French. To follow the influential *Kinyameteka* and the burgeoning private print media, all written in Kinyarwanda, the local language common to all Rwandans, diplomats needed translations. At the U.S. Embassy local employees prepared daily summaries in French for the ambassador covering the most important print, radio, and television reports.

The embassy's public affairs office, then the United States Information Agency (USIA), advocated and encouraged responsible journalism. With the aim of reversing the practice of printing rumors and innuendo as if they were fact, USIA organized a number of workshops for journalists from both the private and the government press. There was little if any evidence, however, that the journalists ever acted upon our message in this cut-throat journalistic environment. We also protested to appropriate high-level government officials the abusive treatment accorded those private journalists who expressed opinions contrary to those close to the president, who controlled the government media content.

Comment

Being a diplomat in Rwanda at the start of its political transition to multiparty democracy was exciting. It was a heady time. Rwandans I met—political party leaders, human rights activists, journalists—

appeared energized by the promise of political reform. Those in the opposition were full of enthusiasm for the prospect of greater participation in the political process. All seemed to have high hopes for a successful transition to democracy. At the U.S. Embassy in the fall of 1991, supporting and encouraging democratization, as President Habyarimana had asked of us, was our highest priority.

The process of change would be neither easy nor smooth. But I had no idea how difficult and how rancorous it could be in cultures not accustomed to the democratic processes of a loyal opposition or to a peaceful alternation of power. Nor did I fully understand the stakes involved for those called to cede power in a culture where winner-take-all was the norm. I had no way of anticipating the kinds of actions they might take to keep from having to give up their power and positions with no guarantee of future participation in the political process. There were already hints of future problems that I failed to fully appreciate.

First, the transition to democracy was regarded in Kigali as a primarily Hutu affair. For the mostly Hutu, mostly southern opposition, political pluralism offered a way to access power and redress their grievances against the nearly twenty-year rule of the president and his northern entourage.

Second, the role and place of the Tutsi in Rwanda, and how they might be better integrated into Rwandan society, were not at issue in Kigali-based political reform discussions. The assumption among politically active Hutu and most observers, including diplomats, was that Tutsi would join the more open political process either through participation in existing political parties or by forming their own. Indeed most Tutsi democracy advocates inside Rwanda had already aligned themselves with Hutu colleagues rather than form separate political parties. How the RPF would participate was not an issue initially.

Third, the unchecked, emotionally charged media campaign championed Hutu supremacy and indiscriminately linked all Tutsi to the cause of the RPF enemy. The widespread fear this caused among Tutsi meant that few dared even join the democratization process, let alone risk overt, public support for the RPF invaders. Initially Rwanda's minority Tutsi had as much reason as the majority Hutu to view the RPF as an external military threat to Rwandan stability and their own security. Only when peace talks made Tutsi participation a factor in the power-sharing equation did these calculations change.

Fourth, despite the valiant efforts of various Rwandan and international human rights organizations to bring violations to light, neither government officials nor the existing judicial system could be counted on to hold perpetrators accountable.

Fifth, power remained concentrated in the ruling MRND party despite promises of a more open political process. There were already indications that many in the president's inner circle and in the MRND had no intention of letting democratization remove them from power.[9]

[2]

War Intrudes

Armed conflict between the Rwandan armed forces and the Rwandan Patriotic Front (RPF) had been simmering at the Ugandan border for nearly a year by the time I arrived in Kigali in August 1991. But it formed only a distant but constant backdrop to the political wrangling dominating discussions among Kigali's political elite. Maneuvering and positioning over the formation of a multiparty coalition government consumed the mostly Hutu dialogue between the ruling and opposition party leaders. Intense political exchanges scarcely acknowledged the ongoing, escalating civil war despite regular radio and press reports of the fighting. War seemed far away from Kigali and the everyday lives of people in the capital. The RPF's armed challenge seemed to be a separate matter from the internal domestic process of democratization.

The war at the border, which began October 1, 1990, with the invasion of RPF forces from Uganda, did affect the government of President Habyarimana and his MRND party. Armed conflict with the RPF forces, who were mostly Tutsi, posed an external threat that was every bit as serious as the political challenge from the predominantly Hutu internal opposition. Throughout the effort to transition to democracy and peace, both the Hutu opposition and the RPF threatened the incumbents' hold on power.

Refugee Roots to the Conflict

The flight of Rwanda's minority Tutsi began in the late 1950s in response to anti-Tutsi violence prompted initially by pre-independence competition among political parties. The parties had formed to contest a 1960 election for internal self-government. The stakes were high: this election would decide whether Hutu or Tutsi would rule Rwanda after independence. Anti-Tutsi violence continued after MDR-Parmehutu, a party advocating Hutu emancipation from both Belgian and Tutsi rule, won the June 1960 election.

Violence escalated after this government, with its support centered in the south, declared Rwanda a republic. This decision, confirmed by a 1961 referendum, effectively ended the Tutsi monarchy. The violence forced about one-third of Rwanda's 1960 Tutsi population to flee to neighboring countries before independence in 1962. Despite the violence, Belgium handed political power to the Hutu-supremacist MDR-Parmehutu party in power at the time of independence.

In the 1960s and early 1970s, this MDR-Parmehutu government, reelected in 1965, carried out periodic pogroms against Tutsi to assert dominance and control. Unsuccessful attempts by various groups of Tutsi exiles to fight their way back into Rwanda were always quashed by the military and countered with more Hutu attacks. Many Tutsi were killed in these episodes of violence. Many others, fearing for their lives, sought refuge in the neighboring states of Uganda, Tanzania, Burundi, and Zaire.

After the army chief of staff, Juvénal Habyarimana, seized power in a 1973 coup, his northern Hutu government enforced a quota system that limited Tutsi representation in higher education and the civil service. Although human rights violations and political persecution against Tutsi continued, there were no reported massacres of Tutsi between 1973 and 1990. Only after the invasion of the RPF in 1990 did the Habyarimana government resort to the pattern of massacring Tutsi.

RPF leaders asserted two reasons for their cross-border invasion into northern Rwanda from Uganda on October 1, 1990. First, they claimed the right of refugees to return to Rwanda, a right President Habyarimana had consistently refused to recognize. His argument against refugee return turned on population density. He repeatedly maintained that there was not enough land in densely populated Rwanda to accommodate the return of all the refugees, mostly Tutsi, who had fled the country since 1959. Many people living in the country already had insufficient land for subsistence farming, he claimed. Space for grazing Tutsi cattle was, in his view, out of the question.

Estimates of the numbers of Rwandan refugees in neighboring countries in 1990 vary. The author Gérard Prunier started with the UN refugee agency's estimates of 150,000 Rwandan refugees in 1960. From there he calculated the 1990 number at approximately 600,000 to 700,000, including their children and grandchildren.[1] The RPF countered that one million Rwandans were living outside Rwanda when the war started in 1990.

Second, the Tutsi-led RPF wanted a role in the political liberalization process the president had announced, which the leaders said would have to include Habyarimana's departure from government.[2] Most RPF leaders left Rwanda as toddlers with their parents in the early 1960s. They had grown up as refugees in Uganda and were in their early thirties when they launched their 1990 attack on Rwanda. Many were also better versed in warfare and guerrilla tactics than those who had mounted failed attacks in the 1960s. They had played a key role in helping Uganda's president, Yoweri Museveni, seize power in 1986. Having gained Museveni's respect and trust as fighters in his insurgent forces, many Tutsi refugees rose to important positions in the Ugandan military once Museveni took over as president.

A third reason influenced the timing of the RPF invasion: Rwandan Tutsi were no longer welcome in Uganda. After thirty years of adapting to life in Uganda and seeing their children integrated into Ugandan institutions—especially the army—Rwandan Tutsi were still viewed as outsiders and resented for holding prominent positions at the expense of Ugandan citizens. This anti-Tutsi sentiment made the Rwandan Tutsi refugees a political liability for President Museveni. Despite his gratitude for their support during his quest for power and the ethnic links between his Hima clan in Uganda and the Tutsi of Rwanda, Museveni began to encourage the Rwandans to return home. In a 1988 petition to President Habyarimana following a conference in Washington DC, Rwanda refugees in Uganda sought the right to return. Their request was rejected. The formation of the RPF and its military wing was the consequence.

Government Forces Receive Help

Both Belgium and France sent troops to Rwanda within days of the RPF's October 1990 invasion. The Belgian troops, intended to protect Belgians living and working in Rwanda, withdrew by the end of October. The French, however, maintained a military presence until the end of 1993 under the terms of a 1975 military cooperation agreement with Rwanda. Throughout this period a contingent of about three hundred French troops rotated every three months with a contingent from the French Foreign Legion. The role of these troops was to protect the approximately 1,200 French civilians living and working in Rwanda. The French withdrew these troops in December 1993 in accordance with provisions of the Arusha peace agreement between the Rwandan government and the RPF.

This French military presence augmented an already large military assistance program that provided advice and training to the Rwandan armed forces. The number of its personnel and the extent of its military cooperation meant that France was gradually replacing the Belgian colonial power as Rwanda's most important European backer. Their close relationship with the Rwandan armed forces marked the French as pro-Habyarimana; French forces repeatedly rescued the Habyarimana government when RPF military pressure increased. The French prioritized state security over democratization.

The Government Responds to the RPF Attack

The government's initial responses to the RPF invasion from Uganda followed historical patterns in the wake of refugee efforts to fight their way back into Rwanda: appeal to Hutu solidarity in the face of a threat from an armed Tutsi enemy and exact reprisals against Tutsi living inside Rwanda.

The government's first ploy was to heighten Hutu fear of the RPF and, by implication, of the Tutsi living inside Rwanda. Four nights after the RPF invasion, the military, under the control of the president's MRND party, staged a simulated attack on the capital and blamed it on the Tutsi-dominated RPF. The masquerade included exploding bombs and shooting into the air, terrifying Hutu and Tutsi residents alike. When the ruse was revealed, people were relieved, but latent Hutu suspicions of their Tutsi neighbors had been awakened and could not be easily suppressed.

Radio Rwanda, also controlled by the one-party government, duly reported this manufactured attack and wasted little time rolling out an anti-RPF, anti-Tutsi media campaign. A steady barrage of verbal vitriol demonized the *inyenzi* (cockroaches), a pejorative reference to the armed Tutsi invaders. The Radio Rwanda campaign also labeled all Tutsi living in Rwanda RPF sympathizers, likely RPF accomplices, and ultimately the enemy of all Hutu.

The government's second ploy was to heighten fear among the Tutsi living in Rwanda of possible reprisals for RPF actions. After the staged attack on Kigali, Tutsi didn't have long to wait. The government began almost immediately to arrest prominent Tutsi. Within a few months, more than six thousand Tutsi—mostly doctors, lawyers, businessmen, and intellectuals—and some Hutu had been jailed. They were accused of being *ibiyitso* (accomplices) of the RPF. The *ibiyitso* label was applied without regard to whether individual Tutsi had dared to support the RPF openly or had any connection with the group at all. Rwandan employees of the U.S. and other embassies were among those arrested. All were imprisoned without charges, many for up to six months. Like Japanese Americans interned in the United States during World War II, the Tutsi detained in this wave of mass arrests felt betrayed by their country. Today many remain deeply scarred by the experience.

To underscore to Tutsi inside Rwanda the threat the RPF invasion posed to their security, Hutu-led massacres began almost immediately. Reminiscent of past government reprisals against Tutsi for unsuccessful Tutsi refugee attacks, the first massacre followed swiftly in the wake of the RPF's October 1 invasion. Just days later, killing began in Kibilira, a commune in the northern prefecture of Ruhengeri. In January and February 1991, the Bagogwe, a Tutsi subgroup, became the victims of killings in several communes of the same prefecture.

War Intrudes

More localized massacres would follow in 1992 and 1993. The prelude to the massacres often involved local authorities spreading rumors to whip up Hutu animosity against their Tutsi neighbors. Communal authorities, sometimes aided by the military, and later in conjunction with political party militia, primed the pump by leading some community members in killing the first few Tutsi targets.[3]

The RPF Attacks, Stumbles, Recovers

The 1990 RPF invasion, like earlier ill-fated attempts by armed refugee groups to fight their way back into Rwanda, suffered early setbacks. Government forces succeeded in pushing the RPF back into Uganda by the end of October, albeit with help from French forces sent under their 1975 defense pact with Rwanda. President Mobutu Sese Seko of neighboring Zaire, a good friend of Habyarimana, also sent troops in early October.[4]

Additionally, on the second day of the invasion, the RPF's popular commander, Maj. Gen. Fred Rwigyema, was killed under circumstances that remain unclear. Together these setbacks could have doomed the RPF effort. But the armed group persisted, resolving its leadership crisis by summoning Maj. Paul Kagame back to Uganda from a military training course he had only just begun at Fort Leavenworth in the United States. Kagame immediately took command of the RPF.

Kagame used the first few months to regroup and reorganize the RPF following its withdrawal from Rwanda. Then, in January 1991, the RPF attacked Ruhengeri, a major town in northern Rwanda, and controlled it for a day before retreating into the bush. Significantly, before its departure, the RPF broke into the Ruhengeri prison and freed a number of longtime Hutu political prisoners.

This successful raid against the government army's northern headquarters in Ruhengeri disturbed Rwandan military and civilian leaders alike. Clearly the RPF had become a force to be reckoned with. Rwandan civilians and the military realized that the border conflict was unlikely to be as brief as they had anticipated.

The Ruhengeri attack had another unforeseen effect: it brought RPF commander Paul Kagame to the attention of military analysts in the West and began to build his reputation as an outstanding military strategist. Kagame told us several years later, after the Arusha Peace Accord had been signed, that he was glad his training course in the United States had started out with military strategy. It had given him, he said, a good grounding for his RPF leadership role.

When I got to Rwanda in August 1991, the war was still simmering at the northern border. I soon learned from the French that, contrary to the government's contention, the RPF had already gained a foothold in a remote area inside Rwanda. The government, however, did not acknowledge an RPF presence on Rwandan soil until much later. By mid-1992, though, after the RPF moved its headquarters to the Mulindi tea plantation not far from Byumba, there could be no denying the RPF presence on Rwandan territory.

Early Peacemaking Diplomacy Goes Nowhere

Diplomatic efforts to end the fighting between the Rwandan government and the RPF began almost immediately after the October 1 invasion. These early efforts involved primarily regional governments as well as local and regional organizations.

Neighboring countries and the Organization of African Unity (OAU), precursor to the current African Union, took the lead. At a Tanzanian-hosted regional summit sponsored by the OAU in mid-October 1990, the neighboring states agreed to help resolve the Rwanda crisis. A second OAU-sponsored summit held a month or so later in Zaire agreed to send a military observer group to Rwanda under the jurisdiction of the OAU Liberation Committee. Though not actually deployed until a year later, this group marked the first ever involvement of the OAU in conflict-resolution activities, now a hallmark of the African Union.

Repeated efforts to fashion a cease-fire and start negotiations to end the conflict, however, made little headway. With prodding by Rwanda's neighbors, government and RPF representatives met several times to discuss how to bring the conflict to an end. At these various meetings, they concluded cease-fires, developed frameworks for future talks, and made commitments to each other and the international community. The United States had even sponsored unsuccessful secret talks in Harare, Zimbabwe. Nevertheless all of these efforts were either short-lived or never got off the drawing board.[5]

Common ground eluded negotiators in large part because each side remained steadfast in its negotiating positions throughout the first year and a half of the conflict. The Rwandan government held the Ugandan government responsible for RPF actions, accused President Museveni of supporting the rebel force, and demanded that Uganda end its interference in Rwanda. Furthermore, Rwanda's negotiators, led by Foreign Minister Casimir Bizimungu, were Hutu hard-liners and MRND loyalists who, along with key ministry officials, held strong anti-RPF views. The historical association of Museveni with the RPF hardened the Rwandan government's position.

Museveni, on the other hand, rejected all allegations of support for the RPF and refused to be drawn into negotiations as its surrogate. Just a day after the invasion, he had insisted to the U.S. assistant secretary of state for Africa, Ambassador Herman J. Cohen, that he had no advance knowledge of the RPF's intentions and was in no position to do anything about it. Cohen became suspicious the following day, however, when he learned that Museveni was urging the French and Belgians not to send troops to Rwanda.[6] It was not long before the United States had intelligence confirming some form of Ugandan involvement in the RPF invasion. Initially U.S. diplomats in Uganda took a hard line with Museveni, stressing his responsibility and pressing him to act to end the RPF invasion.[7]

The RPF denied Rwandan contentions just as adamantly as did the Ugandans, insisting it had received no help from President Museveni or the Ugandan government. Therefore the Rwandan government's position of holding Uganda accountable for RPF actions was a nonstarter. Instead, the RPF maintained, the Rwandan government would have to address its concerns directly with the RPF leadership before any meaningful steps toward peace could take place.

As long as this intransigence held on both sides, there was no hope of a breakthrough. Only after an opposition political party member became foreign minister in the 1992 coalition government did negotiations begin to move forward. Museveni and the RPF never changed their denials of Ugandan support for the insurgents.

At the Arusha peace talks two years later, RPF soldiers assured me that they had in fact deserted from the Ugandan military and taken their weapons and heavy equipment with them to launch their cross-border invasion without the knowledge or support of Museveni. I found this scenario highly unlikely, given Museveni's close personal ties with RPF leaders from their guerrilla war days. Additionally RPF "deserters" circulated freely in Uganda without retribution.

U.S. Embassy Concerns

To keep abreast of the course of the war, we at the U.S. Embassy consulted regularly with colleagues at the French Embassy and its military aid mission. In contrast to the extensive French connections with the Rwandan military, the U.S. Embassy had no resident military attaché, and we sponsored only one small military training program. The U.S. International Military Education and Training program had been sending one or two Rwandan soldiers to the United States for yearlong study programs, much like the one Kagame had briefly attended. The embassy's economic-consular officer, Michael Zorick, managed the program and enjoyed good relations with his Rwandan counterparts. However, once the war began, Rwanda suspended its participation in the program. Top soldiers could no longer be spared for study overseas; the army needed all available officers for the war effort.

Along with other representatives from the diplomatic community, Zorick made several government-organized visits to the war front. There he was able to see firsthand what was happening and its impact on the border region. These visits ceased, however, when being close to the escalating fighting became too harrowing for comfort. That occurred shortly after I arrived in Rwanda.

The U.S. ambassador frequently raised the issue of the war with his contacts in the Rwandan government and with political party leaders. He stressed the urgency of concluding a cease-fire and negotiating a settlement to the conflict. We emphasized the same policy message in discussions with our diplomatic counterparts at other Kigali embassies.

Through Ambassador Flaten, the embassy coordinated policy closely with colleagues in Washington, who took the lead in formulating international and multilateral diplomatic initiatives on Rwanda. Assistant Secretary Cohen and his deputies maintained communication with French representatives concerning Rwanda. Once the

RPF appointed representatives in the United States, the desk officer for Rwanda—first Carol Fuller and then Kevin Aiston—had regular contact with them. By late 1991 both the United States and France were engaged in separate diplomatic initiatives with RPF representatives in their respective countries. Both aimed at finding ways to bridge the divide between the two sides.

Human rights violations also concerned the U.S. Embassy. In the early days of the border conflict, Western ambassadors, including Flaten, made diplomatic interventions calling for an end to the massacres of Tutsi that followed the RPF's October 1990 attack. They were also quick to speak out against the mass arrests of Tutsi in the wake of the attack. Ambassador Flaten worked tirelessly for the release of the most senior Rwandan employee at the U.S. Agency for International Development, a Tutsi who had been swept up in the government arrest net. Flaten acted both in concert with his diplomatic colleagues and on his own. Only after Sylvestre Nsanzimana, a former Hutu diplomat, replaced a hard-line minister of justice in early 1991 were the last of those arbitrarily imprisoned gradually released.

Armed Forces on Both Sides Expand

As the war dragged on with frequent skirmishes but no clear victor, both the government and the RPF built up troop strength. The Rwandan Armed Forces (Forces Armées Rwandaise; FAR) numbered about 5,200 at the time of the RPF invasion; at the end of 1991, there were thirty thousand soldiers, and by mid-1992, when peace talks began, the FAR had expanded to its peak of fifty thousand troops.[8] This rapid troop buildup had a devastating impact on the national budget. Arms and ammunition were in constant demand. The exponential increase in personnel also took a toll on the discipline and professionalism that had once been hallmarks of the Rwandan army.

The RPF force grew almost as quickly. From an estimated five thousand fighters within six months of the invasion, the force reached twelve thousand by the end of 1992. It reportedly peaked at about twenty-five thousand troops at the time the genocide began in April 1994.[9] Some new troops had come from within Rwanda as young Tutsi volunteers left their homes to join the RPF and fight for the cause. Most, however, had come from refugee communities in Uganda,

Tanzania, and Burundi. Even some Zairean citizens of Tutsi descent joined the RPF and later took their fight back to the eastern region of the Democratic Republic of the Congo (previously Zaire). When the RPF turned to the Tutsi diaspora for funding, Tutsi in Canada and the United States became the primary financial backers, though Tutsi from throughout the world regularly contributed to the war effort.

Refugee Return in the Works

President Habyarimana's 1986 declaration that refugees could not return to Rwanda because there was not enough land for them prompted Tutsi refugees to action. In 1988 they held an international conference for Rwandan refugees in Washington DC, with cosponsorship from the U.S. Committee for Refugees.[10] As the result of a resolution passed at that meeting, a group of refugees petitioned Habyarimana for permission to return to Rwanda. When the request was denied, refugees in Uganda decided to transform their refugee welfare association into the Rwandan Patriotic Front, which would take up arms to fight its way back to Rwanda.

On a separate track, the Office of the United Nations High Commissioner for Refugees (UNHCR) began in the late 1980s to urge President Habyarimana to take the return of refugees seriously and begin planning for it. Despite Habyarimana's reluctance, his government did begin to take steps toward refugee return even before the RPF invasion; for instance, in 1989 he established the Commission on Rwandan Refugees in Uganda. In cooperation with the OAU and UNHCR, a revived Rwandan-Ugandan interministerial committee on refugees devised a survey so that UNHCR could determine the demand for repatriation among Rwandans in Uganda and begin to prepare for their return.[11] Indeed on the very day the RPF launched its military attack in 1990, representatives from the refugee community in Uganda were scheduled to travel to Rwanda to assess conditions for their return and report back to their community. Needless to say, this visit never took place.

While I was serving at the U.S. mission in Geneva monitoring UNHCR activity in Africa, I knew of neither this UNHCR initiative nor the Washington DC conference that led to the creation of the RPF and its intention to take up arms. Competing refugee situations, such as the sudden onset of wars in Liberia and Somalia, were emergencies that consumed my attention. I was aware, however, of plans for UNHCR to convene a regional summit in Dar es Salaam on refugee return as part of international efforts to end the fighting in Rwanda.

At that January 1991 meeting, in a significant departure from his earlier position, Rwanda's president affirmed the right of refugees to return and reintegrate into Rwandan society. The agreement emanating from that meeting, the "Dar es Salaam Declaration on the Refugee Problem," called for UNHCR to draw up a plan of action for the return of the refugees, for reintegration projects, and for a donor roundtable to raise funds to pay for this mammoth undertaking. Repatriation could involve upwards of 600,000 Rwandan refugees and other Rwandans living in exile.

Sergio Vieira de Mello led the UNHCR's delegation to this conference. I had worked closely with him and his UNHCR officers a couple of years earlier on the Comprehensive Plan of Action for resolving the Vietnam refugee crisis, and I strongly encouraged him to apply some of the same principles to a regional solution for the Rwandan refugees. I already knew I would be transferring to Rwanda the following summer. I also knew that no one would have a better chance of pulling a rabbit out of this hat than Sergio, an experienced, engaging, and persuasive diplomat. Yet, although useful commitments resulted from this conference, no grand plan emerged.

Nevertheless the "Dar es Salaam Declaration on the Refugee Problem" and the plan of action it called for provided Rwandan government and UNHCR officials an enabling environment to address this critical issue with a plan of their own. During the last quarter of 1991 I met the officials involved in elaborating such a plan. In my discussions with the UNHCR representative in Rwanda, Gesche Karrenbrock, and with Habyarimana government officials responsible for planning refugee return, it was evident that they were making progress assessing the issues and developing a strategy for return and reintegration.

One element of their proposed strategy was an amnesty law that would absolve all returnees of any crimes against the state committed up to the signing of the amnesty. This was to include those who had taken up arms and participated in the RPF attacks. After the draft bill became law in early December 1991, only a few exiled Tutsi businessmen took advantage of it. Later, during peace negotiations in Arusha, the RPF would argue that they had rejected the amnesty because it implied wrongdoing on their part, which they denied. The government's expectation, that this law could help end the fighting, never materialized.

War-Displaced Persons

The armed conflict had its humanitarian consequences. Although the fighting preoccupied the government, it seemed far away from the frenzy of political activity in the capital. It was not, however, distant from the 150,000 or so Rwandans who, by the end of 1991, had been forced to flee their homes in the border region to safer locations in the Rwandan interior. Government-controlled media reported RPF attacks centered on civilian targets: marketplaces, schools, hospitals, and the makeshift settlements of those displaced by the fighting. The impression conveyed to radio listeners was that the RPF considered anywhere civilians congregated a legitimate military target. There were also media reports charging that the RPF kidnapped civilians and took them to Uganda.

Those fleeing RPF attacks or forced to move by the government settled in tent camps in the northeastern and north-central parts of the country. The International Committee of the Red Cross (ICRC) and Catholic Relief Services organized the camps and delivered humanitarian assistance, which kept the internally displaced persons (IDPs) alive. I visited several such camps with an ICRC official. In one, a conglomeration of tent-like structures perched on a sloping hillside. The IDPs had chopped down the ubiquitous eucalyptus trees to make room for their settlement. Water faucets, latrines, and food storage depots installed by ICRC provided for the IDPs' basic needs. The displaced sat at the doors of their tents or milled about in quiet conversation with other IDPs. Children played in the pathways between the tents. Most of the IDPs were women and children, but some elderly men and a few young ones were also about.

The local populations in areas where IDPs settled were indirectly impacted by the war as well. The need for wood in the makeshift camps took a toll on the environment. The rustic shelters intended to keep out the rain and cold, characteristic of the high altitudes of Rwanda's northern hills, required branches supple enough to be bowed and covered by thick plastic sheeting. Limbs of young trees and twigs collected from nearby forests were also used to fuel cooking fires and provide warmth. Continuous, systematic culling of trees for firewood and shelter destroyed forests surrounding the IDP camps. These were often community forests that provided important revenue for local needs. Their destruction became a serious source of friction between the displaced and the local population.

Comment

Promoting peace between government forces and the RPF was as important a diplomatic policy priority for the United States as was support for democratization. However, when I arrived in Kigali in the fall of 1991, Rwanda's second transition—from war to peace—was not yet under way. Each international effort at peacemaking had come up empty-handed. The same Rwandan government and RPF representatives met periodically, made the same uncompromising demands, and arrived at the same results.

The issue central to their intransigence—whether Uganda and President Museveni were supporting the RPF—underscored the regional character of Rwanda's internal conflict. This issue affected not only early regional peacemaking efforts but also U.S. policy formulation toward Uganda and the incipient war in Rwanda. Ambassador Flaten had recommended sanctions against Uganda in response to its support for RPF destabilization of Rwanda, but the U.S. government decided to continue aid and political support to Uganda on grounds that the RPF invasion of Rwanda would likely be short-lived.[12] Ambassador Cohen wrote that in retrospect the United States should have denounced the RPF invasion, pressed Uganda to force an RPF withdrawal from Rwanda, and launched a diplomatic process to address the refugee issue.[13]

Confined as it was to skirmishes at the Rwanda-Uganda border, the war initially seemed to have little, if any, impact on the transition to democratic pluralism that was the talk of Kigali. Democratization and the border conflict were on separate diplomatic tracks. The two tracks merged into one, however, when power sharing became the core issue at the Arusha peace talks. Until then, Rwandans I met from the political parties, the media, and the judiciary had little to say about the war. Their attention was fixed on political jockeying in Kigali rather than on the fighting at the border.

In the early days of my tenure at the embassy, several of my contacts helped me understand what had happened during the year since the RPF invasion, before I arrived. Some had been among those arrested; others had been working to have them released. Human rights activists had documented and reported on abuses committed by both sides during the fighting. They knew what was happening in the countryside.

At that time I felt no concern for my own safety. Like others living in Kigali, Rwandans and foreigners alike, I believed the conflict was contained at the border, far away. The fighting, however, could not have been much more than sixty miles away as the crow flies. The general lack of concern for the armed conflict reflected a profound miscalculation of the Rwandan Tutsi refugees' determination to return home, a goal evidently shared by Museveni.

I once got a stark reminder that the war was real and not that far away. When I showed up one Sunday at the Belgian Club for a swim, there, beside the pool, was a rifle mounted on a small tripod aimed over the water. A second glance revealed a uniformed French Foreign Legionnaire sitting casually nearby. None of the men, women, or children around or in the pool seemed concerned. I didn't stay long.

While I was getting to know Rwandans, I was also meeting my diplomatic counterparts. We often compared notes on our assessments of the situation in Rwanda, as well as on the steps our governments were taking to address the situation diplomatically and through our aid missions. Our consultations showed that we were working in parallel but not necessarily in concert. This would begin to change as our diplomatic goals and objectives converged around the success of the peace talks.

[3]

Rights Abuses and Violence Sow Fear

Human Rights Abuses Mount

Freedom of association and freedom of speech, although guaranteed by Rwanda's constitution and expected as part of political reform, were under assault when I arrived in Rwanda in 1991. The political playing field was anything but level. After nearly twenty years of one-party rule, the president's MRND party still controlled all the levers of power at all levels of society. Habyarimana's stated commitment to multiparty politics notwithstanding, the MRND showed little if any interest in creating space for the newly formed opposition parties to build their following, conduct their business, or communicate with their followers.

The government used RPF attacks as a smoke screen for its own human rights abuses. Both the mass arrests of approximately six thousand Tutsi professionals and the government propaganda campaign denigrating Tutsi and labeling them RPF sympathizers and enemies had stoked the embers of ethnic fear and hatred. By constantly reinforcing these ideas, the media contributed to the reprisals that were perpetrated against Tutsi living in Rwanda, as well as Hutu political opponents. These reprisals came in the form of threats, arrests, detentions, disappearances, and recurring massacres. Victims of human rights abuses were primarily Tutsi, but Hutu democracy advocates also received threats.

Opposition party leaders frequently told embassy officials about being denied permits to hold political rallies with party members and about being harassed by the police even when they had all the proper papers in hand. Opposition political leaders asserted that their party members should be allowed to gather in public places without interference, just as the ruling party did. How else, they lamented, could they motivate and communicate with supporters? This was especially important, they maintained, given that they were regularly denied access to the airwaves of the country's only radio station by its MRND managers. Their party communiqués, they complained, were not broadcast, their announcements did not make the news, and their events were not covered by government journalists. Some opposition party members told us they had been fired from their civil service jobs for changing their political affiliation.

We at the embassy used our diplomatic access to press government authorities for an end to these abuses. We reminded them of their commitment to open the political system to participation by all, urged them to respect basic freedoms of expression and assembly as their constitution and a democratic system required, and warned of the risk of violence should such disregard of rights continue.

Journalists frequently bore the brunt of the government's heavy hand. For publishing articles or cartoons uncomplimentary to the president or his party, many were harassed, arrested, tortured, and even threatened with death. Some journalists reportedly went into hiding to avoid such reprisals.

In one widely publicized case, the opposition journalist Boniface Ntawuyirushintege, editor of *Umurangi*, a paper linked to the largest opposition party, the MDR, wrote about his ordeal of arrest and torture in detention. He revealed that the soles of his feet had been so badly thrashed that he could barely walk; to support his allegations, he published pictures of his injured feet. He named as his assailant Capt. Pascal Simbikangwa, head of the government's intelligence service and a member of the president's inner circle.

Ntawuyirushintege also made the rounds of the embassies to tell his story. As the officer responsible for covering human rights issues, I met with him when he came to the U.S. Embassy. I remember him as a big man who might have been expected to tolerate considerable pain. He vividly recounted his horrifying treatment at the hands of government authorities. The embassy denounced the beating of this journalist, and the intimidation of journalists in general, to the minister of justice.

There is no indication that anything ever came of our representations to government officials. Captain Simbikangwa, whose reputation for torture was well known, was never brought to trial or held accountable by the judicial system for his actions. On March 3, 2014, however, twenty years after the genocide ended, a French criminal court convicted Simbikangwa of complicity in genocide and crimes against humanity for his actions during the four months of killing in 1994.

Massacres Target Tutsi

In early March 1992 violence erupted in the Bugesera region south of Kigali. In a five-day period, March 4–9, at least three hundred Tutsi were brutally killed, and many Tutsi homes were burned to the ground. An estimated fifteen thousand fled to the safety of churches in the area. Although the government-controlled media portrayed the attack as a spontaneous Hutu response to a legitimate Tutsi threat, the reality was quite the opposite. The perpetrators had carefully orchestrated the operation to make it look spontaneous.[1]

Gradually I learned from human rights contacts, other Rwandans, and colleagues at other embassies how the Bugesera massacre had unfolded. In the days and weeks leading up to the massacre, anonymous tracts, false media reports, and rumors warned of imminent infiltration and attacks by the *inyenzi* (cockroaches) intended to arouse Hutu fears of their Tutsi neighbors. For example, following a Liberal Party (PL) rally in the region, an unsigned tract circulated accusing Justin Mugenzi, Hutu president of this multiethnic party, of having incited Tutsi to kill Hutu. Local authorities spread allegations that young Tutsi were increasingly leaving the region to join the RPF in Uganda. On March 3 ruling party ideologues broadcast a Radio Rwanda message warning of imminent Tutsi plans to kill Hutu in the Bugesera region, information later determined by Rwandan human rights groups to be bogus.

The unfounded tracts and rumors spread by local authorities, along with the media's concocted story, were part of an orchestrated strategy to pave the way for violence against Tutsi. The message "Kill or be killed" resonated with Hutu throughout the Bugesera area. Most had migrated there decades earlier in search of land, some from the president's region in the northwest of the country, some from heavily populated areas of the south, and others from neighboring Burundi to escape Tutsi violence there. But Tutsi lived in Bugesera, too, having moved into the then largely empty region even earlier, in 1959, to escape Hutu violence elsewhere in Rwanda.

On March 4, the day after the Radio Rwanda ruse, the slaughter began. It spread quickly. Regular army soldiers and members of the Interahamwe, the militia of the MRND, together with local Hutu civilians, began attacking and killing Tutsi. By March 9, five days later, calm had returned to the area. But unthinkable damage had been done.

The diplomatic community responded quickly to the horror. Canadian, Swiss, and Belgian diplomats traveled to Bugesera to find out what had happened and to serve as an international presence in the area. The U.S. ambassador, Robert Flaten, led a joint diplomatic representation to the president to protest these killings and demand that the culprits be found and tried for their crimes. I was unable to accompany my diplomatic colleagues into the area, however, because the ambassador had put the Bugesera region temporarily off-limits to U.S. citizens for security reasons.

Several hundred persons were arrested and accused of committing these massacres, but they were later released on technicalities. Only one gendarme, who was charged with killing an Italian lay sister during the massacre, was brought to trial. He was convicted and given a nominal sentence. The pattern of impunity for those who engaged in such horrific acts was becoming well established.

The Bugesera massacre, though the first to occur during my tenure in Rwanda, had been only the most recent localized massacre since the RPF's October 1990 invasion from Uganda. Just days after the RPF crossed into Rwanda, Tutsi were attacked and killed in Kibilira, a district in the northwest. In early 1991, after the RPF's raid on the northern town of Ruhengeri, Hutu in the area attacked the Bagogwe, a pastoral subgroup of the Tutsi. As in Bugesera, the appearance of spontaneity in these earlier massacres belied the reality of orchestrated violence. Massacres such as these would occur periodically prior to the 1994 start of the genocide. Between 1990 and 1993 Human Rights Watch counted seventeen such massacres occurring mostly in the president's northwestern stronghold.[2]

Random Violence Claims Arbitrary Victims

About the same time as the Bugesera massacre in March 1992, random violence began to escalate in Kigali and elsewhere in the country. Fear of arbitrary attacks spread among the populace at large. On March 9, the same day the Bugesera massacres ended, a truck hit a land mine buried just under the surface of a dirt road in Kigali. On March 20 a bomb exploded in a taxi minibus that was loading passengers at the Kigali bus station. The wife of a U.S. Embassy workman died in that attack. Grenades, selling for less than three U.S. dollars each in the Kigali central market, were thrown into crowds at the bus station, killing and injuring innocent civilians. Grenades became the weapon of choice for ordinary burglars as well. No one was ever arrested for these crimes. The government claimed that the invading armed Tutsi of the RPF had infiltrated government-controlled areas and were committing these attacks against Rwandan civilians. Cited as proof: most of the victims were Hutu. The RPF denied these and similar government accusations. No arrests were ever made.

We at the U.S. Embassy were appalled by these random attacks on civilians. On the one hand, the government's claim of RPF culpability seemed unlikely. In early 1992 the fighting was confined mainly to Rwanda's northern border with Uganda. Could the RPF have actually infiltrated Kigali and the president's stronghold in the northwest, committed these heinous crimes, and evaded capture afterward? Did the RPF have the means and matériel to conduct such operations? And what interest would the RPF have in making itself look even worse in the eyes of the civilian population?

On the other hand, we did not want to believe that government officials or other adherents of the MRND party would orchestrate such attacks against civilians, Hutu and Tutsi alike, just to feed the anti-Tutsi media frenzy and score propaganda points with the Hutu public. It was hard for me to accept such a cynical interpretation of events.

Although we diplomats did not believe we were targets of this escalating random violence from either side, we realized we were at risk. We began curtailing our movements around town and, to a large extent, around the country. I had enjoyed walking around downtown Kigali, browsing through the market and small, nearby shops. With the area no longer safe, however, I relied on my Tutsi cook to do the shopping for most of my food and household necessities. Sadly, I recognized that he was putting himself at great risk.

One of my pastimes had been to eat out in small, local restaurants that served African food where the clientele was primarily Rwandan. However, after a bomb exploded under a table in one I had frequented, seriously injuring a client, I came to the stark realization that these local restaurants too had to be off limits.

As diplomats of the United States, our primary responsibility is always the safety of our citizens overseas. As the random violence escalated, of particular concern were the nearly one hundred Peace Corps volunteers scattered throughout the rural areas in the south of the country. Even though there were no reports of random violence in the south, taxi buses, like the one in which a bomb exploded, were the volunteers' primary mode of transportation. They had few options should they need to travel from their posts to Kigali or elsewhere. Consequently news of random attacks on taxi buses and land mines planted even on lightly traveled roads was especially worrying. Thinking that time would allow the situation to become calmer, the Peace Corps banned volunteers from all travel for a two-week period.

Even after the two-week travel hiatus ended, however, Peace Corps volunteers remained at risk. When they visited Kigali they were more vulnerable to random violence than the rest of the American community because they were more likely to be in the bus station, the central market, or other places that had been, and might again become, sites of violence. A single incident showed us how true this was. The night after several volunteers enjoyed music and dancing at a local Kigali nightclub, a small bomb went off on the establish-

Rights Abuses and Violence Sow Fear

ment's premises. Although there were no serious injuries, this haunt too I crossed off my list of entertainment possibilities.

Comment

1. *Webs of ambiguity*: As I sought to understand the reasons and motivations for this violence, it gradually became clear to me that Rwandans were masters at weaving webs of ambiguity to mask responsibility for any given situation. Logical analysis could generally suggest several competing, yet plausible, explanations. The multiple possibilities resulting from the webs of ambiguity allowed all sides to sow doubt and deny responsibility for any abuses or violence. This plausible deniability by all possible culprits meant none could be held accountable for their actions or the consequences of those actions. Such carefully crafted webs of ambiguity opened opportunities for propagandists on both sides to exploit preconceived notions and to blame the other.

Even more perplexing was my realization that understanding any given situation might require taking into account seemingly unrelated factors or events totally outside the situation of immediate concern. To use a baseball analogy, the best explanation was likely to come out of left field.

Whatever the explanations, tensions mounted between Hutu and Tutsi as each side blamed the other for the random violence and human rights abuses. These tragedies became a permanent feature of life in Kigali and other parts of the country. The unpredictability of events, the ambiguity surrounding responsibility for them, and the culture of impunity from accountability were the hallmarks of Rwanda's ever-increasing insecurity.

2. *Scapegoating the RPF*: The border conflict, viewed from Kigali as an irritant and a distraction from democratization, made the RPF a convenient scapegoat for any violence or infringements of human rights within the country. According to the government line, RPF infiltrators and their Tutsi accomplices within the country were undoubtedly responsible. With government media promoting this message at every opportunity, Tutsi living inside the country were being set up for individual reprisals and collective punishment.

Such unproven accusations made all Tutsi vulnerable and paved the way for genocide.

3. *The stress of fear*: Constant fear of life-threatening violence created unimaginable stress for everyone. Only much later could I really understand what that meant to Rwandans. When I went to Tanzania for several months in 1993 as the official U.S. observer at the Arusha peace talks, I experienced the sensation of relief that came with the absence of an ever-present threat of physical danger. I could relax for the first time in months, if not years. It shocked me to realize how much stress I had been under in Rwanda. If I had been feeling that much stress without even being a target of the violence, what toll was the constant stress and fear taking on Rwandans?

Rights Abuses and Violence Sow Fear

[4]

Opposition Parties Join a Coalition Government

A Second Multiparty Government Forms

Against the backdrop of increasing insecurity, Prime Minister Sylvestre Nsanzimana and opposition party leaders were negotiating the
formation of a more diverse government than the one announced at
the end of 1991. That first attempt at political pluralism had yielded a
twenty-member cabinet with just one ministerial portfolio held by
a party other than the MRND. Most observers did not yet consider
that one party, the PDC, part of the political opposition. Furious at
this pseudo-multiparty arrangement, opposition parties led over
fifty thousand of their members into the streets of Kigali in January
1992 to express their dissent. This demonstration forced the president and the MRND to reconsider.

On March 14, 1992, President Habyarimana signed a landmark
compromise agreement with the opposition political party leaders.[1]
This unexpected accommodation came as complaints against the government of Prime Minister Nsanzimana increased and as ethnic tensions mounted in the aftermath of the Bugesera massacre. Under the
arrangement, an opposition prime minister from the largest opposition party, the MDR, would lead a multiparty government composed of nineteen ministers proposed by their respective political
parties and appointed by the president. Nine ministers would come
from the MRND, nine from the three opposition parties—three each

57

from the MDR, PSD, and PL—and one from the smaller PDC, considered at the time to lean toward the MRND. With the vote of the MDR prime minister, a united opposition would have ten votes. The president's MRND would need the PDC to vote with its nine cabinet members in order to deadlock the cabinet at ten votes to ten.

This agreement took effect on April 7 with the swearing-in of Prime Minister Dismas Nsengiyaremye and the nineteen members of his cabinet. The MRND retained the critically important defense, interior, civil service, and transport ministries among its nine cabinet portfolios. It had to relinquish to the opposition MDR the key ministries of foreign affairs and education. The PL would head the ministries of justice and commerce among its three portfolios, while the finance ministry was one of the PSD's three portfolios. Only one of the twenty cabinet members was Tutsi: the PL's minister of labor and social affairs.

How to apportion the cabinet seats among the parties had prolonged negotiations over the formation of this new multiparty government. When the president accepted the March 14 agreement, he may have counted on the PDC—with its lone seat in the cabinet—to side with the nine MRND members in cabinet decisions so the MRND could at least match the ten votes of the opposition parties plus the prime minister. The PDC, however, would disappoint the president. It began flirting openly with the opposition parties and would soon identify primarily with them. The vote the president thought he could count on to prevent an opposition 11–9 majority gradually slipped away from him. The PDC became a maverick and an unreliable partner for the president's MRND party.

New Political Party Excluded

The newly formed, hard-line CDR party that positioned itself to the right of the MRND was not included in this coalition government. Because it had launched only in early March, the CDR had not taken part in the months of delicate negotiations between Nsanzimana and the opposition parties over the portfolio distribution formula. Nevertheless the CDR clamored for a seat at the cabinet table. It argued that it was a significant party that deserved a portfolio in the coalition government as much as, if not more than, the PDC. The president sided with the CDR position. With the CDR firmly in the president's camp and the PDC's affiliation uncertain, CDR participation became increasingly important to the president's strategy for holding on to power. President Habyarimana needed a sure ally in the new government.

But the CDR's bid to join this first truly multiparty government failed. The issue of the new party's role in governance, however, would not go away. Twice more in power-sharing negotiations, first at the Arusha peace talks, and then in the stalled efforts to implement the Arusha Peace Accords, CDR participation would become a critical stumbling block.

Mandate for a New Government

The new government would have a one-year mandate. Within that time the president's charge to the Nsengiyaremye cabinet was three-fold: negotiate an end to the war with the RPF, hold a national conference to determine the way forward to multiparty democracy, and prepare for national elections. This was a tall order given the record of the past year and a half of failed negotiations with the RPF and the slow pace of democratization.

A key factor to accomplishing these tasks was the change in leadership at the Ministry of Foreign Affairs and Cooperation. With the new multiparty government, control of the foreign ministry—and leadership in negotiations with the RPF—passed from the MRND to the MDR, the main opposition party. This was a game-changer. Former hard-line foreign minister Casimir Bizimungu had never established good relations with the RPF and had never been able to negotiate a lasting cease-fire. The MDR named party member Boniface Ngulinzira to succeed him.

Minister Ngulinzira immediately laid the groundwork for significant change in the government's approach to the RPF. He sidelined Jean-Bosco Barayagwiza, director of political affairs and a founding member of the CDR party. Because of their hard-line views, both Bizimungu and Barayagwiza had been serious impediments to fruitful negotiations with the RPF. Ngulinzira named to key ministry positions people who were more compatible with opposition thinking favoring power sharing with the RPF and more amenable to the ministry's charge to end the war. He also dropped the MRND contention that Uganda's Museveni was responsible for the actions of the RPF.

Although Barayagwiza no longer had a role at the foreign affairs ministry, under Rwanda's labor laws the government could not dismiss him. So he was able to retain access to a telephone in his office at the ministry, from which, it was rumored, he conducted CDR business.

Comment

Installation of the multiparty coalition government marked the first step toward breaking the power monopoly that President Habyarimana and his MRND party had exercised over both the southern Hutu and the Tutsi in Rwanda for nearly twenty years. However, although the opposition—which was mostly Hutu—would make some significant changes through cabinet decisions, the political playing field was not yet at all level.

The president evidently still thought that he could keep up the appearance of democratization without losing control of the process. The MRND still had full control of the security services, and most civil service employees remained loyal to the MRND even though opposition parties assumed leadership of half of the ministries. Also, for a while yet, the MRND would control Radio Rwanda and continue to disseminate its inflammatory anti-Tutsi messages. Gradually, however, the president, his MRND party, and his more extreme CDR allies would see their control of the democratization process slip from their grasp.

The CDR's absence from the coalition government, whether for practical or political reasons, marked the first of three such exclusions with catastrophic consequences. Each time the CDR was excluded, this hard-line party took a step closer toward concluding that democratization would not only thwart its goal of holding on to power but would also leave the CDR without a role or a voice in the new Rwanda. Each rejection helped turn this radical group of Hutu supremacists from losers in the democratization and peace processes into spoilers who would plan and execute the genocide.

As the multiparty coalition government took charge, democratization and peace remained on separate tracks. The mandate to the coalition government to end the war, however, led to a convergence of the two at the Arusha peace negotiations. At this juncture, though, no one anticipated that peace talks to end the war would become the primary focal point for democratization.

When the Bugesera massacre and the appointment of the multiparty government occurred so close together, I began to see a pattern: human rights abuses and violence seemed to increase each time there were advances in the process of democratization or developments favorable to the RPF in the border conflict. I wasn't sure whether to regard this as a coincidence or as somehow related by cause and effect.

[5]

Peace Talks Begin and a Cease-Fire Takes Hold

Peace Negotiations Explored

Ambassador Robert Flaten had been waiting for the right time to invite a high-level U.S. delegation to Rwanda to encourage the government in its quest for peace and democracy. The April 1992 installation of an opposition-led coalition government, mandated to end the war, provided just such an opening. The ambassador arranged with the Department of State in Washington to have the assistant secretary of state for Africa, Ambassador Herman J. Cohen, visit Kigali in early May 1992, just weeks into the tenure of the new government. Cohen's presence could help accelerate the U.S. policy of promoting the peace process.

Ambassador Cohen went first to Kampala, Uganda, May 8–9, 1992, to talk with President Museveni and with RPF representatives. In both meetings Cohen discouraged further combat and urged negotiations to end the RPF's conflict with the government of Rwanda. Museveni told Cohen he was pleased that the United States did not view the war as Uganda's problem, as the French did, and he promised to use his influence with the RPF to encourage negotiations. Col. Alexis Kanyarengwe, a Hutu and the RPF chairman, led the RPF delegation that included Maj. Paul Kagame, the vice chairman and commander of the RPF's Rwandan Patriotic Army. The RPF delegation indicated to Ambassador Cohen its readiness to negotiate.[1]

Cohen was in Kigali on May 10–11, 1992, carrying these messages for President Habyarimana and the opposition political party leaders. In a one-on-one meeting with Cohen, Habyarimana emphatically linked the RPF to Uganda's leaders and insisted that the RPF return "home" to Uganda. The RPF's interest in refugee return, the president said, could be settled through the commission he had already established.

In his separate meetings with Prime Minister Dismas Nsengiyaremye and Foreign Minister Boniface Ngulinzira, both members of the largest opposition party, the MDR, Cohen stressed the importance of moving from the battlefield to the negotiating table. He underscored the RPF's willingness to begin talks. Based on his discussions in Kampala, he said, the moment was propitious. He found Ngulinzira skeptical of negotiations with the Tutsi-led RPF but ready to consider developing a comprehensive framework for negotiations.

Peace diplomacy moved forward rapidly after Cohen's visit. On May 24, 1992, Foreign Minister Ngulinzira traveled to Kampala to hold the Rwandan government's first direct talks with the RPF. This was a remarkable event. For the first time, a Rwandan delegation disassociated the RPF from the Ugandan government. Also, the delegation was notably free of the ideologues whose hard-line positions had impeded success at all previous efforts to launch negotiations. In their place were moderates who wanted to work with the RPF to end the war. This new approach signaled a new beginning. The government and RPF delegations agreed to meet again on June 6 in Paris, at the invitation of the French, to discuss further the possibility of peace talks.

Violence Flares as Peace Diplomacy Picks Up Pace

Tensions had been increasing in Kigali as the pace of diplomacy about peace talks quickened. In the month prior to the Paris meeting, with prospects for peace talks looking more and more likely, random violence increased. Land mine and grenade explosions became more frequent in Kigali. A sense of insecurity was pervasive.

Three days after the agreement to go to Paris, soldiers in Gisenyi and Ruhengeri in northern Rwanda went on a rampage. Hutu military mutineers killed scores of civilians, mainly Tutsi, and pillaged or destroyed property valued at hundreds of thousands of dollars. Unhelpful rumors—not totally unfounded—about possible large-scale demobilization at war's end had supposedly sparked the rioting. Apparently the soldiers feared losing the job security that had come with the rapid expansion of the army since the beginning of the war.

Violence between political parties was also on the rise. On the American Memorial Day holiday at the end of May, two separate political party demonstrations turned violent when they converged at a traffic circle in the middle of Kigali. One person was reportedly killed in the ensuing melee.

Some American community members, taking advantage of the holiday to shop downtown, were nearly caught in the riot. They complained bitterly to the ambassador and embassy officers for failing to warn them about the demonstrations. However, we ourselves had been caught off guard; we had no advance information about the demonstrations.

This incident was a timely wake-up call for the embassy. Americans were on edge due to the insecurity around them. Fortunately no Americans suffered injury or worse because of the unexpected demonstrations. Nevertheless embassy officers realized they had to become more alert to potential security threats to Americans and more responsive to community anxieties. We needed to inform ourselves about such high-risk situations in advance and be more sensitive to what might endanger Americans. We needed to alert community members quickly whenever necessary to ensure their safety.

As a result of this experience, the embassy began to hold security briefings open to all Americans every two weeks throughout the next two years, as tensions remained high and violence escalated in both magnitude and frequency. At these sessions, which I often chaired, embassy officials, aid managers, consultants, and missionaries all shared pertinent information from their various vantage points. Our community-wide two-way radio network would provide a channel for passing urgent security messages to Americans between briefings, if necessary.

Talks about Talks: Warring Sides Agree to Negotiate

Coincidentally I was scheduled to transit Paris on the eve of the June 6 talks en route to the United States for home leave. I was asked to stop over to brief Senior Deputy Assistant Secretary for Africa Jeffrey Davidow, the State Department Africa Bureau's official observer at the session. Davidow and I talked long into the evening about the military and political situation in Rwanda, about the prospects for the talks, what he needed to know before the meeting, and what pitfalls he should avoid. He was a quick study, an able diplomat, and a personable colleague.

In the morning, before the talks began, we learned via cable from Kigali that the RPF had attacked the northern Rwandan town of Byumba on June 5. It had held Byumba briefly and then retreated, tactics that echoed its Ruhengeri raid a year and a half earlier. This time, however, the rebel force did not return to its original positions at the Ugandan border. Instead, for the first time, the RPF boldly took up positions inside Rwanda. For the duration of the war, the RPF ran its military and political operations from Mulindi, an abandoned tea plantation inside Rwanda, not far from the Ugandan border and the town of Byumba.

With knowledge of the RPF offensive in hand, Davidow, Reed Fendrick, the Africa watcher at the U.S. Embassy in Paris, and I met with the RPF delegation in the hotel lobby for preliminary discussions shortly before its meeting with the government began. Davidow asked Pasteur Bizimungu, the Hutu head of the RPF delegation, to explain the previous day's attack on Byumba. Bizimungu contended that the RPF had acted in self-defense, in response to the killing a few days earlier of scores of Tutsi civilians by the Rwandan soldiers who had gone on a rampage, following rumors of mass demobilization. What Bizimungu didn't mention was that the intent of the attack might have been to strengthen the RPF's bargaining position at the Paris talks with the government delegation.

Much to the surprise of the diplomats observing the talks in Paris, the government and RPF delegations conducted their discussions in Kinyarwanda, the language common to both the French-speaking government officials and the English-speaking RPF delegates. There-fore the two parties did not need the interpreters on hand for French and English. With no Kinyarwanda interpreters available, the delegations had effectively shut out the French hosts and other international diplomatic observers. At the end of the day the two delegations announced their agreement to meet again in July, in either Zaire or Tanzania, to discuss a cease-fire and longer-term peace negotiations.

To determine which venue would be most suitable, a Rwandan foreign ministry delegation traveled to Kinshasa, the capital of Zaire, and to Dar es Salaam, the capital of Tanzania, for consultations. Subsequently the parties settled on holding the talks in Arusha, Tanzania. They invited Ali Hassan Mwinyi, the president of Tanzania, to be the facilitator for the talks. He accepted this role, aware that President Mobutu of Zaire would retain his role as mediator. With talks looking promising, the RPF and the government opposition appeared to distance themselves from Mobutu, whom they viewed as being too closely aligned with President Habyarimana. The Organization of African Unity agreed to cosponsor the peace talks with Tanzania, a ground-breaking decision for Africa's regional political organization.

Arusha Negotiators Conclude a Cease-Fire and a Rule-of-Law Protocol

From the beginning of the Arusha peace talks in July 1992, the United States was committed to their success. To help the two sides prepare for the talks, the State Department sent two officers with considerable experience in cease-fire negotiations to consult with both the government and the RPF delegations. One expert, Charlie Snyder, then a senior political-military advisor to the State Department's Africa Bureau, went to Addis Ababa, Ethiopia, and Kampala, Uganda, before heading to Arusha. In Addis Ababa he held talks at the OAU headquarters with officials who would attend the talks as observers. In Kampala, Snyder, a military specialist on cease-fire negotiations, discussed approaches with the RPF delegation.

The second expert, John Byerly, then an assistant legal advisor on African affairs at the State Department, visited Kigali before heading to Arusha. Byerly, a lawyer experienced in drafting cease-fire agreements, talked with the government delegation. I arranged and attended his meetings with ministry of foreign affairs civilians and defense ministry military personnel. All participants expressed appreciation for Byerly's help in thinking through what to expect at the forthcoming negotiations and how they could craft a successful cease-fire agreement.

Talks began in Arusha on July 12, 1992. Both Snyder and Byerly were on hand to consult with delegates from both delegations. By July 14, after just two days of talks, the two delegations had signed a cease-fire agreement. While observers were stunned by the speed with which the negotiators reached agreement, the talks had not begun at square one. Instead the delegates had tweaked a previously signed, but never implemented, cease-fire accord, the "N'sele (Zaire) Cease-Fire Agreement of March 29, 1991, as amended at Gbadolite (Zaire) September 16, 1991."[2] In an encouraging show of good faith, a truce began as agreed on July 19, and the cease-fire took effect on schedule about two weeks later, at midnight on August 1, 1992.

In accordance with the cease-fire agreement, the OAU established a neutral military observer group (NMOG) to monitor compliance with the agreed terms. Military officers from Nigeria, Senegal, Mali, and Zimbabwe made up this forty-person force. It replaced the OAU's smaller military observer group, deployed in late 1991 to observe regionally brokered cease-fires. The major difference between the two forces was their composition. The NMOG drew troops from outside the immediate region of Central Africa instead of from Rwanda's neighbors, whom the warring parties did not consider neutral observers.

At the suggestion of the American consultants, the Arusha cease-fire agreement also created a Joint Political-Military Commission, which would provide a forum for the discussion and resolution of contentious military issues raised at the peace talks. Five members each from the government and the RPF (as well as international observers) composed the Commission, which met periodically at the OAU headquarters in Addis Ababa. However, the venue and the Commission itself seemed removed from the talks in Arusha, and it never fulfilled its intended role.

A second accomplishment of the July 1992 session of the peace talks was an agreement between the two delegations on a broad outline for the peace negotiations to follow. The outline named four key areas for negotiators to address: rule of law, political and military power-sharing, integration of the armed forces, and repatriation and resettlement of refugees and internally displaced people.

Arusha II, the second session of the peace talks, took place August 10–17, 1992. The result was a protocol on the rule of law signed on August 18 by the head of each negotiating team. This protocol laid out lofty principles that the two sides agreed should guide the Rwandan state. In the agreement both the government and the RPF negotiators committed to create a government of national unity, to abide by the rule of law, and to respect human rights. The protocol also affirmed the right of Rwandan refugees to return to their homeland. Both sides were pleased at having reached this agreement so easily.

U.S. Commits Observers to the Arusha Peace Talks

The United States sent a senior Africa specialist, David Rawson, as its observer to the second round of peace talks in Arusha in August 1992. Rawson knew Rwanda well. He had served at the U.S. Embassy in Kigali in the mid-1970s and in the State Department as desk officer for Rwanda and Burundi in the early 1970s. Furthermore, he had grown up in neighboring Burundi, where his parents were missionaries. As a child he learned to speak Kirundi, the language of Burundi, which is so close to Rwanda's Kinyarwanda that speakers of each language can understand the other.

Rawson came to Kigali for consultations both before and after Arusha II. As the chargé d'affaires while the ambassador was on leave, I accompanied him to his meetings with Rwandan government officials and political party leaders. His interlocutors provided him with useful summaries of the issues on the minds of Rwanda's leaders both before and after Arusha II. Those he spoke with, regardless of their political stance, expressed some degree of mistrust regarding RPF's intentions.

Before heading to Arusha II, Rawson met with the prime minister, foreign minister, defense minister, and several political party leaders. Prime Minister Nsengiyaremye honed in on principles the government delegation would advocate at the next round of Arusha talks. Most important, he said, negotiators needed to define Rwanda as a democratic country and agree on strategies to achieve democracy. Both sides had to accept existing institutions and laws as the foundation for the future. Rwanda, he said, was not a tabula rasa; negotiations did not mean revolution. Integration of the RPF into Rwandan society and institutions was a given, but the question of proportion would be key. Elections, he maintained, were still targeted for April 16, 1993, the end of the one-year mandate for the coalition government. Adhering to this timing would raise questions of participation for nationals outside Rwanda, as not all refugees could return by then. The government delegation, the prime minister told Rawson, would strive to create a climate of collaboration with the RPF at the next round of talks in Arusha. Once they agreed upon the principles, the rest would follow, he predicted. He noted in closing that Rwanda might need U.S. help on several of these difficult issues ahead.

Foreign Minister Ngulinzira, head of the government delegation to the Arusha talks, reviewed the status of the cease-fire implementation, declaring that, despite some minor violations, the cease-fire was holding. Ngulinzira said the NMOG officers were beginning to arrive in Kigali. Ten Senegalese officers were already there, and Nigerian and Zimbabwean troops were expected within the next few days.

Echoing the prime minister on issues anticipated at Arusha II, the foreign minister said that the government delegation at Arusha would insist on the RPF's accepting the legality and legitimacy of Rwanda's existing institutions. The RPF must agree to integrate into the system as it was, and then join with other political forces to modify it. Democratization was in progress. Change would have to come through elections, not force. He expressed unease with an RPF proposal to concentrate both executive and legislative powers in a single national unity council. Democracy, the separation of powers, and civil rights for all must be preserved, he said.

Minister of Defense James Gasana ruminated with Rawson about the difficulties of integrating Rwandan and RPF forces, an anticipated consequence of peace. Faustin Twagiramungu, leader of the main opposition party, the MDR, emphasized the critical need for peace and for elections to change the country's leadership. Justin Mugenzi of the Liberal Party told Rawson that peace was not the president's first priority and that making peace would be easier if he'd just step down. Both Twagiramungu and Mugenzi expressed skepticism about the RPF's proposal to replace both the president and the legislature with a national unity council. Mugenzi was adamant that Rwanda follow the principle of the separation of powers. Twagiramungu said the political opposition was not willing to accept an RPF "coup."

The ambassador was still on leave when Rawson returned to Kigali after Arusha II. Again I accompanied him to his meetings with Rwandan policymakers and political leaders. His interlocutors uniformly expressed support for the rule-of-law protocol and the principles it laid out. Juvénal Renzaho, the president's political advisor, reflected the government's publicly expressed view opposing any constitutional changes that would reduce the powers of the president during the transition period. RPF leaders must recognize, Renzaho declared, that evolution was acceptable but revolution was not.

Twagiramungu of the MDR and Mugenzi of the PL, whose views diverged on when constitutional changes would be appropriate, both believed there needed to be a way to curb the president's powers during the transition period. Mugenzi accused the RPF's chief Arusha negotiator, Pasteur Bizimungu, of being disingenuous by claiming that members of the government delegation at Arusha were all representatives of the Rwandan "dictator." "He knows us," Mugenzi said, "and he knows why others are not on the delegation."

In these meetings Rawson counseled that the nature of negotiations changes discussions from debates into a search for compromises. He speculated that the forthcoming September talks on political power-sharing could be extremely difficult.

The views expressed by these Rwandan leaders from both the ruling party and the opposition foreshadowed some of the issues that would cut deep cleavages between the various political positions. The first issue to entrench and widen the gulf between the hard-line MRND and CDR parties and the opposition MDR, PL, and PSD parties came when the next Arusha session limited the powers of the president to primarily ceremonial functions during the anticipated transitional period.

Comment

Several consequences flowed from the RPF's establishing its head-quarters at the Mulindi tea plantation after its June 1992 attack on Byumba. It put the RPF leadership and its forward military base a scant forty miles north of Kigali. The attack forced more Rwandans from their homes, bringing the total number of internally displaced persons to an estimated 350,000. With RPF-controlled territory straddling the main commercial road north into Uganda and on to the Kenyan ports Rwanda depended on for much-needed imports, the RPF could henceforth control the flow of goods into Rwanda, including food and humanitarian supplies for the increasing numbers of IDPs. RPF leaders also became accessible to Rwandan government officials and Kigali diplomats. This channel, used sparingly for consultations during the negotiations to come, supplemented contacts already occurring in other locations outside Rwanda.

I felt privileged to accompany Ambassador Davidow to the Paris talks; doing so helped me gain an appreciation of Washington's view of developments in Rwanda. More important for me, though, was my first glimpse of the negotiating team that would lead the RPF delegation throughout the peace talks. Of particular note were Pasteur Bizimungu, the Hutu delegation leader, and Patrick Mazimhaka, a Tutsi, who was always at his side. Both would reprise these roles in Arusha. Bizimungu's explanation in Paris for the RPF attack on Byumba had disappointed me. While I understood the RPF's desire to use military gains for political leverage going into the talks, the move made me question the group's sincerity about peace. This would not be the last time the RPF would justify its aggression on the grounds of protecting Tutsi civilians from Hutu aggression.

The four broad issues for the peace talks to resolve, as agreed to in the July session at Arusha, suggested that reaching an agreement to end the fighting might not be as straightforward as most observers had anticipated. The broad scope of the issues to be addressed in the talks suggested the negotiators would have to resolve not only the usual military requirements that follow a cease-fire, such as disarmament of the warring sides, integration of the two armies, demobilization of forces, and reintegration of demobilized fighters into society.

These negotiations would also be deciding highly political issues among the major political forces in Rwanda, such as power sharing in the government and the military. This would involve the very sensitive subject of how to integrate both the RPF, which was predominantly Tutsi, and the southern Hutu into the existing Rwandan political system and the security forces. The implications of such a large-scale change to the system were still unclear.

In Kigali the Hutu political elite and the diplomatic community—even after the first two Arusha sessions—continued to envision the RPF joining the existing political process as a political party that would vie for allies and power within the existing political framework still dominated by the president and his MRND party. Gradually, though, the RPF's not-so-veiled intention at Arusha would come into focus: it would seek an all-encompassing reorganization of the Rwandan power structure, and it would use the peace process to break the president's power monopoly and ensure a substantial role in governance and state security for the Tutsi minority. Government hard-liners and the RPF would be on different tracks, trying to steer the train in opposite directions. The opposition parties would be caught in the middle, suspicious of both drivers and hesitant to jump on either train.

Rapid agreement at the first two Arusha sessions gave diplomats and Rwanda's political players reason to hope for quick, successful peace talks. However, this progress masked the fact that the delegations shared no common vision for Rwanda's political future. Indeed the government delegation itself spanned the gamut from those aligned with the president's efforts to hold on to power to those committed to sharing power, who were members of opposition parties.

The lofty principles laid out in the rule-of-law protocol seem, in retrospect, to have been empty words without substance or meaning. My question at the time was how the Rwandans expected to fulfill these commitments and implement these principles. The question we probably should have asked was whether there was really any commitment to these principles within any of the political factions.

David Rawson's visits to Kigali en route to and from the Arusha II talks were my first introduction to him. Though we did not know it at the time, he would succeed Flaten one and a half years later as the U.S. ambassador to Rwanda.

[6]

Democratization Flounders

Opposition Cabinet Members Win Early Successes

Opening peace negotiations with the RPF—a success spearheaded largely by Foreign Minister Boniface Ngulinzira from the opposition MDR party—was only one front on which newly installed opposition cabinet members took decisive, bold steps. The ministries of education, interior, and information saw significant changes after opposition ministers took over in April 1992.

Minister of Education Agathe Uwilingiyimana, who, like the foreign minister, came from the MDR party, quickly abolished the "policy of equilibrium" in education. That policy had given children from the Hutu majority priority over children from the Tutsi minority for places in schools. It had also favored Hutu from the president's northern region over Hutu from the south. In its place, the minister, a Hutu, instituted a merit system of exams that awarded places in schools to successful applicants regardless of their ethnicity.

The Ministry of the Interior, though still in the hands of the president's MRND party, was forced by a cabinet decision to end the prevailing practice of selecting regional governors (*préfets*) only from the president's party and the northwest region. Instead persons appointed as governors would henceforth reflect greater diversity in regional and party origins.

The MDR-appointed minister of information, Faustin Ruco-

74

goza, dealt a serious blow to media domination by the MRND. He took steps almost at once to fire the powerful head of the Rwandan Office of Information, Ferdinand Nahimana, a historian and hard-line Hutu supremacist. A former Rwandan journalist told me in 2010 that Nahimana's dismissal had provoked an intense, behind-the-scenes political battle. The newly appointed opposition prime minister Dismas Nsengiyaremye had insisted that Nahimana go, and President Habyarimana had insisted that he stay. The prime minister prevailed.

Six months later, in December 1992, a southern MDR member, Jean-Marie Vianney Higiro, took over as head of the Office of Information. He dismissed most of the president's MRND party journalists and replaced them with MDR loyalists. No longer would northern Hutu supremacists be able to use government-controlled airwaves or the government press at will to disseminate their virulent, anti-Tutsi, pro-Hutu propaganda. The messages reaching the populace became decidedly more balanced in the wake of this appointment. Higiro, whom observers considered an MDR moderate, had earned a degree in communications from the University of Texas at Austin.

Another shake-up occurred when the Council of Ministers voted on June 10, 1992, to reorganize the military. President Habyarimana resigned as head of the armed forces to comply with provisions of the 1991 constitution. Key high-level members of the military hierarchy close to the president were forced into retirement in accordance with the recommendations of a secret report from a military conference held the previous December. Habyarimana approved implementing these changes.[1]

Most notable among those retired were Col. Laurent Serubuga, chief of staff of the army, and Col. Pierre-Celestin Rwagafilita, chief of staff of the gendarmerie and a brother of the president's wife. Both were known for their hard-line positions and their membership in the president's inner circle, called the Akazu (little house). Col. Elie Sagatwa was also dismissed from the army, though he retained his position as the president's personal secretary. He was married to the president's sister and was a cousin of his wife. Known collectively as "the three colonels," Serubuga, Rwagafilita, and Sagatwa were reputedly responsible for instigating violence and many of the human rights abuses of the Habyarimana government.

What machinations Serubuga and Rwagafilita might undertake in their certainly unwelcome retirement worried me. I doubted these two MRND stalwarts would easily walk away from their military careers and the positions of power they had occupied for so long. So I was not surprised when I later heard from a reliable source connected to the judicial system in Kibungo that Rwagafilita was engaged in political mobilization in that southeastern town. My source told of secret meetings the retired colonel held at his home with MRND youth. He also reported increasing ethnic tension in the Kibungo area and rising fear among the Tutsi population there.

What, I wondered, were Rwagafilita's secret meetings about? Did his political involvement extend to militia training? Why did these two notorious presidential confidants drop out of public sight after their retirement, just as democratization and the peace process were gaining momentum? While I had reason to believe my Kibungo source accurately reflected the mood there, contacts in Kigali were either unaware or not telling me, an outsider, how these two were spending their newfound leisure time.

Even though opposition members of the coalition government could claim success for relieving these two colonels of their jobs, they could not control the appointment of their successors. That responsibility fell to the Ministry of Defense, which the MRND party still controlled. Their replacements would be other MRND loyalists. Col. Augustin Ndindiliyimana, who succeeded Rwagafilita as chief of staff at the gendarmerie, brought to the position his experience as a former minister of defense and minister at the presidency for military and security. He was reportedly respected both inside and outside the armed forces. The contrary might be said of Col. Déogratias Nsabimana, who replaced Serubuga as army chief of staff. He came to the position with a battlefield reputation for torture and summary executions. Both Sagatwa and Nsabimana died in the plane crash that killed the president in April 1994.

Another senior official caught in this military shake-up was Col. Léonidas Rusatira. For nearly a decade he had been secretary general of the Ministry of Defense, a key position somewhat akin to chief of staff for the minister. Although Rusatira was removed from this key military position, he could not be ousted from the army because, in contrast to the three colonels, he had not yet reached mandatory retirement age. Instead he was sidelined to the position of director at the military training academy.

Even before I met him, Colonel Rusatira intrigued me, and after several productive one-on-one lunches, which I initiated, he became a valuable resource for me at critical points in time. Despite his many years of service in a key military position in the Habyarimana government, Rusatira was not the hard-line Hutu supremacist one might have expected. In retrospect, I believe he was one of the people who tried to warn me about the plotting that would lead to the genocide. His veiled language, however, did not communicate a clear message at the time.

Paralysis Grips the Coalition Government

After this spate of early policy successes for the political opposition, the Council of Ministers became increasingly unable to reach decisions. The formula adopted for divvying up portfolios had established a nearly evenly divided cabinet—a recipe for stalemate. Nine members from the president's MRND party were up against nine ministers from the three principal opposition parties and the opposition prime minister. If the last member of the cabinet, the politically insignificant PDC party representative, voted with the MRND as expected, the president's party could achieve a 10–10 split on controversial votes and thus block action it opposed. If the PDC voted with the opposition, the opposition would prevail 11–9. This swing-vote capability gave the minor PDC extraordinary decision-making power in the coalition government. Initially the PDC sided with the MRND.

In July 1992, just about the time the cease-fire talks began in Arusha, the Council was deadlocked and MRND ministers threatened to boycott the gridlocked cabinet meetings. To explain their side of the story, opposition parties sent two ministers each to several key diplomatic missions in Kigali. Minister of Education Uwilingiyimana, a Hutu from the main opposition party, the MDR, and Minister of Labor and Social Affairs Landoald Ndasingwa, a PL leader and the only Tutsi in the cabinet, called on the U.S. Embassy in early

August. As chargé d'affaires in the ambassador's absence, I received them on a weekend afternoon on the screened-in porch at my residence. After listening to their arguments, I encouraged them to seek common ground with the president's party and make compromises. They replied that they could not even talk to the other side.

I devised a plan for some behind-the-scenes diplomacy that might jump-start discussion across the divide. Two key people from the opposing sides of the political spectrum were already scheduled to be on hand at the airport on a Sunday morning in August to officially receive a planeload of relief supplies from the United States for the 350,000 war-displaced. I could arrange a time for the two to talk privately prior to the ceremony. These two, Enoch Ruhigira, permanent secretary in the Office of the President, and Ndasingwa, whose portfolio included responsibility for refugees and displaced persons, were, in my view, among the most reasonable persons on either side. I was fairly confident the two could have a civil conversation and get to the heart of the issue blocking the Council.

In response to my query, Lando, as Ndasingwa was commonly known, said he would be willing to raise the cabinet stalemate with Ruhigira at this event. Therefore I arranged the schedule so that the two would have at least fifteen minutes alone in the holding room before the ceremony. There they could have a private discussion out of view of any colleagues who might be at the airport. Even if the two could not resolve the differences, they could at least open a dialogue.

All went as planned; the ceremony went on with no one the wiser; and the cabinet stalemate was broken a few days later. At the time I had no idea whether there had been any connection between this discreet airport meeting and the resumption of cabinet business. However, a few weeks later, during an official call on Foreign Minister Ngulinzira, he expressed appreciation for U.S. help in breaking the government deadlock. While pleased that I had been able to help, I was even more excited that my confidence in Enoch and Lando had not been misplaced. Government paralysis, however, continued to plague the multiparty coalition cabinet off and on throughout its nearly two-year existence. The PDC was an unreliable maverick, siding sometimes with the MRND and sometimes with the opposition.

Political Parties Become Vehicles of Violence

While the peace talks were getting under way in Paris and Arusha in July and August 1992, violence waxed and waned in Kigali and elsewhere in Rwanda in parallel with advances in political liberalization and progress in the peace talks. Indeed democratization and peace had increasingly become associated with violence. Rival political party youth groups escalated their interference with each other's recruitment efforts. They disrupted each other's rallies to discourage would-be members from joining the parties of their opponents. Inevitably these clashes devolved into violence.

News reports from the independent, opposition-linked press tended to blame the MRND party youth group, the Interahamwe (Those Who Attack Together), and the hard-line CDR group, the Impuzamugambi (Those Who Have the Same Goal), for attacking opposition party youth. Their targets were youth groups of the opposition parties, the Inkuba (Thunder) of the MDR and the Abakombozi (Liberators) of the PSD.

The MRND's Interahamwe, however, was becoming more than just a youth group turned violent; it was being transformed into a true militia. In mid-August 1992 a Hutu source sent to me by a mutual friend came to my office to tell me—and the U.S. government—that the Interahamwe was no longer the vibrant youth organization he had helped organize. Instead it had become a militant group from which he wished to disassociate himself.

The allegations of this insider source were stunning. President Habyarimana's wife and her family clan, he claimed, were primarily responsible for initiating and carrying out this transformation. Active and retired military personnel and gendarmes were conducting secret Interahamwe training camps at sites outside Kigali. He told me he feared for his life for having made known his disappointment and intention to withdraw from the group. To substantiate his fears, he told me about a bomb that had exploded in a car just outside his office a couple of months earlier. He believed it was a warning to him.

I remembered this car-bomb incident. It had occurred during the U.S. Memorial Day holiday, when two opposing parties had clashed violently in downtown Kigali. At the time there had seemed no logical explanation for the explosion. Now I could fit it into a larger picture that was taking shape. This person's report troubled me greatly; there was enough about it that rang true. It wasn't long before reports from unrelated sources began to echo his allegations about high-level involvement in creating a militia out of the MRND's party youth group.[2]

Interahamwe Blocks Access to Kigali

What I learned about the Interahamwe's transformation into a militia made me reflect on my unnerving encounter with the group a few weeks earlier. It had happened on the morning of July 28, 1992. I was returning to Kigali from the southern town of Butare, where I had attended the opening of a refurbished national museum the day before. To avoid driving the winding road in the dark, I opted to stay overnight. I used the additional time to meet with Butare-based Peace Corps volunteers who joined me for dinner at my hotel.

My driver and I set out early the next morning in order to reach Kigali at the beginning of the work day. In the ambassador's absence, I had a full day of meetings ahead of me. Because I was in Butare on official embassy business, we were in the ambassador's distinctive, official vehicle—a long, white, armored Chevrolet. We had no information to suggest possible problems along the way. This changed, however, when we reached the outskirts of Kigali.

As we approached the crest of the long hill descending from the escarpment into the city, we came unexpectedly upon an extensive backup of cars and trucks. All were just sitting in the road, engines turned off. No vehicles were coming toward us. Curious about this development, my driver maneuvered us to the front of the line. He was hoping to find someone who could explain the cause of the delay. At the front we found several gendarmes, the territorial police, who were preventing the vehicles from descending into the valley. The gendarmes said a political demonstration was in progress on the road below. The line of cars and trucks would have to wait until it was over before they could proceed. The officials were unable to say when that might be. These officers of the law claimed not to know who was demonstrating or why.

Using the two-way radio in the ambassador's official car, we contacted the embassy in Kigali to learn what they knew about the demonstration and what they thought our chances might be of getting around or through it. After checking with some of their contacts, embassy officers reported that the Interahamwe were demonstrating peacefully on the main road leading into Kigali. They didn't know what the reason was, but they thought we could get through it.

My driver and I deliberated briefly. It sounded to us as if the demonstrators' aim was disruption, not violence. We considered it unlikely that peaceful demonstrators, even Interahamwe, would turn violent without provocation. The official U.S. Embassy vehicle was unlikely to have such an effect, we reasoned; as long as the demonstration remained peaceful, our risk was minimal. So, providing the gendarmes would let us pass, we decided we would proceed forward and try to make it through to Kigali. We could reassess the situation as we got closer and stop at any time if necessary.

We relayed our decision to the embassy, and my driver unfurled the two American flags mounted on the front fenders of the Chevrolet to signify that the representative of the United States was in the car.

Although I was uncomfortable about jumping the long queue of waiting vehicles, we pulled out of the line and moved cautiously forward. A Canadian diplomat also caught in the backup asked to follow along behind us, and I agreed. Perhaps there would be safety in numbers should anything go wrong. The road was so narrow there was no turning back. The gendarmes and the other drivers appeared relaxed about our presumptiveness, content to let these foreign diplomats do as they wanted, foolish though it might be. Though anxious about what we might find, I was comfortable with our decision to get a closer look at the situation in the valley.

We wound our way slowly down from the crest of the hill to the river crossing in the valley below. The Canadian diplomat's car followed closely behind. So far, so good. Over the radio, embassy officers continued to reassure us that the demonstration remained peaceful. We crossed the river and turned north up the valley toward Kigali. There was still no evidence of any blockage on the road. Minutes later, however, after passing a major junction in the road, we suddenly came upon the demonstration ahead of us.

To my consternation, the road appeared totally impassable. Trucks of every size and description were parked at right angles to each other in zigzag formation. They blocked the road for about fifty yards. Scores of young people were milling about, some in the road, others along the low riverbank just to our left. Most wore what I came to know as the distinctive costume of the Interahamwe: a pajama-like outfit made from African cloth with blue and yellow swirls. Some demonstrators hid their faces by wearing nylon stockings over their heads or knit balaclava hats. Others had large banana leaves protruding from their hair in several directions. They were truly intimidating.

Despite their menacing appearance, the demonstrators seemed only curious about us; there was no hint of threat or animosity. As we advanced slowly and warily toward the seemingly impenetrable roadblock, we could see gaps between the trucks. Some colorfully clad demonstrators, apparently with some authority, motioned us forward and directed us to drive between and around the parked trucks. They didn't appear troubled by the two diplomatic vehicles. Maybe the U.S. flags had made a difference.

My driver skillfully maneuvered the large Chevrolet slowly and carefully through spaces barely large enough for us to pass. As he kept his eyes on the road and the task at hand, I could see tension mounting in his demeanor. This was not just from the challenge of the driving; I realized what he had probably suspected and feared all along: these militant Hutu from the president's political party might identify him as a Tutsi. If they did, our luck could change. I too became nervous and anxious, worried that at any moment a wrong move or look might trigger a reaction that could jeopardize his safety and mine.

Luck was on our side that day. In what seemed like an age, we and the Canadian diplomat successfully navigated through this odd gamut of vehicles. With the demonstration behind us, my driver and I, both shaken, breathed a sigh of relief. We were still moving slowly away from the blockage when I noticed a small pickup truck parked at the side of the road with three men leaning against it. They were calmly watching the peaceful but disruptive demonstration. Many commercial truckers still at the top of the hill behind us were stranded, losing money and getting behind schedule because of the demonstration.

To my surprise, I recognized two of the three men leaning against the truck as high-level government officials. One was the mayor of Kigali, Col. Tharcisse Renzaho, a strong supporter of the president and the MRND party whom I had met several times in his official capacity. Another was Kigali's attorney general (*procurer général*) François-Xavier Nsanzuwera. In one-on-one working lunches at my house, he had indicated his support for the process of political liberalization and his sympathy for improving the human rights situation in the country. I was surprised to see him with this ruling party stalwart casually observing this demonstration.

I asked my driver to stop. I wanted to know more about the reason for the demonstration and what, if anything, they planned to do about it. I got out of the car and went over to talk with the three. Mayor Renzaho said something about a political party clash in a nearby village over what seemed to me a minor issue. In my view, his explanation hardly justified such a large, disruptive demonstration. When I asked what was being done to unblock the road and get commerce moving into town again, the mayor shrugged his shoulders and said sarcastically, "This is democracy, Madame. What can I do?" My anxiety turned to irritation at such a condescending reply. But I held my tongue, got back in the car, and proceeded into town. I would wait for another opportunity to talk to Nsanzuwera.[3]

The demonstrators had chosen the perfect place to block all travel into Kigali: at the junction of the roads from the north and the south. Their disruption continued well into the afternoon, ending only when the secretary general of the MRND party, Mathieu Ngirumpatse, went to the site and told the assembled crowd of menacing youth to go home. Clearly he could exercise authority over the Interahamwe; he had their attention and they listened to him. Subsequently I learned that Ngirumpatse, a frequent visitor to the embassy in his capacity as a key leader of the MRND, was the party official in charge of the Interahamwe.

Some weeks later, after my meeting with my confidential source on the Interahamwe's transformation, I seized an opportunity to question Ngirumpatse. As I escorted him from the embassy following a meeting with the ambassador, I asked him about reports of retired, and possibly active, gendarmes providing military training to his party's youth group. In a tone conveying supercilious indignation and self-righteousness, he denied any knowledge of such activity. He offered, "Bring me the name of any gendarme involved in such a thing and I will see that he is disciplined."

I found his reply chilling, and my body stiffened. As far as I was concerned, he had just admitted not only to the existence of such training and to his ability to influence it, but also to a high-level cover-up to throw the diplomatic community off the trail of what would prove to be a critical element in preparing for the genocide. Ngirumpatse's response convinced me that the Interahamwe's transformation from a political youth organization into a militia was indeed well under way.

Massacre in Kibuye

About three weeks after my encounter with the Interahamwe and a few days after the rule-of-law protocol had been signed in Arusha, several days of ethnic and political violence erupted in Kibuye, a town west of Kigali on the shores of Lake Kivu. Provoked by inter-party youth clashes, the massacre claimed about three hundred dead and more than five thousand displaced. About five hundred homes were destroyed.[4]

As in Bugesera the previous March, Tutsi were the primary victims of this Hutu-led violence. This time, however, Hutu members of opposition parties also fell victim to the Hutu rioters. This time, too, there were some arrests, mainly members of the president's MRND party. Rumor and innuendo circulating in Kigali linked the violence to President Habyarimana's chief of staff, Enoch Ruhigira. Originally from Kibuye, Ruhigira was a key embassy contact and an authoritative voice on the thinking of the president and his party. He had helped overcome gridlock in the cabinet earlier in August.

Before I heard about the massacre, Ruhigira stopped by my house for a meeting with a visiting diplomat, David Rawson, who was en route to Washington following Arusha II, the rule-of-law talks where he had been the U.S. observer. It was a weekend afternoon, and Ambassador Flaten was still on leave. A phone call interrupted

Democratization Flounders

our discussion to alert me to the outbreak of violence in Kibuye. I conveyed this news to Ruhigira and Rawson. Ruhigira expressed shock and disbelief before abruptly departing.

Had Ruhigira feigned shock for our benefit? Or had he actually been in the dark about the horrendous events unfolding near his hometown? I hoped the latter. He had always given the impression of being genuinely supportive of democratization and peace, and despite his proximity to presidential power, I did not want to think of him as a party to the ever-increasing violence.

Comments

Even after the southern-based opposition parties joined the opposition-led, multiparty government in March 1992, there was no real power shift. With nine ministerial portfolios in the twenty-member cabinet, the MRND could block any decision providing it could gain the vote of the insignificant PDC. The MRND also retained the loyalty of most of the civil servants staffing government ministries and nearly all local government officials. It also controlled the security and intelligence services.

The opposition parties tried to break up this power monopoly by appointing their own members to top posts at the ministries they headed and by removing MRND-affiliated provincial governors (*préfets*). Despite such changes at ministries and regional administrations, civil servants and local officials who remained in place could stymie the plans of their superiors. Only gradually were some of the most outspoken local MRND administrators replaced.

This arrangement suited the president and the MRND. They were able to retain almost all the reins of power while gaining the appearance of a more open governing system with a multiparty government headed by an opposition prime minister. Nevertheless the former ruling MRND displayed an intense rivalry with the opposition parties, competing for members throughout the country, even in regions dominated by the new opposition parties.

Evidence mounted to support my hypothesis about increased violence and human rights abuses accompanying progress toward political liberalization and peace. Diplomats applauded progress in the peace process during May, June, July, and August 1992: the new opposition-led government had launched peace talks, a cease-fire took hold, and negotiators in Arusha signed a rule-of-law protocol. Meanwhile the same four months saw not only government gridlock and a massive Interahamwe demonstration that blocked access to Kigali but also an increase in human rights abuses and violence. These included political party clashes, a deadly massacre in Kibuye, and reports of Interahamwe militarization.

Successes, however small, in either democratization or peacemaking almost seemed to trigger spikes in chaos and conflict. Could the violence be backlash from those holding power against those seeking to gain power? Tutsi and democracy advocates were bearing the brunt of this violence. Were the transitions themselves, so central to U.S. policy in Rwanda, actually provoking this violence? If so, what role was U.S. policy playing in supporting not only democracy and peacemaking but also the escalating violence?

Doubts are necessarily a part of diplomatic life. Like journalists, diplomats must continuously assess what we learn, check and cross-check the information, evaluate and judge the veracity of our sources. This was especially true in Rwanda. No person and no information could be accepted at face value. What appeared to be true always needed reexamination for alternative interpretations. Motives for words and deeds rarely reflected obvious causal links; more likely they had to be gauged by later consequences. Truth and trust had to defer to skepticism and suspicion. "Rwandans tell you what they think you want to hear," several contacts had warned.

"Truth" in Kinyarwanda, according to several of my contacts, refers to the concept rather than to specific situations. "I saw it with my own eyes" is the only way to actually confirm the factual accuracy of an incident. Trust is also a rare commodity in Rwandan culture. "Don't eat anything at a neighbor's house" is an admonition that children hear from their parents, a Hutu embassy employee told me. In a discussion on these issues with another Hutu contact, I exclaimed, "Should I understand, then, that you don't trust anyone?" After ruminating for a moment, he replied, "Only my mother." Then he added, "And you."

[7]

Turning Point

Adversaries Tackle Power Sharing

In the summer of 1992 diplomats in Kigali were optimistic about the peace negotiations in Arusha. The first two rounds of talks had gone smoothly. Negotiators for the government and for the RPF had reached agreement with little difficulty. In July, Arusha I had put in place a cease-fire that was holding. In August, Arusha II had adopted a protocol on the rule of law that laid out agreed principles as the foundation for Rwanda's democratic future. Diplomats had not anticipated that deliberations over political power sharing would consume four months in the autumn of 1992, engender so much rancor along the way, and end with one side—the president's—rejecting the outcome. MRND and CDR leaders accused the opposition parties and the RPF of marginalizing them and their parties in the proposed power-sharing arrangement, a position they refused to accept.

Political Power-Sharing Negotiations Take an Unexpected Turn

Negotiators in Arusha scheduled just ten days, September 7–18, 1992, for political power-sharing discussions. However, the challenges to reaching agreement on this highly complex, emotionally charged issue were formidable. By the time the scheduled session ended, the government and RPF delegations had only agreed on an institutional framework for a transitional period intended to see the country through to multiparty elections for a new Rwandan government and national assembly.

The agreed framework called for the creation of a Broad-Based Transitional Government (BBTG) to replace the multiparty coalition government formed in April 1992. In addition, a Transitional National Assembly (TNA) would replace the existing legislative body, the National Development Council. These new institutions would have a year to prepare for elections and oversee implementation of the peace agreement. Arusha III, as this short session was called, adjourned on schedule, leaving many thorny power-sharing issues undecided.

Negotiators on both the government and RPF sides spent the next couple of weeks conferring with their respective political colleagues and constituencies about the power-sharing issues remaining on the table. What should be the powers of the president during the transition, and what should be his relationship to the broad-based government? What should be the composition of the broad-based government? How should ministerial portfolios be distributed among government ministers? How should seats in the proposed TNA be apportioned among the parties? Should legislators be elected (the position of the president and the nationally well-entrenched MRND party) or appointed (the position of the political opposition)?

Answers to such questions were central to shaping the transitional period that would in turn fashion new political structures for Rwanda. They went to the heart of future power relationships. Depending on how these negotiations played out, the peace agreement could result in profound power shifts in post-Arusha Rwanda. The stakes were high, and vested interests were definitely in conflict. Kigali politicians remained deeply divided over how to organize Rwanda's political future. Positions spanned the gamut from Hutu hard-liners, fixated on retaining their control, to the mostly Hutu opposition, bent on ending the president's monopoly on power. Time was short: the next round of talks was scheduled for early October. There was no common vision either in Kigali or between Kigali and the RPF for a new political order.

Power-sharing talks resumed in Arusha as scheduled on October 6, with the intention of concluding in three weeks, on October 30. As with Arusha III, however, this round of talks, labeled Arusha IV, ended with the substantive issues on political power-sharing only partially resolved. Nevertheless, at the end of this second round, despite apparent disarray in Kigali on power-sharing issues, the delegation heads took an unexpected step: Foreign Minister Ngulinzira for the government and Pasteur Bizimungu for the RPF signed a protocol that locked in the agreements negotiators had reached during these first two rounds of power-sharing talks.

This October 30 Arusha protocol stunned the president and his hard-line, Hutu-supremacist allies who had not yet consented to anything. The protocol provisions stripped the presidency of most of its executive powers and transferred them to the proposed BBTG. The president would no longer be able to veto cabinet decisions, though he could preside at cabinet meetings. No longer would he have sole authority to appoint cabinet members; instead the president's role would be to endorse candidates put forward by the political parties designated to hold specific portfolios. Essentially this remarkable protocol transformed the president from a head of government with substantial power into a ceremonial head of state with little executive authority.

Opposition political leaders had foreshadowed such an outcome in meetings on August 20 with David Rawson and me when Rawson was transiting Kigali after having attended Arusha II as the U.S. observer. Faustin Twagiramungu, head of the main opposition party, the MDR, and Justin Mugenzi, leader of the opposition PL, talked with us separately about power sharing and the Arusha peace talks. Each contended that reducing presidential power would be the price Rwanda would have to pay for peace, and each predicted that the RPF would refuse to participate in a transitional government if the president were able to continue monopolizing power as he had done for nearly twenty years.

Twagiramungu argued that making the president a figurehead would be a reasonable alternative to the RPF proposal for a national council that would exercise both executive and legislative powers. Mugenzi further suggested that the opposition members of the government delegation might be willing to side with the RPF at Arusha on this issue by insisting that the president retain only ceremonial powers or step down.[1] These opposition proposals and the mostly Hutu political opposition's strategy of joining forces with the RPF had seemed to me wishful thinking in August. By the end of October, however, they had become enshrined in a protocol on power sharing at the Arusha peace talks.

President Habyarimana, his MRND party, and its more radical spin-off, the CDR, were outraged at the audacity of the government negotiators at Arusha for agreeing to reduce presidential powers during the transitional period. They accused Foreign Minister Ngulinzira of having exceeded his brief and claimed he had acted on behalf of his MDR party rather than in the best interest of the country.

These hard-line Kigali politicians further asserted that negotiators in the Arusha peace talks had no authority to make any decisions that tampered with Rwanda's constitution. Although they reaffirmed their commitment to the peace process, outspoken MRND leaders—accustomed to being the ruling elite—insisted on renegotiating certain provisions of the power-sharing protocol.

Prime Minister Nsengiyaremye and Foreign Minister Ngulinzira, both leading members of the main opposition party, bore the brunt of the criticism. The president and his allies denounced not only the signed power-sharing protocol but also the unauthorized position the MDR-led government delegation had taken at the power-sharing talks.

Ngulinzira refused to back down despite venomous criticism from hard-liners. He contended that he had acted in the best interest of the country—not that of his party—and he rejected the call to reopen the protocol to renegotiate its provisions. Ngulinzira talked to me privately at the time about his great frustration and anger at MRND criticism. He reiterated that he had acted in good faith and declared that he would refuse to become a scapegoat for the outcome of the negotiations.

Years later, in 2012, a contact who had been a member of the government's negotiating team at Arusha contended in a private conversation that Ngulinzira could actually have claimed a degree of success with this unpopular result. He said Ngulinzira had protected at least some role for President Habyarimana in the proposed BBTG, albeit with reduced powers, while RPF negotiators had argued forcefully for the president to be completely sidelined during the transitional period.

The President and His Hard-Line Allies Respond: Violence Unleashed

Two widely reported speeches delivered in November 1992 in the northern part of the country—one by the president and one by a regional MRND official—aroused Hutu anxieties about the Arusha peace process. Both stimulated anti-Tutsi sentiment and raised suspicions about the intentions of Hutu who joined opposition parties. Both speakers suggested Tutsi and opposition Hutu would be the likely perpetrators of whatever future violence might occur in the region.

President Habyarimana made his disdain for the October 30 Arusha protocol exceedingly clear on November 15, just weeks after it was signed. Speaking publicly to party supporters in the northern MRND stronghold of Ruhengeri, the president denounced provisions reducing presidential powers during a transitional period and dismissed the Arusha agreement as "nothing but a scrap of paper . . . that the government is not obliged to respect."

Habyarimana's blatant public criticism of the signed protocol contradicted his repeated public claims of commitment to the peace talks, undermining the entire Arusha peace process. His cavalier dismissal of the negotiations gave any Hutu supremacist, indeed any Rwandan, license to reject any agreements made in Arusha between the government and the RPF. His position justified disregard for the peace process itself. Tutsi, on the other hand, heard the president's words not only as a rejection of the Arusha process but also as a possible signal of support for more massacres. As a result their anxiety and fear over more Hutu reprisals for RPF actions intensified.

A week after the president's speech, Léon Mugesera, a regional official in the ruling MRND party, further heightened Tutsi fears and put opposition Hutu at risk of Hutu hard-liner violence. On November 22, 1992, speaking to about one thousand MRND party loyalists in the northwestern prefecture of Gisenyi, he played the ethnic card in an incendiary speech that denigrated Tutsi. Mugesera told the Hutu loyalist crowd that the Tutsi did not belong in Rwanda and should return to Ethiopia, from whence they had come. Furthermore, he advised his listeners, the quickest way to get them back to Ethiopia would be via the nearby Nyabarongo River.

Mugesera's message was unambiguous to his Hutu audience: kill Tutsi and throw their bodies into the river. The Nyabarongo, after wending its way south to Kigali and joining the Kagera River, turns northward toward Lake Victoria in Uganda. From Lake Victoria the River Nile flows northward to Sudan and Ethiopia. His reference to sending Tutsi "back" to Ethiopia reflected a widely held belief promulgated by Belgian colonists that Tutsi were foreigners in Rwanda who had migrated from Ethiopia. This unsubstantiated myth contributed to alienating Hutu and Tutsi during the colonial period.

Mugesera went on in his speech to justify his call for summary and arbitrary killing of Tutsi, deemed RPF "accomplices" by many Hutu hard-liners. He argued that if the judicial system was not going to punish people who had betrayed the country, then the people themselves had a right to punish the "traitors."

Mugesera's wrath was not reserved for Tutsi alone. He also vehemently denounced the Hutu-led opposition political parties for destroying Hutu unity. He accused opposition party leaders and members of being "traitors" for advocating power sharing with the RPF, a position common at that time to the three main opposition political parties. Mugesera even blamed the opposition parties for provoking the army mutiny the previous May with their support for a peace settlement that would lead to the demobilization of many Rwandan soldiers.

Despite the remote venue of Mugesera's speech, his words reverberated rapidly around the country.[2] In this one speech, laden with anti-Tutsi, anti-Arusha, and Hutu-supremacist propaganda, Mugesera successfully stirred up the crowd not only against all Tutsi but also against Hutu supporters of opposition political parties. Ethnic tensions escalated in the remote region of the Gisenyi prefecture, and over the next two months, many Tutsi and some Hutu members of opposition parties in that region became victims of violence. Throughout the country Tutsi feared new Hutu attacks against themselves and their families for RPF actions, alleged or real, and Hutu supporters of opposition parties wondered whether being branded as "traitors" for favoring power sharing with Tutsi would bring reprisals against them.

Years later Nsengiyaremye told me that Habyarimana had nearly pulled out of the Arusha process following the highly controversial power-sharing protocol of October 30, 1992. The former prime minister told me that he had worked exceedingly hard to keep the president engaged in the peace process and had finally convinced him that returning to the negotiating table was preferable to returning to war.

The Power-Sharing Debate in Kigali Accelerates

The pace of political activity in Kigali accelerated in the final months of 1992 against the backdrop of the president's public scorn for the Arusha peace process and heightened ethnic tensions. Kigali politicians scrambled to come up with an agreed formula for sharing power in the proposed transitional institutions. Kigali needed a consensus position to instruct and guide government negotiators scheduled to return to Arusha in late November to resume talks.

At issue was the composition of the BBTG and the TNA, the two transitional political institutions agreed upon at Arusha in September and October 1992. At stake was the distribution of political power within these institutions among the three principal political blocs: the mostly northern Hutu bloc of the president, his MRND party, and their hard-line allies, most notably the Hutu-supremacist CDR; the mainly southern Hutu bloc of the opposition MDR, PSD, and PL; and the Tutsi-led RPF, which was not present in the Kigali debate.

The controversial October 30 power-sharing protocol provided scant but key guidance on the composition and functioning of the BBTG. It was silent on the TNA. Significantly, it specified that ministers in the BBTG would be members of the political parties in the existing coalition government, along with the RPF. However, it complicated matters by leaving the door open for other parties to participate, provided a consensus of the BBTG members named in the protocol accepted them. The protocol also spelled out the vote threshold for passing what it called "important" issues in the BBTG. Such issues would require a two-thirds vote to pass or, conversely, a one-third plus one vote to fail. These two BBTG features shaped Kigali power-sharing discussions.

On the surface, Kigali politicians were grappling with which parties should be included in the two transitional institutions, which parties should have which portfolios in the BBTG, and how the numbers of seats for each party in the TNA should be determined. Discussions over the various representation permutations, however, turned on the key critical issue lurking just below the surface: the calculation of the "blocking third." The president's bloc and the opposition bloc were each searching for a formula that would enable it to garner the one-third plus one votes needed to block certain important issues in the BBTG. This blocking third became the criterion each bloc used to judge the acceptability of any power-sharing formula under consideration.

The president's bloc insisted that any power-sharing formula accord a blocking third in each of the transitional institutions to the MRND and its allied parties. Any less, it argued, would marginalize this bloc and be unacceptable. To bolster its assured support in the transitional cabinet and legislature, the president's bloc pushed hard for opposition parties to agree to the inclusion of its principal ally, the hard-line CDR, in the transitional cabinet. This bloc also argued for the CDR and ten newly formed but small, special interest political parties to have representation in the legislature. Most of these new parties, such as the Islamic Democratic Party (Parti Démocratique Islamique), had recently been carved out of the president's constituency. They were expected to be reliable supporters that would vote with the president's MRND party in the proposed TNA.

The opposition bloc of political parties had been emboldened and strengthened by the October Arusha agreement curtailing presidential powers during the transitional period. They rejected any proposed formula that would give a blocking third to the president's party and his allies in either the BBTG or the TNA. The opposition parties also strongly opposed including the CDR or any of the smaller parties in the transitional cabinet, although their presence in the legislature would be acceptable.

The bloc of parties favorable to the president advocated an elected legislature. It apparently believed its candidates would have an excellent chance of prevailing in local elections. Most local officials had remained loyal MRND party members. The opposition bloc, on the other hand, favored having each party appoint its own cabinet members and legislators according to a predetermined list of ministerial portfolios in the BBTG and numbers of seats allocated to each party in the national assembly.

Even though the voices of the hard-liners appeared to have lost resonance in the September and October power-sharing talks in Arusha, the president, his party, and his even more radical CDR allies remained formidable forces in the Kigali negotiations. They were determined to control the process of political transformation. In particular, they wanted to set the terms for creating the transitional institutions.

The question of including the hard-line CDR in the transitional government led to a protracted debate, and for the second time in Rwanda's political liberalization process, the role of Hutu extremists in future governance brought negotiations to a standstill. Excluded from the existing multiparty government, the CDR argued it had sufficient support among the Rwandan people to merit a place in both transitional institutions, namely the government and the legislature.

The MRND strongly supported the CDR's bid for seats in the transitional institutions. MRND leaders reasoned that CDR representatives would inevitably help the MRND avoid being "marginalized" should the opposition side with the RPF on critical issues. The opposition parties stood firm against CDR participation in the transitional BBTG or the TNA. The RPF too expressed strong opposition to CDR participation in either the government or the legislature. The RPF, however, had no voice in the Kigali power-sharing discussions.

The Kigali Power-Sharing Debate Shows Promise, Then Stalls

An ad hoc group of religious leaders stepped in to help facilitate consensus building between and within these two major Hutu political blocs. The clergy, representing the powerful Rwandan Catholic Church and the small Protestant community, became pivotal mediators in this contentious though primarily Hutu dialogue.

In late November the opposition parties agreed to a set of principles and two possible formulas put forward by the clergy for configuring the transitional government. These proposals were then presented to the president for his concurrence. When news of this apparent progress reached Foreign Minister Ngulinzira, who had already returned to the Arusha peace talks, he announced a "breakthrough" in Kigali negotiations to the assembled delegations. However, the president never took a specific position on either of the alternatives offered by the clergy.

Instead, in a December 1 speech to the nation, the president stopped short of endorsing either of the religious group's power-sharing proposals. Even though he publicly reaffirmed his commitment to the peace process and its outcome, he laid down a defiant marker. No one political bloc, he said, should be either marginalized or accorded enough seats in the transitional institutions to control decision making. Additionally he asserted that the principle of "non-exclusion" should guide power-sharing talks, that all political parties should participate in the transitional institutions that would shape Rwanda's future.[3]

In the absence of a clear response from the president to the clergy's proposals, Prime Minister Nsengiyaremye asked the clerical brokers to continue refining their proposals with more specific details. Their second proposal presented only one option for an equitable division of ministerial portfolios among Rwanda's political parties and the RPF. This time the president and his MRND party rejected the proposal outright. MRND leaders claimed it marginalized their party and relegated it to becoming a "permanent minority."

Despite the best efforts of these ad hoc mediators, the impasse persisted into December. Kigali politicians continued to float ideas for various political configurations to break the impasse over the composition of the transitional cabinet and legislature. A solution always appeared to be just around the corner, but it also proved to be just out of reach.[4]

The Role of the International Community

During the seemingly never-ending debate over power sharing in transitional institutions, all political factions in Kigali sought support for their positions from the international community. Ambassador Flaten became deeply involved in helping the parties search for an equitable and politically acceptable solution to this highly emotional issue. He was a willing sounding board for all of the main political parties on both sides of the political divide. They came to him to test their latest ideas, seek his feedback, and listen to his

observations. He was also a key member of the Western ambassador group (France, Belgium, Germany, and the United States) that,
at strategic points in the process, jointly encouraged the president
and prime minister to be flexible in their consideration of proposals on the table. These diplomats urged moving forward on accepting a power-sharing formula.

In his role as a sounding board for political party leaders, Ambassador Flaten had encouraged consideration of the principle of inclusion of all key political factions rather than exclusion. In practice, this
meant that the United States was implicitly backing participation of
the hard-line CDR party in the transitional government. This policy
position was generally shared by the Western diplomatic missions.
However, it put the U.S. and other diplomats at odds with Hutu
opposition party leadership that opposed CDR inclusion. From their
perspective, the United States and, indeed, most of the diplomatic
community appeared to be siding with the president and his hard-
line allies in favor of the status quo.

While the power-sharing debate dragged on in Kigali, the Tanzanian facilitator of the peace talks in Arusha, opposition party leaders,
and government negotiators in Arusha expressed concern to U.S.
diplomats about the future of the peace process.[5] With the president
and the MRND becoming more and more intransigent, the possibility that they might walk away from the talks seemed likely.

The RPF too told U.S. diplomats visiting their Mulindi headquarters that they worried about the delay in reaching agreement on
power sharing in Kigali. The RPF leader Col. Paul Kagame accused
President Habyarimana of undermining the peace process by stalling on a power-sharing decision. Kagame told Flaten that the delay
reflected the president's unwillingness to address the underlying
issues bedeviling peace and democratic progress in Rwanda.[6]

Arusha Talks Resume Despite Political Disarray in Kigali

Foreign Minister Ngulinzira and his government delegation had
returned to Arusha on schedule in late November 1992. In the absence
of agreement in Kigali on power sharing, however, he had no formal instructions to guide the government delegation's negotiations
with the RPF on this issue. His intention was to keep the two sides

talking pending a Kigali consensus. Neither he nor his opposition colleagues in Kigali, including the prime minister, wanted to risk collapse of the peace process.[7]

To keep the talks alive, both the government and the RPF delegations considered, but rejected, shifting the Arusha focus temporarily from power sharing to the next big issue: integration of government and RPF military forces. The RPF argued the political configuration of the transitional institutions should be settled first. The government delegation agreed; it wanted to keep pressure on Kigali to resolve the power-sharing impasse.

After stalling for a few days in anticipation of instructions from Kigali, Ngulinzira announced to those assembled in Arusha that there had been a "breakthrough" in Kigali on a power-sharing formula. He based this on news that the clergy mediators had presented a statement of principle and two possible power-sharing options to the president's side for consideration. As a result, Ngulinzira said— albeit prematurely—that his delegation was prepared to resume power-sharing negotiations.[8] At the same time the foreign minister announced that Kigali had reached consensus on having appointed rather than elected legislators in the transitional national assembly. He also signaled that the government delegation wanted to revisit three clauses in the already signed October 30 protocol.

Ngulinzira named clauses 14, 21, and 46 as those requiring a second look. Clause 14 called for a consensus of the RPF and political parties in the existing multiparty government before any additional parties could be brought into the transitional government. Clause 21 stipulated that a two-thirds vote would be needed in the transitional cabinet to pass important issues, among them any amendment to a peace agreement. Clause 46 would require all local officials, most of whom had remained loyal to the president's MRND party, to be confirmed or replaced within three months of the peace accords' taking effect. All three clauses as written, and already agreed to by both delegations in Arusha, disadvantaged the MRND and its allies. All three made reaching consensus in Kigali on a power-sharing formula more difficult.

Despite the announced breakthrough, Ngulinzira and the government delegation received no formal instructions from Kigali on power sharing. Instead the Kigali debate dragged on. To delay power-sharing discussions further in hopes of receiving instructions, the government delegation began talks with the RPF over political loose ends, including how to implement the provisions of the controversial October 30 protocol.[9]

Kigali Dithers over Power Sharing; Disagreement Deepens, Stalls Again

As December wore on, hopes for a Kigali consensus faded and prospects for the future of the peace talks became more doubtful. Although the president continued to profess commitment to the peace process both publicly and privately, his MRND party and its hard-line CDR ally had dug in their heels. The MRND threatened to boycott the transitional institutions altogether unless its political bloc was accorded enough votes to play a substantial role in them.[10] The party promised to reject any proposal that marginalized it or relegated it to becoming a "permanent minority." This apparently inflexible hard-line Hutu position remained totally unacceptable to the mainly Hutu opposition parties. Negotiations in Kigali seemed to be at an impasse.[11]

On December 22, however, Prime Minister Nsengiyaremye shared with Ambassador Flaten a new proposal. He contended it had come from the opposition parties and was a slightly modified version of the clergy's last proposal, which the president had categorically rejected. This new proposal would give the MRND and the RPF one additional seat each in the transitional government council, for a total of four each. It would be presented that afternoon to MRND representatives. The prime minister and the ambassador agreed, however, that several more days would likely be needed before consensus could be worked out and instructions sent to the government delegation in Arusha.[12]

Arusha Negotiators Sign Power-Sharing Agreement, Preempt Kigali Decision Makers

That very evening, December 22, in a development that astonished everyone concerned about the power-sharing debacle in Kigali, Radio Rwanda reported that the government and RPF delegations in Arusha had reached agreement on a power-sharing formula for the transitional government. If accurate, this report would mean that Arusha negotiators had concluded an agreement without concurrence from the Rwandan capital. They would have bypassed the power-sharing disarray in Kigali and preempted the Kigali politicians.

The next day a cable from the U.S. Embassy in Tanzania confirmed that the delegations in Arusha had indeed reached agreement on an arrangement for power sharing in the BBTG. The formula described in the cable was almost identical to the one Prime Minister Nsengiyaremye had shared with Ambassador Flaten the previous day. The OAU representative in Arusha, Assistant Secretary General Machivenyika Mapuranga, was reportedly unaware that the formula accepted in Arusha lacked consensus in Kigali.[13] The prime minister professed astonishment to MRND leaders that the foreign minister had taken this preemptive move without having received word of a power-sharing consensus in Kigali.[14]

Foreign Minister Ngulinzira dismissed the resounding criticism from Kigali. He also disregarded a letter from the president's chief of staff, Enoch Ruhigira, telling him that the government in Kigali, not the government delegation in Arusha, had sole authority to decide on the distribution of power in the transitional government. Instead Ngulinzira forged ahead to tackle the remaining power-sharing issue: the size and distribution of seats in the transitional legislature.[15]

Ngulinzira's expressed goal was to have a second power-sharing protocol ready for signature in early January. Key delegates from each side—Pierre-Claver Kanyarushoki, Rwanda's ambassador to Uganda and a trusted ally of President Habyarimana, and Patrick Mazimhaka, the RPF's most senior Tutsi delegate—began drafting such a protocol.[16]

On January 9, 1993, the heads of the two delegations in Arusha— Foreign Minister Ngulinzira for the government and Pasteur Bizimungu for the RPF—signed a second political power-sharing protocol. This one laid out power-sharing arrangements in both the proposed government and the national assembly for a twenty-two-month transitional period. It assigned specific ministerial portfolios in the government and specific numbers of seats in the national assembly to participating political parties. It tied participation in the transitional government and assembly to existing political parties and made each party responsible for deciding which of its members would fill the assigned posts. The agreed formula gave the president's MRND and the Tutsi-led RPF an equal number of members in each transitional institution. The balance of power between the MRND and the RPF appeared to rest with the existing, mainly Hutu opposition parties.

The Arusha power-sharing formula for the twenty-one-member BBTG allocated five ministerial portfolios each to the president's MRND party and the Tutsi-led RPF. The opposition parties would control ten ministerial positions. The three main opposition parties—the MDR, the PSD, and the PL—were allotted three portfolios each, and the opposition premiership would remain with the MDR. The swing party in the existing coalition government, the PDC, would have one portfolio in the transitional cabinet. The hard-line, Hutu-supremacist CDR party and presumed ally of the president's MRND party was assigned no ministerial portfolio.

The Arusha formula for distributing the seventy seats in the TNA among the political parties allotted eleven seats each to the MRND and the RPF. Each of the three major opposition parties was also assigned eleven seats. The PDC was accorded four seats. Eleven other parties, most small and considered MRND clones, were allotted one seat each. This included the Hutu-supremacist CDR.

The Arusha power-sharing arrangement had treated the CDR as if it were no more important than a minor-party clone of the former ruling party. Like the minor parties, the CDR had received no seat in the transitional government cabinet and only one seat in the national assembly. The CDR, however, saw itself as a significant political force, which had proven capable of mobilizing both public opinion and political action.

In the prevailing political climate, the Arusha power-sharing arrangement left the MRND without any allies in the cabinet. In the national assembly it could count on only its own eleven votes and those of the eleven smaller parties accorded one seat each. Unless the MRND could win over the PDC and several members of the opposition parties, it would be unable to reach the two-thirds needed to pass important questions or the one-third plus one needed to defeat them in either transitional institution.

These calculations held great significance for all the parties, but especially for the president and his MRND. What the MRND wanted to avoid was a possible move in the future TNA to impeach the president, or worse. Given the political alignments when the Arusha power-sharing formula was concluded, the president's hard-line and Hutu-supremacist supporters saw no way they could prevent an impeachment vote should it come to that. They believed the Arusha power-sharing arrangement had curtailed the MRND's ability to exercise, let alone control, power during the transitional period.

The opposition parties, however, could exercise real decision-making authority in both transitional institutions, providing the parties remained united. The ten opposition representatives, in a cabinet with twenty-one members, could easily muster the one-third plus one votes needed to stop initiatives of either the MRND or the RPF. Conversely, opposition collaboration with either the RPF or the MRND could determine which important issues could reach the two-thirds threshold to prevail. Similarly, in the seventy-member assembly the thirty-three votes of a united opposition surpassed the twenty-four needed for a blocking third. Likewise, if the opposition parties swung their thirty-three votes to the RPF, or even the MRND, they would need just a few votes from the small parties to garner the two-thirds needed to push through an important issue. At the time, it seemed likely that the Hutu opposition would align with the RPF rather than with the MRND on important issues.

U.S. Observer Absent from Arusha at a Critical Time

It is worth noting that the United States did not have a high-level, Washington-based observer present during the December 1992 round of talks. A designated senior U.S. official was waiting in the wings in Washington to be dispatched to Arusha only after Kigali reached a consensus on power sharing. Instead a political officer from the U.S. Embassy in Dar es Salaam, Tanzania's capital, went to Arusha when talks resumed in late November, pending arrival of the Washington diplomat. Arusha negotiators were not expected to take up power-sharing issues in the absence of a consensus in Kigali.

The expectation was that negotiations would shift to military issues pending resumption of political power-sharing discussions. So the

State Department's Africa Bureau sent Lt. Col. Tony Marley, its military advisor, to Arusha. However, when negotiators decided that they needed to resolve the political impasse before turning to military issues, Marley left Arusha for consultations in Rwanda. When power-sharing discussions in Kigali broke down in mid-December, the Dar es Salaam political officer also left Arusha. No one anticipated the sudden turn the peace talks in Arusha would take at the end of 1992 and into early 1993.

Comment

The power-sharing negotiations in both Kigali and Arusha from September through December 1992 were pivotal in setting the stage for the political disintegration in Kigali that followed. At the time, I certainly did not appreciate or even fully comprehend the dynamics at play as a result of the acrimony and increased mistrust that developed among the Rwandan power blocs during these critical negotiations. The decision in Arusha to preempt consensus in Kigali only exacerbated the bitterness among them.

Several of these dynamics are as follows.

1. *A marriage of convenience*: The unexpected Arusha agreement in October 1992 on reducing the power of the president introduced a new dynamic into the peace talks. The mostly Hutu political opposition within the government delegation and the mostly Tutsi RPF insurgents demonstrated, both in October and again in December, that if they could reach agreement on difficult key issues, they could outflank hard-line Hutu within the government delegation.

The common goal of ending the president's twenty-year monopoly on power allowed the Hutu opposition in Arusha and the RPF delegation to reach a compromise agreement on reducing presidential powers during the transition. United in an uneasy alliance, they shut out the Hutu hard-liners who had advocated the status quo. The October 30 protocol diluted the president's unfettered authority to rule during the proposed transitional period. The power-sharing arrangement agreed in December further isolated the president and his party, denying them the possibility of rounding up enough votes in the transitional institutions to prevail on controversial questions unless they could win over to their cause Hutu opposition parties or individual party representatives.

This observation should not be construed to suggest that the RPF and the opposition faction of the government delegation shared a common vision for the future of Rwanda. Nor could they necessarily be expected to collaborate on other issues. Instead their common ground on presidential powers and the distribution of power in the transitional institutions reflected a marriage of convenience based on a convergence of interests. Privately Ngulinzira contended that he remained wary of the RPF and was skeptical about its intentions. At Arusha he spent an enormous amount of time trying to craft common government positions to present to the RPF. Despite Arusha outcomes that both the Hutu opposition and the mostly Tutsi RPF accepted, it is unlikely, in hindsight, that either side fully embraced the compromises it made.

Nevertheless an impression was emerging of a three-sided negotiating table. Any one group—the RPF, the government opposition, or the government hard-liners—could prevail if it could convince one other group to support its position. Rumors suggested that government hard-liners had even approached Hutu RPF leaders, who were former allies of the president, about joining forces in the interest of Hutu solidarity to prevail over the mostly Tutsi RPF.

2. *A Kigali-Arusha split*: The two key power-sharing agreements forged during this period revealed a growing gap between the negotiating environment in Kigali and that in Arusha. In Kigali the president and the former ruling party, the MRND, held considerable sway in determining whether, when, and what instructions would be sent to Arusha. Their immediate adversary was the mostly Hutu internal opposition. The RPF, unrepresented in Kigali, remained peripheral to their deliberations.

In Arusha, on the other hand, the diverse government delegation dealt directly with the mostly Tutsi RPF delegation on a daily basis. What might be acceptable in Arusha, even to MRND supporters in the government delegation, might be totally unacceptable in Kigali. Both power-sharing protocols seemed to have caught the hard-liners in Kigali by surprise. Both were met with virulent opposition—verbal and physical—in Kigali and elsewhere in Rwanda. The emerging gap between the Kigali power structure and the government negotiating team in Arusha would grow greater as the peace process proceeded.

3. *Kigali hard-liners were losing control of the democratization process*: When the president and his MRND party announced political liberalization and democratization two years earlier, albeit somewhat reluctantly, they had apparently believed they would be able to control the process. They anticipated that they could dominate a multiparty political system just as they had controlled a one-party state.

However, with the advent of the peace talks, the locus of decision making on political liberalization and democratization shifted from Kigali to Arusha. Shaping a new political structure became the central issue at the talks. The Arusha peace process, with the opposition political parties and the mostly Tutsi RPF at the helm, seized control of the political liberalization process. The two Arusha power-sharing protocols confirmed this shift. Control of the democratization process was slipping away from the hard-line politicians in Kigali. They were not, however, willing to accept this.

4. *The peace process became a platform for revolutionary change*: During this critical period of power-sharing negotiations, the RPF began to show its hand. In contrast to the concept of evolutionary change prevailing in Kigali, it was becoming clear that the RPF had its sights set on revolutionary change. It had no intention of becoming a benign, minority political party within the existing Rwandan political system. What seemed more likely was that the RPF would seize every opportunity to use the Arusha negotiations to achieve fundamental change in the existing political system and power alignments in Rwanda. The RPF, it appeared, viewed the peace talks as a way to enhance Tutsi security and assure an RPF role in reshaping Rwanda's future.

[8]

Violence Stalks Democratization and Prospects for Peace

Throughout the complex political negotiations over power sharing that absorbed Ambassador Flaten in the fall of 1992, I was closely tracking human rights concerns, civil society developments, refugee return, and security issues. The surge in inter–political party and ethnic violence from July through September continued to escalate throughout October, November, and December. Like the insecurity that had coincided with agreements at the Arusha peace talks in July and August, the later violence again had Arusha links. Hard-line Hutu had been outraged at the Arusha protocol of late October that dramatically reduced presidential powers during the projected transition period. This anger and dismay was reflected in the November speeches by President Habyarimana, who had dismissed the Arusha process, and by the political operative Léon Mugesera, who had encouraged Hutu violence against Tutsi. These, in turn, fueled fear among Tutsi, intimidation of Hutu opposition, and eventually actual violence against both. By the time the second power-sharing protocol was signed in January, the human rights abuses and violence seemed to be spiraling out of control.

Death Squads in Rwanda?

As violence intensified, an announcement in Brussels disturbed many Rwandans and surprised diplomatic observers. On October 2 Filip Reyntjens, a Belgian academic specialist on Rwanda and the Great

Lakes region of Africa, and Willy Kuypers, a member of the Belgian Senate, held a joint press conference in Brussels.[1] They asserted that a network of highly placed persons was operating in Rwanda like a Latin American death squad. They dubbed this clandestine group Réseau Zéro (Zero Network).

The name Réseau Zéro had actually been coined a few months earlier by Christophe Mfizi, a former associate of President Habyarimana, to describe a coterie of persons close to the president, whom he claimed had taken control of the state and were using it to enrich themselves. In an open letter dated August 15, 1992, Mfizi had denounced the activities of this group and resigned from the president's once all-pervasive MRND party.[2]

At their press conference, Reyntjens and Kuypers named nine prominent Hutu with close ties to the president and his family as leaders of the Zero Network. Topping their list were three of Habyarimana's brothers-in-law: Protais Zigiranyirazo and Seraphim Rwabukumba, both brothers of his wife, and Col. Elie Sagatwa, his personal secretary and the husband of one of his sisters. Reyntjens and Kuypers also cited Col. Théoneste Bagosora, the cabinet director at the Ministry of Defense from the president's home area who later featured prominently in the genocide, and the president's son-in-law, Alphonse Ntirivamunda, director of public works.

The Rwandan government made no immediate comment on these allegations. A few weeks later, however, all nine persons Reyntjens and Kuypers had named as "death squad" leaders sent a letter to a Belgian newspaper, contending that they were totally innocent of the charges and that would soon file a law suit in Belgium for defamation of character.[3]

About six months later a Rwandan journalist imprisoned on unrelated charges claimed he had taken part in death squad activities. Afrika Janvier alleged he had attended a planning meeting of the Zero Network where former foreign minister Casimir Bizimungu was present. Bizimungu adamantly denied any such involvement, and the government strongly supported him. Most observers tended to dismiss Janvier's accusation; his testimony was considered suspect and his confession was given little credence. As a result, his finger-pointing was ineffective as proof of death squad activity.

The U.S. Embassy Grapples with the Allegations

The death squad accusations, though never proven or disproven, stirred doubt over whether an organized group such as the Réseau Zéro might actually exist. Could such a group have been behind the increasing insecurity, as well as both random and targeted acts of violence that were becoming more frequent? Deciding how to treat this issue in the Department of State's annual human rights report to Congress for 1992 became a bit of a dilemma for the embassy. The Department, under pressure from human rights groups in the United States, wanted to treat Reyntjens and Kuypers's charges as fact. After all, the two were reputable individuals knowledgeable about Rwanda. The embassy, on the other hand, wanted to be more circumspect until links between the named individuals and actual incidents could be verified.

We all agreed, however, that hundreds of Rwandans had been affected by targeted and random acts of violence during the 1992 calendar year. Additionally we agreed it seemed unlikely that such actions could have taken place without the knowledge or involvement of government officials or persons close to the president. A code of silence protected whoever the perpetrators were, and a climate of impunity shrouded them from judicial or public scrutiny and from accountability for their actions. So we settled on calling these reports "unsubstantiated allegations" of "the existence of death squads with possible links to the president."

The embassy was never able to pin down links between specific individuals and the escalating violence and human rights abuses. Nor could we confirm the existence of an organized group of perpetrators, as claimed by Reyntjens and Kuypers. Nevertheless it seemed plausible that at least some highly placed individuals or groups had been involved in instigating violence to disrupt democratization and discredit the peace process. The absence of accountability for perpetrators of the violence lent support to this thesis.

Réseau Zéro stuck as a pejorative term. Like Akazu, it became synonymous with the small cadre of the president's immediate family and friends who had been at the helm in Rwanda over the previous two decades.

Targeted and Random Violence Breeds Insecurity and Fear

As the president and his allies lost ground in their efforts to control the peace and democratization processes, reports reached the U.S. Embassy of increasing violence among the political parties that was primarily associated with public party rallies. When one party would try to hold a political rally to mobilize its members or attract new ones, members of another party would arrive at the venue to disrupt the proceedings. Violence generally resulted. According to Human Rights Watch, politically motivated attacks by the Interahamwe, the MRND party's youth wing, and other groups during 1992 and 1993 took some two hundred lives and injured scores of people in communities across Rwanda.[4]

Political party officials, party youth groups, and local authorities openly encouraged this chaos. To many Rwandans, it must have seemed that violence was an expected consequence of democratic practice. Few if any culprits were ever prosecuted for engaging in these skirmishes. Rwandans in areas affected by this violence must have longed for the days before political reforms and the revival of multiparty politics.

Random violence too was on the rise in the fall of 1992. Incidents of grenades thrown into houses, land mines detonated by vehicles on major and secondary roads, and bombs exploding on buses, at markets, or in restaurants were regularly in the news. Responsibility for these anonymous and mostly arbitrary attacks depended on one's point of view. Those favoring the president believed accusations prevalent in government-controlled media and official speeches. These sources regularly charged that infiltrators from the invading RPF supported by internal Tutsi "accomplices" were responsible for the violence. Those supporting opposition parties preferred to believe that presidential loyalists were behind these pervasive attacks. Whatever their actual provenance, the result was a climate of increasing insecurity throughout the country, especially in Kigali.

By early December 1992 political and ethnic tensions were running high. Minority Tutsi and Hutu members of opposition political parties were especially wary. The November discourses of the president and his MRND lieutenant Mugesera had instilled fear in these groups in particular. Many Tutsi were genuinely afraid for their own safety and that of their families. Opposition Hutu began to wonder about their security. In this volatile environment, victims of random or targeted violence could count neither on protection from security forces nor on justice from an ineffective judicial system.

As I walked around our embassy, I began to notice that several Tutsi employees were visibly exhausted during the day. Some would even fall asleep at their desks. When I asked them about this, they explained that because they feared possible Hutu attacks at night, several Tutsi families would gather at one family's home—a different one each night. To enhance the safety of the group, the men would take turns standing guard throughout the night while the women and children slept. They believed their security was seriously threatened by increasingly frequent radio messages labeling Tutsi inside Rwanda "accomplices" of the RPF. They had nowhere to turn for protection except to each other. Their explanation sharpened my understanding of the depth of their anxiety and fear.

A Holiday Hiatus?

The 1992 holiday season was anything but cheery. Everywhere a mood of gloom and doom prevailed. On Christmas Day, at a dinner I hosted for a group of humanitarian aid workers and diplomats, we were nevertheless able to enjoy a lighter moment. During our gift exchange, a French aid worker selected from an array of possible gifts a large, deep, open, brown cardboard box. Without looking inside, he reached his hand in to find out what gift he had selected, then instantly withdrew his hand, let out a yelp, and jumped back!

Wide-eyed onlookers held their breath as he reached in again. What he lifted out of the box was a gift no one had anticipated: a live white rabbit! Laughter consumed us. The gift came from our colleague at the International Committee for the Red Cross who, unbeknownst to most of us, had been raising rabbits. He had given all of us the gift of a much-needed moment of comic relief during an emotionally difficult time.

Our reprieve was fleeting, however. Before the guests had even left my house, we heard a large explosion not far away. It shattered our warm, sunny Christmas Day afternoon and brought us abruptly back to reality. We learned later that a small bomb had destroyed an electrical transformer located just off the main road, down the hill from my home. No one had been injured, but it knocked out power to the neighborhood below mine for several days, affecting a number of friends from the international humanitarian aid community, among others.

The Arusha Agreement on Power Sharing Prompts More Violence

The position of the MRND and its Hutu-supremacist CDR ally on power sharing hardened throughout December 1992. After news broke on December 22 that Arusha negotiators had agreed on a power-sharing formula before Kigali politicians had reached a consensus, a deteriorating security situation became even worse. Within days the MRND and CDR parties underscored their rejection of the agreement with violence. Once again, what the diplomatic community viewed as progress toward peace was met with increased violence and insecurity.

The embassy in Kigali received reports daily about death, injury, and property destruction across northern Rwanda. On December 28, 29, and 30 anti-Tutsi ethnic violence broke out in several communes in the northwestern Gisenyi prefecture. The sites were not far from where the MRND party official Mugesera had urged death to Tutsi a few weeks earlier. Not-so-veiled language on Radio Rwanda and in speeches encouraged Hutu violence against Tutsi neighbors. The message: Save yourselves from expected Tutsi aggression. Kill now or be killed later.

One local official reportedly warned a Hutu crowd to expect imminent RPF attacks and advised them to "clear the brush" so the RPF would have nowhere to hide. To the assembled Hutu, this was an unambiguous instruction to kill the Tutsi "accomplices" of the RPF. The Hutu were warned that local Tutsi might shelter RPF troops in preparation for an attack.

Rampaging Hutu subsequently killed three Tutsi in two communes, wounded many others, and destroyed many homes. Hundreds of Tutsi, the primary victims of these attacks, and Hutu members of opposition parties fled their homes to seek safety in churches or local communal buildings. Hutu attacks on Hutu members of the political opposition were consistent with Mugesera's message: Hutu who opposed the president, the MRND, and the CDR but who favored power sharing were as much the enemy as were the Tutsi RPF fighters.[5]

One of the most widely reported incidents of terror involved a girls' secondary school in a remote part of Gisenyi province. Between Christmas and New Year's, militiamen from the MRND and CDR surrounded the school. For five days they held hostage the sixty students and four religious staff members. Only after the gendarmerie chief of staff, Col. Augustin Ndindiliyimana, sent several busloads of gendarmes to the site was the standoff ended and the hostages released.

The northeastern province of Byumba experienced violence similar to that in the Gisenyi province during this period. Here too local authorities failed to provide protection from vigilante groups for Tutsi and opposition party members who feared for their lives. In one case reported to me by an international aid worker, six of the organization's local Hutu staff members operating assistance projects in the Byumba province were chased, caught, and then beaten, two badly enough to need hospitalization. The reason: they could not produce proof of membership in the MRND or CDR and they had refused to reveal the whereabouts of a Tutsi colleague who had gone into hiding. Such accounts of violence, along with the propaganda assaults on so-called Tutsi accomplices of the RPF and the Hutu opposition, were wearing down the resilience and confidence of people in Kigali and around the country. I felt despair and helplessness at hearing these reports. What could we in the international community do to forestall such violence and abuse of human rights? How could we contribute to or facilitate protection for the victims?

On December 31 the Hutu-supremacist CDR party staged a well-coordinated show of its strength by shutting down all commerce between Kigali and the rest of the country. It took only a few strategically placed roadblocks on the outskirts of Kigali to stop all traffic in and out of the city, as the Interahamwe had aptly demonstrated six months earlier. Simultaneously CDR members closed down roads into and out of the major northern towns of Ruhengeri and Gisenyi.

A strident CDR communiqué read on Radio Rwanda that evening, New Year's Eve, accused Foreign Minister Ngulinzira of having committed treason by agreeing in Arusha to a power-sharing arrangement that the CDR claimed handed power over to the Tutsi-led RPF. The CDR statement also denounced the opposition parties for supporting the RPF and accused the Hutu opposition and the RPF of trying to seize power by force. The communiqué threatened more disturbances throughout the country unless the CDR was accorded representation in the transitional cabinet and more than one seat in the transitional legislature.

As if the CDR's threat of violence needed an exclamation point, a bomb exploded that New Year's Eve at a hotel in the southern university town of Butare, the first such act to occur in the south. News of the bombing spread quickly on Radio Rwanda and put a damper on holiday festivities. Butare seemed an unlikely site for such violence. I had no holiday spirit left in me; the violence and threats of violence had deeply saddened me. So I stayed home that New Year's Eve and watched the movie *It's a Wonderful Life* with an equally morose friend. The year was off to an inglorious start.

Comment

During this volatile period I had spent a month on holiday outside Rwanda. A birthday celebration in England and a photography trip in Morocco allowed me to take my mind off events unfolding in Rwanda for a few short weeks. I returned to Kigali just in time for the president's speech denigrating the Arusha process, followed by Mugesera's call to eliminate Tutsi. I also had to grapple with how to handle the death squad accusations in the 1992 human rights report for Rwanda.

It remains unclear to me whether we at the U.S. Embassy grasped fully the consequences likely to flow from the controversial power-sharing agreements at Arusha. Even though the violence across northern Rwanda in late December escalated to a level not seen before, I believe we were still trying to take the violence in stride. Winners and losers were inevitable as the political forces in the country attempted to rebalance power to the greater benefit of the greatest number. We remained committed to supporting this historic shift. There was no thought, at least to my knowledge, of linking our support for democratization and peace in a cause-effect relationship with the violence and human rights abuses. Rather, we saw it as the actions of a few disgruntled hard-liners who were destined to lose power as democratization and peace progressed. We still believed that if President Habyarimana and key MRND leaders would express genuine support for change and cooperation across ethnic lines, the hard-liners would be obliged to follow. Through a process of negotiation and compromise the naysayers could be encouraged to support the process and participate in the future of Rwanda.

Mugesera's speech, however, had not only demonized Hutu and Tutsi proponents of power sharing; it also laid the groundwork for calling them traitors. This label, when applied to Foreign Minister Ngulinzira and others who supported the Arusha power-sharing protocol, made them the enemy and early targets for death when the genocide began.

The significance of the threat in the CDR's New Year's Eve communiqué did not register with me at the time. Its vow to cause further violence unless its demands for greater participation in the transitional institutions were met foreshadowed the willingness of this Hutu-supremacist party to play the spoiler in the peace process. The letter I wrote to family and friends in December 1992, before the sudden and unexpected Arusha agreement on power sharing, summarized my thoughts on the past year in Rwanda and expressed my pessimism and frustration at year's end.[6]

[9]

The January from Hell

Diplomacy at a Crossroads

Rejection and More Violence Follow Arusha Power-Sharing Protocol

The second power-sharing protocol, signed in Arusha on January 9, 1993, without the consent of the MRND ruling party and its hard-line allied parties, set a contentious tone for the year ahead. Government negotiators in Arusha had paid no heed to the firestorm their December agreement for power sharing in a transitional broad-based government had set off among hard-liners in Kigali in the final weeks of 1992. They had disregarded the violence erupting in the countryside—mainly in the president's home area—in opposition to it. Instead they had continued to negotiate and proceeded to agree with the RPF on a second power-sharing formula for the distribution of seats in a seventy-member transitional national assembly. Then, together, the delegations drew up and signed a protocol to enshrine both.

The negative reaction in Kigali to this final Arusha protocol on political power sharing was swifter and even more explosive than that following the October protocol reducing presidential powers during the transition. The MRND and CDR quickly and categorically denounced this signed Arusha agreement. Leaders publicly reiterated their late December accusations: the agreement was an overt power grab by the mostly Hutu opposition and the mostly Tutsi RPF; Foreign Minister Ngulinzira had sided with the RPF instead of paying attention to the views of the government delegation.

115

In short, the Arusha power-sharing agreement was categorically unacceptable to the pro-president, pro-MRND, pro-CDR political and military contingents that continued to control most levers of power in Kigali. They could be in no doubt that their grip on the future was slipping away with each advance toward democratization and peace.

Furious CDR leaders asserted that their party was an established political force that should not have been treated as a minor party. Not only should the CDR have had a place in the cabinet, they argued, but it should also have received more than one seat in the Transitional National Assembly.

To underscore their rejection of the power-sharing accord, the MRND and the CDR organized protest demonstrations in Kigali on January 20, 1993. Party militia from the MRND's Interahamwe and the CDR's Impuzamugambi showed up en masse and paralyzed the town. Barricades of burning tires appeared throughout the city. Not surprisingly, violence ensued. Three persons died and many others were injured.

One person was killed at a barricade just in front of the U.S. Peace Corps office and not far from the headquarters for the U.S. Agency for International Development. This brought the violence very close to the American community. Peace Corps staff began a review of the safety and security of the volunteers stationed at sites in the southern Rwandan countryside. The entire American community was chastened by this tragic event. The embassy and my house were both within a mile of this tragic incident.

The following day, January 21, Mathieu Ngirumpatse, chairman of the MRND, publicly announced what we had been hearing privately for several weeks: that his party would not accept this Arusha protocol, regardless of the fact that it had already been signed. This rejection permeated the MRND leadership and spread to its rank and file. Most offensive to them was the equivalency accorded to the MRND and the RPF. In a refrain we had heard repeatedly from government and party leaders, Ngirumpatse said the MRND would never accept being relegated to the status of a "permanent minority" in Rwanda. Like the CDR, the MRND party that had ruled Rwanda for nearly twenty years made it clear to all that it would not accept the power-sharing arrangement reached in Arusha and enshrined in the January protocol.

Ambassador Flaten soon began to hear from contacts in the MRND and its hard-line allies. They insisted that this power-sharing protocol be reopened and renegotiated. However, the delegations at Arusha took no steps to do so. Apparently neither the government nor the RPF delegation believed it had any incentive to do so. The signed protocol favored their common goal of ending the president's nearly twenty-year monopoly on power.

Furthermore the international community exerted little to no pressure on either the government or the RPF delegation at Arusha to reopen political power-sharing negotiations despite public rejection of the agreement by the still-powerful ruling party and its allies. Diplomats reasoned that reopening the protocol, even if it was imperfect, could endanger the success of the Arusha talks. Renegotiation, the argument went, could put at risk the entire peace process, end progress toward a negotiated settlement, and make return to war inevitable. Though recognizing the pitfalls in this power-sharing agreement, diplomats believed the risk of collapse of the entire peace process, and a likely resumption of war, was the greater danger.

Instead Ambassador Flaten encouraged his interlocutors in the ruling party to accept the idea that political parties, the building blocks for the transitional institutions, were not immutable. He discussed the democratic concept of "shifting coalitions" to describe changing political groupings as interests and issues of various factions changed over time. He counseled flexibility on the issue and acceptance of the fait accompli at Arusha. Alternatively, he suggested using the implementation process instead of renegotiation to redress grievances concerning specific articles in the protocol that the president, his party, and their allies found objectionable.

If we at the U.S. Embassy had failed to fully comprehend the significance of the October 30 Arusha protocol reducing presidential powers, we had no doubt that the January 9 protocol contained intrinsic difficulties. Rejection by the MRND and CDR was unequivocal, as was the refusal of the RPF and the opposition parties to reopen and renegotiate portions of the protocol. Commitment to the success of the peace talks in Arusha kept the diplomatic community from supporting renegotiation and risking total collapse of the peace process.

International Human Rights Commission Visits

MRND party propaganda portrayed escalating ethnic and political violence coincident with the signing of the Arusha power-sharing protocol as spontaneous, a heartfelt response of ordinary Rwandans to objectionable decisions. Curiously, however, despite continuing verbal denunciations of the agreement, overt violence subsided markedly when a coalition of international human rights organizations arrived to conduct a two-week investigation beginning on January 7, 1993.

This independent International Commission of Investigation on Human Rights Abuses in Rwanda had been invited by Rwanda's five human rights groups to investigate abuses committed by both the government and the RPF since October 1, 1990, the date the RPF first attacked Rwanda. The multiparty government installed in the spring of 1992 had authorized this mission in one of its early decisions. It had charged the newly appointed minister of justice, Stanislas Mbonampeka, an opposition Liberal Party leader, with responsibility for the visit. The minister had tapped Alphonse Nkubito, attorney general for Kigali and founder of Rwanda's first human rights organization, ARDHO, to facilitate the work of this commission.

Four well-known and well-respected international human rights groups made up this ten-member panel of experts: Human Rights Watch (New York), the International Federation of Human Rights (Paris), the Inter-African Union of Human Rights (Ouagadougou), and the International Center for Human Rights and Democratic Development (Montreal). The ten commission members divided their two weeks in Rwanda between Kigali and regions of the north most affected by the border war. In pairs they interviewed key local human rights activists, politicians, government and military leaders, as well as victims of violence and abuse. They also crossed into RPF-controlled territory in northern Rwanda, where they were able to meet people living there and listen to their stories. They also talked with RPF leaders at their Mulindi headquarters.

The relative calm that prevailed during most of the visit was shattered the day before the commission members left Rwanda by the deadly January 20 demonstration in Kigali. On January 21 random and targeted killing—so rampant in late December and early January—resumed in earnest. Some incidents were reported later to have been reprisals for cooperation with the human rights investigators. The international commission's March 1993 report of its investigation estimated that government forces killed three hundred to five hundred people in the wake of the visit as punishment for providing testimony.

Alison Des Forges of Human Rights Watch, the only American member of the Commission of Investigation, had been a frequent visitor to the embassy over the course of her many visits to Rwanda during my first year and a half in Kigali. I do not recall, however, whether she briefed us at the embassy on this visit. Commission members would have wanted to safeguard their independence. Also, the group had not yet formed its collective conclusions about the Rwandan human rights situation.

Nevertheless Alison and I did connect by phone before she left Rwanda, on the evening of the deadly January 20 demonstration. I do not remember what we said, but I do remember that we cried together over the phone. The intense emotion of the day's events and the cumulative despair I was feeling over the brutality of physical and psychological abuse of ordinary Rwandans poured out. I felt helpless in the face of the escalation of violence and fear that gripped Rwanda and so many Rwandans. Peace and democratization seemed as elusive as a mirage on a desert horizon.

Intimidation and Fear Intensify

Despite the somewhat diminished violence during the visit of the international human rights organizations, the climate of fear and intimidation continued unabated. One mid-January weekend, in the midst of all this turmoil, a Rwandan friend dropped out of sight. We had arranged to play tennis on Saturday morning, but he did not show up and was nowhere to be found.

After surfacing the following week, this friend explained that he had gone into hiding after friends told him they had seen his name on a list. Rumors of lists containing names of persons designated for harassment or even elimination were nothing new. These lists were infamous, and having one's name on a list was ominous. Evidently my friend believed that the imminent danger had passed and that it was safe enough to resume his normal daily routine. The fear, though, remained close to the surface. This friend, and many others in Rwanda's human rights and civil society organizations—both Hutu and Tutsi—were targets for the killers when the genocide began.

Ambassador Flaten got a firsthand look at the chaos unleashed by Hutu hard-liners on January 18, the U.S. holiday honoring Martin Luther King. On that Monday he took visiting family members, still in town from the Christmas holidays, to see Rwanda's famous mountain gorillas, not far from the northern town of Ruhengeri. On his way back to Kigali, the ambassador reported encountering several military roadblocks set up on the main highway to check the papers of Rwandans. The ambassador and his family, however, had been allowed to pass without incident. He said that the crowds lining the highway appeared terribly menacing. Later reports indicated that many Bagogwe, the Tutsi subgroup living near the Gisenyi-Ruhengeri road, had been harassed, beaten, and even killed at these roadblocks during that time.

New Human Rights Groups Emerge

In the wake of the visit of the international human rights commission, and perhaps in anticipation of what their investigation might turn up, new human rights organizations appeared in Rwanda in January 1993. The first to surface was the Independent League for the Defense of Public Liberties (Ligue Indépendante de Défense des Libertés Publiques), followed shortly by three others: the Rwandan Association for the Respect of Human Rights (Association Rwandaise pour le Respect des Droits de l'Homme), the Rwandan Association for the Defense of the Rights of Victims of the War (Association Rwandaise pour la Défense des Droits des Victimes de la Guerre), and Misericordia.

In contrast to the already established local human rights groups, all of these associations were created by the government and were partial to the president and the hard-line parties. They had as their mission the defense of the Hutu majority against abuse by the insurgent RPF and its so-called Tutsi accomplices inside Rwanda. Whereas the older human rights organizations criticized the abuses against the population by both government institutions and the RPF, the new organizations denounced only abuses against the Hutu majority by the RPF.

Representatives of some of these pro-Habyarimana, pro–Hutu supremacy groups came to the embassy to introduce themselves and seek embassy funding. As the human rights officer, I heard them out, but the embassy declined to help. It was clear that the government had created these groups as a counterweight to the existing human rights organizations. Their objective was evident: to exonerate the president and his hard-line, Hutu-supremacist allies from any responsibility for the escalating violence and human rights abuses. Their strategy was to deflect blame to the RPF and its so-called Tutsi accomplices. They publicly discredited any concrete, factual information to the contrary, accusing the sources of being under the control of Rwanda's enemies. Africa Watch, a division of the U.S. rights group Human Rights Watch, gave little credence to these new Rwandan human rights groups.[1]

In April 1993 these groups issued a joint critique of the report of the International Commission of Investigation on Human Rights Abuses in Rwanda. They charged that the Commission had been a tool of the older human rights groups that were, in turn, tools of the opposition parties.[2]

Comment

January 1993 in Rwanda will always be for me the January from Hell. The acrimony over the power-sharing arrangement agreed at Arusha, the violent political demonstrations in Kigali on January 20, heightened fear among Tutsi from intimidation and orchestrated attacks, and the renewed massacres at the end of the month in the northwestern Gisenyi prefecture brought a gloomy end to a chaotic and most depressing month. These pressures and preoccupations overshadowed some important observations that became clearer somewhat later.

1. *Death lists in preparation*: The incident involving my friend who felt the need to drop out of sight for a few days gave me another glimpse into the Tutsi world of constant fear. This incident later confirmed for me that the lists the killers reportedly used to target designated victims at the onset of the genocide in April 1994 must have been drawn up, or were at least in the process of being prepared, in January 1993.

2. *"Hutu solidarity" becomes a propaganda tool*: When the CDR called Foreign Minister Ngulinzira a traitor for signing the January Arusha protocol on political power sharing, it was echoing the speech of Léon Mugesera, the MRND political operative. Mugesera had not only callously suggested sending the Tutsi back to Ethiopia via the Nyabarongo River; he had also accused Hutu in opposition parties of being traitors by breaking with Hutu solidarity. My ignorance of Rwandan history kept me from understanding fully how this intolerant and antidemocratic remark had registered with Rwandans. I was unaware that the phrase "Hutu solidarity" had been used ever since independence in 1962 to rally Hutu against the perceived Tutsi enemy.

In the course of 1993, the call for "Hutu solidarity" would gain momentum, with dire consequences. Hard-line Hutu supremacists would use it as a propaganda tool to unite the Hutu president's political supporters and the Hutu opposition. It became the rallying cry of the Hutu Power movement, forcing Hutu politicians and democratization activists to choose between allying with the Hutu supremacists or continuing to support power sharing. Choosing the latter meant being called a traitor. The hard-line propaganda machine would need only another short step from labeling Hutu opponents traitors to equating them with the RPF and Tutsi enemy. Hutu solidarity left no room for moderates who had embraced power sharing as a way to bridge the deep-rooted divide between Hutu and Tutsi in Rwandan society.

3. *Diplomacy at a crossroads*: Diplomacy was at a crossroads in January 1993, but we diplomats did not realize it. We plunged ahead with support for democratization and peace, not recognizing or accepting that our policies were leading to neither. We didn't under-

stand the extent to which our unconditional backing for the peace talks might have contributed to the violence that followed the Arusha agreements to reduce presidential powers and deny MRND dominance during the proposed transitional period. We did not understand that instead of helping to build a strong foundation for a smoothly operating democracy, our support was doing just the opposite.

This was probably the moment when diplomats should have reassessed the status of both democratization and the peace process in light of their very negative and violent impact within the society. Instead we were intent on continuing our policies of support for Rwanda's transitions to democracy and peace. We were committed to their success, and a signed power-sharing agreement at the Arusha peace talks seemed like success.

What diplomats viewed as progress toward peace and democratization, those opposed to the Arusha process perceived as existential threats to their future. We failed to realize that we had unwittingly become part of the problem rather than part of the solution. Cavernous ethnic and geographic divides would polarize Rwandans, creating serious obstacles to achieving a functioning, sustainable democracy.

The question still nagging me more than two decades later is whether the diplomatic community should have done more than it did at this juncture. Should diplomats have done more to encourage negotiators in Arusha and in Kigali to take a second look at controversial provisions in the Arusha power-sharing arrangements, even if it risked collapse of the peace talks? After all, the hard-liners most upset by the January power-sharing protocol were the ones most capable of becoming spoilers of its success. They controlled the military and the military hardware.

Should diplomats have threatened to withdraw support from the Arusha process pending adjustments to the power-sharing texts? Should we have insisted on equal consideration being given at the peace talks to the security fears of all groups? Should we have encouraged safety nets not only for the minority ethnicity that stood to gain power but also for those in the majority group who would have to cede some power? Their representatives repeatedly insisted that they needed protection from the minority. What could we have done to help build bridges across the divides that were pulling Rwanda deeper into a quagmire?

This was the time it might have been most appropriate for diplomats to have taken a stand against a deeply controversial and likely unworkable accord, to have disavowed the agreement that seemed unlikely to garner support from those already disaffected Hutu. I do not believe, however, that we fully understood what a critical turning point this moment was for the future of Rwanda. I, at least, did not grasp at the time the significance of this crossroad.

[10]

Diplomats Undertake a Fact-Finding Mission

Increasing violence left a terrible trail of death, destruction, and displacement across the northern region of Rwanda at the end of 1992 and the beginning of 1993. In late January representatives of a number of Rwandan and international human rights and development organizations gathered to compare notes and aggregate their findings. The tally had been staggering. More than 150 Tutsi and Bagogwe had been killed. Several dozen homes of opposition MDR party members had been burned to the ground. Over two thousand Tutsi and opposition party members had fled their homes seeking safety in church compounds or government buildings. The group concluded that ethnicity, regionalism, and political party rivalries, as well as the speeches of political leaders, such as the November rant of MRND operative Léon Mugesera, had inspired this violence.[1] The group called on Rwandan authorities to restore calm quickly.

Some in the diplomatic community believed we needed to do more than make verbal denunciations to government officials condemning this unacceptable escalation of unchecked violence. We wanted to take some action that would demonstrate our opposition to the violence and our support for its victims, and we wanted our action to show government officials how appalled we were at its campaign of fear and its lack of action to end the carnage.

Spurred on by diplomats from Canada and Switzerland, a group of us decided to show our concern by making a one-day fact-finding mission to one of the remote areas hardest hit by the violence. Once there, we planned to call on local officials and visit sites where displaced persons—Tutsi and opposition Hutu political party members alike—had gathered to escape life-threatening attacks by marauding Hutu. We would travel by road in a convoy of vehicles bearing diplomatic license plates, each of us in our own official vehicle with our own driver. We hoped our visible presence would make clear the diplomatic community's concern for the suffering of the people and elicit some corrective action by the government.

We set out at dawn on February 4 in a convoy of four or five diplomatic vehicles. Although our destination was not far to the northwest of Kigali as the crow flies, none of the main roads out of town linked directly with this isolated region west of the meandering Nyabarongo River. To reach the only bridge that would allow us to cross the river into this area, we had to follow the main highway southwest from Kigali to Gitarama and then turn north on a less-traveled but well-maintained dirt road leading to the bridge. The first part of the trip was uneventful.

After about an hour we crossed the bridge over the narrow Nyabarongo River into the Gisenyi prefecture (now called the Western Province). We had reached the southern part of the region where Mugesera had delivered his provocative speech in November and where the violence had been the most severe in December and January. A powerful feeling of dread and foreboding immediately came over me. Crossing the bridge seemed to transport me into another country.

The few people walking along the road certainly did nothing to make us feel welcome. They failed to greet us with a nod, a smile, or a wave. Any of these responses would have been customary and friendly. Instead, when they saw or heard our convoy approaching, they would stop, turn toward the vehicles, and look at us with cold, empty stares. The hoes slung over the shoulders of some suggested they might be Hutu farmers heading to cultivate nearby fields.

I pondered the situation. How had the recent violence touched these people? What horrors might they have witnessed? What stories could they have told? Had they been among the Hutu perpetrators? Or had they perhaps been victims? Had they lost Tutsi or Hutu friends? Might they have opposed the violence and tried to stop the killing? They may not have identified us as diplomats, despite our CD license plates, standing for *corps diplomatique*, or diplomatic corps, but they could not have missed our white faces. How did they view us? Outsiders to be sure. Meddlers, probably. This was unlikely to be an easy day!

It wasn't long before we came to the first administrative center, where we had hoped to engage the local authorities. Nestled in a sparse grove of trees, it was little more than a few tin-roofed, adobe-brick buildings. We stopped, got out of our vehicles, and inquired where we might find the local officials. None of the authorities we wanted to question was in, we were told. Only a few lower-level civil servants were available. No explanation was offered, and we did not ask for one; instead we moved on. We had several stops on our program and did not want to waste any time. When the story was the same at the next village administrative center, we began to speculate about the reasons. Was there some conspiracy about not talking to visitors? Why were all the authorities missing from their offices and their villages? Had they all gone somewhere?

Only at the third administrative site did we finally learn the reason: President Habyarimana was expected to arrive by helicopter at a nearby location at about noon. All the local officials had been summoned to the site to welcome the president and listen while he addressed the anticipated crowd. We realized that to find any local officials to talk with, we would have to go to the site of the president's visit as well. It was still early; we could reach the site and complete our business before the president arrived.

Encounter with Displaced Persons

As we neared the helicopter landing site, the forested area we'd passed through after crossing the Nyabarongo River opened to low, rolling, treeless but grass-covered hills. Shortly after turning onto a dirt track leading to the gathering site among the hills, a school to the right of the road captured my attention. Instead of the cheerful sounds of children playing in the schoolyard, there were about fifty to seventy-five obviously displaced persons. There seemed to be women and children as well as men, suggesting that whole families had fled together. Many of the women were solemnly attending to food preparation. Men were milling about. Some had wrapped blankets around themselves against the morning chill on this high-altitude plateau.

None of the blue plastic sheeting tents characteristic of displaced persons camps was visible; classrooms were evidently providing shelter. Absent too were the noise and energy of children running about, a usual sight in other displaced-persons camps I had visited in Rwanda and elsewhere. A silent pall hung over the people and the place.

Our convoy stopped. Listening to the displaced was one of our objectives. We could also talk with some of the local humanitarian workers from the Rwandan Red Cross organization who had taken charge. As I got out of my four-wheel-drive vehicle, I glanced across the road and realized the reason for the unnatural silence. Just across the narrow dirt road, on a grassy, treeless hillside overlooking this makeshift displaced-persons camp were scores of young men silently watching. Some were standing, others squatting on their heels. Some seemed to be holding sticks. Or were they machetes?

I suspected that these were the very people who had forced the displaced persons to flee their homes, the very people the displaced were trying to escape. Only the narrow, unpaved, rutted dirt track—and a few Rwandan Red Cross workers—separated the hunted from the hunters. No forces of law and order were anywhere to be seen. Based on my previous work on humanitarian relief issues, I was extremely worried for those who had fled to what they hoped would be the safety of the school. Was our unwelcome presence creating a hiatus in the violence? Through interpreters, displaced Tutsi told us of their fear and the trauma of leaving their homes to avoid being killed by their Hutu neighbors. They said they had no intention of returning to their homes any time soon.

Encounter with President Habyarimana

After spending some time talking with these frightened people, we left them in the care of the Red Cross workers. Our procession of diplomatic vehicles continued along the dirt track across the hilltops, toward the helicopter landing site. Soon we saw a cluster of rudimentary, one-story, tin-roofed buildings ahead of us. As we drew closer, we could see people gathered there. Others were finding places to sit on a hillside facing what we presumed to be the helicopter landing pad a bit away from, and higher than, the administrative buildings.

As we drew closer to these buildings, we suspected those milling about—all men in suits and ties—were the officials we had been seeking earlier that morning. They were talking in low voices among themselves as they awaited the president's arrival. We decided to mingle. While they were in waiting mode, we seized the opportunity to fan out among them and ask about the violence in their areas.

All the stories we heard were similar. Spontaneous outrage set Hutu against Tutsi and was responsible for the recent bloody attacks. One group of officials offered to talk with us further at their village at the end of the day. They wanted to show us the damage violence had done in their community. We agreed to meet them later, and they gave our drivers directions to their village.

Not long after we began talking with these officials, including some we recognized from Kigali, the group started to gravitate toward the landing site at the top of the nearest hill. A podium marked the spot from which the president would address the gathering crowd, no doubt entirely Hutu. We diplomats were hanging back. We did not intend to follow the officials to the landing pad. Our instincts told us to keep a low profile at this high-profile gathering.

However, the Kigali authorities had recognized some of us as well, and they knew that we represented the diplomatic community. They insisted that we accompany them to greet the president, so we reluctantly agreed to follow. We soon realized that they wanted to make sure we were not only in the receiving line to welcome the president but also visible to the journalists filming the event. Television had become an established media source in Kigali, even though its reach extended only a short distance outside the town. The evening news either that night or the next would surely cover this presidential event. The president's supporters had their own agenda for us.

The president's helicopter finally arrived. Kigali authorities, local officials, and we members of the Kigali diplomatic corps were lined up to greet the president as he disembarked. He must have been as surprised to see us in this remote region as we had been to learn about his visit falling on the same day as ours.

To my dismay, journalists filming the event featured us prominently in evening television reports of the president's visit, even though we had tried to appear obscure and incidental at the very end of the long welcome line. We had tried in vain to avoid such a public role. We hadn't wanted to give onlookers any opportunity to misconstrue the purpose of our presence in this deeply troubled region. Unfortunately the journalists did just that, their reporting suggesting that we were there in support of the president. This distorted our message and totally undermined the purpose of our trip. Our intention had been to show support for the victims of violence and of concern for the government's failure to intervene to end the horrors. We had not anticipated the presence of reporters, and we had not managed them well.

Our convoy got under way as the president was preparing to deliver his speech to the assembled crowd. We still had several stops on our planned itinerary and wanted time to take up the invitation of the local authorities to visit them at their village. Darkness would be upon us at six o'clock in the evening and it was already after noon.

Encounters with More Displaced and Local Officials

Our next stop was a Catholic mission perched on a hilltop. Scores of Tutsi—men, women, children, and the elderly—had sought safety there from Hutu attackers. A large group of these displaced persons had gathered in the courtyard of the church compound. Rwandan priests interpreted responses to our questions.

Their voices and their body language spoke of desperation and fear. Echoing the earlier group of displaced sheltered at the school, the men told of narrow escapes, helpless vulnerability while crossing the Nyabarongo River, and fear for their lives as they fled from pursuing Hutu. Like the group we'd met earlier, these displaced too indicated no interest in returning to their homes until calm had returned and their security could be assured. We promised to carry word of their plight to Kigali, humanitarian organizations, and the rest of the world.

Our convoy moved on to another Catholic mission about half

an hour away. To get there we followed another dirt road down a long hill, crossed the Nyabarongo River on a rickety log bridge, and drove up a long hill on the other side. It reminded me of my days as a Peace Corps staff member in Zaire, when I visited volunteers at their remote teaching sites. Only then the roads would have been rivers of mud and my vehicle would have been slipping and sliding down to a river crossing, possibly onto a pontoon ferry boat.

Once at the Catholic mission compound we found more people in distress. Some identified themselves as Tutsi, and some said they were Hutu opposition party members. All had fled their homes in search of protection from marauding Hutu. We heard more harrowing tales of fear and narrow escapes. Anxious priests worried about how long they could continue to feed and protect these people. We saw people traumatized by fear, some no doubt dealing with the loss of loved ones. They must have wondered what would come next for them.

Shaken by the extent of the suffering and the depth of the trauma we encountered, we drove back across the Nyabarongo River for our promised rendezvous with the group of local officials we'd met earlier in the day. We found them in a dust-swept village of huts clustered around a large, open, central space.

The officials were waiting for us and immediately took us to one of the nearby communal buildings. It was an approximately fifteen by twenty foot cement-block building, with a tin roof, and now it was an empty shell. They explained that scores of Tutsi had huddled together inside to protect themselves from a throng of over two thousand angry Hutu. The exterior walls were pockmarked by bullet holes. Large metal window frames held no glass. Inside, spots of spattered blood and occasional bloody handprints on the walls told a horrible story of fear, defenselessness, struggle, and undoubtedly death. I tried to imagine what it must have been like for those Tutsi men, women, and children looking out of those two-foot-high windows to see a hoard of attackers carrying—what? Guns, spears, clubs? What had it felt like, packed densely in that room, trying to crouch lower than the low window ledge to escape the advancing onslaught?

The village authorities rather imperiously credited themselves with routing the attackers and escorting surviving Tutsi to safety. In response to our questions, they explained that the attackers were not from their village but had come from a neighboring district. An interesting strategy, I thought, as I struggled to regain my composure. The image of those bloody handprints about eighteen inches above the cement floor is seared in my mind even now, nearly twenty-six years later.

Following this jarring experience, the local officials escorted us into a rather large room that may have been a school classroom. As the light faded from the sky, they offered their explanation for the violence in their area and answered our questions. The senior official, a deputy governor (*sous préfet*) of the region, reiterated the story we'd heard earlier in the day from other officials. The violence against the Tutsi in their village had been spontaneous. His explanation for this spontaneous rampage: the rural people, "simple peasants," he called them, were angered by the early January signing of the power-sharing agreement in Arusha that would bring Tutsi into the Hutu-led government. They were upset because, in the words of the deputy governor, the agreement gave too much power to the Tutsi rebel group, the RPF.

Attributing the violence to popular outrage over the Arusha power-sharing agreement while simultaneously contending the villagers were "simple peasants" struck me as contradictory. From my seat near the back of the group I asked whether he thought the local people had followed the peace talks in Arusha so closely and whether this explanation accurately reflected the thinking of those he had called "simple peasants."

The deputy governor acknowledged that the peasants probably had not followed or understood the Arusha talks in detail. Nevertheless he persisted in justifying the spontaneity of the attacks. The Hutu villagers, he continued, feared that after a peace accord, exiled Tutsi would return to the region, reclaim lands they had left thirty years earlier, and kill the current Hutu occupants. The Hutu villagers, he said, had acted out of fear of the Tutsi and fear of the opposition political party members. He concluded, "The peasants may not understand Arusha, but what they do understand is fear." The deputy governor emphasized the word "fear." His explanation, delivered firmly and with no hesitation in a nearly dark room, made me shudder.

Returning to Kigali in darkness along unlit rural roads, I reflected on the day's events. I wondered how my Tutsi driver had interpreted what he had heard and seen. At home that night I found myself shaken to the core by our excursion. The deputy governor's words echoed in my ears: "What the peasants do understand is fear." Had the local authorities played a major role in instilling that fear in the "simple peasants" of this remote region? We had long suspected local authorities of having a hand in instigating the so-called spontaneous acts of violence. It seemed to me that we had just heard a local official acknowledge as much.

In a surprising turn-around, some authorities from this remote, trans-Nyabarongo region were actually disciplined for their part in causing the violence in this area. One was the deputy governor who had spoken with us that afternoon. Could this be a positive sign of progress toward the rule of law and holding officials accountable for their dastardly acts of inciting violence?

Comment

Our fact-finding mission probably had little impact on either restoring security to the region or changing the views of the authorities who may have inspired the fear and violence. I never even had time to write a reporting cable on this outing. Just four days later the violence of December and January was overshadowed by the resumption of the war. Nevertheless, to see firsthand the situation of the displaced in an area badly affected by violence, to experience the palpable tensions, and to hear the arguments justifying the violence had made our trip worthwhile.

According to the evening press reports in French, the president had said the right things when he addressed the people and the authorities that early February day. He had encouraged the crowd to end the violence and to restore peace and calm to their communities. How much veiled language he might have used to convey a contradictory message I will never know.

Our excursion across the Nyabarongo River into the southern Gisenyi prefecture underscored a key issue that only became worse over time: how to provide protection to those threatened by or faced with deadly violence. Who could those targeted by violence turn to for safety and security? The security institutions of the state—police, gendarmes, military—had proven themselves ill-equipped, unable, or unwilling to protect the victims. National and local officials were partisan and untrustworthy. The churches and the clergy, though willing to help, were unprepared for the long-term care of those who reached their doorsteps.

What might diplomacy have done to enhance protection for the people who lived in fear that each day might be their last? Our diplomatic excursion had certainly confronted us with the urgency of what was happening in the rural areas. If the war had not resumed four days later, could we have used what we had learned to exert pressure or develop strategies for influencing change in the behavior of those committing the violence or supporting it from behind official titles? The rupture in the cease-fire and renewed war, however, preoccupied everyone, including the U.S. Embassy staff, for the next couple of months.

[11]

War Resumes

An RPF Offensive Rocks the Country

Dark days of February followed the January from Hell. On February 8, 1993, just days after my firsthand look at the impact of January's interethnic, interparty violence in rural Rwanda, Kigali awoke to Radio Rwanda reports that RPF forces were on the move. Tutsi-led troops were pushing southward from their Mulindi headquarters near Rwanda's northern border toward Byumba and Ruhengeri, the two major population centers between the RPF base and the capital. Rwandans in the path of the advancing soldiers were also on the move. Tens of thousands were said to be fleeing south toward Kigali in front of the RPF army.

This sudden move by the RPF shattered the July 1992 cease-fire that had paved the way for peace talks in Arusha and had lasted for six months. The RPF justified its attack as retaliation for the January killings of Tutsi across northern Rwanda. It rejected the assertion that it had broken the cease-fire, contending that the Hutu attacks on Tutsi had in fact been the cease-fire violation. This RPF offensive against Byumba and Ruhengeri, though a surprise, was not entirely unexpected. For weeks there had been rumblings among Kigali officials and politicians and even within the diplomatic community of a possible attack.

The diplomatic strategy to avert such a move had been to encourage positive progress at the peace talks. Thus the timing seemed curious to us, coming just a month after the RPF had appeared to win a major victory at Arusha. The January power-sharing protocol had given the RPF a significant role in the anticipated transitional government—one equal to that of the president's MRND party. Was this advance intended to underscore that victory? Or was it a show of force to strengthen the RPF's hand at the next round of peace talks in Arusha? Might it have been prompted by some other consideration not yet evident?

Why, I wondered, would the RPF choose to return to war? Had RPF leaders not anticipated that breaking the cease-fire would be like pouring fuel on a fire in the wake of the widely disparaged January power-sharing protocol? Wouldn't they want, instead, to build up RPF credibility and trustworthiness instead of fanning the flames of the anger, anxiety, and antagonism sparked by the protocol? Why would the RPF deliberately take this step that it surely knew would sully its credibility with Rwandans, particularly the Hutu, even further?

The Peace Process Threatened

Peace negotiations had already resumed in Arusha when the RPF troops moved out of Mulindi and attacked Byumba and Ruhengeri. Despite continuing controversy and violence surrounding the power-sharing protocol, a new round of talks had convened on January 24, 1993. Negotiations were scheduled to take up another sensitive aspect of power sharing between the government and the RPF: power sharing in the military. Discussions on integrating government and rebel RPF military forces would have to address how to distribute leadership positions among the officer corps of the two armies and what proportion of each force would be included in the respective units of the united army.

At issue as well would be which ministry would control police functions. Should the police remain a gendarmerie, a part of the military under the defense ministry, as in the French security structure? This was the government position. Or, should the gendarmerie be transformed into a national police force and transferred to the jurisdiction of the Ministry of the Interior, as in an English-based system familiar to the Tutsi who had grown up in Uganda? This was the RPF position. Under the terms of the power-sharing protocol, the defense ministry would continue to be under the control of the president's MRND party. The interior ministry, however, would become the responsibility of the RPF. Each side wanted to control the police functions.

Defense Minister James Gasana had gone to Arusha to co-chair the government delegation with Foreign Minister Ngulinzira. A Hutu and member of the MRND, Gasana would bring his experience as defense minister to the military discussions. Though not part of the president's inner circle, he may also have been sent to keep an eye on Ngulinzira. The president's supporters and allies—notably the CDR party—had accused the foreign minister not only of giving away too much to the RPF in the January power-sharing negotiations but also of having actually committed treason by doing so.

When the government delegation at Arusha learned of the RPF offensive, it abruptly walked out of the peace talks and returned to Kigali. It wasn't clear whether the peace process could be salvaged. A hard-line member of the Rwanda delegation, Col. Théoneste Bagosora, reportedly said, "I have returned to Kigali to prepare for the apocalypse." He was later tried and convicted of being a key instigator of the genocide.

Kigali Calm at First

The RPF offensive caught the Rwandan security forces off guard and shook the Kigali political elite to its core. Despite the angst and despair renewed fighting had caused, however, the town remained calm. Most people went about their business as usual. I proceeded as scheduled that February 8 morning to deliver opening remarks at a women's seminar on civil rights and democratization. Haguruka, a women's group, had received an embassy grant from the U.S. Democracy and Human Rights Fund to implement an information-dissemination project. Assembled for the one-week training session to kick off the project were women from throughout Rwanda. Participants had no doubt heard the morning news announcing the resumption of fighting, yet all turned up on time for the start of the program. Although they were clearly agitated and nervous, they carried on all week, conducting discussions and training sessions.

Fighting near the northern border was not entirely new, and people in Kigali did not feel immediately threatened.

This time, however, the fighting did not stay at the frontier. Instead RPF forces moved swiftly south, capturing the town of Ruhengeri on the first day of their offensive. They had apparently encountered little opposition. Regular government forces, like the population at large, were reportedly fleeing the advancing RPF army. Rumors spread of pervasive rapes by the retreating troops. Before long, the RPF had moved far enough south to cut the main highway between Kigali and the northern towns of Ruhengeri and Gisenyi. Being cut off from Gisenyi meant Kigali was cut off from Rwanda's only beer brewery, the sole source of the two bottles per day given to every soldier.

French Forces Increased

Within days RPF forces occupied positions no more than twenty miles north of Kigali, and fear mounted among the city's population. Mortar fire boomed periodically both day and night. The sound of war punctuated thoughts we didn't want to contemplate.

Immediately after the RPF offensive began, the French reinforced their troop strength in Kigali by three hundred.[1] Officially sent to protect French citizens and other foreigners, these fresh troops reportedly deployed at roadblocks and other defensive positions around Kigali. They certainly gave Kigali residents a sense of security they might not otherwise have had. And the visible French presence may have contributed to the RPF's decision to halt its advance and declare a unilateral cease-fire.

Numbers of Displaced Mount

In front of the advancing RPF forces and the retreating Rwandan Army, Hutu peasants fled, many already displaced at least once before. Thousands were heading south toward Kigali. Rwandan authorities eventually stopped this massive flow of humanity in a valley just north of the capital along the road leading to the northern town of Byumba. The International Committee of the Red Cross, which aids civilians caught in conflict situations, and the World Food Program came to their aid. Other local and international humanitarian organizations already in Rwanda quickly ramped up their operations. Some had built up stocks of food and shelter materials in Rwanda or nearby that they could draw on to speed the humanitarian response. New international aid organizations flocked to Rwanda, so that almost overnight the international aid community in Rwanda expanded exponentially.

Hillsides flanking the road to Byumba, just outside Kigali, became an instant community. Before long, the once forested hillsides were devoid of trees; in their place were crude tents fashioned from sapling branches and white plastic sheeting. This tent city covered the hillsides as far as the eye could see.

As a result of this RPF offensive, some 600,000 newly displaced persons joined the estimated 350,000 already displaced as a result of the war. This meant that by February 1993, more than one year before genocide gripped the country, nearly one million Rwandans, or about one out of every seven, had become homeless in their own country.

Embassy on Alert

The American community went on alert as soon as the cease-fire broke down. Renewed fighting, a burgeoning humanitarian crisis, and concern for the security of Americans in Rwanda stretched our tiny staff to the breaking point. Security of the American community is always an embassy's top priority. Americans in Rwanda numbered about three hundred, counting all U.S. government employees, contractors, staff of nongovernmental organizations, missionaries, and those in Rwanda on their own or married to a Rwandan. Most lived in Kigali, though a fair number were scattered around the country. This was a large number for our small staff to deal with, but it was far fewer than the estimated six hundred French and about 1,200 Belgian citizens in Rwanda.

Our sole consular officer made contact with every American in Rwanda to assess individual situations. We were especially worried about those living and working in the north, the area most affected by the war and the renewed fighting. One of these was Rosamond Carr, an elderly American living alone on her farm near Gisenyi, an area in the northwest where Tutsi massacres had occurred repeatedly. Also of concern were the Seventh-Day Adventists teaching at a secondary school in the same region. We speculated that neither

Carr, a longtime resident and flower exporter made famous by the movie *Gorillas in the Mist*, nor the Adventist teachers would be eager to evacuate even if we encouraged them to do so.

Embassy staff monitored closely RPF progress toward Kigali so we could assess both political and security implications. We gathered as much information as we could from our Rwandan contacts, NGO friends, and key international organizations such as the ICRC and the various United Nations offices. We also kept in touch with our diplomatic colleagues—particularly the Belgians and the French—to compare information and assessments. Each day I wrote at least one, and sometimes two, situation reports to apprise Washington offices and officials of the security circumstances. The ambassador focused his communications to Washington and other interested embassies on the political aspects and implications of the renewed fighting. We held regular security briefings at the embassy to exchange information within the American community, sharing with community members what we knew, what we thought might happen, and how it might impact us, while they offered information they had acquired from their contacts. We passed messages over our two-way radio network as necessary.

Our general assessment was that the RPF would be unlikely to try to capture Kigali because of the mayhem such a move would undoubtedly unleash. The Tutsi living inside Rwanda would bear the brunt of such an attack, we believed, becoming victims of outraged Hutu in the face of the advancing RPF. We thought the RPF would not want such an outcome and so would exercise restraint and not claim the ultimate prize: the capital city. It was also possible that the RPF would not want the responsibility of occupying and running the town.

Nevertheless the embassy had to plan for the worst-case scenario. Ten days after the cease-fire had collapsed, the outcome of the fighting was still very much in flux. Prospects for restoring the cease-fire appeared dim. The RPF was still advancing toward Kigali. Ambassador Flaten asked, and received, State Department permission for the embassy to go to "Authorized Departure" status. This meant any American government employees declared nonessential, along with their spouses and children, could choose to leave Rwanda at U.S.

government expense and return once the situation improved. All American government personnel, whether employed at the embassy, USAID, the U.S. Information Service, or the Peace Corps, opted to stay for the time being. Several employees' family members, however, left promptly on commercial flights. So far, the Kigali airport remained open.

As deputy chief of mission, I was on the short list of "essential" personnel. Departure was not an option unless our status escalated to "Ordered Departure." That would mean all government employees would have to leave. We all knew that an obligatory drawdown of personnel could begin at any time should the situation deteriorate further, and we needed to prepare for such an eventuality.

Before the embassy went to "Authorized Departure" status, the Peace Corps had summoned its thirty or so volunteers to Kigali. Although the volunteers had been based only south of Kigali and had not been directly in harm's way, the move was intended to offer them greater security and enable a speedier evacuation from the country should that become necessary. Two weeks later, when the volunteers were still unable to return to their posts due to the continuing security concerns, the Peace Corps decided to evacuate all of them to the United States for reassignment or, for those close to the end of their two years in Rwanda, to terminate their service. Without any volunteers to manage, the Peace Corps director and his small international staff also departed.

Ambassador Flaten was not pleased about this decision, which was made solely by our Peace Corps colleagues in consultation with their Washington headquarters. But the ambassador had little recourse. Kigali Peace Corps officials explained that headquarters policy required volunteers to return to Washington if they were absent from their posts for more than two weeks.

I sympathized with the Peace Corps decision. Fifteen years earlier I had been in a similar situation, but then I was on the Peace Corps side of the table. As an associate director in Zaire, I was party to a decision to evacuate and reassign or terminate some volunteers we believed to be in harm's way during the first Shaba war. Embassy officials had tried unsuccessfully to dissuade us.

With no new cease-fire in sight, some American government

employees who had opted to stay began to think about the security not only of themselves but also of their prized possessions. Each family group that left under "Authorized Departure" had been allowed to take five hundred pounds of luggage at government expense. However, there was no special shipping allowance for employees whose families opted to remain or for single employees, like myself, in such a situation. If we were ordered to evacuate on short notice, we would have to leave everything behind. This anomaly in the rules seemed unfair. Our tenacious administrative officer, Larry Richter, lobbied the State Department and won permission for single employees and those whose families had remained at post to ship up to five hundred pounds of unaccompanied personal belongings out of Kigali.

That's when I learned that my irreplaceable African bead collection weighed over one hundred pounds. I bundled it all up in newspaper, bubble wrap, and protective African baskets and sent it out of Kigali in the shipment of one of our officers who was scheduled to transfer back to Washington that summer. Under the circumstances, he had received approval to proceed with the immediate shipment of his personal effects. I would recover my bead collection from him at some future time. Of course, all my other possessions—clothes, the artwork hanging on my walls, files of personal papers—remained at risk of being left behind should we have to evacuate.

Initiatives to Restore a Cease-Fire and Peace Talks

Diplomacy swung into high gear as soon as the fighting resumed. Efforts began almost immediately on multiple fronts to persuade the RPF to return its troops to their Mulindi base and reestablish the cease-fire. The United States pressed both the government and the RPF to restore the cease-fire and resume peace talks. Ambassador Flaten entered into a flurry of discussions with Rwandan government officials. In Washington DC, Uganda, and elsewhere, State Department officials and diplomats at U.S. embassies urged RPF representatives to resume the cease-fire and abandon war in favor of peace negotiations.[2]

On February 20, twelve days into the renewed fighting, the RPF unexpectedly declared a unilateral cease-fire. However, this led only to a stalemate rather than a return to the status quo ante, as the government side did not reciprocate with its own cease-fire declaration. Yet Kigali residents welcomed even stalemate; their nerves, already frayed, were reaching the breaking point. Throughout this trying period, almost everyone attempted to carry on as usual. Shops and offices in Kigali, including embassies and aid missions, remained open for business. French and Belgian commercial air flights maintained their regular schedules. Although the situation remained tense, the RPF's declaration of a cease-fire opened the way for the two sides to talk.

Rwandans too tried to broker an end to the fighting and a return to the negotiating table. Opposition party leaders met with RPF representatives in Bujumbura, Burundi, from February 25 to March 2. Their aim was to find common ground for restoring a lasting cease-fire and resuming peace talks. The meeting issued a final communiqué calling for a durable cease-fire, renewed peace negotiations, the return of the internally displaced to their homes, and legal action against those responsible for the recent January massacres. The Bujumbura meeting also insisted on the withdrawal of foreign troops. This was a pointed reference to the French forces, viewed by those in the meeting as helping to keep President Habyarimana in power.[3]

Almost simultaneously a second, competing meeting took place in Kigali that brought together representatives from nearly all the existing political parties. Ostensibly organized by the Rwandan Bishops' Conference and the Protestant Council of Rwanda, it was a rare example of collaboration across the divide between the ruling and opposition parties. The president's MRND and its allied party, the CDR, along with seven of the ten minor parties generally favorable to the president's positions, sat down with representatives from each of the four main opposition parties—the MDR, PSD, PL, and PDC—to work out a way forward. The RPF wasn't present.

In stark contrast to the Bujumbura meeting, however, the outcome of the Kigali session tilted in favor of the president. It condemned the RPF for resorting to arms, praised the Rwandan armed forces for their bravery, and welcomed the presence of the French troops. This meeting condemned Uganda for supporting the RPF and called for improved coordination between the multiparty coalition government, the president, and the prime minister.[4] After the Kigali meeting, the presidents of the four opposition parties disavowed their parties' representatives on the grounds that they had not been authorized to participate.[5]

According to the author Gérard Prunier, the all-party meeting in Kigali had actually been convened at the initiative of the president.[6] Prunier contends that the president intended to exploit the RPF aggression by wooing opposition leaders and building alliances between his MRND party and opposition party members. Perhaps some could now be convinced to view the RPF differently—to see the Tutsi-led rebel group as the enemy rather than as a political partner. Alliances with disillusioned opposition party members could strengthen the president's and his party's voice in votes in the transitional government and national assembly.

Comment

The RPF's February offensive had a profound impact on the course of events in Rwanda: it caused Hutu in opposition political parties who had bought into the idea of power-sharing with the Tutsi-led RPF to rethink their position. Like shifting tectonic plates, this shifting political ground effectively destroyed the unity of the opposition parties. The contradictory statements from the nearly concurrent meetings in Kigali and Bujumbura first revealed the rifts developing within the opposition. Cohesiveness, both within and among the opposition parties, never recovered. The new political fault line—whether to share power with the Tutsi and the Tutsi-led RPF—defined Rwandan political alignments and loyalties from this time forward. The emergence of these splits in the opposition parties offered President Habyarimana a political opportunity that he was quick to seize and exploit.

An explanation for the RPF offensive was suggested to me many years later by an informed Rwandan Hutu living in exile in Europe. He firmly believes that the RPF's intent had been to weaken the Hutu opposition. This explanation sounds plausible. If true, it could account for the response of RPF delegates in Arusha when I contended that the offensive might have been counterproductive because it had turned so many Hutu supporters of power sharing against the RPF and the peace process. RPF members always smiled and insisted the offensive had not been a mistake from their point of view.

Whether or not weakening the opposition was the RPF's goal, it was indeed the result. The doubts over power sharing that the RPF offensive aroused among opposition political leaders and their rank and file blurred the lines between the former regime and those professing opposition to it. This made the parties ripe for the crippling splits that were to follow. The impact of these splits, however, would become clear to many in the diplomatic community only months later when they were already threatening the stability of post-Arusha Rwanda They provided the basis for the party realignments that resulted in the political polarization that isolated those few Rwandans still daring to support power sharing with the RPF. This polarization and the vitriolic propaganda denouncing those still advocating power sharing would leave no room for moderates in Rwanda's political process.

[12]

A Second Chance for Peace

Cease-Fire Restored

By early March, life in Kigali began to return to a more normal tempo. The RPF troops had halted their advance about twenty miles north of the city. The unilateral cease-fire was holding, and the sounds of war no longer filled the air at unpredictable intervals, day and night. Some displaced persons who had fled south to escape the advancing RPF army began to filter back to their homes. The RPF leader Gen. Paul Kagame contended some were even returning to their homes behind the RPF lines.[1]

The cease-fire, however, had yet to be formalized. President Ali Hassan Mwinyi of Tanzania, the facilitator of the peace process, took on this task. He launched an initiative to end the standoff between the Rwandan government and the RPF and put the peace process back on track. To do so, Mwinyi summoned government and RPF representatives to Dar es Salaam on March 5 for consultations aimed at reestablishing a cease-fire agreement. Resolution came swiftly. On March 7, about a month after the RPF had launched its attack, government and RPF representatives signed a new cease-fire agreement to take effect two days later. The prime minister Nsengiyaremye and the chairman Colonel Kanyarwengwe signed the agreement for the government and the RPF, respectively.

The terms of the new cease-fire called for RPF forces to return to the positions that they had occupied in the north prior to their February 8 offensive and for government forces to stay south of the line they had been pushed back to during the fighting.[2] Negotiations were to resume in Arusha on March 15; talks on outstanding military issues were to conclude within three weeks. The agreement asked the OAU to extend the mandate and increase the funding for its cease-fire monitors, the neutral observer group NMOG.

The vast territory between new front lines of the armed forces would become a demilitarized zone, or DMZ. No troops from either side were to operate in the DMZ, which was intended to reduce the risk of shelling incidents from stationary forces by separating the combatants. These conditions, the reasoning went, would open the way for the displaced persons to return, if they wished, to their homes and, more important, to resume farming in the economically critical DMZ. NMOG would monitor the return of the forces to their prescribed positions and their compliance with the terms of the cease-fire.

The cease-fire agreement also addressed three related but extremely controversial issues: the presence of French troops, sanctions against public officials involved in massacres, and the status of agreements at Arusha. It called for all foreign troops to withdraw from Rwanda and be replaced by a neutral international force under the auspices of the Organization of African Unity and the United Nations. It gave the Rwandan government one week to suspend, fire, or take other administrative action against all public officials involved in massacres or who had failed to prevent them, including some to be named by the RPF. It also committed both the government and the RPF not only to a negotiated settlement within the Arusha framework, but also to accept as binding all protocols and agreements concluded and yet to be reached at Arusha.

The CDR Rejects the Cease-Fire and Splits with the MRND

The hard-line, Hutu-supremacist CDR strongly objected to this cease-fire agreement. On March 9, the day the agreement was to take effect, it issued a vitriolic statement, accusing President Habyarimana of agreeing to an arrangement "obviously detrimental to the interests of the Rwandese people" and calling the agreement "an act of high treason." The statement denounced the president as well as the opposition prime minister for accepting a cease-fire agreement that was too soft on the RPF.[3]

A few weeks later the CDR went a step further. On March 27, it publicly ended its loose alliance with the president's ruling MRND party, from which it had sprung. It was openly repositioning itself as a right-wing party opposed to the president and the MRND as well as to the RPF and the mainly Hutu opposition parties.

Back to the Negotiating Table: Force Integration and Military Power Sharing

Peace talks resumed in Arusha on March 16, 1993, just a week after the new cease-fire was concluded in Dar es Salaam. Negotiators picked up where they had left off in early February, with the divisive issues of force integration and demobilization. The two sides had made little headway in their discussions before the RPF offensive.

The U.S. Department of State's Africa Bureau sent its military advisor, Lt. Col. Tony Marley, to serve as U.S. observer for this round of military-focused peace talks. Marley was well versed on postconflict force integration and the process of military disengagement and demobilization. He also knew the situation in Rwanda well. On several occasions he had participated in meetings with RPF representatives in both Washington and Uganda. He had also attended the Arusha talks briefly in November 1992.

Furthermore, Marley was already in the region when the peace talks resumed so quickly after the renewed cease-fire, consulting key political and military players in Uganda, Rwanda, and Tanzania about pending military issues at Arusha. Twice he had met with RPF leaders, including Commander Kagame, at their Mulindi headquarters in northern Rwanda. For the first meeting, before the renewed cease-fire, he reached Mulindi from Uganda's capital, Kampala, with a U.S. Embassy colleague. For the second, after the new cease-fire, he and Ambassador Flaten drove from Kigali. Also attending this second meeting were UN and OAU representatives and a number of Rwandan journalists.

At this second meeting, Commander Kagame committed to abiding by all the terms of the new cease-fire. He assured the ambassador and Marley that all RPF troops would withdraw from the DMZ

A Second Chance for Peace

by the March 17 deadline. He also unexpectedly agreed to United Nations help to strengthen the OAU's neutral observer force, NMOG, already deployed to Rwanda to monitor compliance with the 1992 cease-fire. Kagame emphasized, however, his preference for having OAU rather than UN troops serve as peacekeepers after an Arusha agreement.[4]

When Marley arrived in Arusha, he found negotiations on force integration dragging on without reaching an agreement. On the table was the government's demand for 80 percent of the officers and troops to 20 percent for the RPF. The RPF delegation leader Bizimungu termed this proposal "provocative" and "an insult" in consultations with the Tanzanian facilitator. Noting the success of the RPF's February offensive, Bizimungu countered with 80 percent for the RPF, before dropping to 55 percent for the RPF and 45 for the government. When briefed on the impasse, the observers began to consider variable ratios at different levels of the army or a 50-50 split.[5]

Marley's reports from Arusha indicated that disagreement on several related questions hampered progress on the central issue of force proportions. One such contentious issue was the size of the integrated security forces. The government advocated a combined army and gendarmerie force of twenty-five thousand, while the RPF insisted on no more than fifteen thousand. Nor could the two sides agree on whether police functions should stay with the gendarmerie reporting to the Ministry of Defense, or whether a new national police force should be created under the jurisdiction of the Ministry of the Interior. Even choosing the name for a proposed high command office to advise the defense minister and president became a point of disagreement and delay.[6]

A UN Force for the Rwanda-Uganda Border?

Just days after the cease-fire was reestablished between government and RPF forces, the UN Security Council made its first move toward military involvement to end the Rwanda conflict. On March 12, 1993, the Security Council unanimously passed Resolution 812 (1993) that laid the foundation for both a UN border-monitoring force and a UN peacekeeping force aimed at facilitating peace in Rwanda.[7] The resolution called for the UN secretary general to examine separate requests from Rwanda (S/25355) and Uganda (S/25356) for UN military observers to be deployed at their common border to monitor any transit of RPF troops or matériel from Uganda to Rwanda.[8] The resolution also called on the UN secretary general to look into how the UN might collaborate with the OAU to strengthen the Rwandan peace process. Not until five months later, however, at the end of August, several weeks after the government and the RPF had signed a peace agreement, did a seventy-two-person force finally deploy to positions on the Ugandan side of the border.

National and International Human Rights Groups Document Abuses

The RPF's February offensive prompted allegations of human rights abuses against both government and RPF troops. International and local human rights groups documented many violations and published reports inside Rwanda and elsewhere over the following six months. Their findings painted an ugly picture of escalating cruelty and ethnic hatred.

Several Rwandan human rights groups traveled in mid-February to Ruhengeri, the northern city targeted in the RPF's February 8 attack. Rights investigators talked to witnesses about what had happened. This coalition of local rights groups documented the killing of numerous Hutu civilians at the hands of the RPF solely because they belonged to the president's MRND party or its then ally, the CDR. These local rights groups publicly condemned the RPF for such attacks.[9]

The international rights group Africa Watch, a division of the U.S.-based Human Rights Watch, condemned violations by both the RPF and government forces. Its report "Beyond the Rhetoric," not released until June 1993, documented the killing of several Ruhengeri Hutu authorities and their families by RPF soldiers at the start of the February fighting.[10] The same report outlined numerous cases of Rwandan government soldiers arresting and beating Tutsi for not carrying proper documentation or for allegedly being accomplices of the RPF. The report identified government gendarmes (territorial police) and political party militia as perpetrators of similar abuses. Africa Watch concluded that soldiers had been responsible for raping many women but noted the assaults generally went unreported and the soldiers unpunished.[11]

On March 8, 1993, just as the peace process was getting back on track with a new cease-fire, the International Commission of Investigation on Human Rights Abuses released its report.[12] The coalition of rights groups had visited Rwanda on January 7–21, 1993, to investigate human rights abuses committed by the government and the RPF since the 1990 invasion.

Its investigation concluded that the Rwandan government had killed or instigated the killing of an estimated two thousand civilians from October 1990 to January 1993. Most of those killed, it reported, were minority Tutsi. However, starting in 1992 Hutu opposed to the president and the MRND were also victims. The Commission found that the president and government of Rwanda had tolerated and encouraged the activities of armed militias attached to the political parties, thus "privatizing" violence that had previously been carried out by the state. The Commission report noted the impunity accorded perpetrators and attributed this to political interference in Rwanda's judicial system, concluding that justice had not been served for the victims. Even when prosecutors arrested those accused of human rights abuses, they were quickly released and never brought to trial. The Commission's report also documented rights abuses by the RPF, which had attacked, killed, and injured civilians, kidnapped and expelled them to Uganda, confiscated their cattle, and destroyed their property.

Although the Commission's report affirmed that many Rwandans had been killed, seriously injured, or forced to flee their homes solely because of their Tutsi ethnicity, it stopped short of concluding that the attacks constituted genocide. To meet the definition set out in Article II of the UN Convention on the Prevention and Punishment of the Crime of Genocide (1948), the killing would have to have been "committed with intent to destroy, in whole or in part" the Tutsi ethnic group in Rwanda.[13] The report posited that this criterion might not have been met because the numbers of Tutsi affected might be too low and because Hutu opposition party members had also been targeted.

The Commission addressed recommendations to the government and the RPF as well as the international community. It urged both the government and the RPF to end human rights abuses and to hold accountable those involved in committing them, and it called on the international community to facilitate an end to rights abuses by encouraging the successful conclusion of the Arusha peace negotiations. It recommended that donors to Rwanda immediately end all military aid to the two sides and make future aid contingent on improvements in the human rights situation.[14]

Initial Rwandan responses to the Commission's findings were swift and sharp, focused mainly on discrediting the report's confirmation of death squad activity. President Habyarimana broke his silence on the death squad issue in a speech to the nation on March 23, when he accused the human rights commission of bias resulting from a subjective choice of witnesses. He asserted that the poor human rights situation in the country was entirely a function of the war, and he blamed the Tutsi-led RPF for any human rights abuses that had occurred. The president also defended Minister of Health Casimir Bizimungu, the former foreign minister, against charges of involvement in death squad activity. A few days earlier, on March 20, Bizimungu had vehemently denied the Commission's conclusion on grounds that it was based on false testimony from a questionable witness.[15]

Not long afterward, however, the president modified this categorical rejection of the findings. On April 7 he and the Hutu opposition prime minister, Dismas Nsengiyaremye, issued a joint statement with a much more conciliatory tone.[16] This was likely the result of the Council of Ministers instructing the two to work together on a suitable reply.[17] In their joint statement, the president and the prime minister recognized and regretted human rights violations and acknowledged the possible existence of "criminal organizations" responsible for the deaths of many persons. They even agreed that undisciplined military forces could have been guilty of looting, rape, and killing and that some authorities might have been "ineffective" in carrying out their responsibilities. The joint statement, however, reiterated the president's earlier rejection of government responsibility for the widespread human rights abuses.

The joint statement concluded by outlining a number of government commitments aimed at ending human rights abuses and sanctioning perpetrators. Notably the president and the prime minister pledged to respect all the accords that would result from the Arusha peace negotiations, echoing one of the terms of the recently renewed cease-fire. A month earlier the prime minister had signaled the importance he attached to this pledge when he told an American delegation that a presidential commitment to abide by all the Arusha Accords would be a precondition for continuing the peace process.[18]

A UN Human Rights Investigator Arrives

On April 7, the same day the government issued this joint statement on human rights, another external human rights investigator arrived in Rwanda, this time from the United Nations Human Rights Commission. Bacre Waly Ndiaye, the UN special rapporteur on extrajudicial, summary, or arbitrary executions, had requested and received an invitation from President Habyarimana to visit the country. Ndiaye, a Senegalese lawyer with extensive background in human rights law, had come to investigate complaints recently received by his office alleging abuses of persons who had talked to investigators from the International Commission of Investigation in January.

Ndiaye used the International Commission's report as the point of departure for his April 8–17 mission. He focused his attention on what had happened between the January departure of the Commission's experts and his April visit. During his ten-day visit, he spoke with Rwandan authorities, including the president; met with human rights advocates and diplomats, including Ambassador Flaten and myself; visited displaced persons camps; and collected data from displaced persons in the DMZ.

The UN special rapporteur's findings were not released until August 11, 1993, a week after the Arusha Accords had been signed. Even then, it received scant distribution and little attention. Its findings, however, would echo those of the International Commission and come even closer to acknowledging the existence of genocide.

Coup Rumors

In the latter half of March 1993, rumors circulated in Kigali that a coup would likely take place at the beginning of April. We had often heard rumors of lists of journalists to be fired or persons to be killed, but rumors of a possible coup were new. I remember discussing this rumor over lunch with Maj. Augustin Cyiza, a respected local human rights activist as well as a member of the Rwandan military. I wanted to understand where such a coup might come from. The political opposition did not have the military backing or access to military hardware that would be needed to mount a coup. The RPF was not an internal player. So it did not seem reasonable that it could come from the left of the political spectrum.

My luncheon guest, who was also the chief judge of the military court, speculated that elements on the right might be moved to mount a coup. But why, I wondered aloud, would the right, which already held the presidency and controlled the military, want to oust the president and take over power? My companion suggested that perhaps the hard-liners did not believe the president was moving firmly enough against the RPF or taking a sufficiently tough stand against objectionable parts of the peace agreement. What would happen to the president in this scenario, I wondered? Who would take over? There didn't seem to be any likely candidates. I recalled that the far right, the extremist CDR party, had recently publicly rebuked the president over the new cease-fire agreement. Could the CDR muster the military might needed to wrest power from the president? It did not seem a likely scenario to me at the time. The embassy did not give the coup rumors much credence.[19]

In retrospect, my analysis was flawed and naive. I was not attributing enough importance to the rupture between the president's MRND party and the Hutu-supremacist CDR. I had thought the break between the two was mostly for show, to allow the president to distance himself from CDR rhetoric espousing firmly held Hutu-supremacist views. I considered the CDR's words and deeds a reflection of the president's views. Nor did I pay enough attention to the appearance within the military of the shadowy, hard-line Alliance of Soldiers Annoyed by the Underhanded Acts of the Unarists (Alliance des Militaires Agacés par les Séculaires Actes Sournois des Unaristes; AMASASU). AMASASU had announced its existence in a January 1993 letter to the president with copies to key diplomatic missions, including the U.S. Embassy. "Unarists" were members of the Rwanda National Union (Union Nationale Rwandaise), an independence-era political party composed of conservative Tutsi monarchists. The letter had been signed only by "Commandant Tango Mike," a pseudonym possibly for someone with the initials T. M.[20]

At a March 17 meeting with the president, some military officers—no doubt linked to AMASASU—criticized him for capitulating to the RPF following its February attack rather than continuing to fight on.[21] Periodically AMASASU released anonymous tracts that were strongly in favor of Hutu supremacy and against Tutsi. I did not know much about this group; neither did I understand the extent of its influence within the military. I had not considered how serious such a division within the military might be, nor did I recognize the significance of a military-civilian link between AMASASU with its Hutu-supremacist ideology and the CDR Hutu-supremacist party.

No coup took place in April 1993. However, this right-wing coup scenario was very close to what actually happened a year later, in April 1994. Hard-line Hutu supremacists took over the government after the president was killed when his plane was shot down. With active participation of right-wing militia and elements of the military— particularly the presidential guard—Hutu supremacists launched the genocide against Tutsi and killed moderate Hutu who had supported power sharing.

Comment

1. *Human rights policy*: The human rights situation in Rwanda clearly deteriorated at the end of 1992 and into early 1993. Local and international human rights organizations publicized carefully documented violations committed by both the government and the RPF. The United States generally responded to such reports with quiet diplomacy, public statements, or both to register concern, dismay, condemnation, horror, or other sentiments evoked by such violations of rights. Behind-the-scenes interventions with high-level Rwandan officials were made either separately or in conjunction with Western allies in Kigali or Washington or somewhere in Europe. Statements were usually released in Washington.

Our human rights policy usually went no further. Once, however, in early 1993, I tried unsuccessfully to persuade State Department colleagues working on human rights issues to have the United States sponsor a resolution condemning the human rights situation in Rwanda at the 1993 UN Commission on Human Rights session. I was told the U.S. priorities at the commission were Cuba, China, and Sudan; the U.S. delegation could not manage any other country cases that year. I should, perhaps, have taken the initiative to discuss this idea with my counterparts in Kigali. Perhaps one of the other concerned Western countries might have wanted to explore this possibility. But I did not pursue this.

Rwanda did come up at the 1993 rights commission under its confidential proceedings. However, not until after the genocide was well under way did the UN Commission on Human Rights debate Rwanda publicly. At a special session on Rwanda in May 1994, the head of the U.S. delegation, Geraldine Ferraro, became the first U.S. official to use the term "genocide" to describe what was happening in the country.

Human rights organizations, especially the U.S.-based Human Rights Watch, repeatedly recommended that Western nations tie aid levels to respect for human rights. In response to the findings of the group of international human rights experts, the United States did issue a statement indicating Rwanda would risk losing its special aid status unless it made serious changes in several domains, including human rights. The statement also said it would review the $19.6 million in aid for Rwanda and prioritize humanitarian over development assistance.[22] The latter was happening in any case as the numbers of displaced persons escalated to over one million following the RPF's February offensive. I am not aware, however, of any aid cuts that were linked explicitly to Rwanda's tragically deteriorating human rights situation.

The time may have been ripe, however, to look beyond quiet diplomacy and public pressure at policy options that might have had greater impact on changing the behavior of Rwandan human rights violators. We might have considered more seriously the option, urged by human rights groups, of applying sanctions or adopting aid conditionality pending an improvement in respect for human rights by the government and government-linked organizations or groups. We might have examined ways human rights

A Second Chance for Peace

advocates we supported might be protected from threats and physical harm. We might have thought more analytically about the root causes of the escalating abuse and violence. That may have turned our policy attention to strengthening the rule of law in the interest of changing the culture of impunity. We might have decided that a program to improve ethnic relations could have helped reduce animosities. It's not clear whether any such policies would actually have influenced the behavior of the abusers. However, doing nothing more than issuing verbal rebukes in the face of documented cases of human rights abuse was ineffective in halting the offenses. It may even have contributed to the cycle of violence by emboldening the abusers' sense of impunity.

Had the findings of the UN special rapporteur's March 1993 mission to Rwanda been released earlier than mid-August, it might have had an impact. Its conclusions, taken together with those of the independent group of international human rights organizations, would have created a powerful picture of Rwanda's deteriorating human rights situation. Both had raised the specter of genocide. Together they might have sounded the alarm and provided early warning signs of possible future genocide. They might have had a potent impact on the international community's policies in Rwanda. Instead, separately, neither had much effect.

2. *Rwanda's political landscape shifts to the right*: The RPF's audacious February offensive triggered a profound shift to the right in Rwanda's political landscape. Hutu across the political spectrum hardened their attitudes toward the RPF and the Tutsi. Power-sharing skeptics saw their interests more closely aligned with those of their Hutu brothers and sisters, regardless of political affiliation or whether they were northerners or southerners. Not only was the Hutu opposition fractured in the wake of the RPF offensive, with many moving toward the anti-RPF, anti–power-sharing views of the MRND and even the CDR. The RPF attack also exacerbated fault lines on the political right within the ranks of the former regime. AMASASU's emergence from within the military underscored this.

Initially I suspected that the CDR's declared split with the MRND was simply another ploy to distance itself further from the president and give the avowed Hutu supremacists more latitude to say publicly what the president politically could not. As a result I underestimated the significant gap that was growing between the president and the Hutu supremacists. Had we given this overt and visible split within the political right more credence, we might have marked this as the point at which the hard-line Hutu supremacists' tactics for holding onto power veered sharply away from those of the president.

Long after the events of 1994, I concluded that the president believed until his death that he could succeed in his quest to retain power by manipulating the political process. By March 1993 he had apparently already formulated—and was beginning to implement—a strategy for wooing support of opposition power-sharing skeptics to bolster his side in the post-Arusha transitional institutions prescribed in the protocols. The all-party meeting in Kigali in early March that revealed opposition party splits was a manifestation of this strategy.

What the CDR-led, hard-line Hutu supremacists viewed as the president's lackluster response to the RPF offensive may have convinced them that the path of violence—not the political process—was their only recourse for retaining power. This may have been the point at which the CDR and its like-minded allies within the MRND—the MRND party militia, the Interahamwe, as well as some elements of the military and the political opposition—lost patience with the president and turned their backs on his strategy for political survival through political manipulation and on what they viewed as the president's appeasement of the RPF and Tutsi.

I doubt that we at the embassy ever considered at the time that this CDR-MRND rift actually reflected a clean break between two right-wing strategies for retaining power, namely, the pursuit of a political solution on the one hand, and all-out violence on the other. We focused instead on the resumption of the peace talks. We continued to believe in the possibility of a negotiated peace and the political process of democratization and pushed ahead with our policies of support. We still had hopes that the peace process would bear fruit.

Meanwhile the Rwandan political and military elite were focused on these internal political realignments. The president's all-party meeting in Kigali in early March may have been his first step in efforts to co-opt opposition party members skeptical of a peace process that made power sharing the central tenant of Rwanda's future. He needed their support to make the proposed institutions that would set the course for Rwanda's political future work for him. Other Hutu skeptics went further, gravitating to the CDR and its rejection of the president's perceived softness on the RPF, power-sharing still advocated by many in the opposition, and indeed the entire Arusha peace process. These included not only some from within the president's party but also some from divided opposition parties and from the shadowy AMASASU, the group of disgruntled military officers.

Such ferment, however, was not evident at the time to this diplomatic observer. The shrill protestations of January against any peace agreement that would marginalize the former ruling party had disappeared from public dialogue, perhaps by design. This suggested to me that perhaps the most vociferous critics of power sharing were resigned to the Arusha peace process. It conveyed to me a false sense of restored unity within the president's camp. Not until June 1993 did the acrimony within the main opposition MDR party burst into public view, when an unruly, widely publicized party meeting ousted MDR president Faustin Twagiramungu, an action which he rejected as illegal.

Serious, enduring political realignment was, nevertheless, under way. Destructive political polarization followed and would eventually render implementation of the Arusha Peace Accord impossible. At the time, we diplomats just didn't see, or perhaps acknowledge, the significance of this shift to the right in the Rwandan political landscape. We failed to fully appreciate the significance of the rupture within the right-wing camp of the former regime. Nor did we grasp the implications of the momentum building within the political opposition, particularly the MDR, against power sharing with the Tutsi-led RPF.

3. *Context for peace talks changed*: The RPF's February offensive had dramatically changed the political and military contexts for the talks. On the one hand, the RPF had strengthened its negotiating position with its show of force. The ease with which its troops had almost reached the Rwandan capital had demonstrated considerable military prowess that government troops could not match. Thus emboldened, when the talks resumed, the RPF hardened its demands and showed little flexibility in its positions.

On the other hand, the offensive had prompted profound political rethinking among Rwandan Hutu. Key Hutu opposition leaders began to question RPF intentions. Many feared the RPF goal might be a complete takeover of Rwanda. Power sharing no longer seemed to these skeptics to be a viable basis upon which to build Rwanda's future. Hard-line Hutu supremacists in the CDR and among the military went even further, rejecting what they viewed as the president's strategy of appeasement of the RPF. Even those opposition Hutu still advocating power sharing were angry at the RPF for the attack that seemed to them a betrayal of their goodwill.

[13]

Arusha Observer

The Setting

Ambassador Flaten was the U.S. Embassy's key interlocutor with the government and political parties on the Arusha peace process. However, as a result of my work on refugee affairs during a previous assignment in Geneva, the Africa Bureau at the State Department asked him to send me to Arusha to serve as the U.S. observer when negotiators took up the issue of refugee repatriation. The Arusha agenda called for refugee issues to follow the military negotiations. U.S. Rwanda watchers in both Kigali and Washington anticipated that the military portion would conclude quickly. So, once the peace talks resumed in mid-March, I was standing by for the military talks to end.

My opportunity came sooner than expected. After spending about a month as the U.S. observer in Arusha, Lieutenant Colonel Marley had to return to Washington. No one from the Department of State was available to replace him. So, on the assumption that the military talks would surely draw to a close shortly, I was instructed to proceed immediately to Arusha. Even though I had no background in military issues, I could be the State Department's eyes and ears at the talks. My primary role would be to follow developments and report to Washington, Kigali, and other interested diplomatic posts on whatever agreements the two sides might reach. I would have the additional role of helping to keep the talks on track by encouraging civility and compromise on the part of the two delegations.

In mid-April I made the journey from Kigali to Arusha. If a direct flight had been available, it would have been a short hop. Instead I had to fly to Nairobi, Kenya, and then travel by a DHL mail bus to Tanzania. The four-hour bus trip across the African savannah was beautiful and largely uneventful, except at the Kenya-Tanzania border crossing. There, despite being a seasoned traveler, I was fleeced by some illegal moneychangers. Fortunately, the only repercussion was that I paid a bit more than I should have for some Tanzanian shillings. I continued my journey with a red face and wounded ego. Once in Arusha, the bus dropped me at the Mount Meru Hotel on the edge of town. It was a large, prominent hotel that would become my home for the next seventy days. The military talks went on much longer than anyone had anticipated.

Background to the Talks

The international community had been urging the Rwandan government and the Tutsi-led RPF to negotiate an end to their conflict ever since the RPF invasion from Uganda in October 1990. Initially the countries within the region were the primary promoters of a peace process. Later, after the coalition government was established in Kigali in April 1992 with a mandate to end the war, the Western countries took a more prominent role in pushing for a negotiated settlement. The Africa-wide Organization of African Unity and its successor group the African Union were involved from the beginning. The United Nations became more engaged after the cease-fire rupture and reestablishment in early 1993.

The peace talks that began in Arusha in July 1992 were, in part, a response to pressure from neighboring and Western donor countries. More important, though, after eighteen months of armed conflict, the two sides concluded that their interests would be better served by moving from the battlefield to the negotiating table. Neither side had been able to win the military conflict outright, and both saw opportunities to win at the negotiating table. Together the two parties determined the structure, content, and pace of the talks. They asked the Tanzanian president Ali Hassan Mwinyi to be facilitator of the talks and invited the OAU to cosponsor them, chose Arusha as the location, invited Western and neighboring countries to send observers, and asked the OAU and the UN to send political and military observers.

The two sides owned the talks and seemed keen to reach accommodation and find a way forward for Rwanda and all Rwandans. The foundation of the talks appeared solid. They aimed to end the fighting and chart a course toward multiparty elections for a new government based on the principle of power sharing. A democratically governed Rwanda with the majority Hutu and the minority Tutsi both participating in the political process was the apparent goal.

The Location for the Talks

Arusha in 1993 was a town with a population of just over 100,000. It was, and still is, known for two basic things. First, it is a center for Tanzania's tourist industry and the starting point for visits to nearby Ngorongoro Crater and Serengeti National Park, with its magnificent animal migrations to Masai Mara, a game reserve just across the border in Kenya. Hikers and mountaineers who come to Tanzania to climb Africa's highest peak, Mount Kilimanjaro, often buy supplies in Arusha, the nearest town to the base of the mountain. Abercrombie and Kent, a prestigious British travel agency, had a prominent presence on Arusha's main street.

Second, Arusha boasts the Arusha International Conference Center, where the Rwandan peace talks took place. Large rooms equipped with simultaneous translation facilities met the needs of the Rwandan belligerents, and lodging was readily available for delegates in the various hotels around town. The Conference Center was built in 1969 to serve as the headquarters for the East African Community, founded in 1967 to facilitate commercial exchanges among the three English-speaking East African nations of Kenya, Tanzania, and Uganda. When the East African Community collapsed over internal differences in 1977, the multistory Conference Center fell into disuse; by 1993 it was rarely used and suffered from a lack of maintenance.

The building's deterioration became abundantly clear one Sunday, when a group of government and RPF delegates were stranded in an elevator on their way to the third-floor conference room where we were to meet. It took about an hour for the Tanzanian facilitator to rouse a caretaker on his day off to come and free the trapped

Rwandans. Today the East African Community has been revived, and its headquarters are again in Arusha. This organization, which now includes both Rwanda and Burundi, hosts about one hundred conferences a year at the refurbished Center.

I was eager to explore my new environment and to figure out ways to get some exercise. Walking into town, swimming in the hotel's outdoor pool, and possibly playing tennis would meet these needs, time permitting. Early on during my stay, I enjoyed walking into town along a dirt path beside a creek edged with tall shade trees. Arusha's paved streets boasted a multitude of cars and trucks, though I doubt rush-hour gridlock had ever brought the place to a standstill. One-story curio shops, boutiques, restaurants, and offices lined the downtown streets, where I purchased several mementos of my first visit to Tanzania.

One colorful batik of tie-dye art caught my eye and made me smile. In it I saw the perfect metaphor for the Arusha peace negotiations. Front and center are two Tanzanian women dressed in long skirts and flowing headscarves sitting on a sandy patch of ground under some coconut palm trees. Judging by the two pots beside them, they are taking time out from fetching water to play an ancient Tanzanian board game called Bao in Swahili. Similar to the game of Warri I knew from West Africa, Bao players rapidly move pebbles from one hole or "pit" to another, until one player has amassed them all or the other cannot play. Each woman depicted in the batik is carefully watching both the board and her opponent (the two sides in the Rwandan negotiations?). In the background are several anthropomorphic thatched-roofed huts that appear to watch the two women intently through round window eyes (the observers?). A late afternoon sun shines down on the scene, appearing to survey both the players and the onlookers (the facilitator?). I snapped up this delightful piece of Tanzanian folk art that still reminds me of my time at the Arusha peace talks.

My tennis adventure was short-lived. In my very first game at a nearby tennis club that welcomed guests, I slipped on some loose gravel on the court's uneven macadam surface. One leg buckled under me and I toppled ungracefully to the ground. Stunned, shaken, and embarrassed, I was helped to my feet. I had scraped my leg from ankle to knee and twisted my foot. I thanked my newfound friends, hobbled off the court, and never saw them again. A kind club member drove me around the block to the Mount Meru Hotel.

Tennis and long walks were over. For about a month I saw little more than the inside of the hotel, where crossing the lobby—which seemed as big as a football field—to purchase bottled water from the bar on the other side was exhausting. After a few weeks, though, my injury—diagnosed by a local Pakistani doctor as torn ligaments—improved enough for me to resume almost daily swims in the hotel pool. A little exercise was better than none!

Mount Meru Hotel: The Hub for Peace Talks

The Mount Meru Hotel was the center of activities relating to the Rwandan peace talks. In 1993 it was not the luxury hotel it now is, with its 178 nicely appointed rooms and four restaurants. Back then this establishment, at the foot of Mount Kilimanjaro's sister peak, Mount Meru, was quite adequate but basic. Throughout the peace talks, from July 1992 through June 1993, people connected with them occupied a majority of the hotel's rooms. Core members of the Rwandan government delegation all stayed there, as did all the RPF delegates. The Tanzanian facilitator and his delegation, OAU and UN representatives, as well as most of the international observers all had rooms there. Only the government delegates, who changed from session to session depending on the issues, were housed in several smaller hotels closer to the center of town and to the Conference Center.

This proximity day in and day out offered us informal opportunities to get acquainted with our observer counterparts, the facilitator and his team of Tanzanian diplomats, and members of the two delegations. All of us staying at the Mount Meru ate most of our meals there, served buffet-style to allow for flexibility in the negotiators' work schedule. Standing in the buffet lines gave us time to chat. I often scheduled working lunches with members of one delegation or the other or with my international counterparts. Our mealtime companions, however, were generally defined by our group. The RPF was typically quite exclusive, taking all its meals together, often seated at a long table set apart from the main dining room. Government delegates generally ate with their colleagues. We diplomatic observers and other international representatives tended to do the same.

After dinner, when the delegates returned to their work, several international observers were likely to congregate in the hotel lobby, where a band played and a female singer crooned the latest pop songs. Each night I was present we heard the singer's rendition of Whitney Houston's 1992 hit song, "I Will Always Love You." This tune is fixed in my head forever! Frequently one of the international observers, Col. Isoa Delamisi Tikoca, a Fijian who was the United Nations military advisor, added his deep, velvety voice to the evening. He usually performed "Green, Green Grass of Home," a rather melancholy ballad that was popular in the 1960s.

With the Mount Meru Hotel effectively "Peace Talks Central," informal encounters with delegates were often possible and could result in insightful discussions. One casual conversation in the hotel garden with an RPF public relations officer underscored to me a fundamental difference in the way the RPF and everyone else was looking at the process of Rwanda's transformation from a single-party dictatorship to a more inclusive, participatory, democratic system. All along it had seemed to me that the Hutu political elite in Kigali, whether from the ruling party or the opposition, envisioned the mostly Tutsi RPF entering the Rwandan political process as another political party, competing for votes like any other. According to this vision, the RPF would integrate gradually into the existing political system, but it would probably remain a permanent underdog unless allied with like-minded Hutu parties. President Habyarimana had projected this mind-set when he announced the legalization of multiple political parties in July 1991 and invited the RPF to become a political party and join the political process. The diplomatic community in Kigali seemed comfortable with this vision.

This RPF public relations officer, however, described a different vision. The RPF's intention, he explained, was to use the Arusha negotiations to effect fundamental change in the organization and operation of Rwanda's political, military, and security systems. Its goal was to break the monopolistic grip the former single party, the MRND, had on the central bureaucracy, the rural administration, and the security services in order to level the playing field. Only then would the Tutsi-led RPF be able to compete in elections on an equal footing with the mainly Hutu parties. Only in a radically different Rwanda could the RPF expect to garner support from throughout Rwandan society, from Hutu and Tutsi alike, and take what it considered its rightful place in governing the country. "So," I reflected to the RPF representative, "the RPF is seeking revolution, not evolution, in the peace process." He agreed with this characterization, and would not accept my arguments for evolution and slower-paced change. I shuddered to think how much more difficult this revolutionary approach would make the RPF's integration into Rwanda.

This wish for revolution by negotiation did not surprise me. I had suspected from the outline for the peace talks agreed by the two sides in August 1992 at Arusha II that the RPF was aiming to win through negotiation what neither side had won on the battlefield. But this reminder of their goal by a member of their delegation was timely; it helped me understand more clearly why the RPF took many of the positions it did at Arusha and why it held so firmly to some of them.

The U.S. Embassy had arranged for several Kigali journalists to visit Arusha to report on the peace talks. We had drawn on the resources of our Democracy and Human Rights Fund with the aim of encouraging broad coverage of the negotiations in the Rwandan press. The RPF too had journalists present. No doubt key newspapers from neighboring Uganda, Burundi, and Tanzania did as well. One day I joined some U.S.-sponsored visiting journalists for lunch at an outdoor restaurant after formal talks at the Conference Center. What stood out for me in our conversation were the concerns over how one-sided Rwanda's official history was. The story, these RPF sympathizers contended, had been told only from the Hutu perspective. That, they declared, would change once the RPF joined the government and could influence the educational curriculum; then the official recounting of key events in Rwanda's history would reflect Tutsi views as well. The determination I heard in their voices suggested that this issue would be contentious long after the peace talks were over.

The Work Environment and the Participants

The Mount Meru Hotel was the site of preparations for the negotiations. Negotiations did not take place at any fixed time or on any fixed schedule, I quickly learned. Each delegation spent most of its time working on its own, preparing for formal discussions with its adversary, consulting with the facilitator, or holding informal direct talks with delegates from the other side. Only when the two sides had reached agreement on a specific issue or had something to announce did the facilitator convene a formal plenary session. Such formal sessions would involve not only the two delegations but also the international observers. These formal sessions were held at the Arusha International Conference Center, where simultaneous translators could keep the English speakers and French speakers on the same page. Kinyarwanda, their common language, was not an option at official sessions.

In addition to our obligatory presence at these formal plenary sessions, observers could be convoked by the Tanzanian facilitator when he wanted to update us on the state of play or seek our advice and counsel on some issue that was blocking progress. At any time, night or day, weekends, meal times, or evenings running late into the night, we observers could be called to a meeting. On occasion the facilitator would invite the observers to meet informally with one or both sides to hear their positions and arguments on a particular issue. These meetings, outside the plenary sessions, were generally held somewhere in the Mount Meru Hotel.

The International Observers

Such an irregular meeting schedule meant that observers had to be standing by most of the time. As a result, my job involved a lot of waiting. Much of the time I spent discussing issues with other observers or the facilitator, talking with members of the two delegations when they were available to better understand their views, or sharing U.S. views or those of the international community generally with delegates. Preparing reports for Washington and Kigali, communicating by phone with Ambassador Flaten in Kigali or with the Rwanda desk officer at the State Department consumed a major part of most of my days in Arusha.

Unlike the government and RPF delegates who had computers at their disposal, we observers had none. Business centers were not yet standard conveniences for hotel visitors in 1993. At the time, I didn't even own a personal computer. Desktop computers had only recently become common equipment at U.S. embassies; laptops were not yet common. The Kigali embassy certainly didn't have one to loan me for my trip. And I hadn't lugged a typewriter with me, so I wrote all my reports by hand and faxed them to the U.S. Embassy in Dar es Salaam. There they were typed and sent through the State Department's communication system to Washington, Kigali, and elsewhere. To ensure legibility on the receiving end, I learned that I needed to print with a felt-tipped pen.

The hotel did have a fax machine in one of its administrative offices that I was permitted to use. It was certainly not state of the art, even for that time, and the first and only time I used it, it took seven minutes to fax two pages to the Rwanda desk officer in Washington. The cost was exorbitant! I wondered how it would look on my travel voucher if I regularly claimed such sums: I would have been investigated for waste, fraud, and mismanagement! So, with a bit of research, I found a nearby hotel with a commercial fax facility and a much more modern fax machine. I became a regular customer there. The total cost, including taxi fare to and from the location, was only a fraction of the cost of sending a fax from the Mount Meru Hotel.

Getting to know the international representatives at the talks and members of the two delegations was one of the best parts of my job in Arusha. Observers came from both Western donor countries and neighboring African countries. Regularly represented while I was at Arusha were Belgium, Burundi, France, Germany, Tanzania, Uganda, the United States, and sometimes Zaire. Among the international observers were representatives of the OAU presidency, the OAU secretariat, the UN political and UN military affairs, and the UN Development Program.

Some of the international observers were especially memorable. Uganda's observer, its high commissioner to Tanzania, Benjamin William Kanyonyozi Matogo, had long-standing, close ties to Ugandan president Yoweri Museveni, dating to the days of Museveni's armed rebellion in the 1980s against President Milton Obote. Instead of following Museveni into the bush as a fighter, Matogo had remained inside Uganda as an underground operative. At one point, Matogo said, he taught at Uganda's Makerere University under a pseudonym while distributing to the students underground propaganda favoring Museveni's rebellion. Following Museveni's takeover and installation as president, Matogo represented Uganda in prestigious positions abroad. He had been his country's high commissioner in London and ambassador to the OAU in Addis Ababa before being assigned to Dar es Salaam.

The United Nations military representative, Colonel Tikoca, was another intriguing observer. He brought twenty years of experience in UN peacekeeping operations to the Arusha peace talks. Tiko, as he was known, had come to Arusha from an ongoing UN peacekeeping mission in Somalia, where he served as deputy commander. His stories of trying to navigate among the various Somali factions were harrowing and humorous. In one example, while briefly jailed by a local warlord, he kept his spirits up by continuously singing, much to the dismay of his jailers.

Before getting into peacekeeping, Tiko had aided an aspiring politician in his island homeland of Fiji to mount a coup. With a chuckle and a twinkle in his eyes, Tiko claimed that the coup leader, still president, preferred having him overseas doing peacekeeping work than at home in Fiji, where he might pose a risk to national stability. A gregarious person with a big presence, Tiko organized opportunities for us observers to connect with local Tanzanians. Once, for example, when a relative of one of the Tanzanian delegates died in a nearby town, Tiko organized a way for us to go there to pay our respects to the family.

The Government Delegation

The Rwandan government delegation was diverse and divided in its approach to the talks. Some who represented the president's MRND party and its more hard-line CDR allies brought their Hutu-supremacist attitudes to bear on the issues under discussion. Others, from the political opposition, wanted to reach an accord based on power sharing, even though they remained skeptical of RPF intentions.

Foreign Minister Ngulinzira led the government delegation by virtue of his position. As a member of the main opposition MDR, he was close to Prime Minister Nsengiyaremye, also from the MDR. The prime minister was his principal interlocutor in Kigali and the person who provided him guidance on government positions on the issues before the negotiators. Ngulinzira had a staff of civil servants from the Ministry of Foreign Affairs to help him manage the substantive and administrative aspects of the talks. Thomas Muliza, head of the office responsible for African affairs at the ministry, was key among the staffers.

Some delegates on the opposite end of the political spectrum from Ngulinzira probably had direct access to President Habyarimana or his close aides. Representing the president's side was Pierre-Claver Kanyarushoki, Rwanda's ambassador to Uganda. He was a mild-mannered diplomat who told me that he did not belong to the MRND. Nevertheless, he said, he had always had the president's confidence. He was known to counsel the president and his aides to be more flexible and more willing to meet the RPF halfway on difficult political and military power-sharing issues.

Kanyarushoki's advice, however, was no doubt overshadowed by that coming from other delegates more committed to Hutu supremacy and opposed to power sharing. Key among those was Col. Théoneste Bagosora, then chief of staff at the Ministry of Defense. He kept largely to himself and appeared to have little interaction with the observers or even other delegates. He never supported the peace talks and later was instrumental in carrying out the genocide.

There was also an array of Rwandan issue experts who filtered in and out of Arusha depending on the agenda items under discussion. While I was there, many were military personnel from the Ministry of Defense who represented the army, gendarmerie, and intelligence services. Several with whom I discussed the issues seemed to approach their work more as civil servants than as political operatives.

The government delegation had no space set aside at the Mount Meru Hotel for either meetings or work, but it still served as a meeting place for the Rwandan delegates who were lodged in a number of smaller hotels around Arusha. Before plenary sessions, government delegates would gather, usually in the hotel garden, to go over the agenda and their plans for that day. Otherwise they worked individually or in groups at their respective hotels.

For access to computers, government delegates had to go to the Conference Center downtown. Muliza told me that he and his colleagues frequently worked late into the night at the Center preparing summaries of the day's work and translating documents adopted by the two sides.

The RPF Delegation

RPF delegates had appropriated one wing of the top floor of the Mount Meru Hotel for both their lodging and their work space. In contrast to the government delegates and the observers, the RPF equipped its office space with several desktop computers, a rather new phenomenon in 1993, to aid in preparation for the negotiations. RPF delegates were extremely disciplined in their approach to the negotiations; they seldom relaxed in the hotel lobby or garden.

Heading the RPF delegation was Pasteur Bizimungu, a Hutu who had joined the RPF in 1990 after quitting the top job at Rwanda's state-owned electric company over a disagreement with President Habyarimana. He had subsequently accused the president of nepotism and corruption. Bizimungu kept to himself during the Arusha talks, seldom accessible for casual encounters or substantive discussion.

In contrast, the RPF deputy delegation leader, Patrick Kayumba Mazimhaka, was outgoing and affable. A Tutsi who had grown up as a refugee and received his education in Uganda and Canada, Mazimhaka had the confidence of the RPF's military head, Paul Kagame. In meetings he always sat beside Bizimungu. Other RPF delegates came either from the group's political or military wings. One or two delegates focused solely on public relations.[1]

The Language of Diplomacy

Language was a critical component of the talks. The Rwandan government delegation made all of its formal presentations in French. The RPF delegates, on the other hand, used English as their official language, a reflection of the English-speaking, Ugandan upbringing of most delegates. Although the two sides could have spoken to each other in their common national language, Kinyarwanda, and did so among themselves, delegates spoke in either French or English in the formal sessions, with simultaneous translation available. All conference documentation was prepared first in French and then translated into English.

Using French and English as the official languages of the peace talks accommodated members of the international community. The Tanzanian facilitator's representative, either a minister of the Tanzanian government or a member of the English-speaking country's diplomatic service, spoke only English. While I was in Arusha, Ami Ramadhan Mpungwe, director for Africa and the Middle East from Tanzania's Ministry of Foreign Affairs, served as the facilitator's representative. Representing the OAU chairman Abdou Diouf was Ambassador Papa Louis Fall, Senegal's permanent representative to the organization.

Comments

Arusha seemed like a good place to be holding these talks: a small town with few distractions or disturbances, where delegates and observers alike could concentrate on the important task at hand, namely, making peace among Rwandans. Only later would some of the challenges and constraints of being rather isolated and distant from Kigali become apparent. At some point in Arusha, I made an astonishing observation: I was relaxed! The omnipresent stress and latent tensions of the Kigali pressure cooker had drained from my body and my mind. I was not worrying continuously about my safety or the security of the American community. No daily news accounts of security breaches heightened my anxiety. No reports of bombs detonating under restaurant tables. No land mines exploding unexpectedly under vehicles on the roads. I had had no idea how much stress I was carrying around in Rwanda. My colleagues, who, like me, had adapted to the situation in which we found ourselves, probably had no idea how much anxiety we had internalized. I wondered whether my Rwandan friends realized the toll these recent years of war, uncertainty, and insecurity had taken on their psyche and physical well-being.

Upon my return to Kigali I shared this realization with a Rwandan Hutu friend. He had been living with recurrent death threats, but he had also had opportunities to travel to Europe from time to time. He said that he had noticed the same feeling of relief each time he had been outside Rwanda. Most Rwandans, though, had no escape from the pressure and stress inherent in their daily lives.

[14]

Arusha Observer

The Negotiations

I had a few days of overlap in Arusha with Lt. Col. Tony Marley, the U.S. observer I was replacing. In that time Marley and I met with all the key players. First, we focused on the observers and other international representatives. Ami Mpungwe, the director for Africa in Tanzania's foreign ministry who was the facilitator's representative at the talks, joined us for lunch upon my arrival and for dinner before Marley departed. Marley and I joined the OAU's political representative, Joe Felli, a Ghanaian, for a breakfast meeting the next day. Over lunch Marley and I discussed the state of play with the UN's two representatives, one on the political front and one on the military side. At dinner we caught up with the leaders of the Rwanda delegation, Foreign Minister Ngulinzira and Labor and Social Affairs Minister Ndasingwa, both of whom I knew from Kigali. The next day we met for three hours with the RPF delegation deputy Patrick Mazimhaka and an RPF military representative to get their assessment of the status of the talks. When Marley left Arusha on my third day there, I was well briefed on issues and had some insight into the perspectives of the various players. Still, I regretted seeing him, and his military expertise, depart.

Contentious Issues

Integration of Government and RPF Forces

Negotiations about force integration had dragged on without resolution during Marley's month-long stay in Arusha. Discussions seemed to turn in circles, becoming more complex with each turning and no closer to agreement. The RPF had scoffed at the government's initial offer of 20 percent. Despite Rwanda's bargaining position having been weakened by the RPF February offensive, the Council of Ministers sent its delegation back to Arusha with instructions to accept no more than 33 percent for the RPF share. The RPF, while dropping its initial 80 percent demand, was unwilling to consider anything less than 75 percent for itself. Both sides stood firm.

In an effort to try to break the stalemate, Mpungwe suggested the two sides try to agree on a figure between 35 and 45 percent for the RPF troop contribution to the integrated army. Foreign Minister Ngulinzira, head of the government delegation, accepted this suggestion even though it was higher than he had been authorized to accept. But the RPF rejected Mpungwe's proposal and held out for more.

With force integration talks at a standstill, Mpungwe decided the two delegations should turn their attention to other outstanding military and security issues. His hope was that progress on peripheral issues would build confidence between the two sides, making the force integration issue easier to resolve. Unfortunately these issues too eluded easy solutions.[1]

Gendarmerie versus National Police Force

When Marley left the talks, the two delegations were still at loggerheads over the type of police force Rwanda should have and which ministry should have jurisdiction over it. Each side had laid its cards on the table.[2] The government delegation wanted the gendarmerie (territorial police) to remain as it was, a paramilitary force attached to the Ministry of Defense, as in the French and Belgian systems. The RPF, accustomed to the Ugandan system based on the English model, wanted to abolish the gendarmerie in favor of a national police force attached to the Ministry of the Interior. These preferences were not surprising. The Arusha protocol on power sharing had assigned the president's MRND party responsibility for the defense ministry and had named the RPF to head the interior ministry.

The very evening of Marley's departure, Mpungwe, the facilitator's representative, called the observers together. From 10:00 to 11:30, in the first of several meetings on this contentious issue, we discussed how to overcome the impasse. In separate, informal sessions on April 23, about a week after I arrived in Arusha, each delegation, separately, presented the rationale for its position to Mpungwe, the observers, and other international representatives. This followed days of Tanzanian shuttle diplomacy, facilitator briefings for observers, and observer discussions with various members of each delegation. I spoke extensively with leaders of each delegation and with various observers.

In its briefing of the facilitator and observers, the RPF argued that a police force would better serve the daily security needs of the population. The RPF denied being motivated by the issue of control, insisting its concern was to have a more effective security force. The government delegation cited Article 13 of the already agreed power-sharing protocol to support its "no change" position. This provision, it argued, precluded any changes in the structure of the government before installation of the Broad-Based Transitional Government. The RPF proposal for change seemed to me a recipe for disaster. It raised the specter of two armed forces in the country: one, the army, controlled by the president's party and the other, a national police force, under the jurisdiction of the RPF.

After listening to the arguments of both sides and discussing the issues again with the observers, Mpungwe proposed a compromise based on the "no change" provision of the power-sharing protocol. This called for the gendarmerie to remain attached to the Ministry of Defense and to continue to exercise the police function; further changes in the function or structure of the gendarmerie would be deferred until the BBTG had been installed following signing of the peace agreement; once revamped, the post-Arusha integrated gendarmerie—composed of both government and RPF forces— would be structured to enhance its civilian protection function. Both sides accepted the compromise at a formal plenary session on April 26. The RPF, however, immediately put forward a new and controversial proposal: whatever disarmament, force integration, or demobilization decisions were agreed for the army would also apply to the restructured gendarmerie.[3]

The government and the RPF delegations agreed that a Neutral International Force (NIF) should be asked to provide the security needed to help Rwandans implement the anticipated peace accord. There agreement ended. The delegations were starting from strongly held but contradictory positions: the government argued forcefully for a United Nations force, while the RPF adamantly supported an operation run by the Organization of African Unity.

The government delegation's insistence on a UN force reflected President Habyarimana's doubts about OAU neutrality in the Rwanda conflict. The president suspected the OAU of tilting toward the largely Anglophone RPF, with its links to English-speaking Uganda. Having the English-speaking Tanzanian diplomat Salim Ahmed Salim as OAU secretary general at that time did not help. Successive deployments to Rwanda of unarmed OAU cease-fire monitors had not assuaged his concerns.

Taking exactly the opposite stance, the RPF pointed out that the OAU was cosponsoring the Arusha peace talks and argued that the organization had been deeply involved in brokering an end to the Rwandan conflict ever since fighting erupted in October 1990. Among its many contributions, within six months of the conflict's beginning, the OAU had deployed an all-African Military Observer Group to monitor the fragile situation in Rwanda. It had reconfigured this group into a fifty-member Neutral Military Observer Group to monitor the July 1992 cease-fire. At the request of both the government and the RPF, the OAU was in the process of expanding the NMOG to 240 soldiers in order to monitor compliance with the March 1993 cease-fire. Therefore, the RPF contended, the OAU—not the UN— should provide the security needed to implement the anticipated peace agreement.

This debate over whether the OAU or the UN should field such a force encumbered the Arusha peace talks for weeks. Complicating the discussions was the need for delegates to take into consideration references to an international force in two previously agreed documents. The first was the March 8 communiqué reestablishing a cease-fire between the government and the RPF.[4] In addition to calling for the OAU to expand NMOG, that bilateral agreement requested that an international force mandated to protect the civilian population in Rwanda, including expatriates, replace the recently arrived three hundred or so French troops in Kigali who claimed civilian protection as their function.

A second document complicating these Arusha discussions was the UN Security Council's Resolution 812 (1993) that first involved the UN in the Rwandan peace process. Not only did it ask the UN secretary general to examine separate requests for a UN border-monitoring force from the presidents of Rwanda and Uganda; it also mentioned the possibility of introducing a UN peacekeeping force into Rwanda. Further, the resolution called on the secretary-general to look into how the UN could work with the OAU to facilitate and support peace in Rwanda.[5]

Sorting out the overlapping and sometimes contradictory imperatives of these different initiatives was akin to juggling apples and oranges. Delegates' discussions kept going around in circles without any agreement.

This persistent controversy had practical ramifications in Rwanda. The OAU slowed down recruitment of forces to expand NMOG, interpreting the government's strong opposition to an OAU-provided international force as a lack of confidence in the organization. The RPF declared it would never sign a peace accord as long as French troops over and above the two companies allowed by the March 8 communiqué remained in Kigali. Furthermore the RPF accused the Rwandan government of foot-dragging in seeking international troops to replace the recently arrived French forces.

In May, with this discussion going nowhere, OAU observer Joe Felli traveled to the OAU headquarters in Addis Ababa, Ethiopia, for consultations. He wanted a definitive OAU position on provision of a NIF for Rwanda. Upon his return to Arusha, Felli produced an unequivocal letter from the OAU assistant secretary general, Ambassador Machivenyika Tobias Mapuranga. The OAU had neither the manpower nor the funds to mount an international peacekeeping force in Rwanda, Mapuranga wrote. It would therefore cede to the United Nations responsibility for monitoring implementation of the expected peace agreement. The OAU would concentrate on expanding its observer group, NMOG, for the large job of monitoring withdrawal of government and RPF troops to their prescribed positions and ensuring the new demilitarized buffer zone remained free of troops from either army. In addition, Mapuranga pledged, the OAU would continue to seek ways to collaborate with the United Nations on assisting Rwanda's peace process.

With such a categorical letter before the Arusha negotiators, the RPF finally, but reluctantly, conceded that the UN should organize and deploy the NIF to help Rwanda implement the peace accord once it was signed. However, the RPF stressed the importance it attached to cooperation between the UN and the OAU in this effort. In the end, the Arusha Peace Accord called for rapid deployment of a much more robust international force with a vastly larger mandate than the UN Security Council ever approved.

U.S. policy in the 1990s was to promote and support regional African organizations so they could address African problems. Thus the United States supported an OAU force to help implement any eventual Rwandan peace accord. Although I was unaware of it at the time, the United States had already contributed $1 million in FY 93 from Department of Defense funds to support the OAU's expansion of NMOG's monitoring operations in Rwanda. An additional $3.1 million had been reserved from FY 94 funds.[6]

I was relieved with the OAU's deference to the UN on the peacekeeping issue. The OAU, though a regional African organization with conflict-resolution potential, lacked experience in managing the challenges of fielding and equipping a full-fledged, postconflict peacekeeping force. Before sending military monitors into Rwanda, the OAU had shied away from conflict resolution or involvement in member states' internal hostilities. Each of its three successive operations in Rwanda had involved a total of between 50 and 130 troops from four or fewer different African states. Any postconflict peacekeeping force for Rwanda, however, would inevitably have to be much larger and more complex than what the OAU had managed to date.

Implementation Start-Up

Both the government delegation and the RPF said they wanted the peace accord implemented as quickly as possible following its signing. However, complex and controversial differences over timing and sequencing prevented easy agreement. Security for RPF participants in the transitional institutions—the government, the legislature, and the security forces—became the pivotal issue. The obvious first step would have been to swear in the Broad-Based Transitional Government. However, there was the question of what protection would be available for the RPF participants. The RPF categorically refused the government's offer to provide security for its representatives.

To circumvent the security issue, the RPF proposed having the government cabinet meetings held outside Kigali, in the DMZ, for example, where neither government nor RPF troops were allowed. The government totally rejected this idea. Finally, both sides agreed that the arrival in Rwanda of the proposed NIF, mandated to provide security in Kigali, should be the precondition for implementation of the peace accord. All steps taken to effect implementation would flow from the date of the UN deployment.

This agreement resulted in two contradictory decisions being written into the peace accord: speedy implementation of the peace agreement and implementation that would begin only after the requested UN peacekeeping force had been deployed. The UN military observer Tikoca had already advised the two sides that the UN would require a minimum of at least three months after the Arusha Accords were signed to field a force to Rwanda. The key word here was "minimum." First, the UN would send a reconnaissance mission to Rwanda to determine the needs of a peacekeeping force. Then the reconnaissance team would compile a report to the UN secretary general laying out its findings and recommending levels of personnel and matériel required to implement a proposed mandate. After that, the secretary general would have to present the report to the Security Council for its consideration. If approved, the next step would be a Security Council resolution setting out the mandate and parameters of a peacekeeping mission for Rwanda. Once this was completed, the secretary general would still have to solicit troops from potential contributing nations. All of this would take time, even if there were no delays, political or otherwise, along the way. Deployment would clearly be a long way off from the actual signing of the peace accord.

Fully aware of an inevitable delay of several months before a UN force could arrive in Rwanda, the two sides nevertheless wrote into the agreement that the Broad-Based Transitional Government should be sworn in within thirty-seven days after the signing of the peace accord. For that to happen, the RPF participants in the BBTG would first have to arrive in Kigali. But this would not happen, the RPF had vowed, until the NIF was in place to provide security for its leaders.

This post-Arusha timetable seemed to me to be a pipe dream. The thirty-seven-day target for installing the BBTG was totally unrealistic. I had never heard of a peacekeeping force being deployed in less than three or four months. Could the fragile situation in Rwanda withstand a four- or even three-month gap between a signed peace agreement and the arrival of a peacekeeping force? I was skeptical.

Therefore I began in early May 1993 to urge Ambassador Flaten in Kigali and the Rwanda Desk officer in Washington to press for the UN to take immediate steps to reduce the time gap between a signed agreement and deployment of a UN force. I suggested that the UN might send a reconnaissance mission to Rwanda before a final peace agreement was signed or that the secretary general might begin to look for potential troop contributors. Either or both of these moves, I argued, could radically reduce the time required to deploy a peacekeeping force in Rwanda once the agreement was signed.

The Africa Bureau at the State Department picked up on this time concern and in late May instructed the U.S. Mission to the UN (USUN) in New York to urge UN Secretary General Boutros Boutros-Ghali to take a step that was not usual UN protocol. USUN was to ask the secretary general to begin contingency planning for an eventual UN force for Rwanda before the peace accord was even signed. The Africa Bureau stressed the urgency of reducing the gap between a signed peace agreement and UN deployment.

The UN secretary general, however, told USUN officers that he wanted to avoid UN interference in the Arusha peace process.[7] He was reluctant to take any concrete steps toward UN involvement in the Rwanda situation despite the UNSC Resolution 812 (1993) calling for him to explore options and possibilities of UN involvement in an international force in Rwanda.[8]

While in Washington on home leave in July 1993, I lobbied the

Africa Bureau's front office on the urgency of rapidly deploying a UN peacekeeping force after the anticipated signing of a peace agreement. A final agreement was expected at any time. It was then, however, that I learned how reticent the White House was to go to bat for new peacekeeping operations. Interagency consultations were already under way in Washington on strategies to limit U.S. participation in UN peacekeeping operations, mainly for financial reasons. In May 1994, when the genocide was already under way in Rwanda, these discussions resulted in Presidential Decision Directive 25, which set out strict guidelines for U.S. involvement in UN peacekeeping operations. It also proposed gradually reducing U.S. funding responsibilities for UN peacekeeping operations to 25 percent of the total cost, down from the 32 percent previously agreed with the UN and its member states.[9]

Disengagement, Disarmament, and Demobilization

Another critical piece of the post-Arusha implementation process that remained unresolved was how to manage the disengagement, disarmament, and demobilization of the two belligerent forces. This process would involve having soldiers on both sides move back from their forward battle positions, lay down their arms, and assemble in holding zones pending integration into the new army or demobilization and reintegration into Rwandan society. Questions abounded: Who would demarcate assembly points for the two forces? How close would they be to cantonment points for heavy weapons? What would be the procedures for protection and security of cantonment points? What was the definition of "heavy weapons" that should go into the cantonment points and "light weapons" that could be kept in magazines at the assembly points? Suspicions on both sides of the other's intentions made finding agreement and compromise on these delicate questions a laborious process. The two sides made little headway.

The Force Integration Issue Comes to the Fore

The key political decision on force proportions for an integrated army and gendarmerie loomed unsettled in the background while these various other issues took center stage. Near the end of May, the

Tanzanians decided to make another attempt at resolving the force proportion issue head-on. Tanzania's minister of defense, Abdulrahman Kinana, returned to Arusha to press the two sides to conclude this seemingly endless debate. He met with each delegation separately to identify common ground on which the Tanzanians might build a proposal that would enable the government and the RPF to reach agreement and move forward. In a plenary session, Minister Kinana urged the two sides not to get bogged down in the details. Their commitment to peace, he said, was more important than the specifics, which could be worked out as long as there was agreement on principles.

One afternoon, while I was swimming my almost daily laps in the hotel's outdoor swimming pool, I experienced an extremely embarrassing few minutes. Without warning, Minister Kinana came out to the pool to consult with me. I had no time to prepare for this unexpected visit. We conversed for several awkward minutes, he standing tall beside the pool in his suit and I, clinging to the side of the pool at the deep end submerged to my neck in water, craning to look up at him. Kinana seemed in a hurry to have the American view on some point. Although my one-piece bathing suit was conservative by American standards, my towel was nowhere nearby. I did not want to climb out of the pool and risk my bare arms and legs offending a Muslim man. Diplomacy, though, had to go on!

The government of Tanzania, as facilitator and cohost, was eager to bring the peace talks to a conclusion. They'd been under way for nearly a year, and the government had invested heavily in both personnel and funding. Sending a high-ranking Tanzanian official such as Minister Kinana to Arusha was intended to signal to both sides the urgency of speeding up negotiations. By late May the Tanzanians seemed to be running out of patience. They started setting deadlines for ending the military talks and signing the full agreement. Yet Kinana returned empty-handed to Dar es Salaam.

In early June the facilitator's representative, Ami Mpungwe, declared the stalemated military talks suspended pending new developments. He announced that he and other members of the facilitation team would travel to Rwanda to consult on the force proportion issue with President Habyarimana in Kigali and with RPF

Commander Kagame at his headquarters in northern Rwanda. In the meantime Mpungwe instructed the two parties to take up the agenda item on refugee issues.

Finally, the Refugee Talks

The right of refugees to return to Rwanda had been one of the principal reasons put forward by the RPF to justify its October 1990 invasion into northern Rwanda that had launched the civil war. For many years the Habyarimana government had denied Rwandan refugees the right to return to their homeland on grounds there was no space for them and their cattle. Despite the contentious history of this issue, the refugee talks reached a speedy conclusion. In just one week, June 2–9, 1993, the two sides concluded their negotiations and signed a protocol covering a range of topics pertaining not only to refugee repatriation but also to the return of internally displaced persons to their homes.

Contributing to the speed of achieving consensus on this issue was the diligent preparation by both sides and their flexibility in the final deliberations. Minister Ndasingwa had developed the government's approach to the refugee negotiations and to refugee return more than six months earlier.[10] The multiparty Council of Ministers had approved the plan put forward by the Ministry of Labor and Social Affairs in December 1992, when the refugee agenda item had been expected to come up for discussion at Arusha during that month in lieu of stalled power-sharing talks. At that time Lando told me he intended to emphasize at Arusha the government's openness and flexibility. His twofold goal would be to lay the groundwork for bilateral talks on refugee return with each of Rwanda's neighbors and to minimize opportunities for controversy with the RPF.

To meet these goals, Ndasingwa, the only Tutsi minister in the Rwandan cabinet, planned first to have the Arusha observers from the neighboring states participate actively in the deliberations on refugees. Each neighboring state hosted thousands of Rwandan refugees, and each had its own ideas about how the issue should be handled. Second, he intended to downplay the controversial option of naturalization in countries of asylum. The RPF regarded support for offering refugees citizenship in neighboring countries as the government's way of escaping its international obligation to accept refugee return. Furthermore neighboring countries were not keen on this option. Instead, Ndasingwa said he would keep the Arusha delegates focused on repatriation modalities and the local settlement option. The latter would allow refugees to remain in their country of asylum if they so chose without necessarily becoming citizens. Ndasingwa, who came to Arusha to help lead the government delegation on this issue, said he wanted to avoid any impression that the government might compromise its international commitments to repatriate all refugees wishing to return.

The RPF too had a prepared strategy for the refugee talks that it had provided to the Rwandan government and to the UNHCR representative in Kigali, Carlos Rodriguez. Rodriguez had shared a copy with me as the representative of UNHCR's largest donor. The RPF document identified four specific areas it considered of key importance for discussion at Arusha: timing of refugee return, reintegration modalities, refugee property claims, and the size of the refugee population. That last issue focused attention on the disparity between the one million refugees the RPF claimed existed and the more modest 500,000 or so counted as refugees on UNHCR's books, the number the government accepted. Rodriguez surmised that this RPF document reflected a somewhat flexible position. By getting down into these specific details the document signaled to me general RPF acceptance of the principles the two sides already had in place. In the August 1992 Arusha protocol on the rule of law, the government and the RPF agreed on the principle that Rwanda's refugees had an "inalienable right" to return to their country of origin, and both pledged not to interfere with that right. The right of refugees to return had plagued relations between Rwanda and the refugee communities in neighboring countries for years. By the time the refugee talks took place in Arusha, this was apparently no longer an obstacle between the two sides.

Another positive factor contributing to the quick resolution of this potentially thorny issue had been the presence at Arusha of a UNHCR representative who served as a resource person and advisor to both parties as well as to the observers and other international representatives at the talks. This was Kolu Doherty, then deputy director of

UNHCR's Africa Bureau. I was glad to see Doherty, a friend from my Foreign Service days in Geneva, where I had covered refugee affairs and had been in daily contact with UNHCR officials. A Nigerian and an articulate spokesperson for UNHCR policy, Doherty rarely intervened at Arusha, but his carefully timed statements and corridor discussions helped ward off controversy before it got started.

Despite Doherty's best efforts, however, a number of thorny issues still came up in the deliberations. The RPF, for example, insisted on the right of all refugees to reclaim property they had left behind, including land long since resettled, most likely by Hutu. This proposal was problematic for the government, but the eventual Arusha protocol found a compromise: it maintained the principle of refugee rights to lost property with the caveat that persons absent for more than ten years—many had been refugees for thirty or more years—would be discouraged from making any property claims.

The RPF also insisted on the right of all refugees to reclaim or be granted land, even if it meant using national park lands. The RPF specifically argued for settling returnees in the Akagera National Park (which it later did). In a country where a large percentage of the people had no access to land, this proposal was a tall order. Eventually, though, the government agreed that any returnee who wanted land would be eligible for 1.5 hectares. Language was another touchy subject. The RPF wanted, and received, guarantees that returnees from English-speaking countries would not face discrimination in the job market.

Both the RPF and the government assumed in their deliberations that refugees not wishing to return to Rwanda would be allowed to remain in their countries of asylum either as locally settled refugees or as naturalized citizens. However, this was not necessarily the understanding or the position of the international observers representing asylum countries at the Arusha talks, despite earlier promises made by their presidents in the 1991 "Dar es Salaam Declaration on the Refugee Problem."[11] Uganda's observer, High Commissioner Benjamin Matogo, for example, made it clear during the Arusha deliberations that naturalization would not be an option in his country. Whether the refugees could retain Rwandan citizenship in their countries of asylum, as Minister Ndasingwa had proposed, was another controversial issue. The UNHCR representative at the talks adroitly suggested that the various tripartite commissions, composed of Rwanda, one of the neighboring asylum countries, and UNHCR, might be a better forum than the Arusha peace talks for resolving such differences. The observers supported this approach, and the parties agreed to defer these bilateral refugee issues to the forthcoming tripartite commissions. This brought the discussion of these unresolved details to a close before a breakdown occurred.

The United States, as a key UNHCR donor concerned about future stability in the region, was keenly interested in the outcome of the refugee talks. We had identified a number of goals we wanted met in these discussions. We wanted to be sure that naturalization would not be totally ruled out as a potential choice for refugees choosing not to return to Rwanda. We wanted the bilateral negotiations with neighboring countries as proposed by the Rwandan government to include UNHCR within the framework of the agency's usual tripartite commissions intended to work out bilateral repatriation modalities. We also wanted to let the parties know that the United States could be counted on to commit resources to repatriation and reintegration when the time came.

As the discussion unfolded, most U.S. concerns were met without direct interventions on my part. Instead our cause was aided by the careful interventions of the UNHCR representative. I do recall, though, lengthy discussions with Uganda's Ambassador Matogo to dissuade him from being so rigid about his country's adamant rejection of the naturalization option for refugees choosing not to repatriate to Rwanda. Matogo would not budge on this position. This issue could, however, be revisited later, in the UNHCR-chaired Tripartite Commissions. I also recall weaving the U.S. commitment to help fund repatriation and reintegration of refugees into my remarks at the conclusion of the refugee negotiations. On June 9, 1993, the government and RPF delegations signed a protocol on refugee repatriation and the resettlement of displaced persons.

Burundi Elections Intrude

During the first week of June, the week devoted to refugee negotiations, the RPF delegates became more and more antagonistic and difficult in their interactions with others at the talks. Although the refugee discussions proceeded with due civility, the atmosphere was tense and strained right from the start. Minister Ndasingwa announced that he would host a reception at the Mount Meru Hotel to kick off the refugee session. He invited both delegations and the international observers. It was one of the few occasions during the Arusha talks that would have brought the adversaries together in an informal gathering. However, the RPF delegates were conspicuously absent from the event. Their leaders sent word at the last minute that the delegates had work to do and could not take time out to attend the reception. Ndasingwa tried to make light of this snub, but the RPF's refusal to have one or two delegates make even a brief appearance was a slap in the face for both the Tutsi minister and the Rwandan government.

This was not an isolated incident. Until then, the RPF delegates had always been cordial, even friendly toward me. But a few days after the reception incident, a couple of RPF delegates were extremely rude to me in the lobby of the hotel. I do not recall the issue, but I too felt slapped in the face.

The Tanzanian facilitator representative Ami Mpungwe nearly reached the limit of his patience with the RPF during this same week. He had just returned to Arusha following consultations in Rwanda on the stalled force proportion issue. When he reported the findings of his trip to the RPF, its leaders rejected outright Tanzania's new, proposed starting point for force proportion negotiations. Mpungwe shared his frustration and exasperation with the observers, seeking their advice on how to proceed. Something was clearly wrong, but at the time the precipitating cause was not obvious to me.

In retrospect, RPF behavior in those first weeks of June was probably linked to the outcome of the June 1 presidential elections in Burundi. In the country's first democratic elections, Burundian voters had elected their first Hutu head of state, Melchior Ndadaye. The overwhelmingly Hutu electorate rejected incumbent president Pierre Buyoya, a moderate Tutsi who had led Burundi for many years and shepherded it through its brief transition to multiparty elections. Though a logical outcome in a country with a Hutu majority, the Hutu victory sent shock waves through the Tutsi community not

Arusha Observer: The Negotiations

only in Burundi but also in Rwanda. With a similar ethnic composition in each country—Hutu majority (85 percent), Tutsi minority (about 15 percent)—events in Burundi often cast a shadow over Rwanda, and vice versa.

The RPF delegates, almost all Tutsi who had grown up in Uganda, had told me before the vote that they believed the Tutsi incumbent would prevail in the election. Burundi's Tutsi military observer in Arusha had talked as if a Buyoya win were a foregone conclusion. Now Ndadaye's victory over Buyoya made the Tutsi communities of both Burundi and Rwanda take another hard look at their commitment to a democratic process. Several RPF Tutsi delegates nevertheless told me after the Burundi elections that they were pleased to see the democratic process work so smoothly. In all discussions about democracy with me, the RPF claimed that, despite their minority status in Rwanda, they could expect to win any election because their platform of unity and equality would appeal to both the Hutu majority and the Tutsi minority. The outcome of Burundi's first democratic elections evidently came as a surprise and dealt a blow to the RPF.

Stalling or Serious?

With the refugee protocol signed and the facilitator's representative back in Arusha, the Tanzanians again had the delegations take up the critical—but confounding—issue of force proportions. Over several intense days there were long meetings between the facilitator and each of the delegations, the facilitator and the observers, and the observers and various delegates. Tanzania's Defense Minister Kinana returned to Arusha to press for agreement.

Under pressure to conclude the military and security issues, the two sides inched slowly closer to resolving their differences. Yet loose ends persisted. The government delegation accepted the facilitator's proposed 60-40 percent split at the troop level for the integrated army in favor of the government. The foreign minister was confident the upcoming Council of Ministers' meeting in Kigali would approve this formula even though the 40 percent accorded the RPF was higher than the 33 percent limit the government had previously set for the negotiations. The RPF delegation, however, was awaiting instructions from its headquarters on the 40 percent figure, which was much lower than it had been insisting on.

Both delegations were now considering Tanzania's proposal for a 50-50 split in the officer corps, with the principle of alternation in the leadership of each unit. This meant that if one side held the position of commander in one unit, the other side would fill the position of deputy commander; in the next unit, the situation would be reversed. Neither delegation was quite ready to accept a 50-50 division in the officer corps; each wanted a larger share.

The two sides did finally agree to apply whatever force proportion figures were accepted for the army to the future, integrated gendarmerie. They were also coming close to agreeing on a demobilization framework that would make the neutral international force responsible for determining the location of troop assembly points and cantonment sites for heavy weapons. The NIF would also be asked to guard the weapons caches.

Still in play were a number of other important issues. The two sides were at odds over the relationship between the peace agreement and the Rwandan constitution. Which would take precedence, and under what circumstances? The RPF dropped its demand to scrap the entire constitution in favor of the peace accord, putting forward forty-five specific articles of the constitution that the peace agreement would supersede. The government delegation was reviewing this proposal.

Nor could the delegations agree on the status of Kigali. Would it be a weapons-free town? If so, how would this be accomplished? How would the security of Kigali—and indeed the country—be assured if all the army and gendarmerie troops were confined to assembly points pending force integration or demobilization? Sequencing implementation of the accord and the length of the transition were still pending issues. Facilitator representative Mpungwe talked with each side separately and both sides together on these final troublesome issues. He briefed the international observers, and they collaborated on lobbying particular delegations on specific issues. Yet no breakthrough occurred.[12]

Mpungwe became more and more frustrated with the dithering of the two sides as they went around and around without agreement on these final, pesky, pending issues. Dar es Salaam was undoubtedly pressing him to end these talks. After a particularly unproductive session, in which the RPF abruptly and rudely rejected one of his proposals as a basis for negotiation, Mpungwe was ready to call it quits.

He turned to the observers for support and help, calling us together and laying out his concerns for the future of the negotiations. He questioned whether the RPF was serious about a negotiated settlement or was deliberately delaying the talks because of something else it might have been planning. Mpungwe told observers that RPF actions a few weeks earlier had suggested intentional foot-dragging. He recalled delayed decisions on issues relating to the disarmament and demobilization of RPF soldiers and cited repeated instances of the RPF insisting on knowing exactly how the government planned to provide security for its leaders if, as expected, a UN force was not deployed before the accord's thirty-seven-day deadline for installing the Broad-Based Transitional Government. On another occasion, he noted, the RPF even suggested taking two weeks at Arusha to develop a military training curriculum. It certainly seemed possible, Mpungwe said, that the RPF was stalling.

By mid-June, with the talks still going around in circles, the Tanzanians increased pressure on the two sides to reach agreement on the outstanding issues and conclude the Arusha Accords. Mpungwe announced that his government had set a signing date of June 19, just before the opening of the OAU summit in Cairo. He reported that President Mwinyi was in the process of extending invitations to regional leaders to attend a signing ceremony on that day. It was therefore, he said, imperative that the two sides finish by that time.

Then the government of Rwanda threw its own wrench into the works. President Habyarimana insisted on a ratification process for the Arusha agreement before he would sign it. This process, the president asserted, would have to involve his review of the agreed protocols, the cabinet's input, and a review by the existing legislature, and the political parties would have to sign off on it. Surprisingly, this Kigali ratification proposal was anathema to both delegations in Arusha. Government and RPF delegates were actually in total agreement: what they had negotiated should be final. The Tanzanian facilitator went even further, calling the Arusha process "sovereign." These Kigali demands starkly revealed how wide the gap had become between the power structure in Kigali and the Rwandan negotiators in Arusha.

The reaction from Arusha neither impressed nor persuaded Kigali. At a mid-June cabinet meeting the coalition government unanimously summoned Foreign Minister Ngulinzira to brief both the cabinet and the legislature on the Arusha Accords. Ngulinzira said he was too busy negotiating to return to Kigali. There was no time, he claimed, if they were to conclude and sign the agreement on June 19, the latest Tanzanian deadline for ending the talks.

Even though various Kigali constituencies promised to ratify the Accords and assured Ngulinzira that the process would be pro forma, he never found time to accede to Kigali's demands. Neither side gave in. A stalemate prevailed between the government delegation in Arusha and the Kigali power structure still dominated by the former ruling MRND party and the president. However, the unanimous cabinet vote to recall Minister Ngulinzira for consultations revealed how far key opposition leaders had moved toward the president's position.

At the same mid-June meeting in Kigali, the cabinet introduced another controversial decision that opened still another opportunity to delay resolving the outstanding Arusha issues. Examining the security issues raised by the RPF, the ministers decided that, pending the arrival of the UN force, Kigali would not be demilitarized and weapons-free. Furthermore the transitional government would not meet outside the capital, a blatant rejection of the RPF's suggestion for meeting the thirty-seven-day deadline for installing the transitional government pending arrival of the UN peacekeeping force to provide security for RPF officials. Attitudes of ministers from Rwanda's political opposition were clearly hardening against making any concessions to the RPF.

Talks Collapse

The Arusha process was on the verge of collapse. Delays from the RPF. Demands from the government. Mistrust and suspicion from both. Negotiations were going nowhere. Then, on the evening of June 24, Ami Mpungwe, the exasperated and undoubtedly exhausted facilitator's representative, suddenly and without warning declared the talks suspended indefinitely. So close and yet so far. Each side blamed the other for the breakdown. Both blamed the Tanzanians.

There was nothing to do but pack up and go home to Kigali. The next day I wrapped up my time in Arusha by writing a cable and distributing to various delegation members and international observers copies of photos I had taken during the talks. Then I held final discussions with RPF delegates whom I would not see for some time.

The following day I hitched a ride on the government delegation's bus to the Nairobi airport and caught a flight back to Kigali. I had decided at the last minute to check my carryon bag, a small, locked canvas duffle, because it seemed particularly heavy. I had not wanted to lug it around as I was browsing the airport shops during the long wait for the plane.

Upon collecting my luggage in Kigali, I was surprised to note that the duffle didn't seem very heavy after all and wondered to myself why I'd checked it in the first place. When I reached my house, I discovered that the lock had been cut off and my new Nikon camera and a short-wave radio were missing. Why had I left my only items of any value in that checked duffle bag? My credibility as a seasoned traveler dropped another notch or two.

Comments

1. *The diplomatic corps differences between Kigali and Arusha*: Diplomats in both Kigali and Arusha functioned increasingly as collective units as the peace talks in Arusha unfolded. The process had become the vehicle for Rwandans to decide how they would manage their transitions to peace, a democratic political system, and multiparty elections. Diplomats in each location embraced the success of the Arusha peace process as their common policy priority, even though policy differences remained on specific issues under consideration. Supporting the Rwandan quest for a signed agreement united the diplomatic communities in each of these venues. Collaborating on ways to nudge the parties toward rapid agreement was their collective goal. The unity of purpose among the miniature version of the Kigali diplomatic corps in Arusha led to close camaraderie among the observers there.

Unique characteristics of the Arusha situation, though, and its geographic distance from Kigali resulted in important differences in how the two groups of diplomats functioned.[13] The key difference in Arusha was the RPF presence and its prominent role in the negotiating process. In Arusha the Tutsi-led RPF had a seat at the negotiating table on equal footing with the government delegation. Diplomats dealt with the RPF delegates in the same manner as with the government delegates. Diplomats in Arusha were in daily contact with the RPF delegates, just as they were with government delegates. In Arusha there were multiple opportunities to listen to RPF explanations of their positions, assess the merit of their views, and lobby for compromise in the interest of a peace agreement. Observers in Arusha viewed their diplomatic role as one of encouraging the two delegations to forge compromises that would result in agreements that could be implemented.

In Kigali, however, diplomats interacted with only one of the parties at the peace talks. Their interlocutors were primarily Hutu from the former ruling party and its political opposition. Diplomats viewed their role as helping these mostly Hutu interlocutors to forge common negotiating positions for the Arusha talks and to accept the Arusha decisions. The Tutsi-led RPF had no presence in Kigali until after the peace agreement was signed, with the exception of a single military liaison officer who had no diplomatic role. Diplomats in Kigali could meet periodically with the RPF in its northern Mulindi headquarters, but access was not as easy as for the diplomats in Arusha. And there was no opportunity for informal contacts between Kigali diplomats and the RPF.

Another difference was the significant role of African diplomats in Arusha, where they had a much greater impact on the process and outcome of the talks than did their Kigali counterparts. Tanzania's prominent role in facilitating the peace talks thrust Africans into the forefront. Tanzania's ministers of foreign affairs and defense and foreign ministry diplomats guided the talks, proposed strategies for breaking stalemates, cajoled delegations toward compromises, and were the link to the observers on the progress of the negotiations. Ami Mpungwe, the facilitator's representative at the talks while I was an observer, became the de facto head of the Arusha diplomatic corps. The rest of us, Western and African diplomats alike, looked to him as our leader.

In Kigali, Western diplomats, particularly those from France, Belgium, and the United States, were generally the de facto leaders of the Kigali diplomatic corps, even though the Vatican representative traditionally served as the dean. Tanzania's central role at Arusha actually increased the importance of African diplomats in the Kigali diplomatic corps. During and after the peace talks, Tanzania's ambassador to Rwanda played a key role as the link between the Tanzanian facilitator and the diplomatic corps in Kigali. She also became the key African interlocutor with Rwandan government officials and political party leaders.

The diplomatic corps in Arusha included two international organizations critical to the course of the peace talks: the regional Organization of African Unity and the United Nations. The prominent political role of these two organizations in the peace process also carried over to Kigali. After the peace agreement was signed, the UN and the OAU each assigned a full-time officer to Kigali whose responsibility was to help facilitate implementation of the accord. In both cases that officer was an Arusha veteran: Ghanaian Joe Felli from the OAU secretariat and Fijian Colonel Tikoca, an experienced UN peacekeeper.

2. *A tale of two cities*: Holding the Rwandan peace talks at a neutral site outside the country had advantages. However, the distance between Arusha and Kigali presented the diplomatic community with communications management challenges. Maintaining consistency in my messages to the Arusha delegates with those the ambassador in Kigali was conveying to his government and party interlocutors was difficult in those days before email and other forms of instant communication. My only connection with the world outside Arusha was over unpredictable, open telephone and fax lines. Although I wasn't dealing with highly classified information, I had to avoid speculating or making judgments in my phone conversations with Kigali, Washington, or Dar es Salaam. At the same time I was cut off from all State Department cable traffic, clas-

sified and unclassified, going into or out of Kigali and Washington. Somehow we nevertheless managed to coordinate our messages.

Another challenge to diplomacy was the difference in perspective that developed between me in Arusha and the ambassador in Kigali. While I tended to encourage U.S. support for compromises forged in Arusha, the ambassador often maintained that his interlocutors in Kigali would consider them too one-sided in favor of the RPF.

The Rwandan delegation had to cope with similar challenges in its communications between Arusha and Kigali. Two different approaches were apparent in the two different locations. The government delegation in Arusha tended toward conciliation and compromise; this made progress possible in the face of often rigid and maximal positions of the RPF. Compromises, however, seldom satisfied the hard-liners in the government delegation or in the Kigali power structure. They accused the foreign minister for being "too soft" on the RPF. The minister's efforts, and sometimes successes, at protecting Kigali and hard-line interests went unrecognized. At one point, some Arusha government delegates loyal to the president even urged him to be more flexible in his negotiating position, a sign of the philosophical distance that had developed between Kigali and Arusha.

3. *My lesson in Realpolitik*: During my July 1993 consultations in Washington with the State Department's Africa Bureau, my eyes were opened to the realpolitik of international relations. Having spent only the first of my five Foreign Service postings in Washington, I had not realized the extent to which domestic considerations rather than the actual conditions in overseas situations drove policy decisions. When I pressed Washington colleagues to minimize the gap between a signed peace accord and deployment of a UN peacekeeping force, the response was one I had not anticipated. I was told that the public just wouldn't understand administration support for a peacekeeping mission in tiny, faraway Rwanda. Such a stance could become politically problematic.

From then on I learned to look at Washington decision making in a new light. Regardless of the merits of action in any given overseas situation, the relevance and efficacy of any policy action would also always have to be assessed within, and balanced against, both the domestic political context and the national interest of the United States, regardless of the humanitarian and security needs at stake overseas.

[15]

The Dénouement

Arusha Peace Accords Signed

Security an Ongoing Concern

When I returned to Rwanda at the end of June 1993 after two and a half months in Arusha, the enormous emotional and physical tension that had been absent in Arusha reclaimed me. While I was away, the security situation in Rwanda had deteriorated markedly. Bombings where ordinary people gathered in the course of their daily business had heightened insecurity within the general population. On April 21, just days after I left for Arusha, a bomb had exploded in an outdoor marketplace in the southern university town of Butare. Such incidents had been rare in the south up to this time. A day later a blast at Kigali's main post office seriously injured twenty-one persons. A short time later, on May 3, a bomb exploded in another outdoor marketplace, this time in the northwestern town of Gisenyi, near the heartland of the president's MRND party. This random violence, attributed to either the RPF or the government forces, depending on one's point of view, had continued with alarming frequency throughout May and June. No arrests, much less convictions, ever gave victims or their families the satisfaction of seeing justice done. No one was held accountable.

Targeted assassinations stirred up a blame game among political parties and Kigali's political elite. On May 18 Emmanuel Gapyisi, a well-known member of the main opposition party, the MDR, was assassinated in front of his house. The MDR accused the MRND; the MRND countered with accusations that MDR members themselves had carried out the assassination. The mutual recriminations nearly caused the collapse of the year-old multiparty coalition government. Gapyisi's killer was never identified.

Gapyisi's murder was significant. A Hutu opponent of the president, he had been the architect and leading promoter of a political movement advocating Hutu solidarity against both the Tutsi and President Habyarimana. This represented a break with his party's position favoring power sharing. His aim had been to unite Hutu across the political spectrum against the Tutsi enemy. This movement, referred to as Hutu Power, had steadily gained momentum and strength among opposition Hutu who were increasingly skeptical of Tutsi intentions following the RPF's February offensive and dissatisfied with the president for not being tougher on the group. That RPF attack had seriously shaken many opposition Hutu and caused them to question their commitment to sharing power with the Tutsi and the president's resolve to do something about it.

Rifts within Political Parties Deepen

The Gapyisi assassination in May occurred against the background of an increasingly serious rift within the opposition MDR between its president, Faustin Twagiramungu, and most of the rest of the party's leadership. The last straw for prominent party members opposed to Twagiramungu occurred in mid-June, when he unilaterally decided to cosign a statement with other political parties in the coalition government calling for Foreign Minister Ngulinzira to return from Arusha to brief the president, the cabinet, the legislature, and the political parties on the Arusha Accords. The leadership also disapproved of his scheming to be named in the Arusha Accords as prime minister of the transitional government.

At an extraordinary party conference in July 1993 the MDR rank and file rejected Twagiramungu as their president and then expelled him from the party. He, however, disavowed this decision as illegitimate on grounds that he, as the party president, had not sanctioned the special conference. He filed suit in the courts against the decisions of the conference and continued to consider himself the leader of the MDR. In fact, Twagiramungu successfully maneuvered to have President Habyarimana appoint his hand-picked supporters to key MDR-held positions when a new coalition government was formed later that month. The new prime minister, Agathe Uwilingiyimana, and the new foreign minister, Anastase Gasana, both belonged to the Twagiramungu faction of the MDR party.[1]

By July the MDR rift had evolved into two distinct, antagonistic wings. Twagiramungu headed the smaller of the two. A continuing belief that the Hutu could cooperate with the Tutsi in genuine power sharing characterized his faction. After the RPF attack of February 1993, the larger, dissident wing became deeply skeptical of RPF intentions. Inspired by hard-line members from the MDR heartland, such as executive secretary Donat Murego and second vice-president Froduald Karamira, this faction turned to the Hutu-supremacist Hutu Power movement and away from supporting power sharing with the RPF. For them, this movement embodied the idea that Hutu solidarity across party lines would serve as a bulwark against what they anticipated the Tutsi-led RPF intended: the takeover of Rwanda.

Twagiramungu, whose strategy for strengthening his political hand had always been to look for allies among the leadership of other parties, lost control of the MDR rank and file. Prime Minister Dismas Nsengiyaremye, who had always nurtured his relationships within the MDR, became the de facto leader of the majority faction of the party. This left Twagiramungu with a small residual following that he continued to claim represented the entire MDR party. At stake in this dispute were seats the political party would fill in the transitional government and legislature, in accordance with provisions of the Arusha protocol on power sharing.

Difficult divisions also developed within the PL. Like the MDR split, the PL divide had ideological overtones. Unlike the MDR split, which had geographic implications, the PL division had ethnic roots. Its leader, Justin Mugenzi, a Hutu who had been an ardent supporter of power sharing, had gradually distanced himself from the party's Tutsi membership as he moved closer to Hutu Power. The Tutsi members of the PL came under the de facto leadership of party vice-president Landoald Ndasingwa, the Tutsi minister of labor and social affairs who had negotiated the refugee protocol at Arusha. Because representation in the transitional institutions would depend on party affiliation, neither faction wanted to leave the PL to the other; both wanted to co-opt both factions.

The party of the president, the MRND, publicly revealed its fault line as well. In mid-July the soft-spoken, moderate, and well-respected minister of defense James Gasana abruptly resigned and secretly left the country with his wife and children. In his resignation letter he cited threats to his security from AMASASU, the secretive Hutu-supremacist group within the military.[2] The hard-line, Hutu-supremacist CDR party had already broken publicly with President Habyarimana and his party over the terms of the renewed March cease-fire.

A New Government Closes the Deal

As the MDR and PL splits were evolving, the multiparty coalition government was under pressure to regularize its situation. This government, appointed in April 1992 under Prime Minister Nsengiyaremye, had a one-year mandate; at the end of that year, elections were to have taken place. However, Arusha negotiations were still ongoing in April 1993 and elections were not yet on the horizon. So the multiparty government granted itself a three-month extension, until the end of June. But neither a peace accord nor elections were any closer as the new deadline arrived. In fact the situation was worse: the peace process had been suspended and the two politicians most closely associated with the Arusha talks, Prime Minister Nsengiyarmeye and Foreign Minister Ngulinzira, had lost the confidence of the president, the MRND, and the Twagiramungu faction of their own MDR party.

As the three-month extension of the coalition government drew to a close, the participating parties agreed that the president should appoint a new interim government. The main opposition MDR party would again provide the prime minister. The question was: Which faction of the party would assume that responsibility? The majority faction led by Nsengiyaremye put forward Jean Kambanda for this position. It was clear President Habyarimana would never agree to reappoint Nsengiyaremye. The smaller MDR faction led by Twagiramungu proposed Agathe Uwilingiyimana, the minister of education in Nsengiyaremye's government. Twagiramungu wanted to save himself for the premiership of the transitional government. In the end, the Twagiramungu faction prevailed, following close consultation and collaboration with the president.

On July 16, 1993, President Habyarimana swore in Agathe Uwilingiyimana as the new prime minister. The new government's mandate was to conclude the Arusha peace agreement and oversee its implementation. This would include installation of the transitional institutions—the Broad-Based Transitional Government and the Transitional National Assembly—as well as integration of the armed forces and demobilization of both government and RPF troops. The new prime minister appointed a new foreign minister, also from the Twagiramungu faction of the MDR. Anastase Gasana took over immediately from Ngulinzira, who had shepherded the peace process for fifteen months.

Out of power and opposed to Twagiramungu, both Nsengiyaremye and Ngulinzira gravitated to the anti-Twagiramungu faction of the MDR. This wing of the MDR also espoused Hutu Power and supported Hutu supremacy, positions that did not fit with my understanding of these two political figures. When questioned on this point many years later, Nsengiyaremye told me the two were driven purely by their strong opposition to what they believed to be Twagiramungu's political betrayal, not by an embrace of Hutu Power.

At the end of July newly appointed Foreign Minister Gasana and his new negotiating team met directly with their RPF counterparts at Kinihira, a site within Rwanda's demilitarized zone. Without a facilitator or observers present, the two delegations quickly reached agreement on the outstanding issues from Arusha. One key decision authorized an arrangement the RPF said would enable its participants in the transitional institutions to come to Kigali. This arrangement called for a battalion of six hundred RPF troops to come to Kigali to provide security for the five RPF ministers and eleven legislators. The troops would be quartered at the top of Kigali's highest hill in the vacant hotel attached to the building housing Rwanda's legislative meeting hall. With the outstanding issues decided, dates were set for concluding the talks.

The Dénouement

On August 3 in Arusha the government and the RPF signed the military integration protocol and a miscellaneous items protocol. On August 4 the two sides signed the "Peace Agreement between the Government of the Republic of Rwanda and the Rwandan Patriotic Front."[3] Known as the Arusha Peace Accords or the Arusha Accords, it is a collection of all the protocols agreed upon during the year-long negotiations. Once signed, the Arusha Accords, along with the 1991 constitution, became the fundamental law of Rwanda. President Habyarimana signed for the government and Col. Alexis Kanyarengwe, the Hutu chairman, signed for the mostly Tutsi RPF.

The signing took place during a grand celebration before numerous high-level international representatives from Tanzania, the facilitator and host of the talks; the OAU cosponsor; the UN; and the observer countries. Leading the U.S. delegation at the signing ceremony was Robert G. Houdek, deputy assistant secretary in the Bureau of African Affairs at the Department of State. Ambassador Flaten attended as a member of the U.S. delegation. He was proud of the role the United States had played in nurturing the peace process through the complex Kigali political scene to arrive finally at the Arusha Peace Accords.

Comment

After more than a year of concerted effort, Rwanda had a revolutionary blueprint for a twenty-two-month transitional period that would integrate the insurgent RPF into key political and security institutions and lead to multiparty elections. The plan was explicit in most of its arrangements, though there were some loose ends that would still need to be resolved in the implementation phase. The entire undertaking depended on three key ingredients: the early deployment of a neutral international force to provide security, the goodwill of the two sides to work together to solve difficulties as they arose, and the determination of the signing parties to keep implementation moving forward. Continuing support from the international community was also essential to successfully implementing the agreement.

No adjustments, however, had been made to assuage Hutu hardliners who adamantly opposed the Accords' power-sharing arrangements. Notably, in a solo act of defiance, the hard-line, Hutu-extremist CDR party refused to send a representative to Arusha for the signing. Its absence reflected its total rejection of the power-sharing protocol and many other provisions it believed had given too much representation and power to the RPF. Because it did not sign the Arusha Accords, the CDR was the only party that failed to accept the political party code of conduct eschewing violence. Consequently, in accordance with Arusha provisions, the CDR would have to forgo participation in the transitional process. This made the CDR ineligible to take up its one allocated seat in the Transitional National Assembly. Its show of defiance would later haunt the party.

Within the diplomatic community and among some OAU and UN officers, there was cautious optimism that the two sides would live up to the terms of the negotiated peace accord. The hope was that they would find ways to make needed adjustments as implementation proceeded toward the prescribed multiparty elections. The U.S. assessment was that if the president signed the accord, he would be able to bring the CDR hard-liners and other vocal dissidents around to accept it, even if grudgingly. For us, implementation of the peace agreement seemed the best strategy for containing those who rejected the power-sharing provisions. Our rationale was that once they saw that power sharing was the only game in town, they would have to play if they wanted to remain relevant.

The Accords, however, remained anathema not only to the CDR but also to other significant groups. Large parts of the president's MRND, members of the opposition MDR, and some in the PL were flirting with the Hutu solidarity message that offered power-sharing skeptics an alternative. Bringing them around to accept the agreement would be a large undertaking, given the state of political play at the time of the signing.

So, one might ask, why did the president sign the Arusha Peace Accords? Perhaps he believed he had no other choice once the negotiations were concluded. Perhaps he took that step to satisfy the diplomatic community that was exerting so much pressure on him to do so. Perhaps, on the other hand, he may have believed even then that he would never have to implement the undesirable provisions. Maybe he already had a plan for overcoming the parts of the agreement that he and his closest allies did not like. In retrospect, the president probably continued to believe that he could use the democratic political process to shape implementation of the peace agreement to his advantage and keep himself in power. The significant schisms in the political parties and rising cross-party support for Hutu Power might have emboldened his resolve.

At the time I was worried that neither side was entirely satisfied with the outcome of the negotiations, particularly the power-sharing arrangements that were the cornerstone of the Accords. I feared that one side or the other might attempt a coup once the Broad-Based Transitional Government was in place and once the security forces were integrated. By then both sides would have recourse to military might to support such a power grab. I did not give serious consideration to the possibility of a coup occurring before implementation of the agreement because I did not think that was a plausible or viable scenario. I couldn't have been more wrong.

[16]

Preparing to Implement the Arusha Accords

On August 4, 1993, the day the Peace Accords were signed in Arusha, Kigali was ominously quiet. There were no celebrations, no jubilation, no dancing in the streets, and no indication of any kind that this day was any different from any other. Indeed Prime Minister Agathe Uwilingiyimana eventually had to declare a holiday to mark the occasion. Yet even the holiday, August 11, passed with no indication that anything special had occurred.

Asked about this reticence to acknowledge, much less celebrate, the peace agreement, Rwandans in our embassy and our contacts in the society at large—both Hutu and Tutsi—said they were skeptical that anything would actually come of the Arusha Accords. They had no confidence it would mean an end to the fighting between the government and the RPF. Nor, they maintained, would the pact end the suspicion and mistrust between the Hutu and Tutsi ethnic groups. They had no hope that random violence would end or security improve with just the signatures of a few people on a few pieces of paper.

Nevertheless, despite the deep skepticism of the average Rwandan, official Rwanda and the political elite would orient all their efforts over the last five months of 1993 toward preparations for implementing the Arusha Accords. The government welcomed the arrival of the UN reconnaissance mission in August. Political parties planned for installation of the transitional institutions. The two militaries prepared jointly for integrating the army. The United Nations Development Program led the planning process for demobilization. By the end of the year the UN peacekeeping force had partially deployed to Kigali and the demilitarized zone. RPF military and civilians tapped to participate in the transitional institutions had come to Kigali accompanied by an RPF battalion to assure their security. Members of the transitional institutions were to be sworn in before the end of the year.

The process had not been without its problems. By year's end the tight deadline written into the Arusha Accords for installing the transitional institutions had long passed. The divided political parties had yet to agree on common lists of members to fill their designated seats in the transitional institutions. Throughout the fall those involved remained patient. As 1993 drew to a close, however, patience was wearing thin. Tensions within the Hutu ranks and between Hutu and Tutsi were rising. Diplomatic optimism and UN hope were waning. Frustration had set in.

The United Nations Prepares

Key to implementing the Arusha Accords was the early presence of a United Nations peacekeeping force to provide security for Kigali and for the transitional institutions that were to be installed after the force was in place. Although forewarned, Arusha negotiators wrote into the peace agreement a thirty-seven-day deadline for installing the transitional institutions with the precondition that the UN force would be deployed by then to provide security. As expected, this proved overly optimistic.

A UN Reconnaissance Mission Arrives

The government and the RPF tried to push the UN along. They sent a joint letter to the UN secretary general from Arusha on June 14, 1993, just days before the Tanzanian facilitator suspended the Arusha talks indefinitely. The letter appealed to the UN to send a reconnaissance mission to Rwanda as soon as possible to facilitate rapid deployment of a Neutral International Force mandated to monitor implementation of the anticipated peace agreement. The letter also supported integrating into the NIF the OAU forces already in the demilitarized zone monitoring cease-fire compliance. But the UN took no action to field a reconnaissance mission before the signing. The OAU observer forces, NMOG, would, however, be integrated into the UN force.

What the UN did move forward on was the border force requested in March by both Rwanda and Uganda and acquiesced to by the RPF. UN Security Council Resolution 846 of June 1993 authorized this border force, known as the UN Observer Mission in Uganda-Rwanda (UNOMUR). An advance party deployed to the Ugandan side of the border on August 18, just a few weeks after the government and the RPF signed the Arusha Peace Accords, and the force became fully operational by the end of September. Its mandate was to monitor border traffic and ensure that no military personnel or matériel crossed between the two countries. The UN named a Canadian, Brig. Gen. Roméo A. Dallaire, to head UNOMUR.

The day after the UNOMUR advance party arrived in Uganda, General Dallaire arrived in Rwanda at the head of the UN reconnaissance mission for a proposed UN peacekeeping force. This mission, in Rwanda August 19–31, may have set a record, arriving in Kigali barely two weeks after the Arusha Accords had been signed. The joint request of the two parties may have helped speed the process. Members of the UN mission met with military, political, and diplomatic officials in an effort to determine what the NIF functions should be and what resources would be needed.

As chargé d'affaires in the absence of the ambassador, I met with General Dallaire to discuss the proposed UN force. I emphasized the need for speed in assembling the force on grounds that the political situation in the country was fragile and might have difficulty withstanding a prolonged period before the formation of the force and implementation of the transitional institutions. We discussed the sentiment in New York and Washington to keep the size of the force as small as could be effective, or the "minimum viable" size. Dallaire explored with me the idea of a force that would start small, grow as the demands on it increased, in accordance with the provisions of the Accords, and then shrink as the demands decreased. Phase I would have the minimum via-

Preparing to Implement the Accords

ble number of troops needed to get the Broad-Based Transitional Government in place. Phase II would begin when the force was of sufficient strength to allow the troop disengagement process to begin. Phase III would draw down to observer level. This proposal sounded like a practical way to have the appropriate number of troops available when they were needed while keeping overall numbers low. Throughout the discussion Dallaire was optimistic about the operation and its chances for success. He said Phase I would be critical.[1]

I was impressed with the general's suggestion for phased deployment of a force that would begin small, expand during the demanding demobilization period, and contract once Rwanda's transitional political and security institutions were in place. This might allow threading the needle between donor and UN concerns over resources and General Dallaire's concern that the force be large enough at any given time to do the job assigned to it.

Rwandans Lobby the UN for Speedy Action

The Rwandans themselves reinforced this optimism when a joint government-RPF delegation arrived in New York to lobby Security Council member states for approval of the proposed international force. Foreign Minister Anastase Gasana and Patrick Mazimhaka, an RPF leader and Arusha veteran, constituted the joint delegation. They met with the secretary general on September 15. Their message urged rapid deployment of the NIF so that the transitional institutions could be established and cautioned that delay could cause the peace process to collapse. The secretary general, in turn, cautioned them that once approved by the Security Council, an international force would take at least two to three months to become operational. He urged the two sides to continue to abide by the cease-fire in the interim.[2]

Meanwhile the United States had yet to decide its position on a peacekeeping operation for Rwanda.[3] While parts of the bureaucracy supported a wholly UN force, other parts wanted OAU forces to play a key role in any Rwandan peacekeeping operation. This latter position envisioned such an operation as a training opportunity for African OAU forces, an occasion for them to gain peacekeeping experience. The United States was also waiting to see the UN recon-naissance mission's report before taking a final position on a UN peacekeeping operation.[4]

General Dallaire submitted his report of the UN reconnaissance mission to Secretary General Boutros Boutros-Ghali on September 21. On that same day, the secretary general briefed U.S. State Department officials, who were in New York on other Africa-related business, about its contents.[5] He said Dallaire's report had described a force that would scale up and down depending on the tasks at hand in a four-phase peacekeeping operation. This tracked closely with the thoughts Dallaire had expressed in Kigali in August.

Quickly thereafter, on September 24, the UN secretary general submitted his report on the reconnaissance mission, S/26488, to the Security Council. His plan followed Dallaire's report and the Arusha Accords protocols closely. The secretary general called for the phased deployment of up to 2,548 peacekeepers. Phase I would deploy 1,428 troops and last until the Broad-Based Transitional Government was in place, estimated to be by the end of 1993. The pro-posal called for a broad mandate for the force, including establishing a weapons-secure area in and around Kigali.[6]

On October 5 the UN Security Council passed Resolution 872 (1993) establishing the UN Assistance Mission for Rwanda (UNAMIR). Although it retained the concept of phased sizing of the force, it defined a mandate that gave the peacekeeping force much less authority than the UN secretary general or the reconnaissance mission report had recommended. For example, it eliminated the recommendation that the force assist in the recovery of arms, and it specified that peacekeepers could only contribute to, not provide for, the security of Kigali. The areas of force activity outlined in the mandate remained broad. In addition to helping secure Kigali, they included the following:

- Monitoring the cease-fire, including the disengagement activities.

- Assisting mine clearance, primarily through training.

- Investigating noncompliance with the Arusha protocol on armed forces integration.

Preparing to Implement the Accords

- Monitoring refugee repatriation and the resettlement of internally displaced persons.
- Assisting with the coordination of humanitarian assistance.
- Investigating and reporting on incidents involving gendarmes or the police.[7]

Despite the broad scope of this mandate, it was a scaled-down version of that proposed by the UN secretary general to the Security Council, and that proposal had itself incorporated only a fraction of what the Arusha Accords had outlined for the international force. Nevertheless, even though the force would number only a few thousand soldiers, many observers and participants in the peacekeeping operation initially held high hopes for success.

UNAMIR Deployment Begins

General Dallaire returned to Kigali as force commander of UNAMIR on October 22. An advance party of twenty-one troops joined him on October 27. This was only about three weeks after the UN Security Council had established UNAMIR, probably a record for UN deployment.

The OAU's military observer force, NMOG, was already deployed in the demilitarized zone to monitor the cease-fire, build confidence between the two sides, and clear mines. Once Dallaire arrived, these African troops—fifty-five unarmed and sixty lightly armed troops whose OAU mandate expired on October 31—were incorporated into UNAMIR, becoming the first UNAMIR contingent in Rwanda. On November 1, to mark this momentous occasion, Dallaire organized a ceremony at Kinihira, a small village in the DMZ. On hand were government and RPF representatives and many villagers from the surrounding area. The Rwanda national anthem blared over loudspeakers, the UN raised its flag, and the OAU troops exchanged their white OAU hats for the blue berets of the United Nations.[8]

Colonel Tikoca, the Fijian soldier who had been the United Nations military observer at the Arusha peace talks, became commander of this military observer contingent of UNAMIR.[9] With twenty years of experience in peacekeeping operations, he very much wanted to be part of the Rwanda peacekeeping mission. He had told me in Arusha that he was more enthusiastic about its prospects of success than for any of the other peacekeeping operations in which he had served.

UNAMIR held a second flag-raising in Kigali on November 17 to mark the official opening of its headquarters at the Amahoro Stadium near the airport.[10] President Habyarimana attended this event even though the only RPF official present was its liaison officer to UNAMIR, Commander Karake Karenzi. Both Dallaire and the president were upbeat in their remarks, expressing high hopes for the successful implementation of the Arusha Peace Accords. The optimism Dallaire and Tikoca shared for their mission would be sorely tested the very next day with a series of unexplained killings in the north, very close to the position of UNAMIR observers.

The civilian side of the UNAMIR operation began to take shape with the arrival in Kigali on November 23 of the special representative of the UN secretary general Jacques-Roger Booh-Booh, a former foreign minister from Cameroon.[11] A few weeks later, on December 13, UNAMIR held its first briefing for representatives of the international community. I attended that meeting with the embassy's consular and economics officer Laura Lane, who developed excellent rapport with key UNAMIR officials. Multiple briefers touched on UNAMIR's mission, its organization, and its strategy for accomplishing its mission. Presiding were Booh-Booh, Dallaire, and Col. Luc Marchal, the Belgian commander of the Kigali sector. Booh-Booh announced December 31 as the target date for installing the transition institutions. Dallaire reviewed the four phases of the UNAMIR operation, with its changing number of troops, and described the sectors in the country where troops would be deployed. Marchal reported that regular military patrols of Kigali had begun and outlined the timetable for establishing a weapons-secure area in the capital.

Both Dallaire and Marchal stressed UNAMIR's role in controlling the circulation of arms in Kigali. Marchal explained how UNAMIR would do this by monitoring the situation from fixed and mobile posts, controlling the roads, conducting searches if warranted, and, as a last resort, cordoning off areas where weapons were known to exist and going in to get them.[12] On at least one occasion, in early January 1994, Marchal seized a cache of arms, ammunition, and explosives.[13]

Preparing to Implement the Accords

Gradually more UN troops began to arrive. The largest contingents came from Bangladesh, Belgium, and Ghana. Bangladesh and Belgium each contributed four hundred troops to the Kigali sector. Some established an observer post at the RPF headquarters at the Mulindi tea plantation north of Byumba. In January 1994 a battalion joined the former NMOG troops in the DMZ. By the end of December enough UNAMIR troops were in place for the government and the RPF to establish the Broad-Based Transitional Government and the Transitional National Assembly. The political parties, however, were not ready.

Political Parties Prepare

The political parties that the Arusha Peace Accords designated to fill specific numbers of seats in the BBTG and the TNA quickly turned their attention to this task once the Accords were signed. There wasn't much time. The Accords called for these transitional institutions to be in place within thirty-seven days of the signing, as long as a neutral international force was in Kigali to provide security for the RPF representatives. As it turned out, the absence of a UN peacekeeping force would not be the only obstacle to meeting the implementation deadlines set out in the Arusha Accords.

Implementation of the Accords also depended on each of the political parties providing a single list of proposed appointments to the cabinet and the legislature. This required political party unity—a foregone conclusion when the power-sharing protocol was written. However, party unity, a fundamental assumption of the peace accord, no longer existed in the two key opposition parties. The MDR, the major opposition party, and the PL, the opposition party with the largest Tutsi contingent, had each become deeply divided. One faction in each party continued to support power sharing; the other faction had rejected it in favor of Hutu solidarity against a feared Tutsi takeover.

The stakes were high for these party factions as they vied for control of the MDR and the PL. Unless they could reach some accommodation, whichever faction gained control would be able to claim all of its party's designated seats and thus control those votes. Forming breakaway political parties was not an option. Only those parties named in the Arusha protocol on power sharing were eligible to present ministerial and legislative candidates.

Each faction of the MDR developed its own separate list for the party's three ministerial positions and eleven seats in the new legislature. Efforts to fashion a compromise between the two sides failed. The Bishops Council tried to help. Diplomats, including Ambassador Flaten, tried to help. From August through December the two sides stubbornly resisted compromise, each claiming the right to name all the ministers and all the legislators allotted to the MDR in the peace agreement. Eventually the Hutu Power faction dropped its objections to having Faustin Twagiramungu, nominally the party's president, serve as prime minister in the BBTG. He was, after all, named to the position in the peace agreement. In exchange, however, this faction insisted on naming all three MDR ministers, a proposal the Twagiramungu faction rejected. This impasse was not resolved by the end of December, the revised target date for installing the transitional institutions.

The two PL factions were also unable to agree on common candidate lists. The faction headed by the PL's Tutsi vice president, Landoald Ndasingwa, organized elections to determine who would fill the three ministerial positions and eleven legislative seats assigned to the PL in the peace agreement. The Hutu Power side, headed by the PL's Hutu president Justin Mugenzi, rejected these election results. As in the case of the MDR, mediators came forward to encourage the two sides to agree on a common list of candidates. One mediation group consisted of representatives of the other parties. Diplomats, including Ambassador Flaten, again urged compromise. Even the RPF pressed for agreement, possibly seeing an advantage to a political party that included both Hutu and Tutsi. But no formula was acceptable to all party members. Like the MDR, the PL could not come up with one common list of party representatives by the end of December.

This haggling within the MDR and the PL preoccupied the politicians, as well as diplomats and the clergy, throughout the fall of 1993. The diplomatic community and the political elite recognized that these party splits posed a serious threat to implementation of the peace accord. Some believed President Habyarimana was manipulating the MDR and the PL so that the final participant lists would enhance his chances of controlling a blocking one-third plus one in both transitional bodies. At one point MDR leader Twagiramungu even called for the president to stop his meddling so the parties could resolve their differences.

Contributing to this prolonged political stalemate was an event in neighboring Burundi that sent shock waves throughout Rwanda. On October 21, 1993, Burundi's Tutsi-dominated military assassinated Melchior Ndadaye, the country's first Hutu president, who had been elected the previous June. Hutu Power adherents hardened even more their attitudes against power sharing: there could be no compromise with their adversaries.[14] This assassination only reinforced Hutu fears about Tutsi intentions in Rwanda. The Hutu Power movement again gained momentum and increased in popularity.

Within days of the assassination in Burundi, a Hutu Power rally in Kigali drew hundreds of participants from a large cross-section of political parties. The MDR vice president Frodouald Karamira, from the anti-Twagiramungu faction, addressed the crowd, railing against MDR members who opposed Hutu solidarity.[15] He specifically denounced Prime Minister–Designate Twagiramungu, Prime Minister Uwilingiyimana, and Foreign Minister Gasana. Karamira referred to them as *inyenzi*, or cockroaches, using a pejorative that implied they sympathized with or were puppets of the Tutsi-led RPF. Any Hutu working against Hutu solidarity, Karamira emphasized, was "the enemy," a term still regularly used to refer to Tutsi and the RPF even after the peace accord was signed.

With UNAMIR claiming it was ready for the installation of the transitional cabinet and national assembly, it was these political-party schisms that effectively prevented formation of the transitional institutions by the end of December 1993.

The Rwandan Military Prepares

The peace accord protocols on integration of the government and RPF militaries called for the formation of a joint army high command and the disengagement, demobilization, and retraining of the troops. This was to occur after the NIF was in place and following installation of the transitional institutions. The two sides began planning for this military integration not long after the peace agreement was signed. By the end of September members of the future high command had already met in the demilitarized zone to lay the groundwork. At that meeting they agreed, for example, on the number of troops that would gather at their respective assembly points: five hundred at each assembly point for the RPF and two thousand for the government. They also discussed retraining for the integrated force; the government wanted trainers from Canada and France, while the RPF wanted trainers from Belgium and Tanzania.

By November joint military commissions were holding regular meetings in the DMZ. One commission focused on military discipline and training; this group prepared the content of the training program that had been outlined at Arusha. Another commission addressed the issue of demobilization; its principal task was to come up with lists of persons who would remain in the integrated army and those who would be demobilized.

These joint meetings were not without their difficulties. Whenever one side was annoyed about something the other side had said or done, it would boycott the meetings. If the RPF boycotted, this could mean a lost day for the government, as it usually took a couple of hours to travel from Kigali to the meeting point; the government representatives would arrive only to discover that the RPF was not planning to show up that day.

By the end of December the UN force was sufficiently deployed for the two sides to contemplate the next step: installation of the transitional institutions. However, before this could take place, an RPF battalion would come to Kigali, as agreed in the peace accord, to provide security for the RPF civilians tapped to participate in the transitional institutions. The RPF said, however, that its troops and civilians would come to Kigali only after the French troops withdrew, as called for in the Arusha Accords. This provision required all French forces, except those in Rwanda under a bilateral agreement, to withdraw from Rwanda as soon as the NIF was in place. These French troops, about three hundred strong, in Rwanda to protect the French citizens and others in the international community, withdrew in mid-December, in anticipation of the imminent arrival of the RPF battalion and the installation of the transitional institutions.

Preparing to Implement the Accords

On December 28 an RPF battalion of six hundred troops escorted to Kigali from the RPF-occupied zone at the Uganda frontier the contingent of high-level RPF civilians named to participate in the BBTG, the TNA, and the military High Command. The road into town from Byumba was lined with silent onlookers as the RPF convoy slowly plied the last few miles along the Kigali hilltops from the airport to the multistory building commanding the best view of the city, where the RPF was to make its Kigali headquarters. Everyone anticipated that the transitional institutions would be installed before the end of the year, as UNAMIR had announced.

International Organizations Prepare

During the fall of 1993 international organizations and agencies devoted considerable time and energy preparing for the implementation of the Arusha Accords. The various United Nations organizations waded into the complex Rwandan situation with enthusiasm and optimism.

The United Nations Development Program took on the mammoth task of preparing for the demobilization of the two armies. While the government and the RPF were identifying which troops to drop from the ranks of their armed forces, UNDP was examining what to do with those no longer in the military. The challenge was to work out a way to reintegrate an estimated fifty thousand ex-soldiers, both government and RPF, into Rwandan society. The U.S. ambassador, recalling the education program for U.S. soldiers following World War II, advocated educational initiatives. USAID was exploring how its funds could be used to strengthen vocational training and the informal education sector to accommodate as many demobilized soldiers as possible.

The United Nations Development Program sent an experienced consultant, Thomas Paquette, to Rwanda to pull together the broad outlines of the demobilization program. He briefed me on his progress in early October. Paquette set up a coordinating committee consisting of the Office of the Prime Minister, the Ministry of Planning, and the Ministry of Defense. He also met with government military commanders. As a guiding principle, Paquette said, demobilized soldiers, whether government or RPF, would have access to programs similar to those available to returning refugees, the resettling displaced persons, and the local population. Most of the integration would occur through local development programs and would be based on current development projects and their absorptive capacity.

The demobilization program would have several components, according to Paquette: a general information program, not only for the persons to be demobilized but also for the general public; a program of practical job training, beginning while those to be demobilized were still in the military holding centers for the disengaged forces; an income-generation component, which would have both credit mechanisms and microenterprise possibilities; and an education component involving vocational training, regular secondary school, and university options. An estimated thirty-one thousand demobilized soldiers were expected to opt for educational opportunities.

Paquette was concerned about how the rather large sums of money promised to the demobilized soldiers in the Arusha Accords would be distributed to them. He had strongly advised the military to make the payments in anything but cash, instead proposing in-kind payments or vouchers for such things such as domestic goods, construction materials, and credit for training, business start-ups, and housing. The money, he said, should pay for goods and services that would contribute to reconstruction, not offer discretionary spending opportunities to the recipients. We at the U.S. Embassy shared his concern about the sums of money involved and supported his proposal to work out a voucher system. We were not in a position to commit funds, however, before extensive discussions with Washington.

The United Nations Office of the High Commissioner for Refugees was also gearing up to implement the Arusha Accords. Its task was to develop a plan of action for the refugees who opted for voluntary return to Rwanda. This plan, UNHCR Representative Carlos Rodriguez told me, would be ready by mid-January. It would include a strategy for sensitizing Rwandans, particularly the majority Hutu, to the return of their compatriots, who were primarily Tutsi. This was to be done in two phases. The first phase, or sensitization phase, was to be conducted by the British NGO Oxfam, which already had a program in Rwanda focused on reconciliation between Hutu and

Tutsi, so it was well placed to take on this responsibility. The second phase would be a campaign in the countryside to involve local government leaders and institutions, such as churches and NGOs, in refugee reintegration.

UNHCR, however, was distracted from these activities by refugee emergencies that impacted Rwanda in the months before and after the August signing of the peace accord. Before the June elections in Burundi, UNHCR was preoccupied with facilitating the repatriation of Burundian Hutu who had sought refuge in Rwanda and wanted to return to vote. Many anticipated that the elections would herald a new era of peace and security for Rwanda's neighbor. After the elections, still more Hutu returned to Burundi, expressing their confidence in the future under a Hutu president.

This hope was short-lived, however. After the October 21, 1993, assassination of Burundi's newly elected Hutu president by Tutsi soldiers, Burundian Hutu fled by the tens of thousands to Rwanda. An estimated 375,000 sought refuge in southern Rwanda to escape a new wave of Tutsi violence and Hutu reprisals that followed the assassination. UNHCR was the lead agency organizing humanitarian assistance inside Rwanda. NGOs and UN agencies already in Rwanda providing humanitarian assistance to the war-displaced in northern Rwanda opened their warehouses to provide immediate emergency food and nonfood relief for the new influx of refugees.[16]

The International Committee of the Red Cross had new demands on its resources in the aftermath of the Arusha settlement as well. Charged with monitoring compliance with the Geneva Conventions on the laws of war, the ICRC organized prisoner exchanges between the government and the RPF. On August 20 it returned three government-held RPF soldiers to the RPF headquarters at Mulindi and twelve government soldiers from Mulindi to Kigali. The ICRC was also involved in organizing food for those returning from displaced-persons camps just outside Kigali to their homes in the DMZ. By one estimate, 500,000 Rwandans had returned to the DMZ, despite the fact that it was heavily mined and that their homes were situated between the two armies. The ICRC established six distribution points where these persons could obtain cooking oil and corn flour. Despite these massive returns to the DMZ, over 300,000 internally displaced Rwandan Hutu remained under ICRC care in makeshift camps on the northern edge of Kigali.

The United States Prepares

During the fall of 1993 the diplomatic community in Kigali was energetically engaged in preparing for implementation of the Arusha Accords. A steady stream of official visitors from the United States kept me busy. The State Department desk officer for Rwanda and Burundi, the Africa watcher at the U.S. Embassy in Paris, representatives of the National Democratic Institute, an assessment team from the Peace Corps, and the military advisor to the Africa Bureau of the State Department came to assess and plan for post-Arusha Rwanda. It was my job to organize their visits, accompany most on their appointments with Rwandan officials or civil society groups, and host luncheons or receptions to enhance their interaction with Rwandans. All the visitors expressed optimism for a successful, though not easy, implementation of the Arusha Peace Accords and transition to a multiparty democracy.

Democracy Building Continues

The U.S. Embassy continued activities aimed at strengthening pro-democratic groups for their roles in Rwanda's post-Arusha democratic process. The ambassador's efforts to broker compromises among and within the increasingly dysfunctional political parties was but one example of this.

In September 1993 the United States Information Service sponsored a training seminar for journalists. The theme was the detection and prevention of conflict. Participants included both government and independent journalists. In one session, journalists examined the extent to which the Rwandan media had covered issues that had contributed to the struggle between the RPF and the government. One speaker, Gaspard Karemera, editor of the monthly journal *Imbaga*, noted that the print media had not done a good job of covering the root causes of the war. He cited an instance in 1990 when President Habyarimana had met with President Museveni of Uganda. The media had reported the leaders' concern about security issues, Karemera said, but had failed to focus on the urgency

Preparing to Implement the Accords

of finding a solution to the question of refugee return. The seminar encouraged participants to think in terms of responsible, investigative reporting.

Representatives of the National Democratic Institute visited Rwanda to explore programming possibilities with the political parties. Launched just a decade earlier, NDI generally focused its projects on skills training to help party leaders strengthen their organizations. Such skills usually included communication techniques and information-dissemination strategies. To emphasize NDI's nongovernmental and nonpartisan status, these visitors met leaders of the political parties without embassy officers present to discuss the kind of training NDI might provide. Party leaders, however, flatly rejected their offer of help. They claimed they had sufficient knowledge about basic party-building skills and said they would hone these skills with practice as they actually developed their parties. They did not want to take time out of their pressing work to participate in training activities.

The visitors from the National Democratic Institute briefed the ambassador and me on this outcome. But the ambassador did not want to let them or the political parties off the hook so easily. He proposed that NDI develop a new training program aimed at fostering cooperation skills among political party members tapped to participate in the post-Arusha transitional government and legislature. The visitors hesitated, arguing that the ambassador's proposal was closer to a conflict-resolution program than to their usual kind of training and technical information. They did agree to study whether NDI could tackle these new areas of consensus building and governance. As it turned out, NDI expanded its training repertoire after 1993 to include encouraging citizen participation in the political process, strengthening civic organizations, and promoting accountability in government. After the genocide it did finally mount a project in Rwanda to train political party youth in leadership skills.

Since mid-1992 USAID had been developing a sweeping democracy project for Rwanda. Its aim was to expand understanding of the democratic process within various segments of Rwandan society and to strengthen the role of individual citizens and groups within each segment. I was involved from the inception of the project in thinking through with USAID officers what institutions and elements of democracy it might tackle. A group of experts in several critical democracy-building fields came to Rwanda to assess how USAID might best target its democracy project. What resulted from our discussions and the consulting group's recommendations was a five-year, $5 million Democracy in Governance project, the largest democracy project in USAID's experience up to that time. This project was just coming on line in the autumn of 1993. A project director arrived in Kigali at the beginning of October to start on-site planning, identify office space, hire a staff, and flesh out the four components of the program.

The project, as conceptualized, targeted four critical elements in the democratic process: the media, the legislature, local government, and civil society. The media component would establish a training center to facilitate expansion of media outlets, especially radio. It would promote the formation of a single journalism association comprising both government and independent journalists, in contrast to the two existing rival groups, one for government and one for private media participants. The project hoped eventually to provide start-up journalistic enterprises access to printing presses and broadcast equipment.

A second component focused on strengthening the legislature. Rwanda's pre-Arusha assembly functioned primarily as a rubber stamp for initiatives of the president and the MRND party. The USAID project would provide training for legislators, computerize the Transitional National Assembly, train assembly staff, and help develop a library for the legislative body. A third component focused on decentralization to help shift authority and resources from Kigali officials to those in various localities. A fourth component was designed to strengthen civil society by supporting and strengthening the skills of political parties and policy advocacy groups.

After the RPF participants in the transitional institutions came to town, the USAID project leaders discussed extensively with both sides how RPF representatives could be integrated into the project's training programs side by side with government participants. RPF members tapped to participate in the TNA were particularly keen to begin as soon as possible to learn all they could about how a legislature worked and what their role would be.

Democracy and the Military

A project of particular interest to the U.S. Embassy was a joint government-RPF military seminar that took place in January 1994, just weeks after the RPF security battalion arrived in Kigali. This three-day event brought together key leaders of both militaries to examine the role of the military in a democracy and the relationship between the military and civilians. It was funded under what was called Expanded IMET, a part of the U.S. Department of Defense's International Military Education Training program that aimed specifically at introducing militaries to democratic concepts and their role in a democratic political system.

The U.S. agency that implemented the program, the Naval School of Justice in Providence, Rhode Island, had sent representatives to Rwanda about a year earlier to determine what subject matter would be appropriate for such a delicate initial meeting between officers of the two sides. At that time the planners talked with government and military officials, as well as with politicians, about the program. After the signing of the peace agreement, a group of four Rwandans went to Rhode Island to help finalize the seminar's curriculum. One of these four represented the RPF, beginning the cross-fertilization that we believed was so important.

The weeklong seminar itself, held at Rwanda's Military Academy, the École Supérieur Militaire in Kigali, was a resounding success. It brought together about twenty members of the government military with about twenty members of the RPF military. I had a chance to observe most of the seminar activities. Vibrant exchanges characterized the classroom sessions. Luncheon discussions were animated. A reception I hosted at my residence on the first evening of the seminar saw the two sides in easy discussion with each other. Of course, there was not complete agreement between the two sides, but they were cordial and respectful of one another throughout. The embassy was proud of this experiment in reconciliation. We believed its success boded well for the future, despite the delays on the political side of the implementation ledger.

In addition to the embassy's democracy-building activities, we were also exploring possibilities for reinstating the Peace Corps in Rwanda. The Peace Corps volunteers and U.S. staff that had been serving in Rwanda had been evacuated because of the serious deterioration in security after the RPF attack of February 1993. Since then I had served as acting Peace Corps director, charged with keeping the office open and the local employees productively engaged in maintenance activities. Now, with a peace agreement signed and the installation of a new power-sharing government apparently just around the corner, the Peace Corps was interested in starting up again.

Peace Corps headquarters in Washington sent two people to Rwanda to assess the current security situation and to determine what sorts of programs might be possible. They looked primarily at the health, education, and agricultural sectors for potential placement opportunities for volunteers. In health, they envisioned doing something to help nutritionists address the enormous malnutrition problem, particularly in the DMZ, where returning displaced persons faced a food shortage because they had not planted crops that year. They also saw opportunities in HIV/AIDS prevention, placing volunteers with workers involved in testing, counseling, or information dissemination.

In education, the Peace Corps looked at both the formal and informal sectors. In the formal sector there was a continuing need for teachers in math, science, and English. In the informal sector the Peace Corps considered involvement in the anticipated training centers that would serve demobilized soldiers. There might also be possibilities, the reconnaissance team thought, in fish farming using ponds abandoned since the Belgian colonial period.

Key to whether the Peace Corps could resume its mission in Rwanda would be the security situation. Peace Corps headquarters sent a resident director to Rwanda early in 1994 whose job was to continue to assess the security environment while laying the groundwork for the arrival of new volunteers. They were considering sending about thirty volunteers in mid-1994 and hoped to find persons with experience working in the region, perhaps third-year volunteers from Burundi or even some who had previously served in Rwanda.

However, it would be fifteen years before the Peace Corps returned to Rwanda. On April 15, 2009, the Peace Corps fielded thirty-two volunteers working in health and community development projects. The program continues today with nearly two hundred volunteers.

The U.S. Ambassador Departs Kigali

In the midst of all this activity, the American community was preparing for a change of leadership. Ambassador Robert Flaten, who had worked so diligently with the political parties to steer them toward cooperation and conflict resolution, left Rwanda on November 23, at the end of his three-year assignment. Before his departure the ambassador made a whirlwind round of calls on government ministers and was the guest of honor at numerous farewell dinners and receptions. There was even a state dinner held in his honor and a private invitation for him and his wife to join the president and his wife for drinks.[17]

A few days before his departure, Ambassador Flaten asked me to accompany him to his farewell call on Col. Alexis Kanyarengwe, the RPF chairman. I was excited. This would be my first visit to the RPF-occupied region and to the Mulindi tea plantation. And I had never met either Kanyarengwe or Commander Kagame, who would surely be on hand for the visit.

So on November 20 we headed north in the ambassador's armored white Chevrolet toward Katumba, the border crossing into Uganda. As we drove through the DMZ, I was impressed by the absence of villages as the road twisted its way up and down the hills. When we reached the RPF-controlled zone, two beat-up pickup trucks driven by RPF soldiers met us and escorted us to Mulindi.

Our small convoy continued on the main road almost to the Uganda border and then turned east, following ever-narrower roads among hills of eucalyptus trees and untended tea plants. At the plantation entrance we followed the access road up and around to the top of a hill, where we found a small collection of somewhat run-down buildings that had once housed plantation managers. From there we could look out over neglected rows of tea plants and across the endless hills and valleys. The RPF had appropriated this property in 1992, after the owner had fled the fighting.

We were greeted by Kanyarengwe, a Hutu, and Kagame, a Tutsi. Several military and political colleagues were with them. Following introductions all around, the ambassador and I were led inside one of the apparently empty houses. The front room was small and bare except for a rough-hewn wooden table, set for ten or so diners, and straight-backed, wooden chairs for each of us. There Chairman Kanyarengwe hosted us for lunch and conversation. Several of the RPF members who joined us had been delegates at the Arusha peace talks when I was there as U.S. observer.

The tone of the visit was cordial and collegial. Rapport with the RPF leaders was easy. My former Arusha colleagues were friendly. Over lunch they talked about their imminent move to Kigali once the United Nations forces were in place. They denied any part in the multiple killings that had taken place a few weeks earlier in four communes around Ruhengeri. Instead they laid the blame squarely on the president and the MRND. They insisted they were committed to implementing the peace process despite such setbacks and expressed guarded optimism for Rwanda's future.

I came away with the impression that the RPF wanted to implement the Arusha Peace Accords and was committed to making the peace process work for them and for the country. This impression was reinforced a few weeks later when I accompanied Lt. Col. Tony Marley, the State Department's visiting political-military officer in the Africa Bureau, on the first of his two visits to Mulindi. After nearly three weeks in Rwanda and two extensive meetings in Mulindi with RPF leaders, Marley's assessment echoed my own.[18]

Comment

Although ordinary Rwandans had little confidence that the Arusha Accords would actually result in peace, the diplomatic community continued to believe that the agreement, if implemented, would provide Rwandans an institutional framework for building a more inclusive, more participatory future for their country. We supported preparations for implementation and were committed to continue

Preparing to Implement the Accords

supporting the process even if stumbling blocks occurred along the way. But I, at least, never anticipated that the situation would unravel as totally as it did.[19]

Divisions within the political parties threw implementation of the Arusha Accords into confusion. If the guiding principle of the Rwandan peace process was power sharing, the political parties were the pillars that were to support this principle. Representation in the transitional institutions depended on cohesive parties, each providing a single list of its nominees. The Arusha power-sharing arrangements had not anticipated divisions such as those in the MDR and PL and could not accommodate them. The party splits jeopardized the careful balance of political forces struck at the negotiating table and put implementation of the Accords at risk.

It seems clear now that the party ruptures were the result of behind-the-scenes manipulation, most probably initiated by the president to maximize his chances of controlling the political process during the transition period. He remained committed, it seems, to hanging on to power by using the political process so favored by the international community.

[17]

Violence Plagues Implementation

While many Rwandans and the international community were gearing up for implementation of the Arusha Peace Accords, others were stirring up fear and insecurity to ensure it would never happen. Continuing violence and human rights abuses formed the backdrop to the flourish of activity undertaken in anticipation of implementing the Accords. The signed peace agreement had not stilled Rwanda's pervasive random and targeted violence. Assassinations, bombs, grenades, and land mines continued to instill fear among the population and threaten stability in the country. A new private radio station used its platform to promote Hutu solidarity, undermine the peace accord, malign advocates of human rights and democracy, denigrate all Tutsi, including the RPF, and discredit the UN peacekeeping force. The assassination of the first elected Hutu president in Burundi reinforced the hard-line Hutu position in Rwanda that the Arusha peace agreement, with its power-sharing provisions, was an unacceptable basis for Rwanda's future.

UN Human Rights Rapporteur Reports Possible Genocide

On August 11, 1993, just one week after the Arusha Accords had been signed, the United Nations released the report on the March mission to Rwanda of Bacre Waly Ndiaye, the special rapporteur on extrajudicial, summary, or arbitrary executions.[1]

His findings echoed those of the International Commission of

Investigation that had visited Rwanda in January. Ndiaye concluded that civilian massacres, death threats, and political assassinations had indeed occurred in Rwanda, and he named several government and government-linked groups as responsible for these violations. He named as human rights violators the Rwandan Armed Forces, local officials, other agents of the state, political party militias, clandestine organizations, and private individuals. While acknowledging that the war complicated the picture, the special rapporteur asserted that these human rights violations resulted from other factors that should have been within the government's power to control. He cited specifically the absence of the rule of law, a deficient judicial system, a tradition of impunity, and the failure to protect minorities. Ndiaye also presented evidence confirming, he said, that the RPF too was responsible for committing human rights abuses.

Ndiaye recommended that the government of Rwanda make improvements in a broad range of areas. He placed high priority on setting up a mechanism for protecting civilian populations from massacres, dismantling violent organizations, and supporting local human rights groups. He called for judicial reform, including an end to impunity, arbitrary arrests, and detentions. He urged reform and restructuring of the media and encouraged creation of a national reconciliation campaign to accompany postwar reintegration of demobilized soldiers, displaced persons, and refugees. He called for the government to issue new identity cards without ethnicity indications and recommended that the president do more to hold accountable those responsible for human rights abuses. He balanced these recommendations with a proposal for an independent investigation into abuses by the RPF.

Like the International Commission of Investigation, Special Rapporteur Ndiaye raised the issue of genocide in his report. And like the Commission, he too declined to judge whether the massacres constituted genocide. Nevertheless, he did assert that events described in his report—the killing of Tutsi because of their ethnicity alone and the abuses of the right to life—fell within the purview of Articles II and III of the UN 1948 genocide convention, to which Rwanda had acceded in 1975. This was the closest anyone had yet come to say-ing genocide was occurring in Rwanda well before the mass atrocities of April 1994 began.

Unfortunately, Ndiaye's important message about the possibility of genocide in Rwanda was virtually lost because his report was neither publicized nor widely circulated. The UN issued no press release and made no public statements. Only those who knew the report existed were likely to request a copy from the UN. In 1993 there was no internet to publicize the document or to make it readily available to interested parties.

As a result, the report received little attention from either the international community or the government of Rwanda. I did not see it until long after I had left Rwanda. This document, with its specific recommendations for holding the government of Rwanda accountable for serious human rights lapses, might have been useful to the diplomatic community. In December 1993, when Ndiaye delivered his annual report to the United Nations Economic and Social Council, he noted that the Rwandan authorities had not yet responded to his recommendations, even though he had provided the report to President Habyarimana in August.[2]

Killings Heighten Insecurity, Test UN Force

In August, just two weeks after the peace pact had been signed in Arusha, a communal leader named Fidel Rambuka, who had played a negative role in the March 1992 Bugesera massacres, was himself killed on his home turf. Not long after, an ICRC vehicle delivering humanitarian relief supplies to displaced persons returning to the DMZ in the north ran over a land mine, killing the driver. A grenade explosion in the yard of his own home injured Alphonse-Marie Nkubito, the attorney general of Kigali and founder of Rwanda's first human rights organization, ARDHO.[3] Nkubito and ARDHO representatives based in various towns around the country had periodically received death threats from the Interahamwe militia of the MRND. Further, within a week of the November 17 UN flag-raising over UNAMIR headquarters in Kigali, at least seventy people were brutally killed, including several children. No individuals or groups were ever identified or punished for any of these killings.

The positive publicity General Dallaire had hoped would follow the flag-raising was overshadowed that same night by simultaneous attacks in four communes near the northern town of Ruhengeri.[4] Of the thirty-five victims, some were members of the president's MRND party, some came from the more extremist CDR party, and others were apparently random victims. The assailants were never identified. One site was very close to a UNAMIR monitoring post.

Curiously, the government radio station announced these killings early the following morning, naming not only the four communes affected but also all thirty-five victims, even though the attacks had occurred in remote, widely dispersed areas only the night before. Government authorities and the media immediately blamed the RPF for the attacks. They cited as proof the deaths of members of the MRND and CDR. Rwandans and diplomats alike wondered how the journalists or their local sources could have gathered this information so quickly. Many suspected possible government or hardline political party involvement.

UNAMIR investigated these attacks but never made any findings public. Colonel Tikoca, who led the UNAMIR investigation, told me that the attacks had been brutal, that the attackers had behaved "like animals." He did not hint, though, at which side he thought might have been responsible. Indeed General Dallaire called the outcome "inconclusive." He subsequently set up a joint government-RPF commission of inquiry, but it never reached a conclusion.[5]

In the absence of a definitive UN conclusion, both the government and the RPF blamed each other for these heinous killings. Both used the incident to accuse the other of being insincere about wanting peace. The doubt each side nourished about the other's intentions heightened anxiety and fear among all Rwandans. A new, private, right-wing radio station began a campaign to undermine and discredit the UN and its peacekeeping force. The station frequently questioned UNAMIR's credibility and sowed doubt about its ability to protect Rwandans.

The thirty-five people who died in these attacks accounted for about half of the people killed in the first seven to ten days after the UN force formally launched its peacekeeping mission. On November 24, the day after the UN's special representative Jacques-Roger Booh-Booh arrived, unknown assailants killed several Hutu in a village in the president's stronghold of northwestern Rwanda. Shortly thereafter UNAMIR soldiers found that six children who had been reported missing had been brutally murdered; a seventh died later.[6] In another incident, a booby-trapped 100-franc note, left lying on the ground, killed six children when one of them picked it up on their way to school. No perpetrator was ever found.

A New Radio Station Encourages Violence

Another kind of violence was being played out in the media. Rwanda's only privately financed radio station, Free Radio and Television of the Thousand Hills (Radio Télévision Libre des Mille Collines; RTLM), started operating in August 1993. Although the station initially attracted a large following with its popular music shows, it gained a reputation as the voice of the extreme right-wing, Hutu-supremacist CDR party, broadcasting extremist views and calling for unsavory actions. This reflected the views of its founders and its financial backers. One of those founders, Ferdinand Nahimana, had returned to his university professorship after the coalition government replaced him as head of Radio Rwanda because of his extreme views. Another, Jean-Bosco Barayagwiza, the ostracized former director of political affairs at the Ministry of Foreign Affairs, was a key ideologue of the extremist CDR party. RTLM's forte was naming people it considered "enemies of the state" and calling for action against them.

In late November 1993 RTLM called for the assassination of Prime Minister Agathe Uwilingiyimana and Prime Minister–Designate Faustin Twagiramungu. This came on the heels of a CDR press release insisting the president and prime minister retaliate or be considered "accomplices of the RPF" following the November 18 killings of thirty-five Hutu near Ruhengeri.[7]

Human rights advocates told me they were cited on RTLM as persons to be eliminated. This kind of hate propaganda, coming across the radio airwaves to which almost all Rwandans had access, greatly influenced the thinking of many Rwandans. Many listeners must have believed that government leaders sanctioned such killings.

As chargé d'affaires after Ambassador Flaten departed Kigali, I called on the president's chief of staff, Enoch Ruhigira, to express concern about RTLM's advocacy of violence and its labeling spe-

Violence Plagues Implementation

cific people "traitors" who should be killed. I had hoped Ruhigira would at least agree to look into what could be done to rein in RTLM announcers and journalists. Instead he blithely answered that the privately owned station was independent of the government; given the constitutional protection of freedom of speech, there was nothing he or the government could do about it. He did not seem concerned over the station's blatant calls for listeners to take violent action. He claimed that the station's founders and financiers had nothing to do with the government. It was common knowledge at the time, however, that a prominent businessman, Félicien Kabuga, whose daughter was married to the president's son, was a key financial backer of the station, and some ministers, highly placed civil servants, leaders of hard-line and extremist political parties, and relatives of the president were among those believed to hold shares in the venture.

Soon after the new U.S. ambassador, David Rawson, arrived in Kigali in January 1994, I invited him to meet Rwanda's key human rights activists at a luncheon at my house. I wanted him to hear their take on the current rights situation in Rwanda. Several cited instances in which RTLM had labeled them traitors and called for them to be killed. Sitting on my veranda looking out over my lush garden on a warm, sunny day, these human rights proponents may have felt a strong enough sense of security to laugh when they described the bounty RTLM had placed on their heads. Or perhaps their laughter reflected apprehension that a radio broadcast might really inspire listeners to violent action against them.

Assassination in Burundi

The event that had arguably the greatest impact on Rwanda between the August signing of the Arusha Accords and the end of 1993 occurred not in Rwanda but in neighboring Burundi. It was the overthrow and assassination of Burundi's recently elected Hutu president, Melchior Ndadaye, by the predominantly Tutsi army on October 21, 1993. This catastrophe had two major consequences for Rwanda.

The first consequence was humanitarian. Refugees, mainly Hutu, fearing a violent aftermath, spilled into Rwanda by the hundreds of thousands. Within a few weeks UNHCR was working with a planning figure of 375,000 persons displaced. Many settled just inside

Rwanda's southeast border with Burundi, not far from the southern university town of Butare. Others arrived in Bugesera, the region south of Kigali that had experienced Hutu massacres of Tutsi eighteen months earlier, in 1992.

The international community mobilized humanitarian relief in response to this sudden influx of refugees. Nongovernmental organizations, in Rwanda to aid the internally displaced in the north, refocused their attention on the new refugee camps that had sprung up in the south. New emergency relief supplies and food poured into the country. The U.S. government declared a humanitarian emergency and provided $25,000 to CARE International for the purpose of installing water sources in the numerous refugee camps.

The second consequence of the assassination of Burundi's first Hutu president was political. This killing convinced the proponents of Hutu Power that their opposition to power sharing was justified: the Tutsi could not be trusted, so power sharing would not work. These attitudes exacerbated the already evident splits in the MDR and PL. Internal compromise over those parties' slates of candidates for transitional government and legislative positions became even more difficult. The Hutu solidarity movement that first gained momentum following the RPF's February 1993 offensive got its second big push with the assassination of President Ndadaye. An ever-growing cadre of adherents to Hutu Power subscribed to the view that the Tutsi-led RPF and its so-called Tutsi accomplices inside Rwanda as well as any Hutu who opposed Hutu Power constituted the enemy. This attitude undermined the Arusha Accords and their core principle of power sharing between the Hutu majority and the Tutsi minority. It also jeopardized any serious chance of implementing the Accords that had as their foundation continuing political party unity.

Government hard-liners seized this opportunity to try to convince the diplomatic community that their open and strident distrust of the Tutsi was justified. The minister of defense found a way to bring home the horror to the diplomats: he invited each embassy to send a representative to join him on a helicopter inspection of Rwanda's rivers, where bloated bodies had floated in on the weak current from Burundi. I expected my counterparts from other Western embassies to participate, but when the appointed day came, I was the only one who turned up. I didn't like the idea of a helicopter ride any more than I liked the idea of viewing dead bodies; however, I thought a U.S. representative should verify the government claims of the extent of the killing in Burundi.

Once aloft I tried to hide my fear of heights as I thought about my vulnerability to harm or injury. I managed to look down as the helicopter swooped in for a closer look at the burden the rivers carried. There was no denying that partially clothed, bloated bodies clogged many of the small rivers and streams meandering from Burundi through Rwanda's countryside en route to Lake Victoria and Uganda farther north. No trees obscured my view either of the dead or the contrasting beauty of the sunny day, the deep blue sky, and the magnificent Rwandan countryside.

Comment

The ugly acts of terror and the subsequent mutual recriminations of responsibility that followed the start of UN operations in Rwanda created fertile ground for an escalation in the tone and volume of the Hutu solidarity campaign against the RPF. And there was a companion message: that the UN force was incapable of protecting Rwandans from the ever-present violence. Regardless of which side was actually responsible for these egregious killings, UNAMIR was the big loser as popular confidence in the UNAMIR operation was seriously undermined. The new private radio station, RTLM, repeatedly called into question its credibility as a force for security. Some wondered whether the intention of this otherwise senseless carnage was to discredit the RPF while testing the response of UNAMIR.

After the October assassination of the president of Burundi, the radio station's anti-Tutsi message and its efforts to undermine the United Nations peacekeeping mission became even more vigorous. RTLM denunciations were spearheaded by ideologues from the extremist CDR party and protected by its MRND benefactors and Rwanda's constitutional guarantee of free speech. RTLM had no trouble painting the moderates it discredited with the brush of "RPF sympathizers" and then labeling them traitors to the cause of Hutu solidarity.

Hutu solidarity became the glue forging a new anti-RPF political alliance among the MRND, the CDR extremists, and those Hutu in opposition parties who rejected power sharing with the Tutsi. This raised the risk for moderate politicians who continued to support power sharing, as well as for democracy advocates, UNAMIR leaders, and the Belgian troops who patrolled Kigali daily. Political space for moderates was steadily disappearing as Hutu Power gained momentum.

I was never convinced by accusations of RPF responsibility for the unexplained violence around Ruhengeri just after the UN raised its flag in Kigali. It was difficult for me to understand what the RPF could gain from committing such carnage. Why would the RPF want to lend credence to its detractors just when it was on the brink of solidifying a substantial role in governance in Rwanda? But the converse explanation was just as difficult to comprehend: Could the hard-line militia or government soldiers actually have killed their own followers in order to blame the RPF and win more converts to Hutu Power and the Hutu-solidarity movement?

It seems reasonable, particularly in hindsight, to suspect that the killings and the intensified anti-Tutsi media campaign, around the time the UN force began operating in Rwanda, aimed to test UNAMIR's response to clear transgressions of the peace accord. Impunity shielded the perpetrators. By the end of the year, General Dallaire's high hopes for the UNAMIR mission began to fade. These adverse events spurred the diplomatic corps in Kigali to redouble its advocacy for speedy implementation of the Arusha Accords as a way to calm the escalating tensions and violence and set Rwanda on a new path. The United States maintained its commitment to democratization and the peace process despite the security challenges.

[18]

Implementation Stalls

December 1993 came and went without the installation of the transitional institutions. Months of wrangling had not resolved who would represent the divided opposition political parties, the MDR and PL, in the transitional government and national assembly. And the delay had opened the way for more violence and unruly demonstrations.

Representatives of the various party factions called at the U.S. Embassy to present their respective points of view. As chargé d'affaires after the ambassador's departure in late November, I received them. Although I encouraged both factions of these two important opposition parties to find compromises with their rivals, their respective positions were far apart. Each side was dug in.

The Tutsi side of the PL described efforts to bring the two sides of its party together but acknowledged they were going nowhere. The MDR too was still wrestling with its schism. Former prime minister Dismas Nsengiyaremye told me his large, dissident wing of the MDR had proposed a deal to Faustin Twagiramungu, who headed the smaller MDR faction but still claimed to be president of the party. Nsengiyaremye said that if Twagiramungu wanted to retain his claim to the position of prime minister–designate in the transitional government, the party's three designated ministerial positions would have to be filled with MDR Hutu Power adherents. This arrangement would give the MDR three votes likely to side with the hard-line Hutu supremacists and only one likely to vote with the RPF. Twagiramungu rejected this proposal.

Meanwhile President Habyarimana, responsible for swearing in the new officials, refused to accept competing lists for ministers and assembly members from the parties. Instead he insisted on their reaching compromises and providing him a single, consensus party list.

Diplomats Press: End Delays, Implement Arusha

When the December 31 deadline set by the prime minister for installing the transitional institutions passed and the stalemate persisted, the dean of the diplomatic corps, Vatican representative Monseigneur Giuseppe Bertello, became alarmed. On the morning of January 1, a Saturday following New Year's Eve, he convened a 9:15 meeting of the diplomatic corps at his residence. The issue for discussion was what the diplomats could do to encourage an end to the political deadlock. We decided that representative groups of diplomats would seek urgent appointments with the prime minister–designate, the president, and the chairman of the RPF. In this show of solidarity and unity, we would express our grave collective concern for the delays in implementing the Arusha Peace Accords and urge our interlocutors to do their utmost to see that the blockages were resolved.

That very afternoon I accompanied a group of Western members of the diplomatic corps to meet with Twagiramungu, who claimed to head the MDR but in fact controlled only the smaller of its two factions. He told our delegation that the president should have nothing to do with deciding who should be government ministers and legislative delegates in the transitional institutions. That decision, he said, referencing the peace accord, was between the prime minister–designate, namely himself, and the political parties. He outlined the anticipated cascade of investiture: first the president would be sworn in, then the members of the new national assembly, and, finally, the government ministers. Twagiramungu contended that the president was refusing to be sworn in—a move that, according to the peace agreement, would trigger the subsequent installations of transitional institution participants—because he wanted guarantees in advance that he would be able to control one-third plus one of the transitional assembly delegates (to avoid impeachment) and one-third plus one of the transitional government ministers (to block cabinet decisions).

Two days later, on Monday, January 3, I was among the members of the diplomatic corps who called on President Habyarimana. He assured us that he accepted the Arusha framework and that implementation would adhere to a strict interpretation of what had been agreed in Arusha. If there were a departure from the text of Arusha, he acknowledged, the parties would "keep going in circles." The president referred to a French radio broadcast that had accused him of blocking implementation by refusing to take the oath of office. He countered that he could take the oath right away, but that doing so would not resolve the impasses in the parties. "What can I do?" he lamented. Only the political parties themselves could end their differences.

The Vatican representative raised the issue of the government's distribution of weapons to civilians. Evading the implied charge of responsibility, the president asserted that arms had been distributed in the border areas when the RPF first invaded in 1990, but all those weapons had been retrieved. He closed the meeting by asking the international community for its help with the drought in Rwanda, the displaced persons, and the refugees. All the while he had a smile on his face. I felt as if I were in a time-warp. The president's request seemed so detached from the crisis of the moment. If this was an attempt to direct the attention of the diplomatic community to other concerns, he failed miserably; we were united and focused on only one issue: implementation of the Arusha Accords.

That afternoon the same group of diplomats called on the RPF chairman, Col. Alexis Kanyarengwe, at the RPF's Kigali headquarters. Kanyarengwe, a Hutu and once a close ally of Habyarimana, had participated in a failed coup attempt in 1980 and fled the country. He blamed the president for the implementation stalemate, noting that the peace accord had deprived Habyarimana of a blocking one-third, preventing him from continuing to monopolize power. He claimed that the president had provoked the divisions within the parties so that his MRND party could secure a blocking one-third plus one. The RPF would not accept all power remaining in Habyarimana's hands. Only the head of the Constitutional Court, not the president, had the authority to accept or reject the lists for ministers or deputies. When asked, Kanyarengwe said he would meet with President Habyarimana, but not alone; in order to guarantee transparency the current and future prime ministers would have to be present.

This round of diplomacy allowed the diplomats to hear from the key players their perspectives on the deadlocked situation, but it did little to break the impasse. Over the next couple of days, these meetings continued with increased urgency. This time I joined a different group of diplomats for another meeting with Kanyarengwe and one with Special Representative of the Secretary General Booh-Booh. I met separately at the embassy with the PSD leader Félicien Gatabazi; PL Hutu Power representatives Justin Mugenzi and Agnes Ntamabyariro, ministers of commerce and justice, respectively; and with MDR leader Twagiramungu.

All these interlocutors wanted to share their perspective on the situation and explore possible ways to break the deadlock. I was astonished at the virulence of Mugenzi and Ntamabyariro against Tutsi in general and the Tutsi wing of their own PL in particular. Only months before, they had been collaborating closely with the Tutsi in their party. Now they were as anti-Tutsi as the MRND or even the radical, Hutu-supremacist CDR. I detected no movement from any of the party factions toward finding acceptable solutions to the stalemate.

If at First You Don't Succeed . . .

Wednesday, January 5, was set as the new date for the installation of the president and the Transitional National Assembly delegates. Everyone concerned filed into the auditorium of the national assembly building for the morning ceremony. Present were members of the Constitutional Court, Prime Minister Uwilingiyimana, Prime Minister–Designate Twagiramungu, Special Representative Booh-Booh, current and future national assembly deputies, current and future government ministers, some RPF soldiers, UNAMIR representatives, bishops, and the diplomatic corps.

Diplomats were directed to the first row of the balcony overlooking the main floor, where persons named to represent their parties in the Transitional National Assembly had already taken seats. After a long delay, President Habyarimana appeared on the stage below us. The president of the Constitutional Court, Joseph Kavaruganda, joined him and spoke to the audience in Kinyarwanda. Court members lined up on the stage and Kavaruganda administered the oath of office to Habyarimana in French, as prescribed in the Arusha Accords. The ceremony was over in five minutes. Juvénal Habyarimana had been sworn in as president of Rwanda for the twenty-two-month transitional period. One transitional official was in place. A measure of success at last!

That afternoon everyone reassembled for the installation of the Transitional National Assembly. We waited and we waited. Eventually the president walked ceremoniously onto the stage and announced that he could not proceed with the swearing-in because the head of the Supreme Court was not present. Furthermore, he explained, some of the persons scheduled to be sworn in were also absent. He did not elaborate.

Before dismissing the gathering, the president said he would swear in the TNA delegates as soon as the political parties had resolved their internal differences and were ready to present their agreed lists of legislators. He appealed to the international community for help so that the delegates and government ministers could be sworn in as soon as possible. After a few moments of stunned silence, then murmuring among ourselves, the diplomats rose and left the hall. Rwanda was now in the awkward constitutional situation of having one transitional institution—the president—in place and the others still in limbo. Those of us in the diplomatic community left scratching our heads.

We later learned that the RPF had boycotted the ceremony; none of its eleven designated TNA members were on hand for the occasion. Likewise the PSD's assembly candidates were absent. We found out later that Landoald Ndasingwa's Tutsi faction of the PL, considered pro-RPF, had been blocked from entering the hall by government security officers. This had left only Mugenzi's Hutu Power faction, the PL wing close to the president, in the hall and ready for its designated representatives to be sworn in.

The next day, January 6, Booh-Booh reported to the diplomats that the UN Security Council had met and decided on a resolution. It would express appreciation for the efforts of the UN in Rwanda and demand the assistance of the parties to establish the Broad-Based Transitional Government as soon as possible. The UNAMIR mandate would be extended, but its continuation would be contingent upon putting the transitional institutions in place. Later that day the Council passed the resolution with a new provision, adding one thousand troops to UNAMIR for its Phase II operations, even though Phase I—installation of the transitional institutions—was incomplete.

In the meeting between Booh-Booh and the diplomats, two avenues emerged as possible ways to break the impasse. One was for the diplomats to encourage a high-level meeting between Habyarimana and the RPF's Kanyarengwe. Another was to involve the Tanzanian facilitator, President Mwinyi or his representative, in negotiations with the two sides. The micro-level, intraparty disputes had become tugs-of-war at the macro level between Habyarimana and the RPF for control of the political institutions during the twenty-two-month transition. This became increasingly clear as the RPF moved toward closer collaboration with the Twagiramungu faction of the MDR and became increasingly influential with the Ndasingwa (Tutsi) faction of the PL.

A Political Quagmire Greets the New American Ambassador

David Rawson arrived in Kigali on January 6, the day after the president was sworn in. He and his wife, Sandy, were quickly immersed in meeting the American community. It did not take long, however, before the ambassador was drawn into the political quagmire surrounding the installation of Rwanda's transitional institutions. Prime Minister Agathe Uwilingiyimana set Saturday, January 8, as the next date for the swearing-in of the national assembly delegates and the government ministers. The president declined to participate on that date, however, on grounds that he already had engagements lined up. He did not specify what they were.

Ambassador Rawson had been in country scarcely fourteen hours when a phone call from the president's office invited him—or rather instructed him—to present his diplomatic credentials on Saturday morning, January 8. All ambassadors go through this formality after arriving in the country to which they are accredited. Once the head of state receives the ambassador's letters of credence, the diplomatic papers of introduction drawn up by the U.S. Department of State, the new diplomat can officially go about his or her ambassadorial duties. Holding this meeting on the second day in country, however, is highly unusual—doing it on a weekend, even more so. Sometimes days, even weeks pass before the arriving ambassador has an audience with the president.

The ambassador grasped the situation immediately: the president was using his credentials ceremony as an excuse to delay installation of the institutions. Ambassador Rawson called several top embassy contacts in the Rwandan government and the president's political party in an effort to have the credentials ceremony rescheduled. However, that proved impossible; not one of our contacts dared to approach the president about changing the appointment. The credentials presentation was set, and I would accompany Ambassador Rawson.

On the morning of Saturday, January 8, the Interahamwe, the MRND's youth group and militia, held a massive, violent demonstration centered at a traffic circle just below the building where the RPF troops and civilians were quartered. It was a place the ambassador and I had to pass through en route from his residence to where the president would receive his credentials. We cautiously approached the traffic circle in the ambassador's large, white, armored Chevrolet with the identifying U.S. flags flying from the front fenders. The area was filled with angry-looking, club-wielding young men, some wearing the distinctive multicolored Interahamwe uniform. Ours was the only vehicle on the road. But luck was with us: the demonstrators let us pass without incident.

The credentials ceremony went smoothly. With his chief of staff Enoch Ruhigira looking on, the president accepted the ambassador's letters of credence and listened to Rawson's remarks about continuing goodwill between our two countries. In his reply, the president welcomed the ambassador, confirmed his commitment to the Arusha Accords, and defended his current stand against swearing in the Transitional National Assembly delegates or the government ministers until each of the political parties had arrived at an agreed list of representatives for these two pending transitional institutions. He appealed to Rawson to continue to provide U.S. assistance to help the parties resolve their differences in support of the peace process.

Later in January UNAMIR learned from an informant that the demonstrations had been intended to provoke Belgian peacekeepers into making a move that would legitimize retaliation against them from the Rwandan militia or military. If enough Belgian soldiers were killed, so the thinking went, the Belgians would withdraw their peacekeeping contingent from UNAMIR and jeopardize the entire UN mission.[1] This time the strategy did not work. It would, however, be repeated successfully at the beginning of the genocide, when ten Belgian soldiers were killed and the Belgians subsequently withdrew their troops from UNAMIR.

UNAMIR and Weapons Caches

The president did not mention to the ambassador the one issue that we diplomats had expressed concern about a week earlier, namely, the distribution of arms to civilians. The reputed existence of arms caches was to become the focus of a January 11 cable between UNAMIR's General Dallaire and his bosses in the Department of Peacekeeping Operations (DPKO) at UN headquarters.[2] In his cable Dallaire informed the DPKO that he intended to seize an arms cache inside the Kigali Weapons Secure Area that had been revealed to him by a credible informant. Additionally he sought authority to provide UN protection to the informant and his family.

In its response, the DPKO, headed at that time by Kofi Annan, who would later become UN secretary general, refused Dallaire's request for protection for the informant and told him to refrain from seizing the weapons cache, on the grounds that he had no authority to do so. UN headquarters further instructed him to brief President Habyarimana on the information about the arms caches. Dallaire was devastated by this response. He had hoped to send a strong signal to the extremists by seizing their weapons.[3]

Dallaire briefed the ambassadors of Belgium, France, and the United States on this issue on January 12, shortly before taking his message to the president.[4] I was not in this briefing and do not recall hearing about it from the ambassador or seeing a cable report to Washington. I do recall knowing that UNAMIR had identified a weapons cache that it wanted to seize. Someone in Dallaire's entourage had told me this as I was leaving the general's office the day we introduced the ambassador to him. A few weeks later, following another meeting at the UNAMIR headquarters, I was told that the weapons had been distributed, presumably to the Interahamwe militia.

Ambassador Rawson quickly became enmeshed in the flurry of diplomatic efforts to resolve the political party differences that were holding up installation of the BBTG and the TNA. I was happy to cede my position as participant in these efforts to him, as the issues seemed intractable. Meetings with diplomats to plan strategy, meetings with the president and representatives of the government, meetings with political party leaders, and meetings with the RPF all came to naught. New dates were set for the swearing-in ceremony, but each passed without results: January 12, February 10, February 22, March 25, March 26, March 28.

New Implementation Obstacle: CDR Demands

By the middle of February intraparty differences within the MDR and the PL no longer stood in the way of a swearing-in ceremony. The PL had found a compromise solution acceptable to both of its factions: two ministerial positions would go to Mugenzi's Hutu Power faction and one to Ndasingwa's Tutsi faction, while six TNA seats would go to Ndasingwa's faction and five to Mugenzi's. Likewise the MDR had reached agreement on who would fill its allocated prime minister, ministerial, and TNA positions.

The new issue holding up implementation of the Accords was the participation of the Hutu-supremacist CDR in the transitional institutions. For the third time in Rwanda's democratization process, how to handle the extremist party's desire to participate became the central sticking point to moving forward.

The CDR had opted out of participating in Rwanda's political transition when it boycotted the Arusha signing ceremony, in protest against the peace agreement and the power it gave to the Tutsi-led RPF. Now, perhaps under pressure from Hutu solidarity advocates leading the Hutu Power movement, the CDR changed its stance and opted for inclusion and participation. Instead of abandoning its one seat in the Transitional National Assembly, the CDR declared it wanted to appoint a delegate.

This would not be easy, however. To claim its seat in the TNA, the CDR would first have to sign both the Arusha Accords and the Political Code of Ethics laid out in Article 80 of the Protocol on Power Sharing, as had all the other political parties. Among other things, the ethics code committed all the political parties to support the peace process, promote national unity and national reconciliation, and abstain from violence and inciting violence.[5]

There was no consensus, however, on whether the CDR should be eligible to join the process. President Habyarimana vigorously defended the CDR's right to sign the Accords and the code of political conduct so it could participate in the transitional institutions. He needed as many allies as he could muster in the government and national assembly. The RPF, on the other hand, remained steadfast in its objections to CDR participation, and it adamantly opposed allowing the CDR to sign the Accords at this juncture. In the RPF's view, the CDR was the antithesis of a party that could meet the standards set out in the code of ethics. In particular, the RPF argued, instead of eschewing violence, the CDR had repeatedly advocated and participated in violence.

The diplomatic community came down on the side of letting the CDR sign the agreement and take up its one seat in the TNA. Although diplomats did not endorse the violence associated with the CDR or its extremist, pro-Hutu, anti-Tutsi position, they had consistently advocated inclusiveness in the political process as a way to ensure all parties would have a stake in the outcome. During the power-sharing negotiations, diplomats had supported including in the new political institutions all those parties that wanted to be involved. Diplomats also argued that having the CDR sign the peace agreement and adhere to the code of ethics would give other parties leverage for holding the CDR accountable for its behavior. Once committed to the standard of nonviolence, so the argument went, the CDR would have to honor this principle or be sanctioned and suffer the consequences.

The diplomatic community could not, however, convince the

RPF to accept the principle of inclusion. The RPF refused to back down and became extremely frustrated with the diplomats' stance on this issue. They viewed it as international support for the president and his continued dominance in Rwandan politics.

Given this controversy, the CDR was having a hard time gaining access to the documents it needed to sign. The original signed copy of the Arusha Accords was secured by the Constitutional Court under the jurisdiction of the court's president, Joseph Kavaruganda, a Hutu. He refused to surrender the peace agreement to the CDR for signing. Ironically, in an effort to obtain the document committing it to nonviolence, the CDR held a demonstration that turned violent outside the Constitutional Court. CDR members even broke into Kavaruganda's office to try to get their hands on it. They also occupied the Ministry of Foreign Affairs, just across the street from the court offices. None of this convinced Kavaruganda to surrender the peace agreement to the CDR for its signature, and it strengthened the RPF's argument that the CDR had not truly renounced violence.

Signing the copies of the Political Code of Ethics posed another difficulty. Each political party and the RPF had its own copy of the code that the CDR would have to sign. Not only were some opposition parties opposed to giving the CDR access to their copy, but the RPF vowed it would never surrender its copy for the CDR to sign.

This stalemate dragged on through February and March. Thus the CDR—not the issue of party lists—accounted for several of the postponed swearing-in ceremonies. This issue was still pending when President Habyarimana's plane was shot down in early April.

Fear and Pessimism Intensify

January, February, and March 1994 saw yet another spike in violence in Rwanda. Inflammatory RTLM radio broadcasts, clandestine distributions of arms, secret military training of militia, bombs, grenades, assassinations, and demonstrations occurred with extraordinary frequency. Exploding grenades, the weapon of choice for burglars, could be heard reverberating throughout the hills of Kigali nearly every night.

Rumors abounded that the Rwandan militia members were not the only ones getting military training. I heard from several sources that Burundi refugees in camps south of Kigali and near the Butare border were being taken away for weeks at a time and given military training. According to the rumors, the refugees would leave and return to the camps in buses. On their return, they were said to be sporting new shoes and clothes. I could never get anyone from the government or the MRND to confirm these rumors. Nor could UNHCR verify the stories, though its staff had also heard them. It did not seem farfetched, however, because the Hutu refugees from Burundi, like Rwandan party militia, were virulently anti-Tutsi. Presumably they could be counted on as allies of the Rwandan extremists should the situation deteriorate further. In retrospect, I suspect that Burundian refugees, if trained in this fashion, were enlisted as killers once genocide reached the southern town of Butare. The region around the town, near the refugee camps, was an area where Hutu-Tutsi animosities were traditionally negligible.

The media was rife with anti-Tutsi propaganda in the early months of 1994. The private radio station RTLM extended its hatemongering to UNAMIR forces in general and in particular to their commander, General Dallaire, and the Belgian troops. In a January 27 broadcast, after denouncing UNAMIR, RTLM called on Hutu to prepare to defend themselves against the Belgian contingent. Otherwise, the announcer claimed, Belgian soldiers would hand Rwanda over to the Tutsi.[6] By the end of March RTLM's inflammatory verbal attacks on UNAMIR, Dallaire, the Belgian troops, and some Rwandan political leaders became increasingly bitter and frequent.[7]

In mid-February the refusal of the RPF and opposition political parties to allow the CDR to sign the peace agreement preceded a series of political assassinations. Causal, coincidental, or unrelated is hard say. On the evening of February 21, following on the heels of the CDR's raucous demonstration in front of the Constitutional Court and its occupation of the Foreign Ministry, Félicien Gatabazi, general secretary of the Butare-based PSD party, was assassinated in front of his Kigali home. The killing was similar to an attempt made a day earlier on the life of Prime Minister–Designate Faustin Twagiramungu and the successful assassination nine months earlier of Emmanuel Gapyisi, an MDR party advocate of Hutu solidarity. Who would want to kill Gatabazi, I wondered, and why? Could it have been to stir up differences among PSD members who had hitherto remained unified and in favor of power sharing in defiance of Hutu solidarity and Hutu Power advocates?

The next day, in the southern university town of Butare, Gatabazi's political stronghold, a mob attacked and killed the president of the extremist CDR party, Martin Bucyana, in apparent revenge for Gatabazi's death. Bucyana reportedly just happened to be traveling in the southern region, where there was strong opposition to the CDR's Hutu-supremacy philosophy. No assailants were ever identified in any of these cases. Such impunity for wanton violence fostered fear among potential victims while emboldening perpetrators. Particularly vulnerable after these political assassinations were political party leaders and democracy activists. It did not go unnoticed that Gatabazi and the PSD—as well as Twagiramungu—had never wavered in their support for power sharing with the Tutsi-led RPF.

For the next four days, the Interahamwe went on a killing rampage in Kigali. For the first time the capital experienced the systematic killings that had caused the death and displacement of so many Tutsi and some Hutu in other parts of the country over the past three years. The militia attacked Tutsi in several Kigali neighborhoods. Nearly seventy persons died. UNAMIR, whose rules of engagement kept it from firing unless fired upon, was virtually helpless. It could not even get past Interahamwe roadblocks to protect or rescue people under assault.

The embassy remained open over these four days of terror in February 1994, which took a terrible toll in certain Kigali neighborhoods. Most Americans were able to come to work each day, but nearly all Rwandan staff, both Hutu and Tutsi, stayed home. Despite these atrocities, and our close look at how easily the extremists could carry them out, we still did not anticipate full-blown genocide in Rwanda. In retrospect, it seems clear that these four days of Kigali violence were intended to test the reaction not only of UNAMIR but also of the international community. It was no doubt a trial run for the mass killings that would soon envelop the country.

In early April RTLM announced that the RPF was planning a coup against President Habyarimana. To support this assertion, the radio station claimed that an RPF attack was imminent.[8] Such warnings worried me and others in the diplomatic community. Rwandans had a track record of masking evil deeds they were planning to commit by threatening in advance imminent danger from the other side. This tactic, used successfully in the March 1992 Bugesera massacre of Tutsi, always stirred up fear and hatred against "the other" and contributed to a web of ambiguity in the event that something did happen.

Visiting U.S. Officials Urge Speedy Implementation of Arusha Accords

During February and March 1994 the embassy welcomed three high-level visitors from the U.S. Department of State. Each had a different mission, but all seized the opportunity to press Rwandan leaders and politicians to compromise on blocking issues and to urge speedy implementation of the Arusha peace agreement. The message from Washington was clear and direct: End prevarication and begin to implement the Arusha agreement or U.S. support will disappear.

The first visitor was Doug Bennett, assistant secretary of state for international organizations, who arrived in early February to discuss issues expected to come before the UN Security Council in the coming session. In January, Rwanda had been elected to one of the nonpermanent member seats on the Council. The assistant secretary normally made such calls on new Council members to familiarize them with U.S. positions on key issues of importance to us and to seek their support on Council votes. Bennett also used this opportunity to stress to the Rwandans the importance the United States and the UN attached to their successful implementation of the Arusha Accords. He asserted that it was vital and urgent for the various political factions to find a way to put the transitional institutions in place at once.

Bennett was the highest-level U.S. official to come to Rwanda since Assistant Secretary for Africa Herman Cohen had visited in May 1992, and the Rwandans rolled out the red carpet. Bennett met with President Habyarimana and Foreign Minister Gasana and had a joint session with Prime Minister Uwilingiyimana and Prime Minister–Designate Twagiramungu. He also met the UNAMIR leaders, Special Representative of the Secretary General Booh-Booh, and General

Dallaire. The foreign minister hosted a state dinner for him. I had never attended such a dinner, and I did not know that it was my responsibility to write Bennett's reply to the foreign minister's toast. Fortunately, when I turned up at the dinner empty-handed, Bennett—an experienced diplomat—spoke extemporaneously, striking all the right notes. I was impressed and relieved but embarrassed at my huge gaffe.

Our next Washington visitor, in mid-March, was Patricia Irvin, assistant secretary for humanitarian affairs at the Department of Defense. Her office identified worthy humanitarian projects to receive excess property, such as school desks, from the department. It also dealt with de-mining. I escorted her to meetings with the foreign minister and the defense minister, and together we visited a couple of the refugee camps for Hutu from Burundi, located in the troubled Bugesera region south of Kigali. We reviewed what humanitarian assistance was already being provided and how her office might offer value-added aid. She left Rwanda without a project firmly in mind, but the dialogue with senior Rwandan officials had begun.

Our next high-level visitors arrived on March 19. Prudence Bushnell, deputy assistant secretary for African affairs at the Department of State, and Arlene Render, director of the Office of Central African Affairs, came to impress upon Rwanda's leaders the urgency the United States attached to implementing the Arusha Accords. They asked their interlocutors to put the transitional institutions into place at once so that the twenty-two-month transition to multiparty elections could begin. Together Bushnell and Render took their message to the president, the prime minister and prime minister–designate, the foreign minister, and the RPF military leader General Kagame.

I accompanied Ambassador Rawson and our visitors on the trip north to the RPF headquarters at the Mulindi tea plantation, where Kagame still made his home. I shall always remember a remark Kagame made at that meeting in response to Bushnell's insistence on peace. He said, "I have found that making peace is much more difficult than waging war." In an aside I urged him to choose peace over war: "Don't take the easy way out."

A Weekend Respite

During the first weekend in April, I enjoyed a respite not only from our spate of Washington visitors but also from the stress of physical insecurity. It was Easter weekend. Both Good Friday and Easter Monday were holidays, so I took advantage of the four-day weekend to have a new adventure in Rwanda. With a camping-enthusiast friend and her visiting sister and ten-year-old nephew, I went on a two-night camping trip to the Nyungwe National Park in the mountainous rain forest of southwest Rwanda. The road leading west to the park from the southern town of Butare was a vast improvement over the one I had traveled fifteen years or so earlier.

Back then I was the U.S. Peace Corps associate director responsible for approximately one hundred education volunteers in Zaire and for several others teaching in Rwanda at the university in Butare. I vividly remember a harrowing trip from Butare to Bukavu, site of the Peace Corps training program in Zaire. A narrow, rocky road wound through the mountains and across barren mountain ridges. Local Rwandan villagers milling along the roadside scattered rapidly, with fear in their eyes, as our Land Rover raced by. We were trying to reach the border before it closed at nightfall, the driver had calmly explained.

This time we drove an expertly engineered, wide, paved, two-lane road, banked appropriately to the mountainous terrain with guardrails as needed for physical security. What a glorious change! We seemed to be the only visitors in the Nyungwe National Park that weekend. We found a lovely, flat place in the densely forested hills to pitch our tents, and well-kept paths offered us several hiking opportunities during our stay. What a feeling of peace and serenity!

We returned to Kigali on Easter Monday, in time to attend a reception hosted by the Senegalese troops in UNAMIR to celebrate their national day. The Senegalese seemed to have invited everyone they knew to the festivities. Their UNAMIR officers and fellow soldiers, the diplomatic community, international and local NGO leaders were all gathered together. The magnificent food included one of my favorites, chicken yassa, a dish covered with caramelized onions and lime juice. The steady rhythm of West African music blared over loudspeakers, prompting many people to dance.

Only when the inevitable speeches began was I jolted back to reality as I pointed out high-level Rwandans to Ambassador Rawson, who had not yet met all of the key players. I remember calling Rawson's attention to one Rwandan military officer in particular, Col. Théoneste Bagosora, the chief of staff at the ministry who had been a hard-line government delegate at the Arusha talks. I told Rawson that Bagosora was known among the observers at Arusha as "Colonel Death."

Another Visitor Arrives to Explore Refugee Issues

The next day, April 5, I welcomed to Kigali the U.S. Department of State's regional refugee officer, Linda Thomas-Greenfield, who was based at the U.S. Embassy in Nairobi. She had come to Rwanda to monitor the situation of the recently arrived refugees from Burundi in the south and to learn about Rwanda's plans for the impending return of Tutsi refugees from neighboring countries in the wake of the peace agreement. Linda and I knew each other well from our days in the political section of the U.S. Embassy in Lagos, Nigeria, about eight years earlier. She would be my houseguest during her visit.

On the following day, Wednesday, April 6, we made several calls on government and UN officials concerned with refugee issues. Our last call was on Jacques Bihozagara of the RPF, who would be responsible for refugee resettlement in the forthcoming transitional cabinet. We met him in the national assembly building, where the RPF security contingent had taken up residence at the end of December pending installation of the transitional government. During that meeting Bihozagara informed Linda and me that many Tutsi refugees had in fact already returned from their many years in exile in Uganda. They were settling in the RPF-controlled territory just inside the Rwandan border. We discussed my traveling with him in the near future to check on the condition of these spontaneous returnees. He and I agreed to fix a specific date for the trip in the coming days.

Etched in my mind from that visit is the stunning view that lay before us as we stepped outside the national assembly building. The day was sunny and warm. The late afternoon air was crystal clear. The sky was deep, deep blue. As Linda and I looked out across the valleys from the highest hill in the city, we could see small, tin-roofed homes in neighborhoods below us. Roads wound down one hill and up another to the center of town. On the valley floor was the stream where young men were often busy washing cars. On a hilltop opposite us stood government buildings and the homes of Rwandans and some diplomats. We paused for several minutes, admiring the view and appreciating the beauty of Kigali. How could there not be hope for Rwanda, I thought. No one we had talked with and nothing we had seen that day gave us any hint of the tragedy that would begin to unfold within hours of this blissful moment.

A Plane Crash

That evening the representative of the UN refugee agency, Carlos Rodriguez, and one of his colleagues joined Linda and me for dinner at my house. We wanted to discuss the refugee issues facing UNHCR in Rwanda and the region in greater depth than we had at his office earlier in the day. At about 8:30, while we were at the table, we heard a distant but distinct explosion but continued talking and eating. Loud noises and explosions weren't entirely without precedent; it was likely another grenade assault on an unfortunate robbery victim.

We couldn't have been more wrong. About half an hour later Ambassador Rawson telephoned to say that the noise had been an airplane crash near the airport. President Habyarimana's plane had gone down. He had been returning from a meeting in Tanzania about impending conflict in Burundi. The president's condition and that of others on the plane was not yet known. Nor was there an explanation for the crash. Our dinner party ended abruptly. My UNHCR guests left agitated and worried. Linda and I were anxious. We wondered what it would mean if the president were dead.

A couple of hours later the ambassador phoned again. UNAMIR sources had confirmed that all aboard the plane were dead: President Habyarimana, President Cyprien Ntaryamira of Burundi, close aides of both, and the entire French crew of the plane. UNAMIR also confirmed that the plane had been shot out of the air by an unidentified missile.

I was charged with drafting the message to the American community. After the ambassador approved the message, consular officer Laura Lane and I used our radio network—in accordance with emergency procedures—to notify the American community in Kigali and elsewhere in Rwanda of the situation. Our message alerted all Americans, both official and nonofficial, to the plane crash, told them that the president and all others aboard were confirmed dead, and advised that they remain indoors while awaiting further instructions.

Comment

Responsibility for shooting down the president's plane has never been definitively determined. Both hard-liners in the government and the RPF had plausible motives. The extremists may have thought that eliminating the president would be the only way to stop implementation of the Arusha Peace Accords and prevent the power-sharing provisions from going forward. The RPF may have thought that removing the president would remove the major obstacle to implementation of the pact that would give them a considerable role in governing Rwanda. Alternatively it could have been a gamble by one side or the other to take over the peace process and scrap the power-sharing arrangement called for in the Accords. Whether either side had the expertise or the means to shoot down the plane was not clear. Whether anyone was still committed to power sharing was doubtful.

[19]

The Exodus

Anxiety Abounds

After receiving the shocking news of the plane crash that killed the presidents of Rwanda and Burundi as well as senior aides and scrambling to alert the American community, I was exhausted. However, my day was not yet over. Into the night Rwandan friends telephoned to say how afraid they were of what might happen next. One, a human rights advocate, was convinced that her life was in danger. She wanted me to have the UNAMIR troops come to her house, not far from their headquarters, and take her to safety. She said she had telephoned them, but the English-speaking Bangladeshi who answered the phone could not understand her French. A journalist who phoned predicted the situation was bound to deteriorate rapidly. I tried, naively, to reassure both of them but persuaded neither. After a long day I fell into an uneasy sleep.

The next morning my house guest, Linda Thomas-Greenfield, the regional refugee officer from the U.S. Embassy in Nairobi, and I were awakened at 5:00 by gunfire very close to the house. Soon it was clear to us that there was shooting throughout the city. By 7:30 I had received two telephone calls reporting systematic, house-to-house killing of Tutsi in a community across the road and down the hillside from the national assembly building, where the RPF troops were quartered. Was this arbitrary killing of innocent Tutsi intended to draw the RPF forces out of their lodging and into a fight? By 8:00 two more calls confirmed that political party leaders—both Tutsi and opposition Hutu—were being killed or taken away by the military. One of the first persons killed, I was told, was the young Hutu cabinet director at the Ministry of Foreign Affairs. He had been killed in his house shortly after midnight. I remembered him as the person who used to hold court almost every evening in a local outdoor fish restaurant where I sometimes ate with American colleagues.

Such violence was not new, but it had never occurred so systematically and with such intensity in Kigali itself. Even the February violence six weeks earlier, following the assassination of PSD and CDR leaders, lacked the sense of organization that was clearly apparent now. Although the actions appeared to be in retaliation for the death of President Habyarimana, it seemed to be something much more. Authority, to the extent that anyone was in charge, was clearly in the hands of the political hard-liners and extremists, and they were wreaking havoc on those they defined as their enemies.

At 8:15 my next-door neighbor, Prime Minister Agathe Uwilingiyimana, telephoned to ask whether she could come over the wall between our two houses to seek safety. I agreed. However, when the blue beret of a Ghanaian UNAMIR trooper apparently charged with organizing this transfer became visible at the top of the wall, shots were fired that seemed to be coming from just outside the gate at the foot of my garden. I surmised that whoever was outside my house with a gun must have been watching the wall to keep the prime minister from slipping away and had spotted the peacekeeper. I told the UNAMIR soldier that we should abandon the attempt, as my house could no longer be considered a safe haven for the prime minister. She would have to look elsewhere. Reluctantly he agreed.

An hour later my day guard advised me of a commotion outside my gate. Presidential guard troops, with their distinctive black berets, were attempting to break down my gate to get inside. They evidently wanted to search for the prime minister, whom they believed had come over the wall and into my house. In order to keep them from breaking down the gate and because I thought I had nothing to hide, I let them in—about fourteen of them.

I was startled when several angrily approached my house guest, a tall, dark-skinned African American. They insisted, in French, that she was a Tutsi. She didn't understand French but knew exactly what they were talking about. We both vehemently denied she was Tutsi, insisting, in French, over and over again that she was an American diplomat visiting from our Nairobi embassy. She produced her passport and desperately waved it in front of her. Eventually, after much shouting—and after seeing her passport—they accepted that she was American and left her alone.

Badly shaken, Linda sat in my front hall holding my four-month-old puppy, Coco, on a short leash while the Black Berets spent more than an hour searching outside and inside my modest, one-level house, including in the space above the ceiling. I kept up a steady barrage of conversation with the soldiers gathered in my kitchen, urging them to go outside while their colleague searched the house, assuring them that the prime minister was not there. Instead, apparently to underscore an order to put the phone down, one of them fired off a couple shots. Of course, I immediately laid the receiver down, but beside the phone so the person on the other end—whoever it was—would hear what was happening. I later learned it was the human rights activist and former Kigali prosecutor Alphonse Nkubito.

Finally the soldier who had climbed into the space above the ceiling to look for the prime minister came to tell me that she was not there. I reminded him that I'd been telling him that all along. So, now that he was convinced, would he please go tell his superiors so they could leave us alone? The soldiers did leave, but not before finding and beating my gardener, Jonathan, a Tutsi who had locked himself in the kitchen pantry. Fortunately, though terribly shaken, he had not sustained any physical injuries or, worse, been killed. At least the soldiers had arrived early in the day and weren't yet drunk or high on drugs.

Half an hour later Linda and I heard a volley of shots and a woman's scream. Then male voices were cheering. We knew immediately that the prime minister had been found and killed. I felt numb. Later I learned that the ten Belgian UN troops that General Dallaire had sent to protect the prime minister never made it to her house. They had been captured en route and taken to a nearby military camp, where they were brutally tortured and killed.

At about the same time, I spoke by phone to an American who worked as a translator for UNAMIR. He confirmed that UNAMIR troops were still under orders not to fire unless fired upon and were stymied in their attempts to get past roadblocks to reach people who needed their assistance. This echoed the situation six weeks earlier, when UNAMIR's rules of engagement had rendered its troops unable to help or protect civilians cut off by militia roadblocks during the four days of terror.

I spent the rest of the day on the telephone, responding to queries from State Department officials in Washington, comparing notes with local diplomats, and gathering information from Rwandan friends and contacts. I reported regularly to the ambassador and to the American community through our radio net. Linda had somehow managed to defrost two turkeys she found in my freezer and cooked them both so that we would have something to eat as long as we were at the house, and something to take with us should we move to the embassy or be ordered to evacuate. These turkeys were to become a lifesaver for us and others.

By afternoon we heard reports that a number of key political opposition figures had been murdered. Topping the list was my neighbor, Hutu prime minister Agathe Uwilingiyimana from the Twagiramungu faction of the opposition MDR party. Former Hutu foreign minister Boniface Ngulinzira had reportedly been killed in the early hours of the morning. His leadership of the government delegation at the peace talks in Arusha had infuriated Kigali hard-liners and extremists in the MRND and CDR. They held him responsible for giving away too much power to the Tutsi-led RPF. Ngulinzira had sought refuge at a secondary school run by a religious group before being found and killed. The PSD minister of agriculture Frédéric Nzamurambaho and his colleague, Félicien Ngango, vice president of the party, were both reported dead. Ngango had been designated to lead the Transitional National Assembly. Their party had never wavered in its support for power sharing with the RPF.

The PL minister of labor and social affairs, Landoald Ndasingwa, who had led the Tutsi faction of the PL, his Canadian wife, Helen, and their two teenage children had been brutally slain in their home that fateful night. I had last seen him a week or so earlier at a dinner at the ambassador's residence for one of our visiting officials. As he approached the door at the end of the evening, Lando spoke what would be his last words to me. He took my hands in his and said with a warm, friendly smile that filled his face and lit up his eyes, "My friend, my friend." Tears still come to my eyes when I think about that moment and recall all the Rwandan talent lost to genocide.

My phone kept ringing. Contacts recounted continuing, systematic killing of Tutsis throughout the afternoon. I was told that military troops were still going house to house seeking Tutsi and Hutu "enemies" in several Kigali neighborhoods. People—mostly Tutsi— were seeking refuge in churches in Kigali. Reports came in of killing occurring also in the north and east of the country. The staff at an American-run Seventh Day Adventist school in the northwest of the country called to say that civilians—probably Interahamwe militia—had entered the campus that morning and killed Tutsi students. A Tutsi judge from the eastern town of Kibungo phoned to tell me that civilian groups he identified as "probably militia" were destroying street lamps, likely intending to take advantage of the cover of darkness to begin killing. I never heard from him again.

We got word that two hundred of the six hundred RPF troops had left the national assembly building under UNAMIR escort. Where they were taken, I do not know. Later information suggested that the RPF forces in Kigali had actually broken out of their lodging—some reports claimed they had constructed a warren of tunnels under the building for just such an eventuality— and were fighting the militia and military. Other reports indicated that RPF troops were beginning to move south toward Kigali from their base at Mulindi in the north. Whatever the facts, a resumption of war seemed imminent.

I relayed all the information coming to me from Rwandan and international colleagues to the ambassador, who was stranded at his hilltop residence in a distant part of town. I talked frequently with State Department colleagues in Washington, where a task force had been set up to monitor the deteriorating security situation in Rwanda in the wake of the downing of the president's plane. Through our emergency contact system that depended on telephones and our two-way radios, we kept all Americans aware of what we knew and advised them to continue staying at home. They shared valuable information and insights with us as well.

As night fell, Linda, Jonathan, and I gathered in the only interior hallway in the house, away from windows and stray bullets. The space, wedged between my bedroom, a second, unfurnished bedroom, and a guest bath, was not much bigger than eight by ten feet. I stretched my phone cord as far as it would go from my bedroom and was able to set up my office there as well. My puppy, Coco, who usually spent nights in the guardhouse at my gate, joined us. I had brought her inside early that morning, even before the Black Berets arrived. I remember vividly a shot ringing out once when Coco ventured into the garden to do her business. Startled by the sound, she came racing across the yard, bounded up the steps to the screened-in porch, and slid across the tile floor, paws spread, into the safety of the house.

Though a bit uncomfortable crammed into the hallway, all four of us were able to get some much-needed sleep. Only twenty-four hours after the president's plane had been shot out of the sky, our lives and the lives of all Rwandans had completely changed. What, I wondered, would the new day bring?

The State Department Orders Evacuation

American community members spent a terrifying Thursday night huddled in their homes listening to gunfire echoing through the Kigali hills. Americans living in the neighborhood known as Kimihurura—on the hill across the valley from the embassy and my house—reported hearing what they believed to be an exchange of fire over their heads between military units based on different sides of the hill. Could one of the Rwandan military units have been challenging another? I never heard any explanation for this event.

I had spent most of Thursday night and into Friday morning on the telephone with Washington. When morning came, gunfire still resonated around my home. I was reluctant to get into my small Toyota Land Cruiser and venture out of my compound as long as I could hear gunfire outside my gate. I suspected road blocks had been erected just outside because of the military school across the road from my house, and the military base not far away.

That Friday morning, however, Laura, the consular officer, and her ex-marine husband successfully drove the several blocks from their home to the embassy. On the way they picked up our visiting defense attaché, who had been staying at the Hôtel des Mille Collines just a short distance from the embassy. She opened a direct telephone line to the task force at the State Department set up to monitor developments in Rwanda and to provide updates to persons seeking information about family members. They also began shredding classified documents, in accordance with protocol.

In a new development, nearly all of the Americans living in Kigali, including Ambassador Rawson, awoke that Friday morning to find themselves without electricity. Only the consular officer and I and some Americans working with nongovernmental organizations never lost power. We lived closest to the embassy and the center of town, where key Rwandan offices were located. Consequently we and the embassy—just next to the Defense Ministry and across the street from the radio station—had electricity and telephones throughout the crisis.

We quickly recognized the lack of electricity as a security liability. No electricity meant no telephones. To communicate we now had to use our two-way radios. However, without electricity to charge the batteries, and a finite amount of fuel to run home generators, it would not be long before we would have no means of communication. Therefore we decided to limit communications with the community to every hour on the hour. In the meantime people could keep their two-way radios turned off. The lack of electricity also jeopardized food supplies in warming refrigerators and freezers.

With no telephone, the ambassador was cut off from most embassy personnel and also from direct contact with Washington. To communicate with the American community, Rawson used his two-way radio. To connect with Washington, his only recourse was to use the high-frequency radio in his house, with which he could reach the ambassador's residence in Nairobi, Kenya. Through Nairobi intermediaries he could then speak to Washington and report our deteriorating security conditions.

Midmorning on Friday, after weighing all the factors at its disposal, State Department officials advised us of their decision to order the evacuation of all official Americans, either by air or overland. We communicated this development to all official Americans and advised nonofficial Americans, including missionaries, of our instructions to depart. Using our two-way radio network, we convened a country team meeting to assess our options. Because everyone on the network could listen in and bring to bear information they were hearing from friends and colleagues, we compiled a pretty good picture of what was happening in different parts of town.

We decided fairly quickly that our best option would be to evacuate south by road to Burundi, driving in convoys of our own vehicles. When I touched base with the French, who were bringing in airplanes and soldiers to evacuate their citizens, I was advised that the Americans could be accommodated, but only after all 1,200 or so French citizens had been evacuated. The Belgians too, who were still working out their plan, told me their priority would be the six hundred or so persons in the Belgian community.

Time, we believed, was of the essence. It seemed to us that we would be safer going out on our own immediately rather than waiting for help from the French or Belgians, both of whom had enemies on one side of the fighting or the other. The United States was more credibly neutral. Also, getting to the airport to meet a French or Belgian plane seemed especially risky. It would require crossing the front lines of renewed fighting between government forces and the RPF army. Going south to Burundi would not.

So far we had no reports of killing in towns south of Kigali. A contingent of U.S. Marines from an aircraft carrier off the coast of Somalia was en route to Burundi's capital, Bujumbura, on a C-130 transport plane. The marines would be on standby should they be needed. We had a regional security officer at the embassy in Bujumbura who proved to be an enormous help in implementing this plan. The U.S. Embassy in Kigali had no marine detachment providing security, as did most embassies around the world. Nor did we have a resident security officer or resident military attaché. Only by chance, the military attaché who covered Rwanda was in Kigali on an official visit from his base at the embassy in faraway Cameroon when the genocide began.

The rest of that day, Friday, April 8, we spent planning the evacuation. The pivotal planner was our consular officer, Laura Lane, who had reached the embassy. Using our embassy evacuation plan as a guide, she worked with the community to appoint convoy leaders, establish times for convoy departures, and designate rendezvous points. The parking lot of the American School on Kimihurura, the hill where most official Americans lived, was one such point; the American Recreation Club, close to the embassy, was the other. She was keeping nonofficial Americans informed of our departure arrangements so they could join.[1]

We wanted assurances from both sides to the conflict that our convoys would be allowed to pass unharmed, even though we didn't expect to have to cross through areas of military operations. We also wanted a Rwandan gendarme escort that could inform any uninformed military or militia our convoys might encounter along the way that we had official authorization to be traveling south on the main highway.

From my house, I contacted Col. Léonidas Rusatira, a high-level military officer with whom I had become acquainted recently, and asked him to help us connect with the authorities who could provide security assurances and a gendarme escort. By chance, he acknowledged, he had himself been appointed by those in charge to be the liaison with the diplomatic community. Instead of agreeing readily to my requests, however, he pleaded with me to abandon the idea of evacuating the American community. He urged us to stay to help restore security and stop the killing. I explained that we were under orders from Washington to leave and that our first responsibility was the safety and security of U.S. citizens. We had no choice. In the end he agreed to help us and arranged gendarme escorts to the edge of town for our convoys.[2]

The ambassador's residence was farthest from the embassy. On the second day of the emergency, Rwandans poured into his walled hillside compound seeking safety, and that afternoon shots were fired into his yard. A child was killed and two persons were wounded. After the ambassador contacted UNAMIR the injured were escorted to a nearby hospital. Only later did he acknowledge that a bullet had narrowly missed him as he was in his yard talking to the Rwandans who had sought refuge there.

The Exodus

On Saturday morning the French head of UN security in Rwanda came to my house. "Moustache," as he was known—a reference to his elegant handlebar mustache—assured me that the streets outside my house were passable. He had someone who wanted to consult with me about the U.S. assessment of the situation, and he suggested we meet at the embassy. I decided that this was my chance to navigate safely the three blocks to the embassy, where I belonged. With the help of a security escort from the United Nations, I drove my own car, taking with me only a blanket and a pillow for my anticipated overnight there. My house guest, Linda, came too, with her suitcase.

When we reached the embassy, I found that Laura Lane and her husband had things well in hand. She was consumed with getting the evacuation convoys under way and seeing that confidential files were destroyed.

Americans Depart Overland to Burundi

That Saturday, April 9, three American convoys left Kigali at spaced intervals for the normally five-hour trip south to Bujumbura. Each convoy included both official and nonofficial Americans. Linda, who thoughtfully volunteered to take my frisky, and now traumatized, puppy along, left in the first convoy. I would retrieve Coco in Burundi. Linda also took with her one of the two turkeys she had cooked during those first tense hours confined to my house.

The first convoy left Kigali shortly after noon and arrived in Bujumbura in the evening. The next two convoys were longer and progressed more slowly. They reached the border after it had closed, but skillful work by the U.S. security officer, who had come to the border from our embassy in Burundi, salvaged the situation. He managed to get the Burundian officials to reopen their side of the border to allow our two convoys to enter the country. They finally reached Bujumbura at 3:00 in the morning, safe but very, very tired.

It was a busy day for those of us still at the embassy. I continued to field phone calls from Rwandans seeking help. I remember talking to Pierre-Claver Kanyarushoki, Rwanda's ambassador in Uganda whom I had worked with in Arusha. He called from Kampala seeking information about the situation because his daughter lived in Kigali. I also remember helping the newly appointed, recently arrived Peace

Corps administrative officer tear bed sheets into one-foot squares. We used these as flags on the vehicles in our convoys to identify us and signal our peaceful intentions. Other embassy workers were still shredding documents. When the shredders broke down, we resorted to burning documents in a trash barrel in the middle of the parking area at the back of the embassy.

We had some help from an American woman married to a Rwandan who had made it to the embassy with her two young children, who were U.S. citizens. She lived in one of the Kigali neighborhoods where killing was rife. In fact there were a number of Rwandans with dual U.S. citizenship for whom the embassy was responsible. Many were children born to Rwandan parents when they were studying in the United States. It was impossible for all of them to get to the embassy or to an assembly point for the convoys. So one of our embassy communicators, Walt Meyers, made several dangerous and heroic trips across the roadblocks into the violence-torn sections of town to facilitate departure of these children and their parents on our convoys. He received a State Department award for his valor.

I must have returned to my house later that day to pack a small duffle bag for the evacuation, now that it was certain I would depart the following day. I crammed the bag with some important papers, my toiletries, and little more than a change of clothes. At the last minute I added a favorite Moroccan wool jacket that I'd bought a few years earlier in the Marrakesh market during a photography trip to that country. I thought it would come in handy in Washington's cool, early April weather. I had neglected, however, to include a comfortable pair of shoes and suffered for that later. We had no idea at that time how long we would be gone from Kigali and Rwanda. My gardener, Jonathan, agreed to stay at the house. He promised to take care of it until my return. We were hopeful that I would not be absent long.

Besides my personal bag, I returned to the embassy with a cooler filled with food from my fridge and all the meat from my freezer. I also took along the second turkey. At the embassy we found some emergency military rations that served as our food while we were there. The turkey went with me on the evacuation trip, providing much needed sustenance for all of us on the long drive south to Bujumbura. I left the cooler with the embassy guards who remained on duty throughout the tragedy. I later learned that they had cleverly kept at bay marauding military keen to enter the embassy by insisting they had no keys and could therefore not open the gates.

That Saturday night, on a thickly carpeted floor upstairs in the area used as a waiting room for visitors to our inner sanctum, I threw down the pillow and comforter I had brought from home and curled up for some much-needed sleep. When I awoke at dawn the next morning, I felt rested for the first time in several days. After a welcome shower in the rather old bathroom behind the ambassador's office, I felt refreshed. I wasn't sure, though, about my readiness to face another day. As I combed my hair, I stood for a moment staring at my reflection in the mirror and listening for signs of activity outside. "Will I make it through this day alive?" I asked the image before me. Then I folded my bedding and went downstairs to join the others.

On Sunday, April 10, two more American-led convoys left Kigali, the first at midmorning. Because some of the cars needed gas to make it to Bujumbura, the organizers decided the entire convoy would drive from the rendezvous point at the American School in Kimihurura to the gas station around the corner from, but within sight of, the embassy. It was a risky move. Laura, our intrepid mastermind for the evacuation, had verified that, miraculously, not only was the station open, but it still had gas for sale. The procession of vehicles, each flying a white flag from its antenna, slowly and cautiously wound its way down from the assembly point, across the valley, and up again to the embassy and the gas station around the corner.

With fuel tanks topped off for the trip—and with a sense of relief that there had been no complications—the convoy made its way out of town. The ambassador's wife was in the lead, driving their personal car as the convoy departed. She had dropped the ambassador off at the embassy on her way to the gas station. This gave him a chance to make a final check of the premises before his own departure. As the group rolled out of town we worried about what they might find on the road south on this fourth day of the crisis.

After what seemed an inordinately long wait, the ambassador's wife finally called in using the two-way radio. She confirmed success in getting all the vehicles across the bridge at the Nyabarongo River in the valley just outside town. We had heard that the military had stationed guards at the bridge, and just hoped that a convoy of foreigners with an escort of gendarmes would be allowed to pass. This good news augured well for our last convoy, which would need to cross the same bridge later that day.

A Friendly Face, an Ominous Message

I remember coming out of the embassy that morning to wait for that first convoy and the arrival of the ambassador. I wanted to wish those in the procession well on their journey south to Burundi. As I stood at the embassy gate, enjoying the first sunshine I'd been in for days, I was struck by the silence and emptiness of the usually bustling intersection that was essentially the center of town. Then I smiled at seeing a familiar Rwandan face. Maj. Augustin Cyiza, head of the military court and a friend to human rights activists, was walking down the road toward me. We had met several times over lunch at my house to talk about the state of affairs in Rwanda.

Major Cyiza, alone on the street, was uncharacteristically wearing his military uniform, and he was in a hurry. Pausing briefly, he told me he was making arrangements to evacuate his family to a safer place in the south and couldn't linger. The uniform, he explained, should make it easier for him to move about the city. He did take a moment, however, to recall the conversation we had had about a year earlier, when coup rumors were rampant in Kigali. He reminded me that I had been unable then to understand who might mount such a coup or how. "This is that coup," he asserted. I wished him well as he departed. Trying to absorb what he had just said, I wondered whether he would succeed in his mission. Judging by his sense of urgency and the way he talked, I gathered he worried that his name might be on the Hutu killers' lists because of his outspoken insistence on respect for human rights. Other Rwandans from the human rights community had confided their fears to me since the downing of the president's plane.

The Last U.S. Convoy Departs

At about 1:15 in the afternoon the Rwandan guards lowered the U.S. flag flying over the embassy. I slammed shut the heavy, armored back door to the building and climbed behind the wheel of my Toyota Land Cruiser. The ambassador was in the passenger seat. As we rounded the corner to the American Recreation Center a few short blocks away, I was stunned by the number of vehicles assembled for this final U.S.-organized convoy. This would be the longest convoy yet.

We began our exodus a few minutes later, with consular officer Laura Lane and her husband in the lead and the ambassador and I bringing up the rear. The last of our five convoys crawled slowly down the long road leading from the center of town south out of Kigali. Young men holding machetes stood on the hillsides both above and below the road, staring at us as we passed. As still as statues, they betrayed no emotion. It seemed apparent that the killing would not end any time soon. I could only guess that they were glad to see us leave. No more prying international eyes. They could get on about their dastardly business. Imbued by the twisted logic of Hutu supremacy, they would justify this horror and their role in it as beneficial for the future of the Hutu community.

When we arrived at the Nyabarongo River bridge, our progress stalled, though from the rear of the procession we could not discern the problem. Soon some military officers appeared at the window of my car. They insisted that Ambassador Rawson had to be at the front of the convoy rather than at the rear. Reluctantly we drove to the front of the long line of vehicles and ceded our position to Laura and her husband.

As we reached the front we saw an altercation between a couple of the soldiers and some Africans in our convoy. The ambassador got out of the car and went over to see what was going on. He understood Kinyarwanda, the language of Rwanda, and could reply in Kirundi, the closely related language of neighboring Burundi, where he had lived as a child. He was able to calm the soldiers, and the Africans from our convoy returned to their car.

As we drove across the bridge, with the long string of vehicles following closely behind, the ambassador told me the story. The soldiers had apparently pulled the wife of a Kenyan diplomat out of their car, accused her of being a Tutsi, and said she could not leave. Her distraught Kenyan husband pleaded and pleaded for her to be allowed to depart with him. But they would not relent. Ambassador Rawson, speaking in Kirundi, had asked the soldiers what gave them the idea that she was a Tutsi. No doubt astonished not only by his question but also by his use of a language they understood, one replied, "Because she speaks Kinyarwanda!" Not missing a beat, the ambassador responded in Kirundi, "How can that be proof? I speak Kinyarwanda too. Does that mean I am a Tutsi?" The soldiers conceded his point. The woman and her husband were allowed to rejoin their vehicle, and the ambassador, humble as usual, had rejoined ours.

The rest of our journey to the Rwandan-Burundi border was uneventful. The ambassador and I were asked a couple of times to show our passports at lightly manned checkpoints as we neared Butare; assured that we were who we said we were, the military allowed the entire convoy to pass. As far as we knew, there had not yet been any killing in the university town, but as we drove along the main street, I sensed an atmosphere of foreboding calm. I remember seeing only a few people walking along the road, but no vehicles were moving.

I had one music CD to distract us as we drove: a recording of the band that had played nightly at the Mount Meru Hotel in Arusha during my time as observer at the Rwandan peace talks. Whitney Houston's song "I Will Always Love You" and Tiko, the UN military advisor, singing "Green, Green Fields" kept us company along the way. They helped put a smile on my face during what was otherwise an emotionally draining experience.

After several hours our long convoy made it to the border. While we were stopped for passport control on the Rwandan side, I got out of my car to stretch my legs and offer my colleagues some of the roasted turkey I had with me. I had plenty of time to take a close look at the composition of our convoy and count the vehicles. It turned out there were 108 vehicles and, I estimated, nearly four hundred people. Only nine persons in the convoy were Americans. German, Swiss, Canadian, and African diplomats, who had no airplanes coming to evacuate them, had joined us. A few pickup trucks piled high with the belongings of several families from the Persian Gulf state of Oman had attached themselves to our group. They said they had family in Burundi to stay with until this latest violence in Rwanda was over. All had decided to take advantage of what they believed would be their last opportunity to leave the country with some degree of safety and diplomatic cover.

By the time everyone completed the border formalities, night had fallen. The ambassador took the wheel of my car and assumed the challenge of navigating Burundi's winding road through the hills to Bujumbura. I fell fast asleep and did not wake until we reached the U.S. Embassy. The convoy had taken ten hours to make the normally five-hour trip.

The following day, with our cars parked and the keys in the care of embassy employees, almost all of the U.S. evacuees flew to Nairobi on the C-130 military transport plane that had brought the three hundred U.S. Marines to Bujumbura from an aircraft carrier off the coast of Somalia. The marines, who had cared for Coco since Linda's arrival in Bujumbura, delivered her to me as I boarded the plane. She trembled in my arms throughout the noisy flight.

After an overnight at a hotel in Nairobi, all of us flew on commercial flights to our respective destinations. Mine was Washington DC, where I continued to follow developments in Rwanda from a tiny, backroom space in the Office of Central African Affairs at the Department of State. I helped the overworked Rwanda Desk officer by writing daily summaries of events, led a humanitarian task force, and participated in other efforts to find a way to end the fighting and resume negotiations on implementing the Arusha Accords. Whether to call the killing genocide, how to protect and aid civilians, and what to do about Rwanda's Hutu-supremacist radio station, RTLM, that continued to spew out inflammatory anti-Tutsi propaganda were three key issues under discussion.

Comment

Somewhere along the way to the Burundi border, not long after we passed through Butare, a huge rainbow arced across the eastern sky ahead of us. The full spectrum of colors was boldly outlined against dark storm clouds in the distance. Could it be a good sign of better things to come for Rwanda? If so, it would be years before its promise could be fulfilled. Over the next four months, from April to July 1994, Hutu—government troops, militias, and ordinary citizens—killed an estimated eight hundred thousand to one million people. The victims were overwhelmingly Tutsi, along with some Hutu moderates.

The killing ended only when the Tutsi-led RPF force successfully defeated the government forces, or more accurately, chased them from the country. In the wake of the government forces followed government officials, civil servants, nearly all of those who had participated in the killing, and thousands and thousands of ordinary Hutu afraid of what an RPF victory might mean and of what the RPF might do to them. In all, nearly two million Rwandans sought safety in neighboring Zaire to the west or in Tanzania to the east.

When I closed the door to the embassy that day, I closed the door on a chapter of vigorous diplomatic activity aimed at supporting Rwanda's transition to democracy and peace. I have always believed that the intensity of the reaction to the downing of the president's plane was in some ways a measure of how close Rwandans had come to achieving both of these goals. Those who had the most to lose politically and economically by restructuring Rwandan institutions as called for in the Arusha peace agreement could not abide the thought of sharing power with the Tutsi or of having less than full control over Rwanda's politics and security.

We all knew there were extremist Hutu supremacists, but no one had anticipated how far they would to go to prevent the realignment of power, the centerpiece of the peace agreement, from coming to fruition. Under the ambassador's leadership, the embassy had always assumed that if the president could be convinced to support the changes, the naysayers would fall in line and support the changes too. We thought that when the president signed the Arusha Accords, he was signing on to the process, only to see him prevaricate and delay at every turn. By signing the agreement he probably signed his death warrant.

Only years later did it become clear to me that the hard-line Hutu supremacists from both sides of the Hutu political and regional divide had made a final break with the president over the strategy and tactics for holding on to power in Rwanda. The hard-liners, or "spoilers" in the parlance of later years, having lost confidence that they could maintain power through the democratic process, concluded that their only path to continuing political control of Rwanda would be through violence and killing their enemies. President Habyari-mana, however, probably believed until his death that he could use the democratic process to manipulate implementation of the peace accord and maintain power in Rwanda. It was the hard-liners' strat-egy of violence, though, that prevailed. Apparently they had not con-sidered the possibility that their strategy might fail.

[20]

Return to Rwanda

Peace returned to Rwanda in July. On July 4 the RPF captured Kigali; on July 13 they captured Ruhengeri in the north; and on July 18, Gisenyi, on the northwestern border with Zaire, fell. The RPF victories ended the killing that had claimed an estimated eight hundred thousand to one million lives, most of them Tutsi, but also Hutu moderates. As the RPF made its final push to end the genocide and the war, more than a million people followed their Hutu leaders into exile in Zaire, and another million or so fled to Tanzania. About a million sought refuge in southern Rwanda, where with UN authorization the French military had established a zone of control in late June called "Operation Turquoise." Many of these people later fled to Zaire after the French withdrew.

The country the RPF had conquered was in shambles. The infrastructure was devastated; the electrical grid was seriously damaged; and the telephones didn't work. The institutions of governance had collapsed; there was no civil service, no legislature, no judicial system, and no central bank. Fleeing government officials had reportedly absconded with all the money from the government coffers and all the vehicles that could move. The banks too were stripped of their money. The economy had collapsed.

Ambassador David Rawson and Lt. Col. Tony Marley, military liaison officer from the Bureau of African Affairs, had returned to Kigali at the end of July 1994 on a reconnaissance mission to assess the feasibility of reopening the embassy. About the same time, the U.S. military intervened to stop a cholera epidemic that was raging in the refugee camps just across the border in Zaire. The military set up its base of operations at the Kigali airport. Because of the U.S. military presence in Rwanda, both the Department of State and the Department of Defense wanted to reopen the embassy immediately to provide diplomatic support for the troops.

Ambassador Rawson raised the flag over the embassy in the presence of Ambassador George Moose, assistant secretary of state for Africa, who was traveling in the region. The U.S. Embassy was back in business. However, the ambassador could not stay. He had not foreseen this precipitous opening of the embassy and had obligations in the United States. So in August, just about a month after the RPF took control, the U.S. Department of State sent me back to Rwanda for two weeks as chargé d'affaires at the embassy in Kigali. With only slight hesitation, I looked forward to the opportunity to return. I did not know it would be one of my most difficult assignments.

There were no regularly scheduled flights into Rwanda, so I flew to Frankfurt, Germany, to connect with a U.S. C-130 military transport plane scheduled to fly to Kigali. The trip was memorable for being noisy and uncomfortable. It was also memorable because the pilot invited me into the cockpit to watch an astonishing air-to-air refueling operation. We landed in Kigali at night. Because of a curfew, I had to stay at the airport rather than go into town. I was shown to a small office equipped with an army cot where I spent the night. The U.S. Army had converted the airport terminal into lodging for arriving troops. The next morning, after a refreshing sleep, I showered in a tent set up on the apron of the runway. As I finished eating a hearty breakfast in a mess tent next to the shower facility, an embassy car and driver showed up to take me into town.

Nothing seemed normal along the way. The route from the airport had always bustled with cars and people. On this morning it was practically empty. Of the few cars I saw, most bore Burundi license plates, a sign that Rwandan refugees, predominantly Tutsi, were already returning. In the center of town occasional groups of people walking along the road turned out to be Tutsi from Burundi who had already traveled north. I learned later that many were living in abandoned houses, some in houses vacated by American personnel. When asked to leave by an embassy officer, Larry Richter, who had returned to supervise packing up the belongings of embassy personnel, they generally obliged, he said. As they left, though, they stole as much as they could and trashed the rest. Most of the houses of our staff and the ambassador's residence had been ransacked either by departing Hutu soldiers or by arriving Tutsi.

My house, however, located only a few blocks from the embassy, was remarkably intact. A mortar shell had hit the foundation at one corner, but the wall had not been damaged. Jonathan, my Tutsi gardener who had been beaten by soldiers searching my house for the prime minister, greeted me as I arrived. He had remained at the house throughout the genocide. My Tutsi housekeeper was also on hand when I returned. She and her entire nuclear family had managed to evade the killers. They had, however, absorbed her sister's children into their family when both parents were killed.

My superb cook, Bernard, also a Tutsi, had not survived. Because the ambassador's residence would need considerable work before anyone could live there again, his cook, a Hutu, had taken over at my house. The cook told me her Hutu husband had been arrested by the new government on charges of having participated in the genocide. She maintained that he had not been involved and was worried about him because of his poor health. He later died during his incarceration.

The U.S. Embassy, in the center of Kigali, was nearly intact. A mortar shell had hit the roof above the second-floor conference room, and sky was visible through the ceiling. The wall below, which framed the back door, bore the pockmarks of shellfire. But embassy vehicles and supplies stored on the compound had not been touched. The loyal guards had refused to admit any would-be pillagers. As a result, I had the eerie experience of finding my office exactly as I had left it four months earlier, when I had closed the embassy door and left Kigali in the final U.S. convoy to Burundi.

At the time of my return in mid-August, a few temporary American staff members were already on board. The economic-consular officer, Laura Lane, who had been back for about two weeks, was just leaving. Her house, also close to the embassy, was one of the few spared the indignity of being ransacked. The former general services officer, Larry Richter, enlisted the help of the Rwandan staff members who were trickling back to work. He too was also leaving. A temporary administrative officer, a clever improviser, would be staying for some time. Tony Marley would also be around for a while, and for that I was thankful. Among his many talents was his knowledge of how to operate the Inmarsat satellite telephone, a bulky, cumbersome phone that needed to be pointed in just the right direction to pick up a signal. It was our lifeline to the outside world. For some reason, though, we could not make it work at my residence.

Most of the returning staff were pleased to see that the embassy was reopening. Our political assistant, a budget analyst, and the receptionist, all Hutu, were among the first to appear. Our Tutsi consular assistant had been brutally killed; Laura, who had worked closely with him, was trying to find a way to get his young daughter assistance to leave the country. A senior local employee at USAID, a Tutsi, had miraculously, with cunning and bravery, survived. He later served as a government minister and played a substantial role in reenergizing Rwanda's private-sector economy. Some Hutu staff, we learned, had fled the country and were in refugee camps in Zaire or Tanzania; over time some of them returned when they learned that the embassy had reopened. It was heartening to see so many staff but devastating to contemplate what they and others who had perished must have experienced. I was on an emotional roller-coaster as I met survivors and learned of casualties.

It could not be business as usual under these circumstances. One of the big challenges to doing my job now was normally a simple one: scheduling appointments. With no telephone service, we had to send cars with messages to persons with whom we hoped to meet. Others looking for us were doing the same, leaving messages with the embassy receptionist seeking appointments.

We learned of one alternative: we could communicate with government offices via the two-way radio. It was while trying to connect with the prime minister's office by radio that I suddenly heard the familiar voice of a Hutu journalist I knew. By chance I had seen him a couple of months earlier in a U.S. television news broadcast, being interviewed from a displaced-persons camp in the Tutsi-controlled part of northern Rwanda. Now I learned that he had returned to Kigali after the killing ended and after the RPF had taken over the government. What's more, he was the cabinet director for the new Hutu prime minister, and just the person I needed to talk to about scheduling an appointment. I was excited to reconnect with him and also to find him with so much optimism for Rwanda's future.

My charge from Washington during my two weeks in Rwanda was to try to convince the RPF leadership to seek an extension of the UN-authorized, French-led Operation Turquoise. The United States believed a continued French presence in the protected zone in the south of the country would contribute to Rwanda's stability. There was still great fear among the Hutu—even those who had taken no part in the killing—because the Tutsi had taken over. To convey this U.S. message, I called on the president, the vice president, and the prime minister.

First I met President Pasteur Bizimungu, a Hutu whom I knew from the Arusha negotiations, at his residence, the former residence of President Habyarimana. I met Vice President Paul Kagame, the former RPF commander, in his office at one of the military barracks. Prime Minister Faustin Twagiramungu, the Hutu who had been named in the Arusha Accords to fill that position and whom I knew well, received me at his temporary office in the Meridien Umubano Hotel. All were adamant that the French should leave Rwanda as scheduled so that the RPF could establish its jurisdiction over the whole country. I conveyed this unanimous rejection of the U.S. proposal to Washington.

Even though the cabinet director was helping me, it was difficult to pin down a time for my meeting with Prime Minister Twagiramungu. In the end, the connection came in a most unusual way. I was just waking up on a Sunday morning when I heard the guard talking to someone at my gate. Moments later this unknown visitor passed in front of the house. From my bedroom window I asked what he wanted. He replied that the prime minister wanted to see me in half an hour, at 8:00. I told him I could be there in one hour.

When I reached the hotel, I had a long wait. This gave me a chance to talk with my journalist friend, the prime minister's cabinet director, and listen to the story of his escape. He had at first entrusted his wife and children to Hutu neighbors and had hidden for several days above the ceiling of his house. Then he put out word that he had been killed. After the killers stopped looking for him, he was able to round up his family and make his way to the RPF-controlled area of Kigali and from there to Byumba, a northern RPF-controlled town. He told of seeing a child walking alone clutching a severed hand. This image gave me chills. How many others were living with such trauma? What does such stress do to one's psychological and physical well-being? How does one recover?

When the prime minister called me into his office, the foreign minister was present as well. Our discussion of an extension for Operation Turquoise took about twenty minutes. After the foreign minister departed, the prime minister continued talking to me for another two hours. He was already upset with the way things were going and apparently needed someone outside the situation to use as a sounding board. He used to enlist the American ambassador for this purpose; this time I would have to do. When I finally took my leave, I found a number of people outside his office waiting to see him. Among them were some Hutu human rights advocates whom I had worked with. I was excited to see them and relieved that they were still alive. I wished them well for the future as they were called into Twagiramungu's office.

One day a Hutu woman whom I knew as a leader of a women's association came to my office to tell me the story of her ordeal during the genocide. She and her husband were known as Hutu moderates, she said, and were afraid they were on the militia or military lists of targeted persons. Fearing for their lives, they left their home with their son to seek refuge in the house of a European neighbor. After a period of time they were able to flee across the battle lines into the part of Kigali controlled by RPF soldiers. Eventually they made their way to Byumba, which had become a haven for Tutsi and Hutu moderates fleeing the killing.

While in Byumba she occupied her time by setting up programs to train other women in income-generating activities. I was deeply moved by her evident ability to retain her equilibrium and task-oriented leadership under such adverse circumstances. I learned several months later that this woman's husband had been assigned by the Tutsi-led government to a local government position in the southern town of Butare. Tragedy struck when he was killed by a band of young, revenge-seeking Tutsi military. With some help from international human rights activists, she managed to send her young son, who was being harassed at school, out of the country to continue his schooling. I do not know what happened to this courageous woman.

One evening Léonidas Rusatira, now a general, came to dinner at my house. He was the Hutu who had declared himself responsible for liaison with the international community after President Habyarimana's plane was shot down. I was surprised to find him in Kigali, as he had been the armed forces chief of staff for many years and therefore not trusted by the RPF. His presence confirmed his own belief in the ability of the new Rwanda to succeed. It marked a clean break for him from his pro-Habyarimana past.

Over dinner he wanted to tell his story of the genocide period. At the time the troubles began he had been director of the military training school in Kigali, the one that had dormitories just across the street from my house. For a while he stayed in Kigali, raising his voice in high-level military meetings against the killing and trying to persuade the political leaders to end it. One person told me that, during this time, Rusatira hid several Hutu in his house until he could spirit them safely out of the city, and he reportedly helped several targeted Hutu pass through roadblocks to escape into the countryside.

Not long after the killing began, though, Rusatira was reassigned to Gikongoro, a town in the south where he was to continue recruiting and training young men for the army. He was still in Gikongoro in late June when it became part of the Safe Humanitarian Zone established by the French under the UN-sanctioned Operation Turquoise. In Gikongoro he led a group of moderate army officers in issuing a statement calling for national reconciliation and an end to the killing. The statement drew virtually no support from Hutu in the military, but it attracted the attention of the French, who saw him thereafter as a liability, a troublemaker, and someone they did not want in their zone for fear he might draw them into political problems.

Consequently the French moved him out of Rwanda and into

neighboring Zaire. He was initially taken to Bukavu, a town across the border from southern Rwanda, and then to a place farther north, just south of Goma. There they confined him to house arrest for a number of weeks. Eventually the French released him but gave him no help in finding his way back to Rwanda; this he had to do on his own, walking and hitching rides, back through Bukavu and southern Rwanda, until he finally arrived in Kigali. He said he was waiting to see what the RPF would do with him, whether and how they would reintegrate him into the army. I learned later that he had to attend a reeducation camp before resuming his army life. His collaboration with the RPF eventually soured, however, and he went into hiding in Nairobi until he could make his way to Brussels.

Abbé André Sibomana, the Hutu priest-journalist and outspoken activist for democracy and human rights, had moved to Gitarama, about an hour's drive outside the capital. After the genocide he became acting bishop of Kabgaye, with his office at the Catholic parish there. During a long chat he recounted his story. He had stayed in his room in a parish in Kigali until he believed he would no longer be safe there. His human rights and anticorruption advocacy had made him a thorn in the side of the Habyarimana government, and he was convinced that he was on the list of persons to be killed. As he was leaving Kigali in his old, beat-up car, Sibomana said, he encountered a problem at a militia roadblock. Just then General Rusatira happened along and ordered the militia to let him pass.

Sibomana headed south to the parish in Gitarama. Some days later he moved on to his parents' home in a village some distance away, thinking he could escape the violence and killing there. But not long after, the killing came to his village. He saw the militia line up Tutsi at a river crossing, kill them, and dump their bodies into the water. Soon Tutsi living in the area started coming to him for help. By day, he said, he hid them in the local church. By night he led them across the fields along the path to the parish church in Gitarama, where a number of Tutsi had already gathered for safety. He took his charges halfway to Gitarama and then left them to make the final part of the journey on their own. The militia was always nearby, making the journey extremely dangerous. Sibomana showed me his shoes and said that he had had both soles replaced twice because of all the walking he had done at night.

He also told the story of a seven-year-old Tutsi boy he had found left for dead at the bottom of a well after being struck on the head with a machete. Sibomana said he nursed the child back to health and then took him one night on the journey halfway to the parish church in Gitarama. The boy, however, instead of continuing on with the others, had turned around to find his way back to the village. En route he had encountered some Hutu militia who asked him about the gash on his head. Savvy enough at age seven to know that he could not tell the truth in such a situation, he lied, telling the men some Tutsi had attacked him. In a second attempt to get the boy to safety, Sibomana took him to an orphanage in Butare. After the war ended he found the child thriving there.

After the genocide Sibomana eventually revived the Catholic-supported weekly newspaper *Kinyameteka*, of which he had been the editor, and wrote a book titled *Hope for Rwanda*. A few years later he died from a recurring disease for which he might have gotten help if the authorities had agreed to issue him a passport.

One Saturday afternoon I walked the couple of blocks from my house to the Diplomat Hotel, where I joined a group of human rights activists on the hotel's front porch. I knew most of them from my embassy work. All had stories to tell about how they or persons they knew had survived the killing. One was Alphonse-Marie Nkubito, the Hutu founder of the first human rights organization, who was minister of justice in the new government. He believed the reason he was still alive was because he had moved not long before the genocide began. The killers had gone to his old house, and—thinking the family living there was his—had killed them.

He had fled to the French Embassy around the corner from his new house. There he discovered that the other Rwandans seeking refuge were high-level officials from Habyarimana's government, many of them hard-line Hutu supremacists. As a human rights advocate and sharp critic of the Habyarimana government, he said he had felt quite uncomfortable in their presence. Nevertheless, he said he had stayed at the embassy because he had nowhere else to go. Eventually he was evacuated south to Bujumbura on a French plane with the other Rwandans, even though at least one had protested his presence. He left the plane in Burundi while the other Rwandans continued on to Paris.

After the RPF captured Kigali, he made his way back to the city. Like the prime minister's cabinet director, he was committed to helping rebuild Rwanda. I saw him a year later when he came to Washington for the presentation of a human rights award to one of his activist colleagues. Within two years, though, Nkubito was dead, reportedly dying in his sleep from an unknown cause. One of his colleagues told me he believed that the circumstances were somewhat mysterious. There was never any inquiry.

Throughout my two weeks back in Rwanda, I kept in close touch with the U.S. military at the airport. I was asked to brief high-level military personnel on the situation when they came to Kigali to assess the progress of their humanitarian operation to combat cholera in the refugee camp in Zaire. One of the visitors was Gen. George A. Joulwan, commander-in-chief, U.S. European Command, and Supreme Allied Commander, based in Germany. I accepted his offer to send some troops to my house to pack up my belongings for shipment to the United States, so one weekend morning four soldiers showed up in a Humvee and went to work. It was apparent they were enjoying being off the airport base. Their packing prowess left something to be desired, however. When I unpacked months later I discovered that glassware they had lightly wrapped and put at the bottom of a large box had been thoroughly crushed. But otherwise everything made it back to the United States in good shape, and I was grateful for their help.

The military had been careful to avoid being drawn into any situations off the airport grounds. The unit had the expertise to repair the city's electricity grid and telephone system, but they would not. The officers were wary of expanding their mission beyond its mandate. The military did have a van of equipment and three telephone technicians based at the embassy whose job was to keep lines of communication open to the United States for the military. These were the only military personnel operating off the airport compound.

On my last day in Kigali a presidential delegation arrived for a one-day visit. There were about ten to fourteen persons, among them a couple of congressmen, congressional staff, the director of the Aspen Institute in Washington (who had attended the same high school I had), and the director of the State Department's Office of Central African Affairs, Arlene Render, who had visited Kigali just prior to the onset of the genocide. Ambassador David Rawson returned with them. The delegation's purpose was to assess the military's humanitarian assistance program and the situation in Kigali. They arrived on a C-5 aircraft, the largest plane in the U.S. fleet. Coincidentally Russia's slightly larger military transport plane, the Antonov-224, was at the Kigali airport at the same time.

We started the visit with a briefing and then escorted the participants to several meetings with key Rwandan leaders, including President Bizimungu and Vice President Kagame. A big challenge was what and where to feed them at lunch time. The military came to my rescue, providing large trays of C-rations that only had to be heated up. We had an excellent, filling buffet lunch on the shrapnel-studded porch of my house. That evening I left on the C-130 military aircraft that came to collect the delegation and returned with them to Andrews Air Force Base just outside Washington DC.

I left Rwanda with sadness and a heavy heart. Throughout my stay Kigali had seemed somewhat surreal. True, I was elated to find many people I knew who were still alive, but their stories of traumatic survival seemed more like miracles than reality. I had also learned that many other people I knew were either in the refugee camps, in exile in Europe, or dead. Rebuilding a vibrant, thriving city and country would be a challenge.

My parting advice to one of my RPF colleagues who had been in Arusha and was now a government minister: Put resources into education for all the people, because an educated population will be less likely to let itself be led into committing the kinds of atrocities Rwanda had just experienced. I doubted the leadership would ever be brave enough to follow this advice, as an educated population can also pose a threat and a challenge. But I was wrong. Expanded opportunities for education became an important part of the RPF government's program.

PART 2

WHY DIPLOMACY FAILED

[21]

Diplomatic Challenges

U.S. policy in Rwanda during the three-year period preceding the genocide never wavered in its support for democratization and peace despite ever-increasing violence within the society. Along with most in the diplomatic community, the United States believed that this support held the key to helping Rwandans resolve their inter- and intraethnic power struggles. As conflict and violence escalated, continuing to support successful democratization and peace became our implicit conflict-resolution strategy. The sooner peace could be established and a transitional government put in place, we reasoned, the sooner multiparty elections could be held that would legitimize a group of leaders to guide the country to inclusive, participatory, democratic governance.

While pursuing pro-democracy, pro-peace policies, diplomats in Rwanda faced numerous challenges as conflict and violence escalated. A messy democratization process, peace negotiation pitfalls, limitations inherent in the practice of diplomacy, and an unresolved refugee situation made diplomacy anything but straightforward. Diplomats aware of such challenges and their implications could become more effective at conflict prevention, mitigation, management, and resolution in future situations where transitions such as democratization or peacemaking—or both, as was the case in Rwanda—are in progress

287

Democratization: A Messy Enterprise

"Democratization" was the policy watchword in Africa in the early 1990s. Most African leaders at the time had come to power through military coups or multiparty elections before subsequently consolidating their authority into one-party or one-man rule. Western governments, including the United States, were urging Africa's authoritarian leaders to end military rule and one-party political systems in favor of more broadly based, multiparty democracies.

Such transitions, however, may not be as straightforward as they may seem. Democratization can be a messy business. Shifts in power relationships that necessarily occur during any transition from authoritarianism or a single-party dictatorship to political pluralism are likely to be profoundly destabilizing. Conflict, for example, lay at the very heart of Rwanda's transition to democracy. The prospect of a more open political process unleashed long-held antagonisms based on ethnicity and geography. In Rwanda, instead of a collaborative process, with all factions working toward common goals, key power groups were intent on dominating the process of change and crafting an outcome favorable to their group. Advocates of change became vulnerable to violence from those holding onto the reins of power.

Those in power—the northern Hutu—undoubtedly believed they could dictate the pace and outcome of the political liberalization process because their party controlled all the levers of power. Those seeking to gain power—the southern Hutu on the one hand and exiled Tutsi on the other—were intent on breaking the monopoly on power held by the northern Hutu for nearly twenty years. Each of these groups believed it could use the democratization process to shape and legitimize a future political system to its advantage.

Rwanda's tumultuous democratization process posed numerous challenges to diplomacy and to diplomats intent on supporting the process. These challenges were not unique, it turns out, to Rwanda's transition process. Similar challenges were prominently in the news in relation to the Arab Spring uprisings fifteen years later. Similar factors and comparable situations will be likely to arise in any new diplomatic efforts to support democratization, or any other such sweeping transformations. Therefore several of the challenges democratization poses to diplomacy are worthy of note.

Creating an Atmosphere Conducive to Democracy

Intra-Hutu animosity, fear and mistrust between Hutu and Tutsi, and the backlash against democratization from Hutu hard-liners created an atmosphere antithetical to a successful transition from authoritarianism to political pluralism. Working toward a common vision for Rwanda's future across political, geographic, and ethnic fault lines was all but impossible. The armed Tutsi-led RPF insurgency exacerbated social divisions, further complicating the situation. There was no shared vision for Rwanda's future political system and little incentive for reaching compromise.

Instead democratization prompted intense competition for position and power within and among Rwanda's principal groups. It also inspired a fierce backlash against changing the status quo. This competition and the backlash were the major sources of the ever-escalating violence that unsettled and destabilized the country throughout my tenure in Rwanda. Nothing less than future control of the country was at stake. Diplomacy focused on helping competing factions find common ground on transition issues without addressing underlying or proximate causes of the intense antagonisms among the groups.

Building Democratic Institutions

Rwandans had little experience with democracy or democratic institutions before embarking on a transition from authoritarianism to political pluralism. They had formed political parties prior to independence and had held multiparty elections both before and after independence. However, the first party elected to power after independence—dominated by southern Hutu—used its authority to consolidate its control and governed as a one-party state in all but name. The 1973 coup brought to power a competing party— dominated by northern Hutu—that did the same. This second postindependence government, though, went one step further, officially declaring Rwanda a one-party state. A legislature existed that had both elected and appointed representatives, but it served as a rubber stamp for initiatives from the president and his party. Rwanda had no tradition of political moderation, power sharing, or compromise. The pendulum of power swung from one extreme to the other. A winner-take-all approach to governance had become entrenched.

As a result, the institutions of democracy—political parties, the judiciary, and the media, for example—were weak, misunderstood, and misused. Political parties became vehicles of violence instead of tools for peaceful mobilization of political participation. Rival party youth groups, instead of respecting constitutionally protected freedoms of speech and assembly, frequently disrupted each other's events. This often led to chaos and violence that resulted in injury and even death to political opponents. Courts offered no recourse for redress of human rights abuses. The media became a tool for propaganda and demonization of "the other."

Embassy pleas to government and party authorities to rein in their youth were rebuffed or ignored. Party leaders, claiming sufficient experience, rejected offers of training in party development from the U.S. National Democratic Institute. Embassy workshops promoting responsible journalism had little impact on inflammatory rhetoric. Diplomats were unable to rectify such misunderstandings and misuse of the institutions of democracy.

Protecting Vulnerable Groups

Advocates of change in authoritarian situations are vulnerable to physical harm, especially from those who reject change or resent those newly empowered by the change. Those in Rwanda whose first priority was maintaining their own power and privilege threatened, intimidated, and subjected to physical violence Tutsi suspected of being accomplices of the RPF insurgents and the Hutu and Tutsi advocates of democracy.

Hate speech played a central role in denigrating and demonizing the Tutsi dubbed "sympathizers" with the RPF and the democracy advocates perceived as threats by some in the Hutu majority. The relentless anti-Tutsi campaign waged by government—and later private—radio, in the print media, and in speeches of political party leaders stirred up ethnic fear, hatred, and mistrust between Hutu and Tutsi. Maligning democracy advocates and labeling them "the enemy" heightened their vulnerability to acts of violence.

The embassy should have done more to make Washington policymakers aware of the destructive role radio, print media, and public addresses were playing in fueling fear and hate. Deliberate words and actions cultivated an attitude toward Tutsi and democracy advocates that made them acceptable targets for retribution and violence. The weak and dysfunctional Rwandan judicial system offered advocates of change little protection or recourse to justice. The system simply did not hold perpetrators of lawlessness or abuse accountable for their deeds. A culture of impunity encouraged and gave free rein to those who abused their waning power. Where the rule of law is weak, the risk to vulnerable groups is great.

Diplomats needed a strategy for countering such irresponsible use of the media and other public speech platforms that would not compromise the principle of free speech and press. Providing brief workshops for journalists was not enough. Diplomats needed strategies for encouraging accountability for human rights abuses. Talking to complicit authorities about respecting human rights was insufficient; it was little better than acquiescing to the existing culture of impunity.

After the genocide the United States poured millions of dollars into a USAID program to help rebuild and strengthen Rwanda's collapsed judicial system. Had such a program aimed at strengthening the rule of law been available before the genocide, it might have offered vulnerable Rwandans some desperately needed protection. Why wait until Humpty Dumpty has fallen off the wall and shattered before providing funding and expertise to help reverse a failing situation?

Today a plethora of nongovernmental organizations specialize in peacebuilding activities. Their programs, intended for early intervention where conflicts appear imminent, address such critical steps between authoritarianism and democracy as a strong, independent judicial system, the rule of law, and protection for vulnerable groups. Peacebuilding programs and strategies are often similar in conceptualization to policies, programs, and interventions usually considered postconflict reconstruction activities.

Where conflict exists or appears imminent, diplomats may want to partner with such peacebuilding organizations to facilitate and support preconflict interventions. Peacebuilding interventions could help societies in transition reach a tipping point whereby those opposed to change would be constrained enough so that those empowered by the change—such as democratization—could act without constant fear of physical harm.

Preventing "Losers" from Becoming "Spoilers"

There will always be winners and losers in societal transitions as broad in scope and implication as Rwanda's attempt to transform its political system from authoritarianism to democratic pluralism. The challenge to diplomats supporting such sweeping change is how to encourage decision makers to ensure all groups involved have a stake in the outcome. If any group—especially one losing power and privilege in the new system—believes it has been left out of the process, the risk is high that it could become a spoiler. All involved need assurances that their interests—and their lives—will be protected during and after the transition process. There can be no single formula for handling this issue. Some proposed solutions have been more successful than others.

In Rwanda the Hutu extremist CDR party was locked out of the democratization process at three critical junctures by opposition politicians and the Tutsi-led RPF. After its third rebuff, CDR members, and others who shared their Hutu-supremacist views, apparently drifted away from or decided to abandon democratization and the peace process. With no apparent alternative route to reaching its goal of clinging to power, the CDR turned to a desperate strategy of apocalyptic violence and the total elimination of its enemies. CDR members and those who joined them in Hutu solidarity believed they had nothing more to lose. Their Hutu-supremacist ideology, overt embrace of violence, and unabashed rejection of the Arusha power-sharing agreement made the CDR a pariah party.

Inclusion versus Exclusion

Diplomats counseled the Hutu opposition and the Tutsi-led RPF to adhere to the principle of inclusion over exclusion. Each time the democratization debate stalled on the issue of CDR participation, diplomats urged them to find ways to keep the CDR and its supporters engaged in the transition process. Their arguments, however, failed to sway those so viscerally opposed to the CDR's increasingly objectionable views and violence. Opponents of the CDR believed there was no reason to modify their exclusionary position or to seek ways to keep the CDR engaged in the democratization process. For its part, the thrice-spurned CDR believed it had been pushed into a corner with no way out other than violence. With no stake in the process, these extremists who would be losers in the transition to democracy became the spoilers of the entire process.

Here the principled stand of the diplomatic community became something of a trap. While diplomats were arguing for including rather than excluding the CDR in the democratization process, the president and his party were also adamantly pressing not only for CDR inclusion in the process but also for giving it an expanded role in the transitional institutions. This unfortunate coincidence of interests between diplomats and the president gave those opposed to CDR inclusion reason to dismiss the diplomatic arguments as mere smoke screens for enhancing presidential power in the transitional period. Diplomats risked their credibility as power brokers over this principle that was resoundingly rejected by negotiators at Arusha. Inclusion versus exclusion remains one of the thorniest issues diplomats can face in resolving conflicts and laying the foundation for sustainable peace.

Addressing Human Rights Abuses

Human rights diplomacy tends to begin and end with verbal denunciations of human rights abuses addressed to appropriate government authorities or pronounced in international fora. However, instead of heeding numerous verbal interventions urging respect for human rights from diplomats of the United States and other countries, Rwandan authorities generally sidestepped the issue. They would deny responsibility for alleged abuses, dismiss calls for redress, or blame others, such as the Tutsi-led RPF, for whatever infraction was under discussion.

Despite such diplomatic interventions in Kigali and ongoing peace negotiations in Arusha, human rights abuses against Tutsi and democracy advocates continued unabated within the country. Diplomacy was unable to thwart the periodic small-scale massacres targeting Tutsi, and it was ineffective at convincing Hutu leaders to curb the violence of political party youth groups.

Making Rwanda's abysmal human rights record more of an issue in international fora might have helped bring greater pressure on authorities to curb abuses. The United States missed an opportunity to raise Rwanda at the 1993 UN Commission on Human Rights, giving priority instead to other pressing human rights situations. Two more missed opportunities came in 1993 with the release of the reports of the two international investigations into the human rights situation in Rwanda. The findings and recommendations of these two credible investigations—one from an international consortium of respected human right groups and the other from the United Nations—could have served as the basis for calling international attention to the deteriorating situation in Rwanda. Highlighting discussions in these reports of whether genocide may have taken place might have evoked a sense of urgency within the international community about the need for a more concerted human rights response than our tiny embassy could sustain. Perhaps taking an outspoken position on the human rights issue—especially in concert with allies—might have provoked UN action or helped protect local rights advocates.

Avoiding Political Polarization and Marginalizing Moderates

In Rwanda the pendulum of governance traditionally swung from one extreme to another when governments changed. This experience of governance from the extremes rather than from the center gave politicians little experience of political moderation, compromise, power sharing, or inclusiveness. Hutu politicians and civic leaders who supported power sharing with Tutsi tried to fill this middle ground during the democratization process. However, once Hutu Power leaders advocating Hutu solidarity successfully rallied most Hutu against power sharing with the Tutsi, the moderates were forced to choose: accept Hutu solidarity over power sharing with the Tutsi or be labeled a traitor to the Hutu cause.

This political polarization turned out to be a divisive and destructive path for Rwanda. It left no space for political moderates whose voices would be critical to democratization and ending the legacy of mistrust between ethnic groups. It was these moderates that U.S. policy counted on to help Rwanda through its transition to democratic pluralism. For the few Hutu who dared to choose power sharing over Hutu solidarity, the price was high: most were killed at the start of the genocide or are still in exile in Europe or elsewhere. Efforts by the United States and other countries to support and strengthen moderates were insufficient; we need to reexamine this strategy and how it can be improved.

Diplomats need to become more effective at using diplomacy to help avoid, slow down, or even reverse political polarization in similar transition situations. One avenue might have been to create opportunities for encouraging better understanding between ethnic and geographic groups. Oxfam U.K. implemented several local-level reconciliation programs in pre-genocide Rwanda with reportedly positive results. Other local or international nongovernmental organizations might have been funded to undertake such reconciliation activities before misunderstandings became wedges driving groups apart. Such reconciliation activities were numerous in the aftermath of the genocide, for example.

Our Western experience with democracy may have dulled our understanding of the impact of such power shifts, especially in countries with little to no history of democracy. We gave little thought to how the winners and losers in Rwanda's democratization process would handle their changing roles and new positions in the political, economic, and social hierarchy. Using our own experience with contemporary democracy as a reference point, we did not adequately anticipate all that lay between authoritarianism and the goal of representative participation in governance. Nor did we recognize any link between our prodemocracy policies and the antidemocracy backlash that fueled Rwanda's ever-escalating violence. We tended to accept verbal commitments to the democratization process as indicative of buy-in to all that democracy entailed. Compromise was expected and a commitment to implementing agreements understood. Our assumptions were misplaced, and they went unrealized.

The simultaneous pursuit of two transitions, democratization and peace, in two different locations, Kigali and Arusha, changed the political dynamics of both transitions. In Kigali the democratization dialogue occurred almost exclusively among the Hutu majority. At the Arusha peace talks, however, the Tutsi-led RPF was negotiating directly—and on equal footing—with the diverse government delegation. The RPF delegation and Hutu opposition representatives on the government delegation, despite their mistrust of each other, managed to find common ground on several critical issues. Over the objections of hard-line Hutu government delegates, the final peace agreement contained controversial power-sharing provisions. The hard-liners rejected the agreement on grounds it granted the Tutsi minority too much power at their expense. They had no confidence that the objectionable arrangement could be altered to their advantage if they deferred action until the proposed transitional government was in place, as counseled by some in the international community. Instead, as the hard-liners saw their prospects for holding onto power slipping away, some turned to an apocalyptic strategy to achieve their goal: killing all their enemies. Mass atrocities and genocide were the result.

The biggest challenge for diplomats seeking to promote or support a successful peace process may be how to help negotiators, mediators, and facilitators craft sustainable agreements that can be implemented over the long term. Diplomacy successfully facilitated bringing Rwanda's warring sides to the negotiating table after armed conflict reached a stalemate. Diplomats and diplomacy also helped shepherd the parties to a final agreement during a year of testy negotiations. But could it be implemented and was it sustainable?

After eight months of effort, implementation of the Arusha Accords still eluded the parties to the agreement, and after steadily escalating violence, genocide enveloped the country. In a series of miscalculations, diplomacy had failed to foster a win-win peace agreement that might have been sustainable. Recognizing some of the potential pitfalls diplomats faced in peacemaking in Rwanda might suggest strategies and policies that could increase diplomatic effectiveness in future similar situations.

A Flawed Agreement

Some international analysts have argued that the Arusha peace negotiations produced a flawed agreement. There is no doubt that the Accords contained seriously problematic provisions that clearly contributed to the delays, manipulation, and violence that dominated the months between the signing of the Accords in August 1993 and the beginning of the genocide in April 1994. These flaws included:

- Retaining power-sharing arrangements for Rwanda's transitional institutions that Hutu supremacists categorically rejected.

- Making representation in the transitional institutions dependent on the unity of existing political parties.

- Setting unrealistic expectations for a proposed United Nations peacekeeping operation.

Diplomats, including those from the United States, continued to support the Arusha peace process despite these flaws. Hutu hardliners had publicly, vociferously, and violently denounced the Accords' centerpiece and its main flaw, its power-sharing provisions. Nevertheless, having failed to convince negotiators to revisit the problematic provisions, diplomats accepted the fait accompli instead of denouncing it or conditioning future support on renegotiation. Intent on seeing negotiations through to a signed accord, diplomats worried that reopening the power-sharing issue could lead to the collapse of the entire peace process and a return to war.

When ideological differences over power sharing blocked two political parties from compiling a unified slate of representatives in the transitional institutions—a manifestation of the second flaw—diplomats urged compromise. Warned that their expectation of having a UN peacekeeping force with nationwide security responsibilities deployed to Rwanda within forty days was unrealistic—the third flaw—negotiators still retained this arrival deadline and expansive mandate assumptions in the Accords.

The veteran American diplomat Herman Cohen has coined the term "signing obsession" to describe the eagerness of diplomats to shepherd negotiations through to their conclusion at the cost of flawed agreements. When he launched his book on peacemaking efforts in Africa, he told a gathering of diplomats that his biggest mistake as assistant secretary of state for Africa in the early 1990s had been to put too much faith in negotiated peace agreements. Flawed agreements, he said, should have been denounced even if the parties were willing to sign them, as in the case of Rwanda. "Frequently," he wrote, "such flawed agreements signal that the peace process is just another aspect of war for some protagonists, a resting and regrouping period between battles rather than a peaceful new beginning. Such was clearly the case in Angola, Ethiopia, Liberia, and Rwanda."[1]

Other Peace Process Pitfalls

The negotiated agreement was the consequence of a peace process that itself had many characteristics that adversely affected prospects for successful implementation. As with democratization, making peace among warring factions involves dialogue and compromise and is likely to produce winners and losers unless a win-win formula is crafted. It requires that all parties maintain a vested interest in the outcome as well as a commitment to implementing it. Several problematic elements in the Rwanda peace process offer warnings to diplomats who might become involved with peacemaking in future.

Dynamics of peacemaking, a voice for the minority: The dynamics of the peace process in Arusha were a stark contrast to those of the democratization process in Kigali. While the Tutsi had minimal impact in Kigali, at the peace talks in Arusha the Tutsi had not only a voice but indeed a critical role in decision making about the future of Rwanda. There the Tutsi-led RPF delegation negotiated as an equal partner with the predominantly Hutu government delegation. Only at the Arusha peace talks did the Tutsi minority have a formal role in discussions about political and military power-sharing. Only in Arusha were representatives of the Tutsi minority talking directly to representatives of the Hutu majority on a daily basis about democracy and peace.

Early on in the peace talks the RPF clearly indicated that it had no intention of joining the existing political process as just another political party vying for power in a multiparty process dominated by the entrenched party of the president. Instead, in the course of negotiations on power sharing the RPF revealed its intention to weaken the president and his ruling party and reshape Rwanda's governance system to include significant Tutsi participation.

Although the Hutu opposition parties in Kigali used democratization to gain leverage over the president and his party, the president and hard-line allies remained the dominant political force. In Arusha the RPF relied on the peace process as its vehicle for assuring a Tutsi role in Rwanda's future. There it was the hard-line, extremist Hutu who were sidelined, not the Tutsi. This unevenness between negotiations in Kigali and Arusha may have enabled the December surprise in 1992, when Arusha negotiators preempted Kigali discussions on power sharing with decisions unacceptable to some.

Dynamics of distance, strange bedfellows: Negotiating dynamics varied significantly between Arusha and Kigali. In Kigali the president and hard-line Hutu could essentially stall or scuttle any negotiating proposals or positions put forward by the Hutu political opposition. In Arusha government delegates representing the Hutu opposition and the Tutsi-led RPF, though suspicious of one another's motives and by no means formally aligned, sometimes saw their interests converge. One common goal was to end the president's monopoly on power. By making common cause with the RPF on this and certain other issues, the Hutu opposition strengthened its voice, to the detriment of the hard-line Hutu delegates.

As a result of their stronger voices in Arusha, the Hutu opposition and the Tutsi-led RPF negotiators could sometimes reach agreement on issues, such as power sharing, that Hutu extremists had blocked in Kigali. Consequently negotiations on political and military power-sharing in Kigali and in Arusha often arrived at very different conclusions.

This cooperation between strange bedfellows at Arusha enabled negotiators—the government opposition and the RPF—to lock in agreements about Rwanda's political and military future that eroded the power and authority of the president and his once omnipotent MRND party. Without the peace talks and their internal dynamics, it is unlikely the RPF could have had such a far-reaching impact in shaping Rwanda's transitional institutions. The negotiations gave the RPF a forum in which it was able to outmaneuver—indeed bypass— the hard-line Hutu on the government delegation and impose its preferences on Rwanda's democratization process.

Absence of a common vision: Just as Rwandans had no common vision for democracy, they had no common vision for the outcome of the peace talks. Even though the government and RPF delegations at Arusha had agreed in the rule-of-law protocol on a set of principles—such as the right of refugees to return to their country and the prohibition of exclusion or discrimination—it was unclear whether the parties shared a common interpretation of these principles. Arusha negotiators and diplomats failed, however, to refer to these concepts embodied in this protocol to prevent the Arusha process from veering off center. One provision, for example, rejected any form of exclusion or discrimination as antithetical to national unity. This might have been relevant to diplomacy over exclusionary treatment of the hard-line Hutu-supremacist CDR party.

Pacing the process of change, evolution versus revolution: The government delegation and the RPF negotiators held opposing views about the pace of change in Rwanda. While Kigali decision makers pursued an evolutionary transition from a one-party state to a democratic system of government, RPF negotiators were locking in agreements at Arusha that would restructure Rwanda's system of governance and revolutionize its power relationships. The president no doubt expected that he and his party could control the pace of change toward the outcome they desired. They lost control, though, of the revolutionary pace in Arusha.

Decisions at Arusha were definitely moving faster and calling for more sweeping changes than the politicians in Kigali were prepared for. The tendency of Arusha negotiators to get out ahead of the Kigali politicians created strong animosities that did not subside with the signing of the Accords. Instead lingering hate fed into the violence that escalated to genocide.

Legitimacy question: The preamble to the Arusha Accords explicitly stated that the protocols agreed at Arusha and the Rwandan constitution would henceforth constitute the fundamental law of the country.

Diplomatic Challenges

Where the two were in conflict, according to the Accords' preamble, the Arusha agreement would prevail. Rwanda's hard-liners—in the president's dominant MRND party, the Hutu-supremacist CDR party, and those from the Hutu opposition who joined them under the Hutu Power banner—never accepted this premise. Arusha negotiators, however—particularly government delegates from the Hutu opposition and the RPF delegates—maintained throughout that their agreement prevailed. The hard-liners apparently believed that the lack of legitimacy they attributed to the Arusha Accords gave them license to disregard the negotiated settlement.

Dynamics of diplomacy, Kigali versus Arusha: The role of the diplomatic corps in Kigali with regard to the peace talks differed from that in Arusha. Although diplomats in both locations shared the goal of achieving a negotiated settlement, they were working in two totally different environments. Kigali diplomats sought to facilitate compromise across the Hutu geographic divide within Rwanda to enable the government to take a united position to Arusha.

Diplomats in Arusha worked across the Hutu-Tutsi ethnic divide and across the gap of the parties to armed conflict to encourage compromise between the warring factions. As observers at the peace talks, they interacted daily not only with the mostly Hutu government delegation but also with the united, disciplined, mostly Tutsi RPF negotiators.

This difference in diplomatic dynamics between Kigali and Arusha often put the Kigali perspective and policy recommendations at odds with those of diplomatic observers at Arusha. These differing assessments reflected the location where the diplomats were operating and the objectives of their respective missions.

Limitations on the Practice of Diplomacy

Diplomacy at its core aims to help prevent, mitigate, manage, or resolve conflicts within, between, or among states through peaceful means: dialogue and negotiation. Nevertheless, despite working with Rwandans in support of their transitions to democracy and peace, the Kigali diplomatic corps was unable to prevent the steadily escalating violence that ultimately led to genocide. Some reasons for this failure derive not only from the situation in the country of assignment but also from limitations inherent in the practice of diplomacy. Systemic and structural aspects of diplomacy can and often do interfere with diplomatic success.

With no discernible strategic or geopolitical national security interests for the United States, Rwanda was a low-priority country for the U.S. Department of State. Even within the Bureau of African Affairs, Rwanda took a backseat to countries where greater national interests were at stake: Somalia was collapsing, civil war was tearing Sudan apart, and an insurgency threatened Liberia. Although the bureau's Office of Central African Affairs paid attention to this small, poor, landlocked, French-speaking country in a region where stability was the only U.S. interest, policy decisions routinely rose no higher than the assistant secretary of state for Africa, three levels below the secretary of state. Two major consequences impacted the Kigali embassy's efforts to implement U.S. policy in Rwanda.

First, few U.S. security interests translated into few resources, both personnel and funding. With just seven American officers at the embassy and only slightly more at USAID, both the embassy and the aid mission had to focus their activities narrowly and work closely with colleagues at other diplomatic missions to heighten the impact of U.S. policy initiatives. Neither the embassy nor USAID had any surge capacity to expand diplomatic or programmatic activities in response to Rwanda's deteriorating security situation.

Second, where U.S. security interests are low, high-level decision makers at the State Department or other relevant departments rarely pay attention to information about emerging problems. During the turmoil of the pre-genocide years, embassy cables reported persistent human rights violations and periodic, geographically confined massacres. Even though the information received broad distribution within the foreign affairs agencies in Washington, it received little attention. No established channels existed for increasing Rwanda's visibility among Washington policymakers. When the president's plane went down in April 1994 and the killing began in Kigali, intelligence analysts throughout the U.S. government scrambled to figure out where Rwanda was and why it was disintegrating. With little to no understanding of the situation, policymakers wondered what, if anything, the United States should do about it.

U.S. Influence Matters

The effectiveness of U.S. diplomacy often depends on the ability of diplomats to influence and convince their various interlocutors of U.S. positions. In Rwanda both Belgium, the former colonial power, and France, the source of significant military support to the government, had far greater influence than did the United States. Both had larger embassy staffs, larger assistance programs, more resources to support policy initiatives, and greater access to a broader array of Rwandan government officials than did the United States. Rwandan authorities, including the president and political party leaders, did seem to pay attention to the views and counsel of successive American ambassadors. Nevertheless the U.S. diplomatic mission in Kigali had little leverage with Rwanda's decision makers.

Diplomatic Culture Traps

Diplomatic culture binds diplomats together. Regardless of their nationality, diplomats share many common professional values that often lead them to similar professional assumptions and judgments. However, these assessments can reflect misunderstandings or misinterpretations of events and actions occurring around them.

For example, the diplomatic culture of negotiation suggests a set of accepted norms: committing to resolve differences peacefully, accepting adversaries as legitimate negotiating partners, seeking common ground and compromise through dialogue, arriving at mutually acceptable arrangements, and working together to implement the agreed program. Diplomats in both Kigali and Arusha may have assumed that by agreeing to negotiate, the parties were also committing to abide by these norms.

If so, such assumptions turned out to be erroneous in the case of Rwanda. They masked competing intentions and goals that were motivating the various factions at the negotiating table. Dominance rather than cooperation seems to have been the guiding principle of the negotiators. There was no fundamental agreement on power sharing, the central premise of the peace talks. There was little evidence that the parties, despite professing commitment to democratic values, had embraced compromise, multiparty elections, respect for minority rights, responsible journalism, or other key building blocks of democracy.

Diplomatic culture also places a priority on success. Having the parties at Arusha reach a signed agreement became a powerful goal and unifying force within the diplomatic corps in Kigali and its counterpart in Arusha. Achieving this goal apparently justified going along with controversial power-sharing provisions that helped lock the parties into an agreement that Hutu supremacists openly opposed and violently rejected.

Consistent with striving for success, diplomats tend to report positive developments to headquarters rather than deliver bad news that might reflect poorly on their accomplishments. Reporting from the Kigali embassy during these troubled times highlighted advances in democratization and progress toward peace. Reports of policy successes, however, needed to be better balanced with reports of threats to successful transitions to democracy and peace: the anti-Tutsi media campaigns and other "hate" radio broadcasts, the culture of impunity for massacres and other human rights abuses, the formation and training of militias, and the distribution of guns to civilians. Greater attention to the actions of the antidemocratization forces would have presented a more complete picture to Washington of what was happening in Rwanda. More reporting on these unintended, negative consequences of U.S. support for democratization and peace might have served as vivid early warning signs for the chaos that eventually engulfed Rwanda.

Knowledge Traps

The core of a diplomat's job overseas is to understand what is happening in a given country in relation to U.S. policy interests and to report coherently and concisely to Washington decision makers. How to make accurate assessments given multiple and often contradictory sources of information presents a series of challenges to any diplomat.

Information gathering: To piece together as accurate a narrative as possible, diplomats generally develop a broad spectrum of local contacts to help them understand why something is happening and how to interpret various, often contradictory explanations. Identifying and building trust with persons who are credible and who will speak honestly and openly takes time. Even then, assessing the credibility of interlocutors and understanding their biases must be taken into account. As Rwandans told me, the local rule of thumb is that people will tell you what they think you want to hear.

Information processing: Americans tend to be very literal, so we are likely to take people at face value until proven wrong. We need to understand that in other cultures people are often much more nuanced. While we want to know the facts and tend to ask *what* happened, in Rwanda the relevant question is usually *why* something happened or *why* someone is telling you something. The most obvious or logical explanation would usually be incorrect and could lead to misinterpretations or skewed analyses. Observers needed to think outside the box, look at the gamut of possible explanations for something, and examine tangential or seemingly totally unrelated events to comprehend any given situation. Rwandans were, in my experience, masters at weaving webs of plausible deniability around any significant or sensitive event.

Little historical context: Generally assigned for two or three years to any one country, diplomats often lack sufficient historical context for understanding contemporary events, especially those deeply rooted in the past. This short-term view can become a serious handicap in grasping fully the context for contemporary events or assessing their significance. Diplomats may not even be aware of the questions to ask about past events in order to elicit key information that would provide a context for current events.

Significant gaps in my knowledge of Rwandan history led me to:

- Underestimate the depth of the split between the president's political party and its more radical Hutu-supremacist offshoot.

- Overestimate the president's ability to convince Hutu extremists to accept the peace settlement.

- Misunderstand the emotional appeal of Hutu Power and its roots in the preindependence slogan "Hutu solidarity," used to rally and unite Hutu against Tutsi.

- Fail to anticipate how far the Hutu extremists were willing to go to prevent implementation of the Arusha Accords.

Limited regional context: Too often the significance of regional and cross-border dynamics is lost in bilateral diplomacy. In the Great Lakes region of Africa, where the history of the countries is so intertwined, a limited grasp of the regional context can adversely impact a diplomat's understanding of any single country in the region. Relations between Rwanda and its neighbors were critical to events unfolding in Rwanda before, during, and after the genocide.

Bilateral (state-to-state) diplomacy, which dominates U.S. relations with other nations, usually downplays the significance of regional and cross-border contexts. The organization of the U.S. Department of State reinforces this bilateral approach. An officer in the Office of Central African Affairs in the Africa Bureau, for example, manages the relationship between the United States and one specific country. If the countries are small and of little national interest to the United States, one officer might handle two or even three country relationships, though each is normally treated as separate. On any given day the manager of U.S. relations with Rwanda, for example, has little knowledge of what is happening in neighboring Uganda; the two are situated in different regional offices at the State Department. Diplomats stationed at embassies abroad focus almost exclusively on the country to which they are assigned, with little time or encouragement to look beyond its borders.

Responsibility for integrating these disparate bilateral policies into a holistic regional perspective generally falls to the office director or the front office of the bureau. These officers, however, may be consumed by several problematic bilateral relationships at once, leaving little time for reflecting on the larger regional picture. In some cases a special envoy might be named to advance U.S. policy with one country or a set of countries within a region. But this person might report directly to the assistant secretary or even higher. The envoy's activities may be poorly coordinated with the relevant regional office.

After the genocide a series of Great Lakes envoys and other special regional arrangements partially rectified this regional knowledge gap. To ensure policymakers receive the best advice possible, however, the Department of State and diplomats abroad need to pay greater attention to regional perspectives in formulating policies, especially when conflict may be involved.

Dealing with Unsavory Characters

Diplomats must maintain good access to key opinion shapers as well as decision makers. This can mean cultivating relationships and spending time with the good, the bad, and the unsavory. Even though it may be uncomfortable to deal with human rights abusers or those behind demeaning media campaigns, maintaining such contacts can be critical to developing a full picture of what is happening in a country and why. Nevertheless diplomatic neutrality or impartiality is often misunderstood, especially where there is high-stakes competition for power, charged with suspicion and mistrust, as was the case in Rwanda. Talking to "them" must mean you are against "us," some host country interlocutors tend to reason.

Domestic Considerations Often Drive Foreign Policy Decisions

When on leave in Washington in July 1993, I urged Africa Bureau leaders to support rapid deployment of a robust United Nations peacekeeping force for Rwanda once the anticipated peace agreement was signed. Such a force, I argued, would be indispensable to creating a secure environment for implementing the peace accord. I was told that, despite my compelling argument, neither the State Department nor other departments of the administration would likely agree to commit the resources needed for such a force in such a small, low-priority country. Furthermore the American public would neither understand nor accept a robust UN force for a place where U.S. security interests were negligible.

I should probably already have understood the extent to which domestic political considerations could override a critical humanitarian need to bring a conflict to an end in a faraway country. Still, I was disheartened by the reply to my advocacy.

Taking steps to overcome or minimize the limitations of the practice of diplomacy could help improve the effectiveness of diplomacy. Effective diplomacy, however, is only part of the story, particularly in conflict situations where ending, mitigating, or managing conflict is the goal. Diplomacy alone can never resolve conflicts within other sovereign nations. Effective diplomacy needs a willing partner. Such conflicts can be resolved only when the parties themselves develop the political will to work together to find solutions. In Rwanda the prospect of profoundly reordered power relationships among various political, geographic, and ethnic groups as a result of simultaneous transitions to democracy and peace led to heightened mistrust among the groups and widespread uncertainty and fear.

Only when the parties to a conflict are genuinely committed to finding common ground, to making compromises, and to achieving a solution acceptable to all will sustainable peace be possible. Diplomacy is most successful and effective when it works with the parties concerned to help create the atmosphere within which these goals can be realized.

When Humanitarianism Is Not Enough

Between 1960 and 1990 the Rwandan refugee situation attracted little international attention. In fact most of that time it was barely on the humanitarian agenda of the Office of the United Nations High Commissioner for Refugees. Rwanda's refugees—numbering up to one million by 1990—seemed settled enough in neighboring countries.

Sadako Ogata, the United Nations High Commissioner for Refugees throughout the 1990s, lamented this thirty years of neglect and the lack of any strategic approach by the world's major powers to resolving the underlying problems in the region. In the concluding chapter of her memoir, *The Turbulent Decade: Confronting the Refugee Crises of the 1990s*, Ogata wrote, "Since the 1960s UNHCR had been faced with refugee problems in the Great Lakes region [of Africa]. . . . Large displacement of Tutsis from Rwanda to all neighboring countries remained unaddressed until 1990, when the Tutsis in Uganda created the Rwandan Patriotic Front (RPF) and achieved a military return." Ogata considered this neglect a contributing factor to the escalating violence that culminated in Rwanda's 1994 genocide: "In spite of serious warnings from UNHCR field representatives, no political solution was found for the Rwanda refugees. . . . The lack of local as well as international commitment to seek solutions to the refugee problems [in the Great Lakes region of Africa] led to a recurrence of violence on an ever-greater scale."[2] Unfortunately there continues to be a lack of commitment on the part of the international community to finding political solutions to refugee problems, especially those of long duration.

Diplomats should be on the front lines of seeking political solutions for refugees. Displaced persons, whether they cross international borders as refugees or remain within their home countries as internally displaced persons (IDPs), signal a magnitude of problems at home that beg for international attention. Initially, assisting people forced to flee their homes is usually an international humanitarian concern. Typically the international community responds quickly and effectively to humanitarian emergencies, providing generous international financial, material, and logistical support to concerned international agencies and nongovernmental organizations.

Too often, however, the international community stops short of going beyond humanitarianism to find political solutions for the displaced. The tendency is to treat the necessary life-saving humanitarian response as a solution. As long as the displaced are supplied with food, shelter, medical care, and education, the international community can claim to have done its duty by the uprooted people. Instead of involving diplomats in a search for solutions to root causes of displacement, the international donor community channels resources into improving the lives of refugees—often confined to camps—in their countries of first asylum. This has often translated into long-term support for expanded health services, schools, and skills training for income-generation activities in anticipation of the day the displaced will repatriate. This is important assistance where repatriation is not an option. But it should not be at the expense of a continuing commitment to seeking political solutions in the home country that could allow for voluntary repatriation.

Finding sustainable solutions for displaced populations has become increasingly difficult, however, as refugee populations have increased. Repatriation, the solution usually preferred by refugees and UNHCR, has slowed or stalled as conflicts have lasted longer and conditions in the homeland have failed to change. Integrating refugees into the societies of their host countries, which often have weak economies and pervasive poverty, has become less likely. Resettlement to a third country, if an available option, can be extremely selective and often politically difficult in light of anti-immigrant sentiment in many of the usual Western resettlement countries. Without recourse to one of these three solutions to their plight, refugees and IDPs are likely to languish in limbo for years.

Refugees or IDPs who remain in long-term situations of displacement risk becoming sources of destabilization for their countries of origin, for neighboring countries where the refugees have been given asylum, and, indeed, for the region as a whole. Such protracted refugee or IDP situations are becoming more and more common as numbers have mounted with new, prolonged conflicts in Syria, Iraq, Afghanistan, and elsewhere. In 2015 UNHCR estimated that of the 20 million refugees worldwide—up from about 15 million in 2013—about 6.7 million were in long-term, protracted situations. These statistics do not include the hundreds of thousands of long-term Palestinian refugees who come under the mandate of the United Nations Relief and Works Agency (UNRWA), a totally different UN organization from UNHCR.

If the protracted Rwandan refugee situation that eventually led to armed conflict and civil war had not caught the attention of the international community for thirty years, surely the escalating numbers of IDPs between 1990 and 1994 should have sounded the alarm. One year before the genocide began, Rwandans displaced by war—mostly Hutu—numbered one million persons, or one out of every seven Rwandans. The massacre victims—mostly Tutsi, at the hands of government-supported Hutu militia, the military, and ordinary citizens—numbered tens of thousands displaced and thousands dead.

High Commissioner Ogata argued in her memoir that humanitarianism alone could not resolve the problems of displacement. She contended that UNHCR, with its essentially legal and humanitarian mandate, needed the international community as its partner in order to reach truly durable solutions for refugee situations: "I have often been quoted as having stated, 'There are no humanitarian solutions to humanitarian problems.' What I wanted to emphasize was that refugee problems are essentially political in origin and therefore have to be addressed through political means. Humanitarian action may create space for political action but on its own can never substitute for it."[3]

This is the inherent contradiction in UNHCR's mandate. Although political, economic, or social considerations frame the refugee context, UNHCR's protection mandate confines it to legal and humanitarian actions. UNHCR is therefore dependent on the broader international community for the diplomatic and political interventions needed to go beyond humanitarianism to address the political, economic, or social root causes of displacement. UNHCR cannot arrive at sustainable solutions for refugees without the diplomatic support and engagement of the international community.

Ending such protracted refugee and IDP situations and being alert to early warning signs of conflicts likely to produce refugees should be high on the diplomatic priority list. The international community must not sidestep or delay addressing the underlying political, economic, and social causes that prompt people to flee their homes or homeland in the first place. This diplomacy cannot be relegated or delegated to humanitarian agencies and assistance organizations. Diplomats of donor states in particular must take the lead in moving beyond humanitarianism in any response to refugee and IDP situations, especially protracted ones.

[22]

Making Conflict Prevention a Foreign Policy and Diplomatic Priority

Despite Rwanda's tumultuous and violent path to democracy, the United States and its diplomatic colleagues failed to recognize or acknowledge that diplomacy in support of democratization and the peace process was leading to neither democracy nor peace. To the contrary, violence always increased following any progress toward either of Rwanda's transition goals. The greater the violence, the more the international community pressed Rwanda's policy makers to quicken the pace of democratization and peace. We had not made the link between our pro-democracy, pro-peace policies and the violent backlash against democratization and the peace process that our policies inspired. Our focus was on the positive advances—however small—in democratization and peace, not on the unintended, negative consequences that accompanied them. The U.S. and other diplomatic missions persisted in this single-pronged policy direction; there was no diplomatic Plan B.

By failing to prevent or curb the violent backlash from Hutu extremists against democratization and peacemaking, the United States and others in the international community that supported Rwanda's two transitions became unwitting parties to the escalation of violence. More and better promotion of democracy and peace could not have stopped this backlash; advances toward democratization and peace only fanned the flames of conflict.

Balancing Promotion Diplomacy with Prevention Policies

What we needed was a two-pronged policy to address not only the *promotion* of democracy and peace but also the *prevention* of escalating conflict and violence unleashed by Hutu extremists to stall or thwart progress toward achieving these transitions. To counterbalance our promotion diplomacy, we needed prevention diplomacy aimed at curbing the violence rooted in profoundly changing power relationships and the empowerment of new political actors. Pro-democracy and pro-peace policies were no substitute for an explicit conflict-prevention strategy aimed at ending, managing, or mitigating the violence and conflict escalation that led to genocide.

A two-pronged strategy, however, with specific, overt policies to address the unintended consequences of support for democratization and peacemaking was apparently not in the cards. Not only were resources for conflict prevention unavailable, but the will to pursue conflict resolution did not exist at the highest policymaking levels of the foreign affairs bureaucracy.

Herman Cohen, assistant secretary of state for Africa under President George H. W. Bush (1989–93), recounted in his book *Intervening in Africa* his desire to make conflict resolution and democratization the policy centerpieces of his tenure. Secretary of State James A. Baker III, Cohen recalled, gave him a green light on democratization but offered only lukewarm concurrence for conflict resolution. Baker's caveat: Find a way to make conflict resolution in Africa consistent with the president's foreign policy priorities elsewhere. Cohen understood this to mean improving collaboration with the Soviet Union on resolving regional problems in Africa. Consequently diplomatic contributions to conflict prevention during his tenure occurred under the radar: ambassadors engaged in conflict resolution activities with encouragement—but not instruction—from the Africa Bureau of the State Department.[1] It is little wonder, then, that during the pre-genocide period in Rwanda, U.S. diplomacy centered on support for democratization and the peace process without linking them to an explicit conflict-resolution strategy. Instead achieving these goals became an implicit conflict-resolution strategy.

Soul-Searching after the Genocide

The genocide in Rwanda in 1994 prompted considerable soul-searching within the international organizations, governments, non-governmental organizations, and civil society. How, they asked, had such unspeakable atrocities been able to take place on their watch? What had they missed? What could have been done differently or better to prevent conflict in Rwanda from escalating to genocide? What changes should agencies and organizations make to avoid similar mistakes in the future? What new capacities and programs could help them be better prepared to prevent or contain conflicts in countries where they work?

The United Nations and the Organization of African Unity set up independent commissions to examine what had gone wrong with their peacekeeping operations and cease-fire monitoring in Rwanda. The parliaments of Belgium and France investigated and assessed the actions of their respective governments during the crisis. International NGOs reviewed their policies and practices. Human Rights Watch published a definitive book on why and how genocide had occurred in Rwanda.[2]

Out of this considerable introspection came new thinking about how international organizations and institutions might respond more effectively to future conflict situations. Conflict prevention was central to this thinking. Recurring themes emphasized conflict prevention through improved information gathering, enhanced early-warning capabilities, and strengthened capacity to analyze the risk or threat of conflict.

Significantly NGOs in particular concluded that their policies and assistance activities, however well-intentioned, were likely to have unintended consequences. Many determined that their approaches could exacerbate tensions and stimulate latent or overt conflict in the societies where they worked. This, they realized, would undermine any good they hoped to do. The remedy they advocated was to become more aware of and responsive to the negative as well as the positive impact of their policies and programs on the intended beneficiaries.

The NGOs integrated their findings into future plans, policies, and programs. Modified service-delivery procedures and new programs were developed aimed at avoiding exacerbating intergroup frictions and minimizing possible adverse consequences of their aid interventions. These changes provided them with new capacity for identifying emerging conflicts and for responding more quickly and appropriately to temper conflict escalation.

Integrating Conflict Prevention into Policy and Practice

Although progress toward making conflict prevention a policy priority has been uneven, it is worth recalling what has been accomplished by international organizations, NGOs, and the United States in the decades since the 1994 genocide in Rwanda.

The United Nations

The UN led the way when it issued "Agenda for Peace" in 1992. In this report Secretary General Boutros Boutros-Ghali argued for the UN to make the peaceful settlement of disputes a top priority by engaging in four action areas: preventive diplomacy, peacemaking, peacekeeping, and postconflict peacebuilding.[3] This framework emphasized prevention and has guided the UN and the international community in conflict prevention, mitigation, and management ever since.

Peacekeeping operations: Improving the effectiveness of UN peacekeeping operations became an important concern for the UN following its failure to avert genocide in Rwanda and in Srebrenica. Recommendations for stronger mandates, more rapid deployment, improved headquarters support, and better coordination of operations, as put forward in 2000 by the key "Brahimi Report," have contributed to strengthening peacekeeping.[4] When the Security Council reauthorized the UN peacekeeping mission in the Democratic Republic of the Congo (DRC) in 2010, it strengthened the mandate by making its centerpiece civilian protection by "all necessary means."[5] The Council went even further in 2013, when it gave the DRC peacekeeping force an offensive capability, authorizing the formation of a rapid intervention brigade of three thousand soldiers drawn from within the nineteen-thousand-strong force. This UN brigade effectively intervened to end the rebellion of the M23, a key rebel militia in eastern Congo, and forced it to disband.

Genocide prevention and the responsibility to protect: Genocide prevention became a key element in the UN conflict-prevention strategy after 1999. In that year an independent investigation into the UN role in Rwanda recommended that the secretary general put in place a system-wide plan to prevent genocide.[6] In response secretary general, Kofi Annan, created the position of special adviser to the secretary general on the prevention of genocide. Launched in 2004, the position became full time in 2007, with a mandate that emphasized improving UN early-warning capabilities through enhanced information gathering and management in order to identify and prevent conflicts that could escalate to genocide.[7]

In 2008 Secretary General Ban Ki-moon created a companion position, a special adviser to the secretary general on the responsibility to protect. World leaders had unanimously endorsed the principle of the Responsibility to Protect at the UN's 2005 World Summit.[8] Known in UN jargon as R2P, the principle embraces the notion that sovereignty, the organizing principle of the United Nations, carries with it responsibilities as well as rights. If a state is unable or unwilling to fulfill its primary responsibility of protecting its citizens, the international community has the responsibility to intervene either to help the state provide that protection or to provide that protection itself. Situations that would trigger international action were specifically named: genocide, war crimes, ethnic cleansing, and crimes against humanity. This special adviser is charged with translating the R2P principle into practice.

After issuing his report "Implementing the Responsibility to Protect" in 2009, Secretary General Ban Ki-Moon created a single office for these two positions, the Office on Genocide Prevention and Responsibility to Protect.[9] It emphasizes early warning and prevention activities, consistent with the original intent of the report of the Canadian commission that first laid out the R2P concept.[10] Central to the Canadian report is the idea that states at risk as well as the other states in the international community should initiate prevention activities at the first sign of inter- or intrastate conflicts.

These two advisers jointly developed the "Framework of Analysis for Atrocity Crimes: A Tool for Prevention."[11] This analytical tool aims to help UN officials, and others working in conflict situations, identify gaps in prevention capabilities and heighten awareness of early warning signs of genocide, crimes against humanity, and war crimes. The release of this framework in 2014 coincided with a UN initiative making human rights and the prevention of mass atrocities a centerpiece of UN concerns.

UN *offices and agencies*: Several United Nations offices and agencies have expanded considerably their capacity for incorporating conflict prevention into their policies and programs since the 1994 genocide in Rwanda. Structures exist, mandates confer authority, and personnel are operational.

- The Department of Peacekeeping Operations, aside from implementing changes to strengthen peacekeeping, has integrated postconflict stabilization and reconstruction activities into peacekeeping missions.

- The Department of Political Affairs created a dispute mediation unit with field offices to provide support for conflict prevention or postconflict reconstruction to UN member states.[12]

- The UN Development Program established a Conflict Prevention Unit in its Bureau of Crisis Prevention and Recovery.

- The Office for the Coordination of Humanitarian Assistance organized an Early Warning and Contingency Planning Section focused on impending humanitarian emergencies. Since 2005 this office has coordinated the UN's "cluster approach," intended to improve UN effectiveness in assisting and protecting internally displaced persons.[13]

Regional and Subregional International Organizations in Africa

In Africa regional as well as subregional organizations have also made conflict prevention a more important part of their standard operating procedures since 1994.

The African Union: The African Union, which replaced the Organization of African Unity in 2002, endorses intervention in member states in cases of genocide, war crimes, or crimes against humanity. This departure from the OAU principle of noninterference in member states led the African Union to establish conflict-prevention mechanisms. Its Continental Early Warning System and its Peace and Security Council provide the organization with both an early warning and conflict response capacity. It has mounted peacekeeping operations in Darfur, Sudan, and Somalia.

International Conference on the Great Lakes Region: This twelve-member intergovernmental organization, sponsored by the UN and the African Union, was formed in 2006. Among other things, it is committed to punishing genocide. In 2010 the Conference established a committee aimed at finding ways to prevent genocide in member states, and in early 2013 it took a large step toward regional stability when it helped broker a peace deal for the Eastern Congo.

International Nongovernmental Organizations

Many international humanitarian and development NGOs now integrate conflict-prevention activities into their programs in conflict-risk areas where they work.

Catholic Relief Services: A relief and development organization of the U.S. Catholic Church, Catholic Relief Services determined after its "jarring" experience in Rwanda that maximizing its aid effectiveness would require minimizing its negative impact. It resolved to do this by making peacebuilding and social justice central to its activities.[14] Its programs began using their primary assistance asset—food—as a tool for addressing inequities and social imbalances within communities in order to foster understanding and reconciliation rather than competition and conflict among community groups. Catholic Relief Services was well-known in Rwanda before the genocide.

CARE International: This relief and development organization introduced a strategy aimed at avoiding or unintentionally exacerbating conflict rather than mitigating it. CARE International integrated conflict sensitivity, a human-rights-centered approach to development and strategic peacebuilding, into its relief and assistance strategies. The organization was active in Rwanda before the genocide, including in northern conflict regions.

The Fund for Peace: This Washington DC–based, antiwar NGO developed a methodology in the early 1990s for assessing conflict risk in countries around the world. While not intended to predict conflict, this risk-assessment tool can help policymakers identify and understand more clearly the signs and sources of conflict in their societies.[15] National, regional, and local conflict-prevention policies and programs have resulted from staff guiding officials and civil society representatives in many countries through the risk analysis. Each August the Fund releases a report that uses its methodology to identify and rank the most conflict-prone countries in the world. Its methodology served as a model for the UN's genocide analysis framework.

Other international NGOs: In addition to these older, more-established nongovernmental organizations, several advocacy groups established in the early 2000s—such as Save Darfur and the Enough Project—focus solely on ending genocide. Environmental NGOs have become involved in conflict prevention through campaigns to end exploitation of illegal minerals fueling conflict in the Democratic Republic of the Congo; Global Witness is one such organization. Umbrella organizations that group together like-minded conflict-resolution and peacebuilding organizations have also emerged, such as the Alliance for Peacebuilding and the Alliance for Conflict Transformation.

World courts: Courts, both international and intergovernmental, have played important roles in reducing impunity for the commission of genocide, war crimes, and crimes against humanity. The International Criminal Tribunal for Rwanda was established by UN Security Council Resolution 955 (1994) with a mandate to prosecute high-level individuals suspected of responsibility for genocide and violations of international humanitarian law in Rwanda during 1994.[16] Modeled on a similar but separate criminal court set up in May 1993 for Yugoslavia, the Tribunal for Rwanda closed down in 2015.

The International Criminal Court, an intergovernmental organization established under the Rome Statute of 1998, has the authority to indict and try individuals suspected of genocide, war crimes, or crimes against humanity.[17] Unlike the ad hoc tribunals for Rwanda and Yugoslavia, the International Criminal Court is outside the UN framework. The United States is not a signatory to the Rome Statute and therefore not a party to the Court.

Conflict-prevention approaches and the structures to implement them developed slowly within the U.S. government. The initial impetus was the collapse of the Soviet Union in 1990 and the genocides in Rwanda and Srebrenica a few years later.

U.S. Agency for International Development: USAID led the way in making conflict mitigation part of its policies and practice. In 1994 it set up the Office of Transition Initiatives to support and strengthen political transitions already under way in former countries of the Soviet Union. Several years later the new Office of Conflict Mitigation and Management developed a series of pamphlets to help field staff integrate conflict-reduction strategies into their programs in conflict-prone countries in Africa and elsewhere.

The Department of State: Not until 2004 did the Department of State begin incorporating conflict prevention into its operations. A new office situated within the Office of the Secretary, the Office of the Coordinator for Reconstruction and Stabilization Operations, had a mandate to coordinate conflict-prevention activities and policies across the U.S. government. In 2011 the State Department replaced this office with the Bureau of Conflict and Stabilization Operations, whose broader mandate aimed to make conflict prevention and mitigation a priority for U.S. policy and practice. Although the Bureau has mounted individual creative projects to mitigate conflict in the midst of extreme violence, it has never had adequate funding for its comprehensive mandate.

The Africa Bureau of the State Department launched an effort to facilitate peace and reconciliation in the Great Lakes region of Africa a decade after Rwanda's genocide and following two bitter, genocide-related wars that left the eastern region of neighboring Zaire in perpetual turmoil. In 2004 the Bureau initiated a peacebuilding project aimed at preventing a return to regional war by Rwanda, the Democratic Republic of the Congo, and Uganda. The Tripartite Plus Commission—as it was called after Burundi joined the group in 2005—brought together diplomatic and military personnel from these core Great Lakes countries in a series of conferences to discuss and find solutions to their common security problems.[18]

When this project ended in 2009, the participating countries were on the verge of restoring diplomatic relations, were discussing modalities of refugee repatriation, and had each joined the International Conference on the Great Lakes Region. Many problems remained, however, and several successive U.S. special envoys, in concert with European counterparts, helped keep the countries working together on peaceful resolution of their differences. Chaos and violence, however, have continued sporadically ever since in areas of the Eastern Congo (formerly Zaire) that border Rwanda, Uganda, and Burundi.

Reports endorsing prevention: Several reports furthered this emerging U.S. government interest in conflict prevention. The 2006 National Security Strategy joined diplomacy and development to defense preparedness as the three indispensable elements to safeguard U.S. security. In 2008 a Genocide Prevention Task Force chaired by former secretary of state Madeleine K. Albright and former defense secretary William S. Cohen recommended, among other things, expanding U.S. capacity for "preventive diplomatic action" in emerging crises.[19] In 2010 two documents, the State Department's first Quadrennial Diplomatic and Development Review and the National Security Strategy, linked U.S. security to being proactive on conflict prevention.[20]

The White House: The White House went even further in August 2011 when President Barack Obama elevated conflict prevention to a U.S. policy priority. Presidential Study Directive 10 on Mass Atrocities asserted that prevention of mass atrocities and genocide is "a core national security interest and a core moral responsibility" of the United States.[21] It called for creating an interagency Atrocities Prevention Board to identify atrocity threats and coordinate the government response. Six months later, when the president launched the Board with a speech at the U.S. Holocaust Memorial Museum, he reaffirmed that preventing genocide was both a national security and a moral responsibility.[22] The Pulitzer Prize–winning author Samantha Power, then senior director for multilateral affairs and human rights at the National Security Council, was tapped to head the new entity. The Atrocities Prevention Board reflected the Albright-Cohen task force's recommendation for an Atrocities Prevention Committee.

The Department of Defense: The U.S. Department of Defense identified conflict stabilization operations as one of its core missions in a 2005 U.S. military directive. By this time U.S. troops were already active in interagency provincial response teams aimed at stabilizing rural areas in Afghanistan and Iraq. In 2010 the Carr Center at the Harvard Kennedy School in conjunction with the army's Peacekeeping and Stability Operations Institute laid out a framework for how the U.S. military could respond to mass atrocities with an eye toward prevention. In 2012 the military updated its Doctrine on Peace Operations, adding an appendix addressing protection of civilians.[23]

Governments, the United Nations, other international organizations, and nongovernmental organizations have invested much energy and thought into integrating conflict-prevention strategies and activities into their policies and programs. Nevertheless all still have a long way to go before conflict prevention becomes an institutionalized part of their policies and practices. Funding for conflict-prevention diplomacy and related activities is not yet at sustainable levels, although nongovernmental organizations seem to be doing better in this area than are governments and international organizations.

Making Prevention a Priority

[23]

Fixes for the Future from Failures of the Past

The U.S. government is still far from making conflict prevention a cornerstone of diplomatic policy and practice, and there are many reasons this is not as easy as it should be. Our bureaucracy is governed by a culture of *response* to conflict rather than by a culture of conflict *prevention*. Even though a few initiatives, such as the formation of an Atrocities Prevention Board (APB), the creation of the State Department's Bureau of Conflict Stabilization Operations (CSO), and USAID's Office of Conflict Mitigation and Management, have conflict prevention, mitigation, and management as their overall goal, the idea of conflict prevention as a policy priority is not part of mainstream thinking or action in the U.S. foreign affairs bureaucracy. There is no widespread commitment to early diplomatic and programmatic activities aimed at preventing, mitigating, or managing conflict.

Securing funding or personnel resources for early action to prevent a potential or low-level conflict that *might* occur or *might* escalate, especially in a distant country where the United States has little or no national security interest, is a hard sell. President Obama launched the APB in 2012 with great fanfare, but without any provision for funding critics predict its demise.[1] For now it is still in operation. The CSO too has struggled to secure funding for its current, modest conflict-prevention work. The foundation for deciding how to allocate such resources is weak to nonexistent.

The landmark 2001 Canadian report, *The Responsibility to Protect*, emphasizes the responsibility of all nations to prevent conflict.[2] It advocates actions aimed at quelling conflict before it reaches the level where military intervention might be needed to arrest its spread. The UN office charged with translating into practice the principle of Responsibility to Protect made prevention a key element in its strategy. Nevertheless institutionalizing the responsibility to *prevent* conflict as part of the UN-endorsed framework remains a challenge not only for the United States but also for the international community.

In January 2010 the U.S. Institute for Peace, a think tank in Washington DC, addressed the issue of prevention when it hosted a public forum titled "Can We Prevent the next War?" This forum highlighted the need to make conflict prevention a critical part of U.S. foreign policy and diplomacy. In response to the question in the provocative title, each panelist urged greater U.S. government attention to preventing or reducing the number of new conflicts, and each argued for a more balanced allocation of resources between prevention and postconflict reconstruction activities.[3]

There are, I believe, a number of lessons that can be drawn from the diplomacy leading up to Rwanda's catastrophic tragedy that underscore the urgency of making conflict prevention a centerpiece of U.S. diplomacy. I hope this initial list of lessons based on my experience in Rwanda can contribute to a continuing dialogue about how to make conflict prevention a U.S. diplomatic priority both in policy and in practice.

An Agenda to Strengthen Conflict-Prevention Diplomacy

Lesson 1: Prioritize a Culture of Conflict Prevention
over a Culture of Crisis Response

Before conflict prevention can become a centerpiece of diplomatic policy and practice there will need to be a profound shift in thinking, from a culture of crisis response to a culture of crisis prevention.[4] Until genocide in Rwanda became a full-blown international crisis, this small Francophone country of negligible security interest to the United States was invisible to high-level U.S. policymak-

Fixes for the Future

ers in Washington. The consequence of this prevailing culture of crisis response was a lack of new resources—either personnel or funding—for increased attention to the root and proximate causes of Rwanda's escalating violence.

Conflict prevention will need to become an integral part of mainstream policy thinking, policymaking, and policy management if early diplomatic preventive activities are to become routine. Preventive diplomatic action cannot wait until Responsibility to Protect thresholds—war crimes, crimes against humanity, ethnic cleansing, and genocide—are crossed. If such high bars are reached, the doctrine of Responsibility to Protect calls for collective international action under United Nations auspices. But the philosophy of responsibility expects preventive action to have begun long before. A culture of conflict prevention would aim for early diplomatic and programmatic support for local initiatives, while low-level interventions can still make a difference. Building a foundation for preventive diplomatic activities requires broad commitment within the U.S. government to prioritizing prevention as a way to deal with incipient conflicts that risk escalation that could eventually threaten U.S. security.

Lesson 2: Strengthen the Bureaucratic Foundation for Conflict-Prevention Diplomacy

Institutionalizing a diplomatic culture within the U.S. government that prioritizes conflict prevention will require a supportive bureaucracy that has a widespread commitment to early diplomatic and programmatic conflict-prevention activities. Developing the infrastructure needed to support policies and actions for conflict prevention will require some structural modifications within the government's foreign affairs bureaucracy. Whatever changes occur should integrate conflict prevention into mainstream policymaking offices and bureaus, not marginalize it.

DEVELOP AN EARLY WARNING CAPACITY

Early warning capabilities depend on the systematic collection and analysis of information about countries at conflict risk by relevant departments throughout the government, including the departments of state, defense, intelligence, health and education, and any others with international activities. Aggregated data would be the basis for developing conflict watch lists and other information for dissemination to all relevant government departments.

The strategies that the Bureau for Conflict Stabilization Operations and the Atrocities Prevention Board are already using to identify conflicts of highest priority should be reviewed and augmented as required to ensure they operate government-wide and function within the mainstream of the departments in question, not on the periphery. In the State Department, for example, such a system might entail creating a unit within the regional affairs office of each geographic bureau to collect and analyze data from its region, develop prioritized conflict watch lists, and disseminate them to bureau leaders, the CSO, and the APB. Otherwise the CSO and the APB must depend on voluntary cooperation from offices with no mandate, resources, or reason to cooperate.

PRIORITIZE CONFLICTS OF CONCERN

Developing some sort of triage system that uses the early warning data to alert high-level decision makers about simmering conflicts at risk of escalating is critical. In practice the existing APB could serve this function. It could receive early warning data, determine which situations are the most critical, and channel them to an appropriate level of decision makers. Again the process should be reviewed to ensure it captures the types of situations deemed to need immediate attention. Are they flagged soon enough for early diplomatic and programmatic activities? Do they meet the "Rwanda test" of an incipient conflict at risk of escalation? An effective triage methodology is integral to decision making about the allocation of conflict-prevention resources, both personnel and financing. It is important to ensure nothing falls through the bureaucratic cracks, as Rwanda did.

DEVISE A PERSONNEL SURGE CAPACITY

The bureaucracy will also need the capacity to respond quickly in countries where help is needed. In Rwanda the embassy staff was too small to do more than provide modest support for democracy and peace initiatives. It had no capacity for conflict-prevention activities. Currently the State Department's rigid personnel system precludes responding rapidly to changing staffing needs; there is no surge capacity as situations change and conflicts escalate. Relying on local resources for surge capacity personnel and expertise—as I understand is the way the CSO operates—would be helpful where possible. Where this is not possible, the United States should work with allies and international NGOs to ensure the availability of specialized resources required for early diplomatic actions aimed at conflict mitigation and management.

STRENGTHEN REGIONAL CONSIDERATIONS IN POLICYMAKING

Many, if not most, intrastate conflicts have regional dimensions. Events in Rwanda did not occur in isolation from Rwanda's neighbors. Regional interests greatly influenced the country's civil war, the peacemaking process to end it, and its transition to democracy. U.S. policymakers needed to understand these influences and relationships better in order to factor them into U.S. policy.

Insurgents, for example, generally require overt or covert support from neighboring governments.[5] The RPF clearly benefited from Ugandan support. The troops faced no consequences for deserting Uganda's national army or for absconding with weapons and heavy equipment. Ugandan hospitals treated injured RPF soldiers. U.S. policy downplayed ties between Uganda's government and the RPF when it opted not to take a tough line with President Museveni or sanction Uganda for its involvement.

Likewise the assassination of Burundi's first elected Hutu president doomed Rwanda's chances of successfully implementing the Arusha Accords. Hard-line Hutu, suspicious of Tutsi intentions in Rwanda, believed their fears vindicated. From then on, most Hutu rejected the peace agreement and its power-sharing provisions. U.S. diplomats and policymakers failed to grasp the depth and intensity of anti-Tutsi revulsion that the Burundi event sparked among Rwandan Hutu across the political spectrum.

We at the embassy did not fully understand the dynamics and interrelationships between events in neighboring countries and their impact on attitudes of Rwandans. Too often the prevailing bilateral orientation of U.S. embassies and the Department of State obscures, neglects, or even dismisses the regional optic in policymaking. The

State Department and other departments with foreign affairs responsibilities will want to devise ways to enhance the regional component of policymaking for conflict prevention.

In reports to Washington, embassy officers are generally inclined to emphasize positive rather than negative developments. In Rwanda the unintended negative consequences of U.S. policies and actions of support helped fuel the violence. But only when policymakers in Washington have the full picture can they develop approaches that make the most sense not only for the United States but also for the countries and regions involved.

Lesson 3: Reinforce Diplomatic Policymaking for Conflict Prevention

To improve diplomatic effectiveness, diplomats in conflict or conflict-prone situations need to broaden the scope of their thinking when considering U.S. policies and actions for conflict prevention and resolution. Some possible strategies for strengthening diplomacy for conflict prevention might be the following.

ENHANCE UNDERSTANDING OF TRANSITIONING SOCIETIES

Societies in transition often face difficult, sometimes destabilizing changes in power relationships. Such shifts are likely to accentuate existing societal fault lines, making tensions, acrimony, conflict, and even violence a possibility. Diplomats in transitioning societies need to look for and seize peacebuilding opportunities to avoid or minimize the unintended consequences, including conflict, that can be unleashed by policies supporting change.

DEVELOP PARTNERSHIPS FOR CONFLICT PREVENTION

Diplomats could strengthen conflict-prevention diplomacy by reaching out beyond the usual bilateral and Western policy contacts. They could draw more fully on the extensive conflict-prevention expertise not only within USAID and elsewhere in the U.S. government but also in organizations outside government. Collaboration and coordination with nongovernmental organizations that specialize in strengthening democratic institutions or in peacebuilding would complement diplomatic efforts. Those groups with expertise in human rights education, institution building, ending historical grievances, or improving livelihoods would reinforce diplomatic policies promoting democracy and peace. Such peacebuilding activities could help create an atmosphere amenable to change. Partnerships with diplomatic colleagues and organizations based in the region of the country at risk might offer new perspectives that could enhance the effectiveness and impact of conflict-prevention policies.

APPLY POSTCONFLICT RECONSTRUCTION APPROACHES TO CONFLICT PREVENTION

Many of the policies and programs now considered part of postconflict reconstruction should be incorporated into prevention strategies aimed at heading off, mitigating, or managing conflicts. A functioning judicial system that applies the rule of law, for example, is just as important to redressing complaints of aggrieved citizens and protecting advocates of change before a conflict becomes a crisis as it is to reconstructing a society that has fallen apart under the weight of unjust treatment and the lack of accountability for abuses. Peacebuilding should be as integral to diplomatic actions and development activities aimed at avoiding or minimizing conflict as it is to postconflict rebuilding.

EXPAND THE DEFINITION OF NATIONAL SECURITY INTEREST

To ensure countries like Rwanda, where U.S. geopolitical security concerns are minimal, rise to the top levels of a triage system and reach high-level decision makers, the definition of a U.S. national security interest should be expanded. It should not only include the commonly accepted definition: the security of the state. It should also incorporate two other critical criteria: the concept of human security—the security of the individual—and the principle that preventing mass atrocities and genocide constitutes a "core national security interest and a core moral responsibility of the United States," as put forward in 2012 by President Obama.[6]

Lesson 4: Improve Preparedness for Conflict-Prevention Diplomacy

Training is critical to building a foundation within the U.S. foreign affairs bureaucracy for improved effectiveness of early, conflict-prevention diplomacy. U.S. Foreign Service officers and relevant personnel from other government departments and agencies need to be aware of the early-warning signs of conflict and of the policy dilemmas they are likely to face in conflict-prone situations. There should be regularly scheduled training opportunities to prepare for operating in conflict or conflict-prone areas. Such training should be an integral part of the Foreign Service Institute's training curriculum and be available to officers and others throughout their careers, but particularly when they are assigned to conflict zones.

The Rwanda experience suggests several areas of concern that should be core elements in such training:

- The dynamics at play in societies in transitions such as democratization or peace-making.
- Early warning signs of countries at risk of conflict or conflict escalation.
- Strategies and resources for supporting democratic institutions and capacity building.
- Options for responding to policy dilemmas characteristic of social and political transitions.
- Biases of diplomatic culture.
- Diplomacy and the protection of vulnerable populations in transitional societies or conflict-prone situations.
- Countering hate speech and human rights abuses.
- Regional implications of conflicts.
- Pitfalls of peace processes and negotiated settlements.
- Use of diplomacy to address proximate and root causes of displaced populations, both refugees and internally displaced persons.
- Reporting in conflict situations, to include both positive and negative policy consequences.
- Balancing policies of support for transitions with policies to address negative consequences, including mounting violence.
- The importance of conflict prevention as a diplomatic priority.

Lesson 5: Seek Political Solutions to Refugees and the Internally Displaced as Soon as Possible

Resolving refugee and IDP situations needs to be an integral part of diplomacy for conflict prevention. Too often, displaced persons who remain in refugee or refugee-like situations for extended periods threaten the stability not only of their home country but also of their country of asylum and often the region as a whole. Rwandan Tutsi refugees who led an armed rebellion against the government exemplify the security risks posed by protracted, unresolved refugee situations. Any protracted refugee or IDP situations, or new movements of refugees or IDPs, should alert diplomats to the urgent need for diplomacy to address and find solutions for both the proximate and root causes of the displacement.

Diplomats need to be at the forefront of the dialogue about political solutions to humanitarian catastrophes. They should partner with the UN refugee agency UNHCR and with countries of origin, countries of asylum, and regional states in search of solutions leading to sustainable voluntary repatriation, viable integration into the country of asylum, or resettlement in a third country. Such diplomacy must become an integral part of mainstream political diplomacy, not left to humanitarian organizations or government assistance agencies.

Humanitarian agencies and aid workers—essential for assuring protection and humanitarian assistance for refugees and IDPs—can help pave the way for this political dialogue. However, humanitarian action can never substitute for a political solution. In the words of Sadako Ogata, a former UN high commissioner for refugees, "There are no humanitarian solutions to humanitarian problems."[7]

Lesson 6: Build Political Support for Making Conflict Prevention a Diplomatic Priority

Declaring genocide prevention a moral responsibility of the United States, as President Obama did in 2012, is not enough to make it so. Whether conflict prevention can become the centerpiece of U.S. diplomatic policy and action will depend on political will. Until there is a commitment within the U.S. government and Congress to prioritize prevention and provide resources—both funding and personnel—early preventive diplomacy will remain elusive. Broad-based political will is a prerequisite for integrating conflict prevention into mainstream policymaking and the practices of diplomacy, development, and defense. Widespread support both inside and outside government is essential if the pervasive culture of crisis response is to be transformed into a culture of conflict prevention where preventive diplomacy is the norm. Only then can President Obama's pronouncement that genocide prevention is a moral responsibility of the United States become an integral part of diplomatic policy and practice.

The State Department, and other government departments as well, will need both personnel and funding for programs to implement early preventive actions in response to early indications of conflict risk. Congress will need to be on board to appropriate such funds. This will be challenging but not insurmountable.

One model for making resources available when conflicts escalate or unforeseen ones arise might be the emergency fund of the State Department's Bureau for Population, Refugees and Migration. The Bureau must respond repeatedly to unforeseen, unbudgeted emergencies in the course of any given year. To make this possible, it can supplement its regular annual budget for emergencies by accessing emergency funds controlled by the White House. Requests from the Bureau to tap into these funds must be submitted, with sufficient documentation, and approved on a case-by-case basis. Congress generally replenishes this fund annually, and more frequently if required. It is useful to note that putting Humpty Dumpty together again after he has fallen off the wall will generally demand more from our country's resource bank than would prevention.

Implementing "An Agenda to Strengthen Diplomacy for Conflict Prevention" could help transform the current diplomatic culture of crisis response to conflict to a diplomatic culture of conflict prevention. It could provide a framework for effective diplomatic conflict-prevention activities supported by early identification of emerging hot spots and early access to funding and personnel for preventive diplomatic activities. This approach could help avoid another Rwanda.

Conclusion

Changing the Paradigm

It is better to invest in prevention today than
potentially pay a bigger price tomorrow.

—PAUL B. STARES and MICAH ZENKO,
Enhancing U.S. Preventive Action

The failure of diplomats and diplomacy to prevent the escalation
of violence to mass atrocities and genocide in Rwanda had monu-
mental consequences that continue to impact that country and the
other countries of the Great Lakes region of Africa. The genocide
and its aftermath reshaped Rwanda's political and social landscape
and left deep scars throughout the population. Rwanda's economy
has mostly recovered, but the country struggles to find a balance
between the security needed for stability and the freedoms so critical to democracy. Emotions from the experience of genocide remain
raw. Witness the twenty thousand children born of war-time rape
who are turning twenty-five years old—some hated by their moth-
ers, some called "children of killers" by their peers.[1]

Rarely are intrastate conflicts contained within the borders of a
single state. The eastern part of the neighboring Democratic Republic of the Congo has known no peace since the genocide in Rwanda.[2]
In the wake of a massive initial influx of refugees and two wars with
Rwanda, the economy of this devastated region is in shambles and
the people continue to suffer. An estimated five to six million have

died from conflict-related causes, and the region is still awash with guns. Competition for control of lucrative mines and wildlife poaching fuel conflicts and violence among a multitude of foreign-backed and domestic militias, remnants of the former Rwandan army, others who participated in the genocidal killing in 1994 and their descendants, and an unruly Congolese army.

The catastrophic consequences of diplomatic failure in Rwanda should shake diplomats to their core. Diplomats became so invested in the Arusha Peace Accords and implementation of the power-sharing provisions that they failed to realize or acknowledge that the process was leading to neither. Rwandans trying to hold on to power and those trying to wrest it from them were undermining both. Diplomats did not understand that the successes of democratization and peace—the small steps forward that diplomats supported—were fueling the backlash of violence and leading to genocide.

The failure was not, however, a failure of the actions taken by the diplomatic community to support Rwanda's transitions to democracy and peace, as some critics have contended.[3] Instead it was the failure to balance policies of support for democracy and peace with policies to prevent or mitigate the unintended consequences of these transitions. In Rwanda diplomacy failed because of a failure of omission rather than a failure of commission.

Diplomats and diplomacy focused on the success side of the ledger, the small advances toward democracy and peace. They paid too little attention to the unintended negative consequences of democratization and peace-making. Both transitions posed profound threats to those in the ruling group intent on maintaining the status quo. Both foreshadowed significant disruption to existing power relationships and social order. They opened new avenues to political participation for those inside and outside Rwanda who opposed the one-party state's power monopoly. The prospect of such sweeping change was unacceptable to those Rwandans who feared losing their power and privilege if these transitions succeeded.

Rwandans with the most to lose lashed out at threats to their continued domination. They responded with orchestrated massacres, random and targeted bombs and land mines, political-party violence, militias, assassinations, human rights abuses, media campaigns intended to denigrate minority Tutsi and intimidate and deter democracy and peace advocates. In the absence of the rule of law, there was no way to hold perpetrators accountable for their actions. Nor could the prospect of democratization and peace dissuade those opposed to a more open political system from becoming the spoilers who doomed both of Rwanda's transitions when they launched the genocide.

Historic enmities provided a shaky foundation for the profoundly disruptive transitions to democracy and peace. As power relationships began to change, existing antagonisms exacerbated and fueled the violence that surged with every step toward democracy and peace. An ethnic fault line between the Hutu majority and the Tutsi minority prompted armed conflict. A geographic fault line between the northern Hutu rulers and their southern Hutu opponents led to endless wrangling for dominance in the political liberalization process. An ideological fault line pitted Hutu supremacists against Hutu advocating power sharing with the Tutsi, a schism that led to political polarization and the isolation of Hutu moderates. A further division within the northern Hutu ruling group, over whether democratization or violence offered the better strategy for retaining power, eventually resulted in genocide.

Although Rwanda's leaders appeared to have embraced both democratization and peace-making, each of the three key power centers—the northern Hutu rulers, the southern Hutu challengers, and the Tutsi-led refugee insurgents—was using democratization and peace-making to further its own goals.

Policies supporting democratization and peace—embraced by the Kigali diplomatic community—offered no antidote to the violence. More, better, or different policies in support of democratization and peace could not have quelled the violence that was rooted in opposition to both. Even though such policies had helped move Rwanda's transitions forward, they had also inadvertently contributed to the backlash of violence. This backlash thwarted both transitions and eventually degenerated into catastrophic genocide.

Pro-democracy, pro-peace policies sidestepped deep-seated, conflict-generating issues such as the fears stemming from ethnic and regional mistrust; the lack of protection or judicial recourse for vulnerable populations, including minorities and civil-society advocates of change; the climate of impunity for perpetrators of inflammatory propaganda, human rights abuses, or massacres; and the rise of the interparty violence and political-party militia. However much we may have thought so at the time, diplomatic support for democracy and peace was not synonymous with conflict prevention. It could not change the calculation of those opposed to change.

Despite some examples of high-level support in the United States for prioritizing conflict prevention over a crisis response approach to foreign policy and diplomacy, the principle is far from becoming entrenched in the bureaucracy or sustainable in practice. Funding and personnel resources for preventive diplomacy continue to be minimal to nonexistent. The Atrocities Prevention Board needs congressional budget support if it is to continue to exist at all, let alone to strengthen its role in early warning and policymaking. It's unclear to me whether the APB process—as currently structured—would enable the next Rwanda to receive an appropriate level of early attention from policymakers.

A paradigm shift to concentrating resources on crisis prevention rather than on or in addition to crisis response has not yet taken place. Although some diplomatic preventive action is evident, much more sensitization will be necessary before such an approach can make a significant difference in stemming conflicts before they escalate to mass atrocities and genocide.

Could Diplomats Have Predicted the Genocide?

U.S. diplomats in Rwanda were focused on the positive prospects of democracy and peace, not on the possibility of failure that could lead to full-blown genocide. The better question might be whether there were warning signs that were missed or ignored that should have turned our attention to the possibility of mass atrocities on a national scale and genocide.

When asked about "tipping points" that might have signaled the onset of genocide in Rwanda, Samantha Power mentioned a number of early warning signs to a 2003 audience in Washington DC. Power, whose 2002 book, *A Problem from Hell: America and the Age of Genocide,* won a Pulitzer Prize, cited fragile democracies, ethnic violence, the media demonizing "the other," polarization within society and insisting people take sides, compilation of lists of people to be killed, and small-scale massacres.

All of these elements were present in Rwanda during the three years prior to the genocide. Should we therefore have concluded that genocide *would* occur? Although these factors could—and did—add up to genocide, their presence does not, in my view, make genocide inevitable. There also had to be morally bankrupt people willing to commit atrocities aimed at exterminating "the other." This turned out to be the case in Rwanda. Unlike the more observable warning signs Power mentions, however, such an indicator is subjective and more difficult to discern.

Nevertheless the presence of any of these indicators should trigger an alert within the international community that would activate early preventive diplomacy and actions. The reports of the Canadian-sponsored International Commission on Intervention and State Sovereignty, which lays out the "Responsibility to Protect" principle, and the U.S. Genocide Prevention Task Force advocate such early preventive interventions. Both elaborate what that might entail.[4]

Could Diplomacy and Diplomats Have Changed the Outcome in Rwanda?

No amount of more, better, or different support for democracy and peace could have prevented the escalating violence that preceded genocide in Rwanda. To the contrary, while helping to advance peace and democracy, the pro-democracy and pro-peace policies of the international community fueled the violent backlash against these two transitions. That violence escalated to mass atrocities and genocide. Policies promoting democracy and peace were ineffective by themselves as a strategy for resolving conflicts rooted in the profoundly destabilizing prospects of altered power relationships expected as a result of an anticipated liberalized political system.

The diplomatic community in Kigali might have united against the controversial power-sharing provisions of the Arusha peace agreement instead of working together to avoid collapse of the peace process and the probable return to war. Early conflict-prevention diplomacy might have contributed to alleviating the unintended negative consequences of pro-democracy and pro-peace policies if implemented before political polarization took root. Genocide became possible because there was no explicit conflict-resolution policy, no credible threat of force, no actual show of force, and no political will to end the atrocities.

Is All of This Just Fighting the Last War?

Rwanda's tragic slide from democratization and peace-making into genocide offers insight into the dynamics of conflicts arising from destabilizing change. Though contexts may differ, wherever transitions impact political, social, and economic power relationships, they are likely to generate similar insecurity and instability. We saw this in the Arab Spring of 2011, when elected governments that came to power after internal uprisings were trying to make the shift from dictatorship to participatory democracy. Egypt and Iraq are failing for lack of inclusion. Tunisia is teetering, but its respect for human rights is helping bring competing groups together.

Transitional situations will continue to create opportunities for conflict to take hold and flourish. Root causes may be similar: group enmities, ethnic or religious rivalries, and competition over control of scarce resources. Proximate causes will undoubtedly vary: access to fresh water, climate migration, food insecurity, cyber security.[5] New tools for engaging in conflict prevention and resolution will also become available: social media, satellite imagery, drones, robots, and new technologies we have yet to imagine.

The one thing likely to remain constant, unfortunately, is conflict itself, its characteristics and its provocations. Improved early-warning capabilities and better assessments of countries at risk of violence could help diplomats better anticipate and identify the next conflicts. Lessons from past conflict-prevention efforts will still be relevant and will help inform strategies in the future.

What Role for Diplomacy in Future Conflict Prevention?

Diplomacy rooted in negotiation and compromise has the potential to contribute to mitigating, managing, or preventing emerging conflicts and to limiting escalation. Bringing adversaries together to find common ground and ensuring contact with all sides in a conflict is central to diplomacy. Diplomats are well positioned to help parties lay the foundation for dialogue within, between, and among states; build an atmosphere in which healthy dialogue can take shape; envision solutions in a new light; and build the trust needed to make discussions possible. Diplomacy can help the parties stay on track in their effort to seek common ground, find inclusive solutions, make compromises, work together to implement agreements, and then accept modifications as needed and appropriate. In short, diplomats can encourage parties to take stock of their situation, discuss their differences, examine their options, and negotiate a mutually acceptable solution.

Now is the time for diplomats to take the next steps toward making diplomacy a more effective tool for conflict prevention than it was in Rwanda in the early 1990s. Diplomats need to understand that good diplomatic intentions do not always generate good consequences. Indeed after the horror of Rwanda's genocide, diplomats should, as their development colleagues have realized, be wary of unintended adverse consequences of well-intended policies and develop and apply approaches and strategies to limit or counter them. Today diplomatic conflict-prevention and peacebuilding activities offer strategies and activities to address potential, incipient, and escalating conflicts and violence.

The challenge for diplomats is to recognize and acknowledge when diplomacy and diplomatic activities are contributing to unintended, potentially negative consequences. They need to be alert to warning signs and have a tool kit of strategies for addressing the unintended impact of their policies.

What Would It Take for Conflict Prevention to Become a Diplomatic Policy Priority?

Making the paradigm shift needed for conflict prevention to become a diplomatic priority would depend on the extent to which diplomacy can move from a culture of crisis response to a culture of conflict prevention. Although the obstacles to such a paradigm change may seem insurmountable, it is important to try to make the change happen.

U.S. support for societies in transition and its growing interest in conflict prevention are likely to continue. Although it does not explicitly identify democratization or conflict prevention as U.S. interests abroad, the 2017 National Security Strategy asserts that stable countries with accountable governments are most likely to offer trade and investment opportunities that will make America stronger. The document contends that it is therefore in the U.S. national interest to help countries realize their potential as prosperous and sovereign states by advancing American principles that will "spread peace and prosperity around the globe."[6]

The strategy states that to minimize threats to its security, the United States will "work with promising nations to promote effective government, rule of law, and develop institutions accountable and responsive to citizens," "partner with governments, civil society and regional organizations to end long-running violent conflicts," and help fragile states and developing countries become "successful societies." The security strategy expects diplomacy to encourage states to make choices toward improvement, and it calls diplomacy "indispensable" for finding solutions to conflicts in unstable regions.[7]

Based on the Rwanda example, policies providing such support are likely to have the greatest possibility of success when counterbalanced with policies aimed at preventing, mitigating, or managing the unintended negative consequences of such policies. Diplomatic support policies for two transitions that would emulate American values failed in Rwanda in 1994. We had no explicit conflict-prevention diplomacy or activities to address the violent backlash to change. Without fundamental change to a diplomatic culture of conflict prevention from one of crisis response, diplomacy is likely to repeat the mistakes of Rwanda.

We Must Make the Paradigm Shift

Making the paradigm shift from a culture of crisis response to a culture of conflict prevention is imperative if diplomacy and diplomats are to become more effective at supporting change in countries at risk of conflict. The U.S. administration, the foreign affairs bureaucracy, and Congress will have to take the steps needed to translate verbal commitment to the principle of ending genocide into the policies and practice of conflict prevention. Preventive diplomatic activities must truly become a policy priority if diplomats are to have early access to appropriate resources when they are in conflict or conflict-prone situations.

In the wake of the Rwandan tragedy, I believed that whenever circumstances forced a significant number of people to become internally displaced inside their country or refugees across borders, alarm bells would surely sound in the international community. I wanted to believe that the world would never again stand by as it had a year before the genocide, when one out of every seven Rwandans had already been displaced by conflict. I wanted to believe that the world would move quickly to address the proximate if not the root causes so people could return home and resume their normal lives.

So far, however, my hopes have not been realized. When mass atrocities in Darfur, Sudan, burst into international consciousness in 2004, a divided Security Council and UN adherence to the principle of absolute national sovereignty—and the threat of a Chinese veto—blocked action at the United Nations. A few years later Somalia counted one million internally displaced as violence surged among armed ethnic rivals. Somalia remains a failed state and is still plagued by sporadic violence. Conflict in Syria has forced more than half the population, or over twelve million people, to flee violence. Initially most remained displaced internally, but after relentless bombings of populated areas, hundreds of thousands of Syrians, many already internally displaced, fled across international borders and became refugees seeking relief, security, and safety as far away as Europe. These three conflicts, marked by rampant violence and enormous numbers of displaced persons, remain unresolved despite international diplomatic and military efforts to stabilize the situations.

Today there are more than sixty-eight million forcibly displaced persons in the world, according to UNHCR 2018 figures, with a staggering twenty-four million of these considered refugees, most as a result of conflict. This is more than double the number of just a few years ago. We cannot abandon such unfathomable numbers of people to lives devoid of any goal but survival. We must develop the understanding and the tools needed, especially as diplomats, to help channel conflicts, however incipient or intense, into dialogue and peaceful resolution. As diplomats, we must always be wary of the unintended consequences of our support and actions and be prepared to help address the proximate and root causes of antagonisms that could result in violence.

Restoring lives in limbo to lives with meaning and fulfillment, poverty reduction, economic growth, stability and security, all depend on becoming smarter about preventing, mitigating, and managing conflict in the face of old and new provocations. The challenge is to develop capacities for recognizing potential conflict early, addressing root and proximate causes early, and committing resources early to diplomats and others with the skills and knowledge to apply them.

Making conflict prevention—indeed ultimately the prevention of mass atrocities and genocide—a diplomatic policy priority not only in principle but also in practice is a worthy goal. The legacy of the 1994 genocide in Rwanda reverberates today in that country and throughout the Great Lakes region of Africa. Finding effective ways to prevent mass atrocities and genocide is the unfinished business of our time. Changing the paradigm for how diplomacy handles conflict situations—from a culture of crisis response to a culture of conflict prevention—would be a good start. Diplomacy backed by resources for early preventive diplomatic action, especially in situations where political or societal transitions are involved, can play a significant role as the world strives to make the words "Never Again" a reality.

CHRONOLOGY OF EVENTS, 1959–1994

1959   Tutsi king dies in July. A subsequent Hutu rebellion and violence between newly created political parties prompt ten thousand Tutsi to flee to neighboring countries.

1960   In June and July southern-based MDR-Parmehutu wins violence-plagued local elections. More Tutsi flee to neighboring countries.

1961   Referendum ends Tutsi monarchy, affirms Rwanda's status as republic. MDR-Parmehutu wins overwhelming victory in September legislative elections.

1962   Belgium grants Rwanda independence on July 1. MDR-Parmehutu leader Gregoire Kayibanda becomes president. Failed Tutsi refugee raids provoke Hutu reprisals against Tutsi in Rwanda. More Tutsi flee the country.

1965   President Kayibanda and MDR-Parmehutu win reelection. Periodic violence against Tutsi continues to spur Tutsi flight.

1973   After renewed attacks on Tutsi, Maj. Juvénal Habyarimana, a northern Hutu, takes power in coup.

1975   President Habyarimana declares MRND the sole political party. Government largesse channeled to president's home region in the northwest.

July 5, 1990	President announces political reform prompted by internal and external pressures.
September 1990	Thirty-three intellectuals and civil society leaders publish democracy manifesto demanding multiple parties and immediate democracy.
October 1, 1990	Rwandan Patriotic Front, an armed group of mainly Tutsi refugees, invades Rwanda from Uganda.
October 1990	In response, government moves against Tutsi for allegedly being RPF accomplices with a massacre in Kibilira in northwest of country and mass arrests of intellectuals in Kigali.
January 23, 1991	RPF attacks Ruhengeri and holds it for a day; opens the prison, freeing political prisoners.
January 27, 1991	Massacres of Bagogwe, a Tutsi subgroup, begin in northwest and spread to surrounding areas in reprisal for Ruhengeri attack.
February 19, 1991	OAU, UNHCR, and regional governments sign the Dar es Salaam accord providing for voluntary repatriation of Rwandan refugees.
April 1991	Government releases remaining Tutsi arrested in October 1990 and held without charges. Heavy diplomatic pressure may have helped.
June 10, 1991	President issues a revised constitution legalizing multiple political parties and officially ending one-party rule. Four opposition parties register in short order.
October 13, 1991	President appoints prime minister from ruling party and charges him with forming a multiparty government.
January 8, 1992	Massive peaceful demonstration in Kigali—fifty thousand strong—protests composition of prime minister's first government for including only one non–ruling party minister.
January 15, 1992	A second protest fizzles. Opposition parties denied permit to march; defiant marchers arrested.

March 4–9, 1992	Massacre of Tutsi in Bugesera, south of Kigali. Attacks leave three hundred dead and fifteen thousand displaced.
March 6, 1992	CDR, radical Hutu supremacist party, announces its formation.
April 7, 1992	President appoints prime minister from MDR opposition party to head a five-party coalition government and charges it to end the border war and prepare elections; half the portfolios go to ruling MRND.
May 25, 1992	Government of Rwanda and RPF hold first direct talks when new foreign minister Boniface Ngulinzira, from MDR opposition party, goes to Uganda to meet with RPF. This follows early May discussions in region with RPF and government of Rwanda by U.S. assistant secretary of state for Africa, Herman J. Cohen.
June 5, 1992	RPF attacks and holds the northern town of Byumba for a day on the eve of discussions in Paris about peace talks.
June 6, 1992	Government of Rwanda and RPF delegates meeting in Paris decide to hold peace talks.
July 12, 1992	Peace talks begin in Arusha, Tanzania, between the government and the RPF, as interparty violence escalates in Rwanda.
July 14, 1992	Parties agree to cease-fire beginning August 1.
August 1, 1992	Cease-fire takes effect. Next day MRND youth wing, the Interahamwe, stages a demonstration blocking access to Kigali.
August 17, 1992	Parties in Arusha sign a protocol on the rule of law that lays out governance principles for the future.
August 20, 1992	Massacres of Tutsi begin in Kibuye in the west. Interparty and interethnic violence leave three hundred dead and five thousand displaced.
September 7–18, 1992	Arusha talks on political power-sharing begin, but issues remain unresolved at the end

	of two weeks allotted to subject. Parties agree to resume in October.
October 31, 1992	Government and RPF sign partial power-sharing protocol that places power in hands of government at expense of president.
November 15, 1992	President, addressing a political rally in Ruhengeri, refers to the October 31 Arusha protocol as just a "scrap of paper."
November 22, 1992	At a rally in Gisenyi prefecture regional MRND official Léon Mugesera urges Hutu to send Tutsi back to Ethiopia via the Nyabarongo River and labels opposition party members traitors.
January 9, 1993	Government and RPF sign final Arusha power-sharing protocol that locks in a formula for distributing portfolios in the transitional government and seats in the national assembly. Presidential supporters reject agreement on grounds it relegates their MRND party to "permanent minority status." MRND and extremist CDR anger sparks violence primarily in Kigali and across the north.
January 7–21, 1993	International Commission of Investigation composed of five international human rights groups investigates abuses since October 1, 1992.
Late January 1993	Hutu massacre Tutsi in northwest Rwanda. Attacks leave three hundred dead.
February 8, 1993	RPF breaks cease-fire, claiming retaliation for January massacres of Tutsi in northwest Rwanda. Its troops advance on Kigali, displacing one million Rwandans.
February 22, 1993	RPF declares unilateral cease-fire. Government does not reciprocate. Throughout February groups of clergy, political parties, and diplomats all try to broker new cease-fire and return to peace talks. Rwanda and Uganda ask UN Security Council for military observers at their border.

March 8, 1993	The International Commission of Investigation releases its report on its January mission. It criticizes both government and RPF for human rights violations but stops short of determining whether genocide is occurring.
March 9, 1993	Cease-fire is reestablished. The RPF withdraws to pre—February 8 positions, the government to the line it was pushed back to. A demilitarized zone is created between the two forces with OAU monitors to assure compliance.
March 16, 1993	Arusha peace talks resume. The two sides continue discussing military integration and, eventually, take up refugee return.
April 7, 1993	President and prime minister sign joint declaration on human rights. It acknowledges and regrets human rights violations but rejects government responsibility for them.
April 8–17, 1993	UN special rapporteur on summary or arbitrary extrajudicial executions arrives in Rwanda. His August 1993 report echoes that of the International Commission of Investigation but notes possible genocide.
May 18, 1993	MDR leader Emmanuel Gapyisi, advocate of Hutu solidarity and opponent of both the president and the Tutsi-led RPF, is assassinated. Assassins are never identified.
June 1, 1993	Presidential elections take place in neighboring Burundi. The electorate—majority Hutu, minority Tutsi, as in Rwanda—chooses its first Hutu president.
June 9, 1993	Arusha parties sign protocol outlining policies and procedures for return and reintegration of refugees and displaced persons.
June 14, 1993	Government and RPF send joint letter to UN secretary general requesting neutral international force to oversee implementation of anticipated peace agreement.

June 22, 1993	UN Security Council authorizes peacekeeping mission at Rwanda-Uganda border, with six-month mandate.
June 24, 1993	Peace talks in Arusha break down and are suspended over unresolved force integration issues.
July 16, 1993	President appoints new government. Agathe Uwilingiyimana, protégée of MDR president Faustin Twagiramungu, becomes prime minister. Anastase Gasana, from same MDR faction, named foreign minister.
Late July 1993	Peace talks resume in the demilitarized zone in Rwanda. Outstanding issues are rapidly resolved.
August 3, 1993	Arusha protocol on military integration signed.
August 4, 1993	The Arusha Peace Accords, a collection of all agreed protocols, are signed in Arusha. In Kigali skepticism, not celebration, greets the signing.
August 19–31, 1993	UN reconnaissance mission for neutral international peacekeeping force visits Rwanda. Headed by Gen. Roméo Dallaire, mission recommends phased deployment to UN secretary general.
September 30, 1993	UNOMUR border-monitoring force of eighty-one soldiers is fully operational. Canadian General Dallaire named its head.
October 5, 1993	UN Security Council approves peacekeeping force UNAMIR for Rwanda, encouraged by joint lobbying in New York by government and RPF representatives.
October 21, 1993	Burundi's Hutu president is assassinated by Tutsi soldiers.
October 22, 1993	UNAMIR force commander General Dallaire arrives in Kigali.
November 17, 1993	UN peacekeepers raise UN flag in Kigali. Within a week seventy persons are killed virtually under the noses of peacekeeping force.

Chronology of Events

November 23, 1993	Special representative of the UN secretary general, Cameroonian Jacques-Roger Booh-Booh, arrives in Kigali.
December 13, 1993	UNAMIR briefs diplomats, affirms UN intent to seize weapons in Kigali.
December 28, 1993	RPF battalion of six hundred troops arrives in Kigali, anticipating installation of Broad-Based Transitional Government before year's end. Its role: to provide security for RPF officials named to government.
January 5, 1994	President Habyarimana sworn in as president of transitional government. Party disputes over representative lists block formation of government and national assembly indefinitely.
January 6, 1994	New U.S. ambassador arrives in Kigali. UN Security Council approves resolution extending UNAMIR mandate, adding one thousand troops, and making future support contingent on installation of Broad-Based Transitional Government.
January 13, 1994	General Dallaire cables UN his intention to seize identified weapons cache. UN headquarters orders Dallaire not to seize weapons but to report matter to president instead.
February 21, 1994	Hutu-supremacist CDR demonstrates for right to participate in Transitional National Assembly after disqualifying itself by not signing the Arusha Accords and its code of conduct for political parties. Demonstration turns violent.
February 21, 1994	PSD leader Félicien Gatabazi assassinated. Four days of violence in Kigali follow, with seventy deaths, mostly Tutsi.
February 22, 1994	CDR president Martin Bucyana assassinated, apparently in revenge for Gatabazi's murder.
March 22, 1994	UNAMIR completes Phase 2 deployment, bringing troop strength to 2,539.

April 5, 1994	UN Security Council extends UNAMIR mandate, again making it contingent upon implementation of Arusha Accords.
April 6, 1994	President's plane shot down on approach to Kigali airport, killing all on board, including presidents of Rwanda and Burundi. Genocide begins with random and targeted killing of ethnic Tutsi. Hutu considered traitors to the Hutu cause are also killed. War between government forces and the RPF resumes.
July 4, 1994	RPF takes control of Kigali, and on July 19, after capturing northern towns of Ruhengeri and Gisenyi, establishes a government. Between eight hundred thousand and one million Rwandan Tutsi and some moderate Hutu die in one hundred days of brutal violence at the hands of extremist Hutu military, militia, and local citizen groups. In mid-July nearly two million Rwandans flee the country, about half to Zaire and half to Tanzania.

NOTES

For more information on how to access the declassified cables cited below, please see page 368 in the bibliography.

Preface

1. Fund for Peace, "Fragile States Index, 2019"; Baker and Weller, *Analytical Model*; Fund for Peace, "CAST: Conflict Assessment Framework Manual."

Introduction

1. Leader, "Genocide in Rwanda," 175–83.

1. Political Liberalization Takes Off

1. Prunier, *Rwanda Crisis*, 128–35. Prunier details the background of the emerging political parties and their leaders.

2. Prunier, *Rwanda Crisis*, 134–35.

3. Association Rwandaise pour la Défense des Droits de la Personne et des Libertés Publiques (hereafter ADL), *Rapport, Septembre 1991–Septembre 1992*.

4. Prunier, *Rwanda Crisis*, 131n8. Prunier describes the political party links of the various human rights organizations.

5. Sibomana, *Hope for Rwanda*, 19–27.

6. Sibomana, *Hope for Rwanda*, 25; Des Forges et al., *Leave None*, 47.

7. International Press Institute, "World Press Freedom Heroes."

8. Higiro, "Rwandan Private Print Media," 73–89.

9. In December 1991, after four months in Rwanda, I wrote the following to family and friends:

> These are exciting times in Rwanda, as the country struggles to transform itself into a democratic, multiparty system after eighteen years of single-party, one-man rule. Three principal opposition parties are challenging the former sole party. Together, government and the opposition are seeking to chart a course that will bring Rwanda through a transition period to elections. Deep-rooted ethnic and regional tensions make it

nearly impossible for either side to believe the other is sincere. As if this were not enough, a rebel group based in neighboring Uganda is attempting to take power by force. So far, the rebels have refused the invitation of both government and opposition to lay down their arms and join the democratic process.

2. War Intrudes

1. Prunier, *Rwanda Crisis*, 62.

2. Des Forges et al., *Leave None*, 48.

3. Des Forges et al., *Leave None*, 87–90; ADL, *Rapport, Septembre 1991–Septembre 1992*, 100–134.

4. Jones, *Peacemaking*, 54.

5. Jones, *Peacemaking*, 53–68. These pages summarize the first one and a half years of international peacemaking efforts.

6. Cohen, *Intervening*, 164.

7. Gribbin, *Aftermath of Genocide*, 64.

8. Prunier, *Rwanda Crisis*, 113.

9. Prunier, *Rwanda Crisis*, 117.

10. Des Forges et al., *Leave None*, 48; Higiro, "Rwandan Private Print Media," 77–78.

11. Adelman, Suhrke, and Jones, "Study 2: Early Warning," 18.

12. Gribbin, *Aftermath of Genocide*, 63–64; Cohen, *Intervening*, 167.

13. Cohen, *Intervening*, 224

3. Rights Abuses and Violence Sow Fear

1. ADL, *Rapport, Septembre 1991–Septembre 1992*, 203–34; Des Forges et al., *Leave None*, 89–92; Prunier, *Rwanda Crisis*, 138; Des Forges, "Call to Genocide," 42.

2. Des Forges et al., *Leave None*, 87.

4. Opposition Parties Join a Coalition

1. Prunier, *Rwanda Crisis*, 145.

5. Peace Talks Begin

1. American Embassy cable Kampala 02581, "A/S Cohen's meeting with representatives of the RPF and the RPA," May 12, 1992; Cohen, *Intervening*, 169–71.

2. American Embassy cable Dar es Salaam 04011, "Text of Joint Communiqué and N'sele Amendments," July 14, 1992.

6. Democratization Flounders

1. American Embassy cable Kigali 02336, "Council of Ministers Retires Top Military Officers," June 11, 1992.

2. American Embassy cable Kigali 03478, "Internal Insecurity: An Ongoing Problem," August 21, 1992. This report provides the author's assessment of the security situation in Rwanda at the end of August 1992.

3. Voices of the Tribunal: UNICTR, "François Nsanzuwera." Nsanzuwera, Kigali's attorney general when the genocide began, recounts his experiences before, during and after the genocide in an hour-long United Nations interview. https://www.youtube.com/watch?v=lufADtenYyE.

4. ADL, *Rapport, Septembre 1991–Septembre 1992*, 257–60.

7. Turning Point

1. American Embassy cable Kigali 03503, "Challenge to the Constitution Brewing," August 24, 1992.

2. Des Forges et al., *Leave None*, 86.

3. American Embassy cable Kigali 04972, "New Hope for Arusha Talks," December 2, 1992.

4. American Embassy cable Kigali 05197, "The Politics of Peace: Internal Dialogue," December 16, 1992.

5. American Embassy cable Dar es Salaam 06841, "Arusha V: Update," November 30, 1992.

6. American Embassy cable Kigali 04929, "Visit with RPF Commander Kagame," November 30, 1992.

7. American Embassy cable Dar es Salaam 06819, "Arusha V: Waiting for Religious Leaders' Proposal," November 27, 1992.

8. American Embassy cable Dar es Salaam 06786, "Political Negotiations Resume," November 25, 1992.

9. American Embassy cable Dar es Salaam 06819, "Arusha V: Waiting for Religious Leaders' Proposal."

10. American Embassy cable Kigali 04936, "Arusha to Continue but Major Issues Unresolved," December 1, 1992.

11. American Embassy cable Dar es Salaam 07089, "Arusha V: Habyarimana wants Tanzanians to Break Impasse," December 11, 1992.

12. American Embassy cable Kigali 05287, "Political Negotiations and Arusha," December 23, 1992.

13. American Embassy cable Dar es Salaam 07326, "Arusha V: Negotiators Settle on Cabinet, Move on to Transitional Assembly," December 24, 1992.

14. American Embassy cable Kigali 05319, "Arusha Agreement: Kigali Reaction," December 23, 1992.

15. American Embassy cable Dar es Salaam 07371, "Arusha V: Talks Continue over Christmas despite Anger in Kigali," December 29, 1992.

16. American Embassy cable Dar es Salaam 07371, "Arusha V: Talks Continue."

8. Violence Stalks Democratization

1. Prunier, *Rwanda Crisis*, 168.

2. Des Forges et al., *Leave None*, 44–45.

3. American Embassy cable Brussels 13386, "Fall-out from Reyntjens/Kuypers Report on Rwanda Death Squads," October 22, 1992.

4. Des Forges et al., *Leave None*, 56.

5. Africa Watch, "Beyond the Rhetoric," 5–6.

6. In December 1992, I wrote the following in my holiday letter to family and friends.

> Rwanda continues to be interesting and challenging. The year has been turbulent, though, as the ship of state lurches toward a multiparty political system after thirty years of independence and nineteen of single-party, one-man rule. On the political front, the entire year has been a prelude to a transition period. The struggle has been intense between the old guard, fighting to *retain* as much power as possible, and the challengers, fighting to *gain* as much power as possible.
>
> Power-sharing negotiations devolved twice into prolonged wrangling over how to divide up ministerial portfolios in a transition government. Initially, the battle was a duel between the president's party and three principal opposition parties. In April, they agreed to a half-and-half formula for a multiparty government led by an opposition Prime Minister. The struggle became more complex, however, with the multi-party government's success in bringing to the negotiating table the Rwandan Patriotic Front (RPF), a rebel force that has waged a war at the northern border since October 1990. At year's end, a new transition government, to include the RPF, is in the making. The President and his party are hanging on with all their might to avoid the moment of truth, when they will no longer have a monopoly on decision making nor unilateral control of the state security apparatus. While the internal political forces are tearing each other apart, the RPF waits at the negotiating table in Arusha (Tanzania) ready to veto whatever government proposal puts it at a disadvantage.
>
> Shifting power is a painful process, especially when the power holder doesn't want to let go. The consequences for the population have been devastating: ethnic massacres (not unlike "ethnic cleansing"), vicious interparty violence, random terrorism (land mines and bombs), armed robbery (guns and grenades), and intimidation. Insecurity, stemming primarily from random terrorism, reached a fever pitch in late May and westerners thought seriously about pulling out. After diplomatic protests to the President, this form of ethnic violence subsided, and we stayed.
>
> A recent upsurge in ugly interparty and ethnic violence has brought insecurity again to a fever pitch. Rwandans, especially the Tutsi minority, are frightened to death that each day may be their last. After one particularly grueling day recently, with lots of bad news about heinous crimes against innocent victims, I mentioned to a Tutsi friend how depressed I felt. In a tone of helpless resignation, he said: "Add to that the fear." I cannot imagine. The forces of law and order are unable or unwilling to put an end to it.
>
> At least the cease-fire that took effect August 1 has held reasonably well. Vicious attacks by the RPF during the first half of the year brought to 350,000

the number of persons driven from their homes [in the north] by the war. The displaced, living in atrocious conditions near the front lines, are deteriorating rapidly for lack of food. Local markets have been stripped bare in an effort to fill the gaps in donor contributions. Food shipments on the horizon are insufficient to make up the deficit. A tragedy is in the making.

The bright spot in all of this has been getting to know some of the Rwandans who are speaking out against injustice and abuse and actively working to shape a more just society. Journalists, human rights activists, women, lawyers, and even some politicians, are telling it like it is. These are people who know the score and the risks they are taking, yet they manage to keep at it day after depressing day. The embassy supports their work in small ways under the rubric of contributing to the development of civil society. I feel privileged to know these courageous Rwandans and to call them my friends.

Weekends out of town, movies and dinners at the American club, tennis and swimming at the Belgian club, restaurants (we have two first class French and several African restaurants), and the occasional dancing party offer some relief from the daily pressures and tensions. . . .

Rwandans are incurable pessimists. No matter how much they accomplish, instead of looking back and noting how far they have come, they always look forward and groan about how far they have yet to go and the obstacles that lie ahead. I feel a bit like that, too, just now. The task ahead seems formidable. . . . All the best for 1993.

9. The January from Hell

1. Africa Watch, "Beyond the Rhetoric," 21.
2. Africa Watch, "Beyond the Rhetoric," 21.

10. Diplomats Undertake Fact-Finding

1. ADL, *Rapport, Septembre 1992–Septembre 1993*, 159–64.

11. War Resumes

1. Prunier, *Rwanda Crisis*, 176.
2. U.S. Department of State cable 57946, "AF DAS Houdek Meets with RPF Representative," February 26, 1993.
3. Prunier, *Rwanda Crisis*, 179.
4. Prunier, *Rwanda Crisis*, 179.
5. Prunier, *Rwanda Crisis*, 181n46.
6. Prunier, *Rwanda Crisis*, 179, 179n44.

12. A Second Chance for Peace

1. American Embassy cable Kampala 01485, "U.S. Meeting with RPF Military Commander," February 27, 1993.

2. American Embassy cable Dar es Salaam 01189, "Dar es Salaam Meeting and Communiqué," March 8, 1993.

3. Prunier, *Rwanda Crisis*, 182.

4. American Embassy cable Kigali 01065, "Visit with RPF Commander Kagame," March 12, 1993.

5. U.S. Department of State cable 91736, "Update on Rwanda Negotiations in Arusha: 3/26/93," March 27, 1993.

6. U.S. Department of State cable 102691, "Rwanda Negotiations Weekend Update," April 6, 1993.

7. United Nations Security Council, "Resolution 812 (1993)."

8. United Nations Security Council, "Letter Dated 28 February 1993"; United Nations Security Council, "Letter Dated 3 March 1993"; U.S. Mission to the United Nations cable 02343, "Ugandan Permrep Letter on Rwandan Border Force," May 12, 1993 (search terms: 93 USUN 02343).

9. ADL, *Rapport, Septembre 1992–Septembre 1993*, 171–72.

10. Africa Watch, "Beyond the Rhetoric," 23.

11. Africa Watch, "Beyond the Rhetoric," 7–12.

12. International Commission of Investigation on Human Rights Abuses in Rwanda, "Final Report."

13. International Commission of Investigation on Human Rights Abuses in Rwanda, "Final Report," 29, 51.

14. International Commission of Investigation on Human Rights Abuses in Rwanda, "Final Report," 53–54.

15. International Commission of Investigation on Human Rights Abuses in Rwanda, "Final Report," 44; ADL, *Rapport, Septembre 1992–Septembre 1993*, 181.

16. International Commission of Investigation on Human Rights Abuses in Rwanda, "Final Report," 20–21; ADL, *Rapport, Septembre 1992–Septembre 1993*, 180–81.

17. American Embassy cable Kigali 01474, "UNHRC Special Rapporteur on Summary Execution to Visit Rwanda," April 7, 1993.

18. American Embassy cable Kigali 00920, "Meetings with the Prime Minister and Foreign Minister," March 4, 1993.

19. American Embassy cable Kigali 01218, "Peace and Politics," March 22, 1993.

20. ADL, *Rapport, Septembre 1992–Septembre 1993*, 123–26.

21. American Embassy cable Kigali 01218, "Peace and Politics."

22. ADL, *Rapport, Septembre 1992–Septembre 1993*, 117.

13. Arusha Observer: The Setting

1. American Embassy cable Nairobi 09675, "Conversations with the RPF," May 3, 1993.

14. Arusha Observer: The Negotiations

1. U.S. Department of State cable 129206, "Rwanda: Update on Arusha Negotiations 4/28/93," April 29, 1993.

2. American Embassy cable Dar es Salaam 01522, "Background to Rwanda Talks Concerning Military Force Size," March 26, 1993.

3. U.S. Department of State cable 129206. "Rwanda: Update on Arusha."

4. American Embassy cable Dar es Salaam 01189, "Dar es Salaam Meeting and Communiqué."

5. United Nations Security Council, "Resolution 812"; Ruhigira, *Rwanda*, 19, 37; U.S. Mission to the United Nations cable USUN 00790, "Rwanda Requests UN Military Observers," February 23, 1993.

6. U.S. Department of State/Diplomatic Security Agency document, "Peace-keeping History in Rwanda," July 7, 1993.

7. U.S. Mission to the United Nations cable USUN 03036, "USUN Conveys to UN Concerns about Rwanda," May 22, 1993.

8. United Nations Security Council, "Resolution 812."

9. U.S. White House, Executive Office of the President, "President Clinton Signs PDD 25."

10. American Embassy cable Kigali 04871, "Arusha V: Refugee Discussions," November 25, 1992.

11. United Nations Office of the High Commissioner for Refugees, "The Dar es Salaam Declaration."

12. U.S. Department of State cable 177847, "Rwanda: Arusha Peace Talks Winding Down," June 11, 1993; American Embassy cable Dar es Salaam 03236, "Arusha Peace Talks: Inching Toward Conclusion," June 21, 1993.

13. Leader, "Genocide in Rwanda," 175–83.

15. The Dénouement

1. American Embassy cable Kigali 02761, "The MDR vs. the MDR," July 26, 1993.

2. American Embassy cable Kigali 02761, "The MDR vs. the MDR."

3. *Arusha Peace Accords, Peace Agreement*; United Nations General Assembly and Security Council, "Letter dated December 23, 1993."

16. Preparing to Implement the Accords

1. American Embassy cable Kigali 03188, "UN Reconnaissance Mission Head Discusses Thoughts on UN Involvement in Rwanda," August 27, 1993.

2. United Nations Security Council, "Report of the Independent Inquiry," 7.

3. U.S. Department of State cable 250796, "Talking Points for Meeting with French on Rwanda," August 17, 1993.

4. U.S. Mission to the United Nations cable USUN 04735, "Rwanda and Criteria for New UN PKO," September 28, 1993.

5. U.S. Mission to the United Nations cable USUN 04653, "UN Plans for Rwanda PKO," September 23, 1993.

6. United Nations Security Council, "Report of the Secretary General," 8–9; United Nations Security Council, "Report of the Independent Inquiry," 7.

7. United Nations Security Council, "Resolution 872 (1993)"; United Nations Security Council, "Report of the Independent Inquiry," 9.

8. Dallaire and Beardsley, *Shake Hands*, 103–5.

9. Dallaire and Beardsley, *Shake Hands*, 108.

10. Dallaire and Beardsley, *Shake Hands*, 109–10.

11. Dallaire and Beardsley, *Shake Hands*, 114–15.

12. American Embassy cable Kigali 04551, "Critical Analysis of UNAMIR's Phase I Operations," December 23, 1993.

13. Des Forges et al., *Leave None*, 147.

14. American Embassy cable Kigali 03854, "Burundi Coup, Rwanda Reaction," October 25, 1993.

15. Des Forges et al., *Leave None*, 138.

16. American Embassy cable Kigali 03855, "Burundi Refugees in Rwanda at 200,000," October 25, 1993.

17. American Embassy cable Kigali 04163, "Rwandans Want the U.S. Involved," November 24, 1993.

18. American Embassy cable Kigali 04381, "RPF Perspective on the Peace Process," December 10, 1993.

19. American Embassy cable Kigali 03060, "The Rwandan Peace Process: Problems and Prospects for Implementing the Peace Accord," August 19, 1993.

17. Violence Plagues Implementation

1. United Nations Commission on Human Rights, "Report by Mr. B. W. Ndiaye."

2. United Nations Commission on Human Rights, "Report by the Special Rapporteur," 117, paragraph 517.

3. American Embassy cable Kigali 04082, "Assassination Attempt on Human Rights Leader," November 16, 1993.

4. American Embassy cable Kigali 04098, "Civilians Killed in DMZ," November 18, 1993; American Embassy cable Kigali 04117, "Civilians Killed in DMZ," November 19, 1993; Dallaire and Beardsley, *Shake Hands*, 110–12.

5. American Embassy cable Kigali 04193, "UNAMIR Sidesteps Naming Culprit," November 26, 1993; Dallaire and Beardsley, *Shake Hands*, 112.

6. Dallaire and Beardsley, *Shake Hands*, 115–18.

7. Des Forges et al., *Leave None*, 143–44.

18. Implementation Stalls

1. Des Forges et al., *Leave None*, 150–51.

2. Dallaire and Beardsley, *Shake Hands*, 145.

3. Dallaire and Beardsley, *Shake Hands*, 146–47.

4. Dallaire and Beardsley, *Shake Hands*, 148.

5. *Arusha Peace Accords, Peace Agreement,* "Protocol of Agreement between the Government of the Republic of Rwanda and the Rwandese Patriotic Front on Power Sharing within the Framework of a Broad-Based Transitional Government, Section 4: Political Code of Ethics Binding the Political Forces Called upon to Participate in the Transitional Institutions, Sub-section 1: Fundamental Principles, Article 80."

6. Des Forges et al., *Leave None*, 158.

7. Des Forges et al., *Leave None*, 171.

8. Des Forges et al., *Leave None*, 171.

19. The Exodus

1. American Embassy cable Bujumbura 01299, "NED from Kigali and an Analysis of What Happened Following the President's Death and Why," April 15, 1994.

2. American Embassy cable Nairobi 06551, "[Colonel] Blames Right Wing Military for Kigali's Nightmare," April 12, 1994.

21. Diplomatic Challenges

1. Cohen, *Intervening*, 223.

2. Ogata, *Turbulent Decade*, 322, 172, 272.

3. Ogata, *Turbulent Decade*, 25–26.

22. Making Prevention a Priority

1. Cohen, *Intervening*, 2–4, 225.

2. Des Forges et al., *Leave None to Tell the Story*.

3. United Nations General Assembly and Security Council, "An Agenda for Peace."

4. United Nations General Assembly and Security Council, "Report of the Panel on United Nations Peace Operations."

5. United Nations Security Council, "Resolution 1925 (2010)," paragraph 11.

6. United Nations Security Council, "Report of the Independent Inquiry," 53–54.

7. United Nations Security Council, "Outline of the Mandate."

8. United Nations General Assembly, "2005 World Summit Outcome," paragraphs 138–40.

9. United Nations General Assembly, "Implementing the Responsibility to Protect," 33.

10. International Commission on Intervention and State Sovereignty, *Responsibility to Protect*.

11. United Nations Office on Genocide Prevention and the Responsibility to Protect, "Framework of Analysis." The fourteen factors used by the UN in its assessment framework echo those which the Fund for Peace developed earlier and uses to rank countries at risk of conflict in its Fragile States Index.

12. Stares and Zenko, *Enhancing U.S. Preventive Action*, 14.

13. United Nations Office for the Coordination of Humanitarian Affairs, "OCHA On Message: The Cluster Approach."

14. Hackett, Piraino, and Rivera, "One Organization's Journey," 4–6.

15. Fund for Peace, "CAST: Conflict Assessment Framework Manual."

16. United Nations Security Council, "Resolution 955 (1994)," Annex, Article 6, Individual Criminal Responsibility.

17. International Criminal Court, *Rome Statute*, part 2, "Jurisdiction, Admissibility, and Applicable Law," Articles 5–8.

18. I served as the State Department's coordinator for the Tripartite Plus Commission from 2005 to 2009.

19. Albright et al., *Preventing Genocide*, 68.

20. U.S. Department of State and U.S. Agency for International Development, *Leading through Civilian Power*; U.S. White House, Executive Office of the President, "National Security Strategy, May 2010."

21. U.S. White House, Office of the President, "Presidential Study Directive."

22. U.S. White House, Office of the Press Secretary, "Remarks by the President."

23. U.S. Department of Defense, U.S. Joint Chiefs of Staff, "Joint Publication 3-07.3, Peace Operations," Appendix B, 1–8; Sewell, Chin, and Raymond, *Mass Atrocity Response*, 9–10.

23. Fixes for the Future

1. Norris and Malknecht, *Atrocities Prevention Board*, 2, 6–7.

2. International Commission on Intervention and State Sovereignty, *Responsibility to Protect*, 19–27.

3. United States Institute for Peace, "Can We Prevent the Next War?"

4. International Commission on Intervention and State Sovereignty, *Responsibility to Protect*, 27.

5. Cohen, *Intervening*, 224.

6. U.S. White House, Office of the Press Secretary, "Remarks by the President."

7. Ogata, *Turbulent Decade*, 25.

Conclusion

1. Paquette and Shefte, "Turning Pain into Hope."

2. Prunier, *Africa's World War*; Reyntjens, *The Great African War*; Stearns, *Dancing in the Glory*.

3. Jones, *Peacemaking*, 3.

4. International Commission on Intervention and State Sovereignty, *Responsibility to Protect*, 19–27; Albright et al., *Preventing Genocide*, 35–71.

5. Koppell and Sharma, *Preventing the Next Wave of Conflict*.

6. U.S. White House, Executive Office of the President, *National Security Strategy*.

7. U.S. White House, Executive Office of the President, *National Security Strategy*.

BIBLIOGRAPHY

Adelman, Howard, and Astri Suhrke, eds. *The Path of a Genocide: The Rwanda Crisis from Uganda to Zaire*. New Brunswick NJ: Transaction, 1999.

Adelman, Howard, Astri Suhrke, and Bruce Jones. "Study 2: Early Warning and Conflict Management." In *The International Response to Conflict and Genocide: Lessons from the Rwanda Experience*, ed. David Millwood. Copenhagen: Steering Committee of the Joint Evaluation of Emergency Assistance to Rwanda, 1996. http://www.oecd.org/derec/unitedstates/50189764.pdf.

Africa Watch. "Beyond the Rhetoric: Continuing Human Rights Abuses in Rwanda." *News from Africa Watch* 5, no. 7 (June 1993). https://www.hrw.org/sites/default/files/reports/RWANDA936.PDF.

———. "Rwanda: Talking Peace and Waging War. Human Rights since the October 1990 Invasion." *News from Africa Watch* 4, no. 3 (February 1992). http://hdl.handle.net/2152/5221.

Albright, Madeleine. *Madam Secretary: A Memoir*. New York: Miramax Books, 2003.

Albright, Madeline K., et al. *Preventing Genocide: A Blueprint for U.S. Policymakers*. Washington DC: U.S. Holocaust Memorial Museum, American Academy of Diplomacy, and the Endowment of the United States Institute of Peace, 2008. http://www.ushmm.org/m/pdfs/20081124-genocide-prevention-report.pdf.

Association Rwandaise pour la Défense des Droits de la Personne et des Libertés Publiques. *Rapport sur les Droits de l'Homme au Rwanda, Septembre 1991–Septembre 1992*. Kigali: Pallotti-Presse, November 1992.

———. *Rapport sur les Droits de l'Homme au Rwanda, Septembre 1992–Septembre 1993*. Kigali: Pallotti-Presse, November 1993.

Arusha Peace Accords, Peace Agreement between the Government of the Republic of Rwanda and the Rwandese Patriotic Front. August 1993. International Conflict Research Institute. http://www.incore.ulst.ac.uk/services/cds/agreements/pdf/rwan1.pdf.

Baker, Pauline H., and Angeli E. Weller. *An Analytical Model of Internal Conflict and State Collapse: Manual for Practitioners*. Washington DC: Fund for Peace, 1998.

Carnegie Commission on Preventing Deadly Conflict. *Preventing Deadly Conflict: Final Report with Executive Summary*. Washington DC: Carnegie Com-

mission on Preventing Deadly Conflict, 1997. http://www.dtic.mil/dtic/tr
/fulltext/u2/a372860.pdf.

Ceasefire Agreement between the Government of the Republic of Rwanda and
the Rwandese Patriotic Front. N'Sele, Zaire, March 22, 1991. United Nations
Peacemaker. http://peacemaker.un.org/rwanda-nsele-ceasefire92.

Cohen, Herman J. *Intervening in Africa: Superpower Peacemaking in a Troubled
Continent.* New York: St. Martin's Press, 2000.

Commission on Human Security. *Human Security Now: Protecting and Empowering People.* New York: Commission on Human Security, 2003. https://reliefweb.int/sites
/reliefweb.int/files/resources/91BAEEDBA50C6907C1256D19006A9353-chs
-security-may03.pdf

Crisp, Jeff. "No Solutions in Sight: The Problem of Protracted Refugee Situations in Africa." *New Issues in Refugee Research* No.75. Geneva: UNHCR, 2003.
http://www.unhcr.org/cgi-bin/texis/vtx/home/opendocPDFViewer.html
?docid=3e2d66c34&query=protracted refugee situations.

Dallaire, Roméo, with Brent Beardsley. *Shake Hands with the Devil: The Failure of
Humanity in Rwanda.* Toronto: Random House Canada, 2003.

Des Forges, Alison. "Call to Genocide: Radio in Rwanda, 1994." In *The Media
and the Rwanda Genocide,* edited by Allan Thompson, 41–54. London: Pluto
Press, 2007.

Des Forges, Alison, et al. *Leave None to Tell the Story: Genocide in Rwanda.* New
York: Human Rights Watch, 1999.

Fédération Internationale des Droits de l'Homme. *Rapport de la Commission Internationale d'Enquête sur les Violations des Droits de l'Homme au Rwanda depuis
le 1er Octobre 1990, le 7–21 Janvier 1992.* Paris: FIDH, March 8, 1993. http://
www.usip.org/files/file/resources/collections/commissions/Rwanda93
-Report.pdf.

Feil, Colonel Scott. *Preventing Genocide: How the Early Use of Force Might Have
Succeeded in Rwanda. Report to the Carnegie Commission on Preventing Deadly
Conflict.* New York: Carnegie Corporation, April 1998. https://www.carnegie
.org/media/filer_public/02/45/0245add3-b6aa-4a08-b9fc-6eb91f4e2975
/ccny_report_1998_genocide.pdf.

Finkel, James P. "Atrocity Prevention at the Crossroads: Addressing the President's Atrocity Prevention Board after Two Years." *Center for the Prevention
of Genocide Series of Occasional Papers* No. 2. Washington DC: USHMM Center for the Prevention of Genocide, September 2014.

———. "Moving beyond the Crossroads: Strengthening the Atrocity Prevention Board." *Genocide Studies and Prevention: An International Journal* 9, no.
2 (2015): 138–47. https://scholarcommons.usf.edu/gsp/vol9/iss2/17.

Fund for Peace. "CAST: Conflict Assessment Framework Manual." Washington DC: Fund for Peace, 2014. https://fundforpeace.org/2014/03/10/cast
-conflict-assessment-framework-manual-2014-reprint/.

———. "Fragile States Index, 2019." Washington DC: Fund for Peace, 2019. https://
fundforpeace.org/2019/04/10/fragile-states-index-2019/.

Gribbin, Robert E. *In the Aftermath of Genocide: The U.S. Role in Rwanda*. New York: iUniverse, 2005.

Hackett, Ken, Dave Piraino, and John Rivera. "One Organization's Journey with Catholic Social Thought and Corporate Social Responsibility." Baltimore MD: Catholic Relief Services, October 2006. https://www.academia.edu /19610969/Catholic_Relief_Services_One_Organization_s_Journey_with _Catholic_Social_Thought_and_Corporate_Social_Responsibility.

Higiro, Jean-Marie Vianney. "Rwandan Private Print Media on the Eve of the Genocide." In *The Media and the Rwanda Genocide*, edited by Allan Thompson, 73–79. London: Pluto Press, 2007.

International Commission on Intervention and State Sovereignty. *The Responsibility to Protect*. Ottawa: International Development Research Centre, 2001. http://responsibilitytoprotect.org/ICISS%20Report.pdf.

International Commission of Investigation on Human Rights Abuses in Rwanda. "Report of the International Commission of Investigation on Human Rights Violations in Rwanda since October 1, 1990." Translated by Alison Des Forge. Washington DC: Human Rights Watch, March 1993. http://www.hrw.org /report/1993/03/01/report-international-commission-investigation-human -rights-violations-rwanda.

International Criminal Court. *Rome Statute of the International Criminal Court*. Rome: International Criminal Court, July 17, 1998. https://www.icc-cpi.int /nr/rdonlyres/ea9aeff7-5752-4f84-be94-0a655eb30e16/0/rome_statute _english.pdf.

International Press Institute. "World Press Freedom Heroes: Symbols of Courage in Global Journalism." N.d. https://ipi.media/ipi-heroes/.

Jones, Bruce D. *Peacemaking in Rwanda: The Dynamics of Failure*. Boulder CO: Lynne Rienner, 2001.

Koppell, Carla, with Anita Sharma. *Preventing the Next Wave of Conflict: Understanding Non-Traditional Threats to Global Stability. Report of the Non-Traditional Threats Working Group*. Washington DC: Woodrow Wilson International Center for Scholars, 2003.

Kuperman, Alan. *The Limits of Humanitarian Intervention: Genocide in Rwanda*. Washington DC: Brookings Institution Press, 2001.

Leader, Joyce E. "Genocide in Rwanda and the Kigali Diplomatic Corps: Consultation, Cooperation, Coordination." In *The Diplomatic Corps as an Institution of International Society*, edited by Paul Sharp and Geoffrey Wiseman, 168–96. New York: Palgrave Macmillan, 2007.

Lemarchand, René. "The Rwanda Genocide." In *Century of Genocide: Critical Essays and Eyewitness Accounts*, edited by Samuel Totten, William S. Parsons, and Israel W. Charny, 395–412. New York: Routledge, 2004.

———. *The Dynamics of Violence in Central Africa*. Philadelphia: University of Pennsylvania Press, 2009.

Longman, Timothy. *Christianity and Genocide in Rwanda*. New York: Cambridge University Press, 2010.

Lund, S. Michael. *Preventing Violent Conflicts: A Strategy for Preventive Diplomacy.* Washington DC: United States Institute of Peace, 1996.

Melvern, Linda. *Conspiracy to Murder: The Rwandan Genocide.* London: Verso, 2004.

———. *A People Betrayed: The Role of the West in Rwanda's Genocide.* London: Zed Books, 2000.

Norris, John, and Annie Malknecht. *Atrocities Prevention Board: Background, Performance, and Options.* Washington DC: Center for American Progress, June 13, 2013. https://www.americanprogress.org/wp-content/uploads/2013/06/AtrocitiesPrevBoard.pdf.

Ogata, Sadako. *The Turbulent Decade: Confronting the Refugee Crises of the 1990s.* New York: Norton, 2005.

Organization of African Unity. *Rwanda: The Preventable Genocide: The Report of the International Panel of Eminent Personalities to Investigate the 1994 Genocide in Rwanda and the Surrounding Events.* Addis Ababa: OAU, July 2000. http://www.refworld.org/pdfid/4d1da8752.pdf.

Paquette, Danielle, and Whitney Shefte. "Turning Pain into Hope." *Washington Post,* June 12, 2017. https://www.washingtonpost.com/sf/world/2017/06/11/rwandas-children-of-rape-are-coming-of-age-against-the-odds/?utm_term=.2c3369158593.

Petersen, Soren Jessen. "Multilateralism, Sovereignty, and the Political Consequences of Humanitarian Intervention." Senior Fellow Project Report. U.S. Institute for Peace, May 29, 2007. http://www.usip.org/events/multilateralism-sovereignty-and-political-consequences-humanitarian-intervention.

Power, Samantha. *A Problem from Hell: America and the Age of Genocide.* New York: Basic Books, 2002.

Prunier, Gérard. *Africa's World War: Congo, the Rwandan Genocide, and the Making of a Continental Catastrophe.* New York: Oxford University Press, 2008.

———. *The Rwanda Crisis: History of a Genocide.* New York: Columbia University Press, 1995.

Rawson, David. *Prelude to Genocide: Arusha, Rwanda, and the Failure of Diplomacy.* Athens: Ohio University Press, 2018.

Reyntjens, Filip. *The Great African War: Congo and Regional Geopolitics, 1996–2006.* New York: Cambridge University Press, 2009.

Ruhigira, Enoch. *Rwanda: La Fin Tragique d'Un Régime.* Vol. 2: *Une Vision étouffée par des intérêts partisans.* Orléans: Editions La Pagaie, 2011.

Sewell, Sarah, Sally Chin, and Dwight Raymond. *Mass Atrocity Response Operations (MARO): A Military Planning Handbook.* Cambridge MA: Carr Center for Human Rights Policy, Harvard Kennedy School and U.S. Army Peacekeeping and Stability Operations Institute, 2010. https://www.ushmm.org/m/pdfs/MARO-Handbook-091117.pdf.

Sharp, Paul. "The Idea of Diplomatic Culture and Its Sources." In *Intercultural Communication and Diplomacy,* edited by Hannah Slavik, 361–79. Malta: Diplo Foundation, 2004. http://www.diplomacy.edu/sites/default/files/IC%20and%20Diplomacy%20%28FINAL%29_Part22.pdf.

Sibomana, Andre. *Hope for Rwanda: Conversations with Laure Guilbert and Hervé Deguine.* London: Pluto Press, 1999.

Smith, Dane F., Jr. *U.S. Peaceforce: Organizing American Peace-Building Operations.* Santa Barbara CA: Praeger, 2010.

Stanton, Gregory H. "Could the Rwandan Genocide Have Been Prevented?" Washington DC: Genocide Watch, 2002. http://www.genocidewatch.org /couldrwandangenocide.html.

——— . "The Rwandan Genocide: Why Early Warning Failed." *Journal of African Conflicts and Peace Studies* 1, no. 2 (2009): 6–25. http://scholarcommons .usf.edu/jacaps/vol1/iss2/3/.

Stares, Paul B., and Micah Zenko. *Enhancing U.S. Preventive Action: Council Special Report No. 48.* New York: Council on Foreign Relations Press, October 2009. https://www.cfr.org/report/enhancing-us-preventive -action.

Stearns, Jason K. *Dancing in the Glory of Monsters: The Collapse of the Congo and the Great War of Africa.* New York: Public Affairs, 2011.

Strauss, Scott. *The Order of Genocide: Race, Power, and War in Rwanda.* Ithaca NY: Cornell University Press, 2006.

Suhrke, Astri, and Bruce Jones. "Preventive Diplomacy in Rwanda: Failure to Act or Failure of Actions?" In *Opportunities Missed, Opportunities Seized: Preventive Diplomacy in the Post–Cold War World*, edited by Bruce W. Jentleson, 238–64. Lanham MD: Rowman and Littlefield, 2000.

Thompson, Allan, ed. *The Media and the Rwanda Genocide.* London: Pluto Press, 2007.

United Nations Commission on Human Rights. "Report by Mr. B. W. Ndiaye, Special Rapporteur, on his mission to Rwanda from 8 to 17 April 1993." E/CN.4/1994/7/Add.1. Geneva: UNCHR, August 11, 1993. http://www .preventgenocide.org/prevent/UNdocs/ndiaye1993.htm.

——— . "Report by the Special Rapporteur, Mr. Bacre Waly Ndiaye, Submitted Pursuant to Commission on Human Rights Resolution 1993/71, December 7, 1993." E/CN.4/1994/7, 116–18. https://www.hr-dp.org/files/2015/08/07 /Report_of_the_SR-_country_situations,_1993.pdf.

United Nations Environment Programme. "From Conflict to Peacebuilding: The Role of Natural Resources and the Environment." Nairobi: UNEP, February 2009. http://www.unep.org/pdf/pcdmb_policy_01.pdf.

United Nations General Assembly. "Early Warning, Assessment, and the Responsibility to Protect." Report of the Secretary-General. A/64/864. New York: United Nations, July 14, 2010. https://undocs.org/A/64/864.

——— . "Implementing the Responsibility to Protect." Report of Secretary-General. A/63/677. New York: United Nations, January 12, 2009. https:// undocs.org/A/63/677.

——— . "2005 World Summit Outcome: Resolution Adopted by the General Assembly on 16 September, 2005." A/Res/60/1. New York: United Nations, October 24, 2005. https://undocs.org/A/RES/60/1.

United Nations General Assembly and Security Council. "An Agenda for Peace: Preventive Diplomacy, Peacemaking and Peace-keeping." Report of the Secretary-General. A/47/227-S/24111. New York: United Nations, June 17, 1992. www.un-documents.net/a47-277.htm.

———. "Letter Dated 23 December 1993 from the Permanent Representative of the United Republic of Tanzania to the United Nations Addressed to the Secretary-General." A/48/824/S/26915. New York: United Nations, December 23, 1993. https://nsarchive2.gwu.edu/NSAEBB/NSAEBB469/docs/DOCUMENT%2017.pdf.

———. "Report of the Panel on United Nations Peace Operations." A/55/305-S/2000/809. New York: United Nations, August 21, 2000. www.un.org/en/ga/search/view_doc.asp?symbol=A/55/305.

United Nations Office for the Coordination of Humanitarian Affairs. "OCHA on Message: The Cluster Approach." Geneva: United Nations, May 25, 2012. https://www.unocha.org/node/3213.

United Nations Office of the High Commissioner for Refugees. "Convention and Protocol Relating to the Status of Refugees." Geneva: UNHCR, July 25, 1951. http://www.unhcr.org/3b66c2aa10.html.

———. "The Dar es Salaam Declaration on the Refugee Problem." February 19, 1991. https://www.refworld.org/pdfid/4dde22d22.pdf.

———. "Protracted Refugee Situations: High Commissioner's Initiative." Geneva: UNHCR, December 2008. http://www.refworld.org/docid/496f041d2.html.

United Nations Office on Genocide Prevention and the Responsibility to Protect. https://www.un.org/en/genocideprevention/office-mandate.shtml.

———. "Framework of Analysis for Atrocity Crimes: A Tool for Prevention." New York: United Nations, 2014. https://www.un.org/en/genocideprevention/documents/about-us/Doc.3_Framework%20of%20Analysis%20for%20Atrocity%20Crimes_EN.pdf.

United Nations Security Council. "Letter Dated 28 February 1993 from the Permanent Representative of Rwanda to the United Nations Addressed to the President of the Security Council." S/25355. New York: United Nations, February 28, 1993. http://www.un.org/en/documents/index.html.

———. "Letter Dated 3 March 1993 from the Permanent Representative of Uganda to the United Nations to the President of the Security Council." S/25356. New York: United Nations, March 3, 1993. http://www.un.org/en/documents/index.html.

———. "Outline of the Mandate for the Special Adviser on the Prevention of Genocide." S/2004/567. New York: United Nations, July 13, 2004. http://www.un.org/ga/search/viewm_doc.asp?symbol=S/2004/567.

———. "Preventive Diplomacy: Delivering Results. Report of the Secretary-General (S/2011/552). New York: United Nations, August 26, 2011. https://reliefweb.int/report/guinea/preventive-diplomacy-delivering-results-report-secretary-general-s2011552.

————. "Report of the Independent Inquiry into the Actions of the United Nations during the 1994 Genocide in Rwanda." s/1999/1257. New York: United Nations, December 16, 1999. https://undocs.org/en/S/1999/1257.

————. "Report of the Secretary General on Rwanda." s/26488. New York: United Nations, September 24, 1993. http://www.un.org/en/sc/documents/search.shtml.

————. "Report of the Secretary General on Rwanda." s/26488/Add.1. New York: United Nations, September 29, 1993. http://www.un.org/en/documents/index.html.

————. "Resolution 812." s/Res/812 (1993). New York: United Nations, March 12, 1993. https://documents-dds-ny.un.org/doc/UNDOC/GEN/N93/146/16/IMG/N9314616.pdf?OpenElement.

————. "Resolution 872." s/Res872 (1993). New York: United Nations, October 5, 1993. https://documents-dds-ny.un.org/doc/UNDOC/GEN/N93/540/63/PDF/N9354063.pdf?OpenElement.

————. "Resolution 955." s/RES/955 (1994). New York: United Nations, November 8, 1994. https://documents-dds-ny.un.org/doc/UNDOC/GEN/N95/140/97/PDF/N9514097.pdf?OpenElement.

————. "Resolution 1925 (2010)." s/RES/1925 (2010). New York: United Nations, May 28, 2010. http://www.un.org/ga/search/view_doc.asp?symbol=S/RES/1925%20(2010).

————. "Second Progress Report of the Secretary-General on the United Nations Assistance Mission for Rwanda." s/1994/360. New York: United Nations, March 30, 1994. https://www.un.org/en/ga/documents/symbol.shtml.

U.S. Agency for International Development. "Conflict Assessment Framework: Version 2.0." Washington DC: USAID, June, 2012. http://pdf.usaid.gov/pdf_docs/pnady739.pdf.

U.S. Department of Defense, Joint Chiefs of Staff. "Joint Publication 3-07.3, Peace Operations." Washington DC: Department of Defense, March 1, 2018. http://fas.org/irp/doddir/dod/jp3-07-3.pdf.

U.S. Department of State, Bureau of Conflict and Stabilization Operations. "Our Mission." Washington DC: U.S. Department of State. http://www.state.gov/j/cso/.

U.S. Department of State, Bureau of Population, Refugees, and Migration. "Protracted Refugee Situations." Washington DC: U.S. Department of State, 2011. http://www.state.gov/j/prm/policyissues/issues/protracted/.

U.S. Department of State, Office of the Coordinator of Reconstruction and Stabilization. U.S. Department of State Archive, 2001-2009. "Core Objectives." Washington DC: U.S. Department of State. http://2001-2009.state.gov/s/crs/c15212.htm.

U.S. Department of State, Office of the Spokesperson. "U.S. Department of State Launches Bureau of Conflict Stabilization Operations." Fact Sheet. November, 22, 2011. http://www.state.gov/r/pa/prs/ps/2011/11/177636.htm.

U.S. Department of State and United States Agency for International Development. *Enduring Leadership in a Dynamic World: The Quadrennial Diplomacy*

and Development Review (QDDR). Washington DC: Government Printing
  Office, 2015. https://2009-2017.state.gov/s/dmr/qddr/2015/index.htm.
———. *Leading through Civilian Power: The First Quadrennial Diplomacy and
  Development Review*. Washington DC: Government Printing Office, 2010.
  https://2009-2017.state.gov/s/dmr/qddr/2010/index.htm.
United States Institute for Peace. "Can We Prevent the Next War?" Washington
  DC: United States Institute for Peace, January 15, 2010. http://www.usip.org
  /events/can-we-prevent-the-next-war.
U.S. White House, Executive Office of the President. "Fact Sheet: The Obama
  Administration's Comprehensive Efforts to Prevent Mass Atrocities over
  the Past Year." May 1, 2013. https://obamawhitehouse.archives.gov/sites
  /default/files/docs/fact_sheet_-_administration_efforts_to_prevent_mass
  _atrocities5.pdf.
———. *National Security Strategy of the United States of America*. Washington
  DC: White House, December 2017. https://www.whitehouse.gov/articles
  /new-national-security-strategy-new-era/.
———. "U.S. Policy on Reforming Multilateral Peace Operations." Presidential Decision Directive 25 (PDD 25). May 6, 1994. http://www.fas.org/irp
  /offdocs/pdd25.htm.
———. "Presidential Review Directive/NSC-13:" Multilateral Peacekeeping
  Operations." Memorandum. February 15, 1993. https://fas.org/irp/offdocs
  /prd/prd-13.pdf.
———. "Presidential Study Directive on Mass Atrocities." Memorandum. August 4,
  2011. http://www.whitehouse.gov/the-press-office/2011/08/04/presidential
  -study-directive-mass-atrocities.
U.S. White House, Office of the Press Secretary. "Remarks by the President at
  the United States Holocaust Memorial Museum." Washington DC: White
  House, April 23, 2012. https://www.whitehouse.gov/the-press-office/2012
  /04/23/remarks-president-united-states-holocaust-memorial-museum.
Uvin, Peter. *Aiding Violence: The Development Enterprise in Rwanda*. West Hart-
  ford CT: Kumarian Press, 1998.
Voices of the Tribunal: UNICTR. "François Nsanzuwera–Appeals Counsel, ICTR."
  May 2, 2016. https://www.youtube.com/watch?v=lufADtenYyE.
Waxman, Matthew C. *Intervention to Stop Genocide and Mass Atrocities: Interna-
  tional Norms and U.S. Policies*. Council on Foreign Relations Special Report
  No. 49. New York: Council on Foreign Relations, October 2009. http://
  www.cfr.org/genocide/intervention-stop-genocide-mass-atrocities/p20379.
Zartman, I. William, ed. *Preventive Negotiation: Avoiding Conflict Escalation*. Car-
  negie Commission on Preventing Deadly Conflict. Lanham MD: Rowman
  & Littlefield, 2001.

Declassified State Department, Embassy, and U.S. Mission to the UN Cables

The U.S. Department of State declassified cables referenced in this book
in 2011. They can be accessed through its Freedom of Information Act

Virtual Reading Room Documents Search page at https://foia.state .gov/Search/Search.aspx. To read a cited cable, go to this URL, enter the search term provided, click on "Search" for the cable title to pop up at the top of a list, and, finally, click on the cable title to see the text.

American Embassy Cable Brussels 13386. "Fall-Out from Reyntjens/Kuypers Report on Rwanda Death Squads." October 22, 1992. https://foia.state.gov /Search/Search.aspx (Search Terms: 92 Dar es Salaam 13386).

American Embassy Cable Bujumbura 01299. "NED from Kigali and an Analysis of What Happened following the President's Death and Why." April 15, 1994. https://foia.state.gov/Search/Search.aspx (Search Terms: 94 Bujumbura 01299).

American Embassy Cable Dar es Salaam 04011. "Text of Joint Communiqué and N'sele Amendments." July 14, 1992. https://foia.state.gov/Search/Search .aspx (Search Terms: 92 Dar es Salaam 04011).

———. Dar es Salaam 06786. "Political Negotiations Resume." November 25, 1992. https://foia.state.gov/Search/Search.aspx (Search Terms: 92 Dar es Salaam 06786).

———. Dar es Salaam 06819. "Arusha V: Waiting for Religious Leaders' Proposal." November 27, 1992. https://foia.state.gov/Search/Search.aspx (Search Terms: 92 Dar es Salaam 06819).

———. Dar es Salaam 96841. "Arusha V: Update." November 30, 1992. https:// foia.state.gov/Search/Search.aspx (Search Terms: 92 Dar es Salaam 06841).

———. Dar es Salaam 07089. "Arusha V: Habyarimana Wants Tanzanians to Break Impasse." December 11, 1992. https://foia.state.gov/Search/Search .aspx (Search Terms: 92 Dar es Salaam 07089).

———. Dar es Salaam 07326. "Arusha V: Negotiators Settle on Cabinet, Move on to Transitional Assembly." December 24, 1992. https://foia.state.gov/Search /Search.aspx (Search Terms: 92 Dar es Salaam 07326).

———. Dar es Salaam 07371. "Arusha V: Talks Continue over Christmas Despite Anger in Kigali." December 29, 1992. https://foia.state.gov/Search/Search .aspx (Search Terms: 92 Dar es Salaam 07371).

———. Dar es Salaam 01189. "Dar es Salaam Meeting and Communiqué." March 8, 1993. https://foia.state.gov/Search/Search.aspx (Search Terms: 92 Dar es Salaam 01189).

———. Dar es Salaam 01522. "Background to Rwanda Talks concerning Military Force Size." March 26, 1993. https://foia.state.gov/Search/Search.aspx (Search Terms: 93 Dar es Salaam 01522).

———. Dar es Salaam 03236. "Arusha Peace Talks: Inching toward Conclusion." June 21, 1993. https://foia.state.gov/Search/Search.aspx (Search Terms: 93 Dar es Salaam 03236).

American Embassy Cable Kampala 02581. "A/S Cohen's Meeting with Representatives of the RPF and the RPA." May 12, 1992. https://foia.state.gov/Search /Search.aspx (Search Terms: 92 Kampala 02581).

———. Kampala 01485. "U.S. Meeting with RPF Military Commander." February 27, 1993. https://foia.state.gov/Search/Search.aspx (Search Terms: 93 Kampala 01485).

American Embassy Cable Kigali 02336. "Council of Ministers Retires Top Military Officers." June 11, 1992. https://foia.state.gov/Search/Search.aspx (Search Terms: 92 Kigali 02336).

———. Kigali 03478. "Internal Insecurity: An Ongoing Problem." August 21, 1992. https://foia.state.gov/Search/Search.aspx (Search Terms: 92 Kigali 03478).

———. Kigali 03503. "Challenge to the Constitution Brewing." August 24, 1992. https://foia.state.gov/Search/Search.aspx (Search Terms: 92 Kigali 03503).

———. Kigali 04871. "Arusha V: Refugee Discussions." November 25, 1992. https://foia.state.gov/Search/Search.aspx (Search Terms: 92 Kigali 04871).

———. Kigali 04929. "Visit with RPF Commander Kagame." November 30, 1992. https://foia.state.gov/Search/Search.aspx (Search Terms: 92 Kigali 04929).

———. Kigali 04936. "Arusha to Continue but Major Issues Unresolved." December 1, 1992. https://foia.state.gov/Search/Search.aspx (Search Terms: 92 Kigali 04936).

———. Kigali 04972. "New Hope for Arusha Talks." December 2, 1992. https://foia.state.gov/Search/Search.aspx (Search Terms: 92 Kigali 04972).

———. Kigali 05197. "The Politics of Peace: Internal Dialogue." December 16, 1992. https://foia.state.gov/Search/Search.aspx (Search Terms: 92 Kigali 05197).

———. Kigali 05287. "Political Negotiations and Arusha." December 23, 1992. https://foia.state.gov/Search/Search.aspx (Search Terms: 92 Kigali 05287).

———. Kigali 05319. "Arusha Agreement: Kigali Reaction." December 23, 1992. https://foia.state.gov/Search/Search.aspx (Search Terms: 92 Kigali 05319).

———. Kigali 00920. "Meetings with the Prime Minister and Foreign Minister." March 4, 1993. https://foia.state.gov/Search/Search.aspx (Search Terms: 93 Kigali 00920).

———. Kigali 01065. "Visit with RPF Commander Kagame." March 12, 1993. https://foia.state.gov/Search/Search.aspx (Search Terms: 93 Kigali 01065).

———. Kigali 01218. "Peace and Politics." March 22, 1993. https://foia.state.gov/Search/Search.aspx (Search Terms: 93 Kigali 01218).

———. Kigali 01474. "UNHRC Special Rapporteur on Summary Execution to Visit Rwanda." April 7, 1993. https://foia.state.gov/Search/Search.aspx (Search Terms: 93 Kigali 01474).

———. Kigali 02761. "The MDR vs. the MDR." July 26, 1993. https://foia.state.gov/Search/Search.aspx (Search Terms: 93 Kigali 02761).

———. Kigali 03060. "The Rwandan Peace Process: Problems and Prospects for Implementing the Peace Accord." August 19, 1993. https://foia.state.gov/Search/Search.aspx (Search Terms: 93 Kigali 03060).

———. Kigali 03188. "UN Reconnaissance Mission Head Discusses Thoughts on UN Involvement in Rwanda." August 27, 1993. https://foia.state.gov/Search/Search.aspx (Search Terms: 93 Kigali 03188).

———. Kigali 03854. "Burundi Coup, Rwanda Reaction." October 25, 1993. https://foia.state.gov/Search/Search.aspx (Search Terms: 93 Kigali 03854).

———. Kigali 03855. "Burundi Refugees in Rwanda at 200,000." October 25, 1993. https://foia.state.gov/Search/Search.aspx (Search Terms: 93 Kigali 03855).

———. Kigali 04060. "Progress on the GTBE." November 15, 1993. https://foia.state.gov/Search/Search.aspx (Search Terms: 93 Kigali 04060).

———. Kigali 04082. "Assassination Attempt on Human Rights Leader." November 16, 1993. https://foia.state.gov/Search/Search.aspx (Search Terms: 93 Kigali 04082).

———. Kigali 04098. "Civilians Killed in DMZ." November 18, 1993. https://foia.state.gov/Search/Search.aspx (Search Terms: 93 Kigali 04098).

———. Kigali 04117. "Civilians Killed in DMZ." November 19, 1993. https://foia.state.gov/Search/Search.aspx (Search Terms: 93 Kigali 04117).

———. Kigali 04163. "Rwandans Want the U.S. Involved." November 24, 1993. https://foia.state.gov/Search/Search.aspx (Search Terms: 93 Kigali 04163).

———. Kigali 04193. "UNAMIR Sidesteps Naming Culprit in Ruhengeri Incident; Parties to Explore Reconciliation." November 26, 1993. https://foia.state.gov/Search/Search.aspx (Search Terms: 93 Kigali 04193).

———. Kigali 04381. "RPF Perspective on the Peace Process." December 10, 1993. https://foia.state.gov/Search/Search.aspx (Search Terms: 93 Kigali 04381).

———. Kigali 04551. "Critical Analysis of UNAMIR's Phase I Operations." December 23, 1993. https://foia.state.gov/Search/Search.aspx (Search Terms: 93 Kigali 04551).

American Embassy Cable Nairobi 09675. "Conversations with the RPF." May 3, 1993. https://foia.state.gov/Search/Search.aspx (Search Terms: 93 Nairobi 09675).

———. Nairobi 06551. "[Colonel] Blames Right Wing Military for Kigali's Nightmare." April 12, 1994. https://foia.state.gov/Search/Search.aspx (Search Terms: 94 Nairobi 06551).

U.S. Department of State Cable State 57946. "AF DAS Houdek Meets with RPF Representative." February 26, 1993. https://drive.google.com/file/d/0B5uQnFUS4VhKLWpCdndsS0dNTEE/edit?pli=1.

———. State 91736. "Update on Rwanda Negotiations in Arusha: 3/26/93." March 27, 1993. https://foia.state.gov/search/search.aspx (Search Terms: 93 State 91736).

———. State 102691. "Rwanda Negotiations Weekend Update." April 6, 1993. https://foia.state.gov/Search/Search.aspx (Search Terms: 93 State 102691).

———. State 129206. "Rwanda: Update on Arusha Negotiations 4/28/93." April 29, 1993. https://foia.state.gov/Search/Search.aspx (Search Terms: 93 State 129206).

———. State 177847. "Rwanda: Arusha Peace Talks Winding Down." June 11, 1993. https://foia.state.gov/Search/Search.aspx (Search Terms: 93 State 177847).

———. State 250796. "Talking Points for Meeting with French on Rwanda." August 17, 1993. https://foia.state.gov/Search/Search.aspx (Search Terms: 93 State 250796).

U.S. Department of State/Diplomatic Security (DS) Agency Document. "Peacekeeping History in Rwanda." July 7, 1993, https://foia.state.gov/Search/Search .aspx (Search Terms: 93 State Peacekeeping History Rwanda).

U.S. Mission to the United Nations Cable USUN 00790. "Rwanda Requests UN Military Observers." February 23, 1993. https://foia.state.gov/Search/Search .aspx (Search Terms: 93 USUN 00790).

———. USUN 02343. "Ugandan Permrep Letter on Rwandan Border Force." May 12, 1993. https://foia.state.gov/Search/Search.aspx (Search Terms: 93 USUN02343).

———. USUN 03036. "USUN Conveys to UN Concerns about Rwanda." May 22, 1993. https://foia.state.gov/Search/Search.aspx (Search Terms: 93 USUN 03036).

———. USUN 04653. "UN Plans for Rwanda PKO." September 23, 1993. https:// foia.state.gov/Search/Search.aspx (Search Terms: 93 USUN 04653).

———. USUN 04735. "Rwanda and Criteria for New UN PKO." September 28, 1993. https://foia.state.gov/Search/Search.aspx (Search Terms: 93 USUN 04735).

INDEX

Abakombozi, 79

Abercrombie and Kent, 163

ADL (Association Rwandaise pour la Défense des Droits de la Personne et des Libertés Publiques), 24, 25

Afghanistan, 310, 322

African Union, 3, 40, 162, 317–18. *See also* OAU

Africa Watch, 121, 150–51. *See also* Human Rights Watch

"Agenda for Peace" (UN), 315–17

An Agenda to Strengthen Conflict-Prevention Diplomacy, 324–32

Aiston, Kevin, 43

Akagera National Park, 186

Albright, Madeleine K., 321

Alliance des Militaires Agacés par les Séculaires Actes Sournois des Unaristes. *See* AMASASU

Alliance for Conflict Transformation, 319

Alliance for Peacebuilding, 319

Alliance of Soldiers Annoyed by the Underhanded Acts of the Unarists. *See* AMASASU

all-party peace meeting (February 1993), 143–44

AMASASU (Alliance des Militaires Agacés par les Séculaires Actes Sournois des Unaristes): death threats from, 201; emergence of, 154–55, 157; political repositioning of, 159

amnesty law, 45–46

Annan, Kofi, 244, 316

APB (Atrocities Prevention Board), 321, 323, 326, 336

Arab Spring (2011), 288, 338

ARDHO (Association Rwandaise Pour la Défense des Droits de l'Homme), 23–24, 25, 118, 230

armed conflict, 34, 47–48; cease-fire violation and renewed fighting, 135–39; diplomacy during, 40–43, 142–44, 146–47; expansion of military forces in, 43–44; foreign involvement in, 37–39, 41–42, 138, 149, 177; refugee origins of, 35–36, 44–47; reorganization of RPF during, 39–40, 65. *See also* DMZ; FAR; massacres; random and targeted violence; RPF

arms control, 190, 212, 244–45

ARP (Agence Rwandaise de Presse), 27, 31

Arusha (town), 163–64

Arusha International Conference Center, 163–64

Arusha Peace Accords, 6–7, 8; CDR and, 59, 204, 245–47; diplomatic corps on implementation of, 238–40, 250–52; implementation of, 206, 296; Political Code of Ethics, 246–47; preparations for transition, 213–20; signing of, 203–5. *See also* power-sharing arrangements

Arusha peace negotiations: on cease-fire, 65–68, 142–44, 146–48; conclusion of, 201–3; diplomacy leading to, 62–66; facilities for, 163–64; government delegation at, 170–72; on implementation and sequencing, 179–82; international observers at, 68–73, 161, 168–70, 193–94; on military and security integration, 148–49, 189–92; pitfalls of, 296–301; pressure to conclude, 191–92; procedures of, 167–68, 194–95; on refugee repatriation, 184–87; RPF delegation at, 172; on rule of law protocol, 68, 89; violence due to, viii, 63–64, 135–36. *See also* cease-fire agreements; diplomats and diplomacy; power-sharing arrangements

373

Christian League for the Defense of Human Rights. *See* LICHREDOR
chronology of events, 343–50
civil society groups, 22–27
CLADHO (Collectif des Ligues et Associations de Défense des Droits de l'Homme au Rwanda), 25
Clinton, Bill, 24
CND (Conseil National de Développement), 20, 188, 253. *See also* TNA
Coalition pour la Défense de la République. *See* CDR
Cohen, Herman J.: on armed conflict resolution, 41, 47, 62–63; French diplomatic communication by, 42; policy priorities of, 313; on signing obsession, 298
Cohen, William S., 321
Collectif des Ligues et Associations de Défense des Droits de l'Homme au Rwanda. *See* CLADHO
colonial history in Africa, 2–4, 92, 224
Commonwealth of Nations, 3
communication challenges, 168–69, 195–96
conflict prevention: Agenda to Strengthen Diplomacy for Conflict Prevention, 324–32; as policy priority, 312–24, 336–40. *See also* diplomats and diplomacy; humanitarianism vs. political solutions
conflict-risk assessment tool, xii
Conseil National de Développement. *See* CND
constitutional revisions, 190–91
coup, rumors and suspicions of, 153–55, 205, 249–50, 268
CSO (U.S. State Department Bureau of Conflict and Stabilization Operations), 320, 323
Cyiza, Augustin, 154, 268

Dallaire, Roméo: on arms cache, 244–45; threats to, 248; on troop deployment, 208–9, 210; as UN force commander, 208–9, 211–12, 231, 258
"Dar es Salaam Declaration on the Refugee Problem" agreement, 45–46, 186
Darfur, Sudan, 341
Davidow, Jeffrey, 65, 71
death lists, 119–20, 122. *See also* random and targeted violence
death squads, 106–8, 151–52. *See also* random and targeted violence
demobilization: Arusha discussion on, 148, 176, 182, 190–91; of military, 64–65, 92, 217–18
Democracy in Governance project, 222

Democratic Republican Movement. *See* MDR
Democratic Republic of the Congo (DRC), 315, 319, 321, 333–34. *See also* Zaire
democratization process: overview, 5–6, 288–95; as messy enterprise, 288–95. *See also* Arusha peace negotiations; elections; power-sharing arrangements
demonstrations, 20–21, 64, 80–83, 112–13, 116
Des Forges, Alison, 24, 119
Dialogue (publication), 28–29, 31
Diouf, Abdou, 173
diplomats and diplomacy, 7–10; 1993 fact-finding convoy of, 125–34; as Arusha observers, 169–89, 193–97; Authorized Departure status of, 140–42; communication challenges of, 168–69, 195–96; culture of, 303–4, 325–28; and democratization process, 5–6, 288–95; evacuation of, 140–42, 261–71; failures of, 333–38; limitations of, 301–8; after October 1990 invasion, 40–42; optimism of, 8–9, 87, 212; peace process pitfalls and, 296–301; policy challenges of, 287–95, 302–8; population of, 139; in power-sharing negotiations, 96–97, 102; pressure to implement Arusha Accords by, 238–40, 250–52; random violence and, 53–55, 63–64, 139–42; signing obsession of, 298. *See also* armed conflict; Arusha peace negotiations; cease-fire agreements; conflict prevention; *and names of specific nations*
displaced populations. *See* internally displaced persons; refugees
DMZ (demilitarized zone): declaration of, 147; IDPs return to, 219, 224, 230; investigation of, 153; negotiations at, 180, 202, 216; UNAMIR celebration in, 211; UNAMIR deployment at, 213. *See also* armed conflict
Doherty, Kolu, 185–86
DPKO (UN Department of Peacekeeping Operations), 244–45, 317
DRC. *See* Democratic Republic of the Congo

East African Community, 3, 163–64
École Supérieur Militaire, 223
economy, 3, 274, 333
educational programs, 74, 284
L'Église de la Sainte-Famille, xv
Egypt, 338
elections: in 1950s and 1960s, 2, 16; in Burundi, 188–89, 219; multiparty participation in, 15, 163, 166–67, 203; steps toward multiparty, 59, 69, 87–88, 201, 214, 251, 287

English language, 3, 30, 172–73
Enough Project, 319
ethnic cleansing. *See* genocide
evacuations, 140–42, 261–71
Expanded IMET program. *See* U.S. International Military Education and Training program

Fall, Papa Louis, 173
FAR (Forces Armées Rwandaise): coordination with French forces, 37, 138; leaders of, 75, 76, 280; military integration plan for, 71–72, 148–49, 174–75, 176, 215–18; reports of human rights abuses by, 229; troop expansion of, 43; violence by, 63. *See also* armed conflict; military forces; MRND; political transitions
fear: among displaced persons, 127–28, 130–31; from death lists, 119–20, 122; of random and targeted violence, 109–10, 139–42; rural officials on village violence and, 131–33; strategies to elicit, 37; among Tutsi, 354n6. *See also* media; stress of fear and violence
Felli, Joe, 174, 178, 195
Fendrick, Reed, 65
Ferraro, Geraldine, 156
Flaten, Robert: Arusha Accords implementation and, 161, 168, 214; at Arusha Peace Accords signing, 203; Authorized Departure status by, 140–41; departure of, 25; diplomacy against violence, 52; diplomacy on democratization and power sharing, 18–19, 22, 42, 96–97, 99–100, 117, 120, 142, 272; diplomacy on peace talks and, 62, 148, 162; diplomatic work on democratic development, 225; meetings with leaders, 13, 148, 153; on Peace Corps departure, 141; principle of inclusion and, 97; on Uganda sanctions, 47. *See also* diplomats and diplomacy; U.S. Embassy, Kigali
food shortages and relief programs, 138–39, 224, 234, 354–55n6
Forces Armées Rwandaise. *See* FAR
forest destruction, 46–47
"Framework of Analysis for Atrocity Crimes" (UN), 316–17
France: defense pact with Rwanda by, 39; diplomats in Rwanda, 139, 140, 263, 314; Kigali embassy of, 42, 282; military forces in Rwanda, 37, 138, 143, 147, 178, 216, 274. *See also* Operation Turquoise

freedom of expression and assembly, 49–50, 233, 291. *See also* media
Free Radio and Television of the Thousand Hills. *See* RTLM
French language, 3; Arusha peace talks in, 172–73; presidential swearing-in ceremony in, 241; print media in, 27, 28, 31
Fuller, Carol, 43
Fund for Peace, ix, xii–xiii, 318–19

Gapyisi, Emmanuel, 198–99, 248
Gasana, Anastase, 200, 202, 209
Gasana, James, 69, 137, 201, 215, 250
Gatabazi, Félicien, 17, 240, 248–49
gendarmerie: as evacuation escorts, 264, 268; leaders of, 75, 76, 112, 171; power-sharing negotiations on, 136, 149, 175–76. *See also* military forces; police forces
genocide: death toll of, 9, 271–72, 274; early warnings of, 77, 83–84, 156–57, 294, 336–37; first use of term regarding Rwanda, 156; historical seeds of, 3–5; investigative reports on, 150–53, 229–30; personal stories of trauma, 276–84; prevention of, 316–17, 319, 321, 329, 331–32; refugee toll of, 272, 274; responsible parties of, 5, 60, 155, 171, 229–30, 272–73, 290–91; in Srebrenica, 315, 320; UN definition of, 151. *See also* massacres; random and targeted violence
Ghana military forces in Rwanda, 213, 257
Gisenyi violence, 63, 91–92, 112, 130–34, 198
Global Witness, 319

Habyarimana, Juvénal, 5; agreements with, 57, 75; Arusha Accords implementation and, 205, 238–39, 272–73; Arusha ratification proposal by, 191–92; assassination of, 7, 254–55; BBTG arrangements for, 89, 90; coup rumors against, 153–55; encounter with diplomatic corps convoy, 129–30; political reform proposals by, 5, 15–16; political repositioning of, 158–59; on refugee return, 35–37, 44, 63, 184; reports on human rights abuses by, 150–53, 229–30; response to power-sharing talks, 91–93, 104–5, 106, 239; rise to power of, 35; speeches by, 91, 96, 152; swearing-in as BBTG president, 241. *See also* MRND
Haguruka, 26, 137
hate speech, 51, 60, 111, 247, 248, 290–91. *See also* RTLM
Higiro, Jean-Marie Vianney, 75

historical overview, 1–10

HIV/AIDS programs, 224

holidays, 110, 113

Hope for Rwanda (Sibomana), 282

hostage incident, 112

Hôtel des Mille Collines, xiv–xv, 262

Hotel Rwanda (film), xv

Houdek, Robert G., 203

humanitarianism vs. political solutions, 308–11, 331. *See also* conflict prevention; refugees

human rights abuses: during armed conflict, 46; documentation of, 150–53, 155, 228–30; investigations into, 23, 24–26, 118–19; against journalists, 50–51. *See also* armed conflict; genocide; hate speech; massacres; random and targeted violence

Human Rights Watch, 24, 53, 108, 118, 121, 150, 156, 314. *See also* Africa Watch

Hutu: overview of political control and, 2–3, 15–16, 32–33; population statistics of, 2, 189. *See also names of specific persons; names of specific political parties*

Hutu Power movement: Arusha Accords implementation and, 202, 214, 215, 237, 241; diplomat's interpretation of, 305–6; on power sharing, 215, 234, 245–46, 294, 301; rise of, 199–200, 205, 234–36, 295, 301. *See also* CDR; "Hutu solidarity"; MDR; MRND; PL

Hutu Social Revolution, 15–16

"Hutu solidarity": as propaganda tool, 37, 91–92, 104, 106, 122, 395. *See also* Hutu Power movement

"Hutu Ten Commandments" (*Kangura*), 29

ibiyitso charges, 38

ICRC (International Committee of the Red Cross), 46, 138, 140, 219–20

identity cards, 3, 229

IDPs. *See* internally displaced persons

Imbaga (publication), 220

"Implementing the Responsibility to Protect" (Ban), 316

Impuzamugambi, 79, 116. *See also* CDR

Imvaho (publication), 27

Independent League for the Defense of Public Liberties, 120–21

Inkuba, 79

Inter-African Union of Human Rights, 118

Interahamwe: Bugesera massacre and, 52; death threats from, 230; establishment of, viii, 79–

80, 83–84; Kigali violence by, 249; media and human rights organizations on violence by, 79, 109; political protests in, 116; roadblocks by, 80–82, 112, 243; transformation to militia, 71; violence and, 52, 109, 112, 243, 249, 260; weapons of, 245. *See also* MRND

internally displaced persons (IDPs): aid for, 71, 78; on policy for, 309, 310, 331; return to DMZ, 146, 219, 224; settlements of, 46–47, 127–28, 130–32; statistics on, 51, 71, 83, 139, 156, 219, 233, 310, 355–55n6. *See also* refugees

International Center for Human Rights and Democratic Development, 118

International Commission of Investigation on Human Rights Abuse, 151

International Commission on Intervention and State Sovereignty, 337

International Committee of the Red Cross. *See* ICRC

International Criminal Court, 319

International Criminal Tribunal for Rwanda, 319

International Federation of Human Rights, 118

International Military Education. *See* U.S. International Military Education and Training program

International Press Institute, 28

Intervening in Africa (Cohen), 313

inyenzi (term), 38, 215

Iraq, 310, 322, 338

Irvin, Patricia, 251

Isibo (publication), 29

Islamic Democratic Party, 94

Janvier, Afrika, 107

Joint Political-Military Commission, 67

Joulwan, George A., 283

journalism. *See* media

judicial system: deficiency of, 33, 51, 92, 151, 229, 274, 291; importance of functional, 110, 329

Kabuga, Félicien, 233

Kagame, Paul: on cease-fire restoration, 146, 148–49; meetings with leaders, 183, 225–26, 251; on power-sharing negotiations, 97; as Rwandan vice president, 278; term limits as president, 3; U.S. training of, 39–40

Kajeguhakwa, Valens, 30

Kambanda, Jean, 201

Kameya, André, 30

Kanguka (publication), 30

257; NMOG, 67, 69, 147, 178–79, 211; post-Arusha training seminar on democracy for, 223; post-conflict integration of, 148–49, 189–91, 215–17; power-sharing negotiations on, 136–37, 148–49, 174–75; Senegalese troops in Rwanda, 69, 252; of UN, 147, 149–50, 177–79, 192, 208, 211. See also AMASASU; cease-fire agreements; FAR; gendarmerie; NIF; police forces; RPF; UNAMIR

militia. See Impuzamugambi; Interahamwe

Ministry of Commerce (Rwanda), 58

Ministry of Defense (Rwanda), 75–77, 136–37

Ministry of Education (Rwanda), 58, 74

Ministry of Finance (Rwanda), 58

Ministry of Foreign Affairs and Cooperation (Rwanda), 58, 59, 249

Ministry of Information (Rwanda), 31, 74–75

Ministry of Interior (Rwanda), 74

Ministry of Justice (Rwanda), 43, 51, 58

Ministry of Women's Affairs (Rwanda), 26

Misericordia, 120

Mobutu Sese Seko, 39, 66

Moose, George, 275

moral responsibility, genocide prevention as, 321, 329, 331–32

Mount Meru Hotel, 162, 165–66, 167, 188

Mouvement Démocratique Républicain. See MDR

Mouvement Républicain National pour le Développement et la Démocratie. See MRND

Mouvement Révolutionnaire National pour le Développement. See MRND

Mpungwe, Ami Ramadhan: as Arusha peace talk facilitator's representative, 173, 174–76, 183–84, 188, 194–95; on force and security stalemate, 190–91, 192–93

MRND, 15–16; at all-party peace talks, 143–45; armed conflict threat to, 34; divisions within, 21, 148, 201; mass arrests by, 38; name of organization, 15; opposition parties and pushback from, 49–50, 57–58, 60, 198–99; on peace talks, 90, 91; response to BBTG of, 93–95, 104–5; response to power-sharing negotiations, 115–18. See also FAR; Habyarimana, Juvénal; Interahamwe; political transitions

Mugenzi, Justin: criminal conviction of, 17–18; as leader of PL, 17, 51, 200, 214, 240; meetings with leaders, 14, 240; on peace talks, 69–70, 89

Mugesera, Léon, 91–92, 106, 109, 111, 122, 125

Mujawamariya, Monique, 24, 26

Mulindi tea plantation, 40, 65, 71, 225–26

Muliza, Thomas, 171–72

multiparty coalition government, 57–61. See also BBTG

Murego, Donat, 200

Musamgamfura, Sixbert, 29

Museveni, Yoweri: rise to power, 169–70; RPF and, 36, 41–42, 47, 60, 327; on Rwandan refugees, 36–37, 48; in talks with other leaders, 62, 220. See also Uganda

Mwinyi, Ali Hassan, 66, 146, 162, 191

Nahimana, Ferdinand, 75, 232

National Development Council. See CND

National Republican Movement for Development and Democracy. See MRND

National Revolutionary Movement for Development. See MRND

Nayinzira, Jean-Népomuscène, 18

Ndadaye, Melchior, 188–89, 215, 219, 233–34, 327

Ndasingwa, Landoald: at Arusha peace talks, 188; author's recollection of, 259–60; background of, 18; democracy diplomacy and, 77–78; as minister of social affairs, 174; murder of, 259; as PL leader, 200–201, 214, 242; on refugee repatriation, 184–85, 186, 188

NDI (National Democratic Institute), 220, 221, 290

Ndiaye, Bacre Waly, 153, 228–30

Ndindiliyimana, Augustin, 76, 112

negotiations. See Arusha peace negotiations; power-sharing arrangements

Neutral International Force. See NIF

Neutral Military Observer Group. See NMOG

Ngango, Félicien, 21, 259

Ngeze, Hassan, 29

Ngirumpatse, Mathieu, 83, 116

Ngulinzira, Boniface: accusations against, 90, 112, 114, 122, 199; at Arusha peace talks, 89, 90, 96–98, 100, 115, 137, 170–71, 192; MDR party schism and, 202; as minister of foreign affairs, 59–60, 74, 174–75; murder of, 259; resistance to accusations of, 90, 100; RPF and, 104, 115; in talks with U.S. diplomats, 63, 78

NIF (Neutral International Force): Dallaire on troop deployment, 208–9; peace agreement on, 147, 149–50, 177–79, 190, 203; U.S. policy on, 209. See also UNAMIR

Nkubito, Alphonse-Marie, 23–24, 25–26, 118, 230, 258, 282–83

press. *See* media
prisoner exchanges, 219
A Problem from Hell (Power), 336–37
Protestant community, 95
Protestant Council of Rwanda, 143
protests, 20–21, 57, 80–84, 116, 245. *See also*
   political rallies; rioting
Prunier, Gérard, 36, 144
PSD (Parti Social Démocrate), 17; at all-party peace
   talks, 143–44; BBTG implementation and, 241;
   opposition to MRND by, 20–21; youth group of, 79

Radio Muhabura, 30
Radio Rwanda, 27, 30; anti-Tutsi messag-
   ing from, 51, 60, 111; monopoly of, 49, 50; on
   power-sharing agreement, 99–100; on RPF
   attacks, 38. *See also* media
Radio Télévision Libre des Mille Collines. *See*
   RTLM
rallies. *See* political rallies
Rambuka, Fidel, 230
random and targeted violence: against Bagogwe,
   38, 52, 120; in Butare, 113, 198, 249; in Gisenyi, 63,
   91–92, 112, 130–34, 198; Human Rights Watch on,
   109; in Kibilira, 38, 52; in Kibuye, 84–85; in Kigali,
   53–55, 63–64, 79–80, 109–11, 198, 247–49, 256–61;
   in northern Rwanda, 63–64, 212; in post-Arusha
   environment, 228–36; in Ruhengeri, 39, 52, 63–
   64, 112, 135, 138, 150, 226, 230–31. *See also* assassinations; genocide; human rights abuses; massacres
rape, 150–51, 333
Rawson, David: as ambassador to Rwanda, 73, 233,
   242–44, 251, 253; April 1994 crisis and evacuation, 262, 269–71; Arusha implementation and,
   245; as Arusha peace talks observer, 68–70, 84–
   85, 89; on Habyarimana's death, 254; in meetings with leaders, 251; reopening of embassy in
   July 1994, 274–75. *See also* U.S. Embassy, Kigali
refugees: Arusha talks on, 184–87; assistance
   for, 14, 44, 46, 78, 253–54; from Burundi in
   Rwanda, 219, 233–34, 247–48; as policy priority, 309–11, 331; proposed repatriation of, 44–
   46, 161, 184–87; right of return denied to, 36,
   184; as RPF troops, 43–44; Rwandan Tusti
   communities of, 4, 16, 35–37, 43–44; statistics
   on, 2, 36, 219, 272, 310, 341; in Tanzania, 35,
   43–44, 272, 274, 277; UNHCR on, 44–45, 185–
   87, 308–9; in Zaire, 35, 272, 274–75, 277, 280–
   81, 283. *See also* internally displaced persons

La Relève (publication), 27, 31
religious mediators, 95–96, 214
Render, Arlene, 251, 284
Renzaho, Juvénal, 70
Renzaho, Tharcisse, 83
Republic of Congo/Brazzaville, 20
Réseau Zéro (Zero Network), 106–8
Responsibility to Protect (R2P), 316, 324, 337
Reyntjens, Filip, 106–7
Richter, Larry, 142, 276, 277
rioting, 63–64. *See also* political rallies; protests
roadblocks, 80–82, 120. *See also* protests
Rodriguez, Carlos, 185, 218, 254
RPF (Rwandan Patriotic Front): amnesty offered
   to, 46; on Arusha talks stalemate, 239–40;
   Burundi presidential election and, 188–89; on
   CDR's role in transitional institutions, 246–47;
   cease-fire declaration by, 142–43; cease-fire violation and resumption of war, 135–39, 142, 144–
   45; criticisms of, 25–26; establishment of, 5, 37,
   44; funding of, 44; invasions and violence by, 5,
   6, 37–40, 135–36; military integration and, 174–75,
   215–17; Mulindi headquarters, 40, 65, 71; Museveni and, 36, 41–42; on NIF, 177–79; peace talks
   with, 62–73, 87, 165–67, 172–73, 187–89; power-
   sharing negotiations and, 87–90, 93–105, 160, 241;
   radio station of, 30; on refugee repatriation, 184–
   85; reports on human rights abuses by, 150–53,
   155, 229; as scapegoat for random violence, 26, 55–
   56, 293; sources of troops for, 43–44; troops in
   Kigali of, 202, 217, 260; war and genocide ended
   by, 274. *See also* armed conflict; military forces;
   political transitions
RTLM (Radio Télévision Libre des Mille
   Collines), 26, 232–33, 235, 247, 248. *See also*
   CDR; hate speech; human rights abuses;
   media; UNAMIR
Rucogoza, Faustin, 74–75
Ruhengeri violence, 39, 52, 63–64, 135, 138, 226,
   230–31
Ruhigira, Enoch, 78, 84–85, 100, 232–33, 243
rule of law: 1992 protocol on, 67–68, 72; 1992
   protocols on, 70; reports on lack of, 229
Rusatira, Léonidas, 76–77, 264, 280, 281
Rwabukumba, Seraphim, 107
Rwabukwisi, Vincent, 30
Rwagafilita, Pierre-Celestin, 75–76
Rwandan Armed Forces. *See* FAR

of the Crime of Genocide (1948), 151; "Dar es Salaam Declaration," 45–46, 186; Development Program, 207, 217–18; DPKO (Department of Peacekeeping Operations), 244–45; examination of Rwandan mission of, 314; Human Rights Commission, 153, 156, 228–30, 294; involvement in peace talks, 162–63, 195; military force of, 147, 149–50, 177–82, 192; peacekeeping force arrangements of, 207–11, 297, 315; Resolution 812 (1993), 149–50, 178, 181; Resolution 846 (1993), 208; Resolution 872 (1993), 210–11; Resolution 955 (1994), 319; Responsibility to Protect (R2P) mandate, 316–17; Rwanda and the Security Council of, 149, 178–80, 208, 209–11, 242, 319; Rwanda's membership in, 3; UNHCR (UN High Commissioner for Refugees), 44–45, 185–87, 218–20, 309–11, 341; UNOMUR (UN Observer Mission in Uganda-Rwanda), 149–50, 208, 210; UNRWA (UN Relief and Works Agency), 310. See also Arusha peace negotiations; NIF; UNAMIR

United States: conflict prevention policy of, 312–21, 325–28, 339–40; Democracy and Human Rights Fund, 23, 167; on International Criminal Court, 319; policy on Rwanda, 7–9, 155–56, 250–51, 287–95, 302–8; policy on Uganda, 47; Presidential Decision Directive 25, 182; support of UN peacekeeping operations by, 182, 196–97, 209–10; WWII veteran reintegration in, 217. See also diplomats and diplomacy

USAID (U.S. Agency for International Development): democracy project in Rwanda by, 221–22; funding for Rwanda reconstruction from, 217; judicial system support by, 291; Office of Conflict Mitigation and Management, 320, 323, 328; personnel of, 43, 141, 277, 302

U.S. Army, 275, 283

U.S. Committee for Refugees, 44

U.S. Department of Defense, 179, 223, 251, 275, 321–22

U.S. Department of State: April 6th crisis and, 256–65; on Authorized Departure status, 140–41; bilateral diplomacy process of, 306–7; Bureau of African Affairs, 181, 196, 203, 313, 320; Bureau of Conflict and Stabilization Operations, 320, 323; conflict prevention policy of, 320, 325–28; Democracy and Human Rights Fund, 23, 137, 167; financial support by, 23; support of post-

Arusha integration by, 220, 236. See also diplomats and diplomacy; names of specific diplomats

U.S. Embassy, Kigali: evacuation of, 261–71; priorities of, 42–43; reopening of, 274–84; on safety of U.S. citizens, 64, 139–42. See also diplomats and diplomacy; Flaten, Robert; Leader, Joyce; Rawson, David; U.S. Department of State

U.S. Embassy, Paris, 65

U.S. Genocide Prevention Task Force, 337

U.S. Information Service (a part of the former U.S. Information Agency), 18–19, 31, 141, 220

U.S. Institute for Peace, 324

U.S. International Military Education and Training program, 42, 223

U.S. Mission to the UN (USUN), 181

U.S. National Democratic Institute. See NDI

U.S. Peace Corps: author's work with, 14, 131, 141, 252; effects of random violence on, 54; evacuation of, 141; exploration of return of, 224–25; Kigali offices, 116, 141

Uwilingiyimana, Agathe: appointment as prime minister, 200, 202; Arusha Peace Accord recognition by, 206; on BBTG implementation, 242; call for assassination of, 232; educational reforms by, 74; murder of, 258, 259; safety of, 257

Vieira de Mello, Sergio, 45

voucher system, 218

weapons control, 190, 212, 244–45

women: as victims of violence, 26, 150–51, 333

women's organizations, 26–27, 137–38

World Food Program, 138

World War II, 217

youth groups and violence, 79–80, 290. See also children; Impuzamugambi; Interahamwe

Zaire: author's position in, 14, 131, 141, 252; Mobutu's military aid to Rwanda, 39; peace talks in, 20, 40, 66–67; representation at peace talks by, 169; RPF troops from/in, 44; Rwandan refugees in, 35, 272, 274–75, 277, 280–81, 283; violence in, 320–21. See also Democratic Republic of the Congo

Zenko, Micah, 333

Zero Network, 106–8

Zigiranyirazo, Protais, 107

Zorick, Michael, 42

Related ADST Book Series Titles

Claudia E. Anyaso, ed., *Fifty Years of U.S. Africa Policy: Reflections of Assistant Secretaries for African Affairs and U.S. Embassy Officials*

Herman J. Cohen, *Intervening in Africa: Superpower Peacemaking in a Troubled Continent*

Herman J. Cohen, *The Mind of the African Strongman: Conversations with Dictators, Statesmen, and Father Figures*

Peter D. Eicher, ed., *"Emperor Dead" and Other Historic American Diplomatic Dispatches*

Peter D. Eicher, *Raising the Flag: America's First Envoys in Faraway Lands*

Harriet Elam-Thomas, *Diversifying Diplomacy: My Journey from Roxbury to Dakar*

Robert William Farrand, *Reconstruction and Peace Building in the Balkans: The Brčko Experience*

Christopher Goldthwait, *Ambassador to a Small World: Letters from Chad*

Brandon Grove, *Behind Embassy Walls: The Life and Times of an American Diplomat*

Robert E. Gribbin, *In the Aftermath of Genocide: The U.S. Role in Rwanda*

Judith M. Heimann, *Paying Calls in Shangri-La: Scenes from a Woman's Life in American Diplomacy*

Michael P. E. Hoyt, *Captive in the Congo: A Consul's Return to the Heart of Darkness*

Edmund J. Hull, *High-Value Target: Countering Al Qaeda in Yemen*

Cameron R. Hume, *Mission to Algiers: Diplomacy by Engagement*

Joanne Huskey, *The Unofficial Diplomat*

Richard L. Jackson, *The Incidental Oriental Secretary and Other Tales of Foreign Service*

Dennis C. Jett, *American Ambassadors: The Past, Present, and Future of America's Diplomats*

John G. Kormann, *Echoes of a Distant Clarion: Recollections of a Diplomat and Soldier*

Jane C. Loeffler, *The Architecture of Diplomacy: Building America's Embassies*

Terry McNamara, with Adrian Hill, *Escape with Honor: My Last Hours in Vietnam*

William Morgan and C. Stuart Kennedy, *American Diplomats: The Foreign Service at Work*

Ronald C. Neumann, *The Other War: Winning and Losing in Afghanistan*

David D. Newsom, *Witness to a Changing World*

Raymond F. Smith, *The Craft of Political Analysis for Diplomats*

James W. Spain, *In Those Days: A Diplomat Remembers*

James Stephenson, *Losing the Golden Hour: An Insider's View of Iraq's Reconstruction*

William G. Thom, *African Wars: A Defense Intelligence Perspective*

Jean Wilkowski, *Abroad for Her Country: Tales of a Pioneer Woman Ambassador in the U.S. Foreign Service*

For a complete list of series titles, visit adst.org/publications.